Young Workers in the Global Economy

Young Workers in the Global Economy

Job Challenges in North America, Europe and Japan

Edited by

Gregory DeFreitas

Hofstra University, USA

Edward Elgar

Cheltenham, UK   Northampton, MA, USA

HD
6270
.Y665
2008

© Gregory DeFreitas 2008

All rights reserved. No part of this publication may be reproduced, stored in a retrieval system or transmitted in any form or by any means, electronic, mechanical or photocopying, recording, or otherwise without the prior permission of the publisher.

Published by
Edward Elgar Publishing Limited
Glensanda House
Montpellier Parade
Cheltenham
Glos GL50 1UA
UK

Edward Elgar Publishing, Inc.
William Pratt House
9 Dewey Court
Northampton
Massachusetts 01060
USA

A catalogue record for this book
is available from the British Library

ISBN 978 1 84720 457 8

Printed and bound in Great Britain by MPG Books Ltd, Bodmin, Cornwall

Contents

List of Contributors *vii*
Preface *ix*

1. Youth Employment: Crisis or Course Change? An Introduction 1
Gregory DeFreitas

PART ONE CURRENT JOB TRENDS AND CHALLENGES

2. The Youth Labor Market Problem in Cross-Country Perspective 21
Rebekka Christopoulou
3. Out of School, Out of Work, Out of Luck? Black Male Youth Joblessness in New York City 59
Mark Levitan
4. Still With Us After All of These Years: Youth Labor Market Entry, Home-Leaving and Human Capital Accumulation in Italy, 1993–2003 89
Niall O'Higgins
5. Youth Employment in Japan after the 1990s Bubble Burst 109
Naoki Mitani

PART TWO SCHOOL-TO-WORK TRANSITIONS

6. Youth Employment Problems and School-to-Work Institutions in Advanced Economies 137
Paul Ryan
7. Work and Non-Work Time Use of US College Students 161
Lonnie M. Golden

PART THREE DYING FOR A JOB

8. Occupational Fatalities among Young Workers 175
Janice Windau

University Libraries
Carnegie Mellon University
Pittsburgh, PA 15213-3890

9. Falling Private Health Insurance Coverage Among Young Workers in the United States 189
Niev J. Duffy

PART FOUR HOW DOES IMMIGRATION AFFECT AMERICAN YOUTH?

10. Immigration and Youth Employment: Recent Debates and Research Findings 203
Gregory DeFreitas

11. Unauthorized Mexican Immigration and Youth Labor Market Outcomes in California in the 1990s 227
Enrico A. Marcelli

PART FIVE STRATEGIES FOR IMPROVING FUTURE JOB PROSPECTS

12. How Can We Improve Employment Outcomes for Young Black Men? 245
Harry J. Holzer

13. Does Job Corps Training Boost the Labor Market Outcomes of Young Latinos? 265
Alfonso Flores-Lagunes, Arturo Gonzalez and Todd Neumann

14. Have Young Workers Lost Their (Collective) Voice? Youth–Adult Preferences for Workplace Voice in Canada 287
Michele Campolieti, Rafael Gomez and Morley Gunderson

References 311

Index 335

Contributors

Michele Campolieti is Associate Professor at the University of Toronto Department of Management at Scarborough, Canada, and at the Centre for Industrial Relations, Toronto, Canada.

Rebekka Christopoulou is a doctoral candidate in the Faculty of Economics and Politics, University of Cambridge, UK.

Gregory DeFreitas is Professor of Economics and Director of the Labor Studies Program at Hofstra University, New York, US. He is also Director of the Center for the Study of Labor and Democracy, US, and the founding editor of *Regional Labor Review*.

Niev J. Duffy is President of Eastern Economic Research, Inc. in New York City, US, and Research Associate at the Center for the Study of Labor and Democracy, US.

Alfonso Flores-Lagunes is Assistant Professor of Economics at the University of Arizona, and Visiting Assistant Professor of Economics, Princeton University, US.

Lonnie M. Golden is Associate Professor, Economics and Labor Studies and Industrial Relations at Penn State University, Abington College, US.

Rafael Gomez is Assistant Professor at Glendon College, York University, Canada, and Lecturer in Management at the London School of Economics, UK. He is also Research Associate of the Centre for Industrial Relations and the Centre for International Studies at the University of Toronto, Canada.

Arturo Gonzalez is Research Fellow at the Public Policy Institute of California, in San Francisco, US, and at the Institute for the Study of Labor (IZA), in Bonn, Germany.

Morley Gunderson is the CIBC Chair of Youth Employment at the University of Toronto, Canada, and Professor at the Centre for Industrial Relations and the Department of Economics. He is also Research Associate of the Institute for Policy Analysis, the Centre for International Studies, and the Institute for Human Development, Life Course and Aging at the University of Toronto.

Harry J. Holzer is Professor and Associate Dean of Public Policy at Georgetown University. He is also a fellow at the Urban Institute and at the Program on Inequality and Social Policy, Harvard University, US.

Mark Levitan is Director of Poverty Research at the New York City Center for Economic Opportunity, US.

Enrico A. Marcelli is Assistant Professor of Economics at the University of Massachusetts, Boston, and Research Associate at the Center for Society and Health, Harvard University, US.

Naoki Mitani is Professor of Labour Economics at the Graduate School of Economics, Kobe University, Japan.

Todd Neumann is Assistant Professor of Economics at the University of California, Merced, US.

Niall O'Higgins teaches economics at the University of Salerno, Italy.

Paul Ryan is Professor of Labour Economics, King's College London, and a Life Fellow, King's College, University of Cambridge, UK.

Janice Windau is an epidemiologist in the Office of Safety, Health, and Working Conditions, Bureau of Labor Statistics, US Department of Labor.

Preface

This book weaves together original studies by an international set of labor scholars in the hope of offering the latest findings and fresh insights into a wide range of high-profile issues affecting youth in advanced economies – from declining job, wage, and training prospects to workplace health hazards and health insurance coverage, immigration, union activism, and new policy strategies. The main focus is on the United States, but in the context of other major developed nations, including: Canada, France, Germany, Italy, Japan, the Netherlands, Sweden, and the United Kingdom.

The goal here is to provide a clear and accessible introduction aimed at a broad, non-specialist readership ranging from college students to employers, unions, career counselors, human resource professionals, vocational trainers, policy analysts, government officials, immigration and health care activists, as well as to the wider public concerned about the future of youth career prospects. We hope that all readers may find something of interest in the host of controversial topics of lively public debate that we cover, including: youth unemployment, earnings mobility, racial/ethnic and gender inequalities, training quality and access, job hazards, health insurance coverage, immigration, minimum wage laws, union organizing, and global economic competition.

This collection of studies originated at an international scholarly conference, "Youth Employment in the Global Economy," held at Hofstra University in New York in September 2005. In planning this conference, we sought to bring together an interdisciplinary mix of scholars from several nations and a variety of representatives of different perspectives from the worlds of labor, business, government, immigrant, and youth activist organizations. In seeking the latest research and freshest new ideas on these issues, we encouraged all of the participants to prepare their presentations in a style accessible to a broad audience.

A great number of individuals and organizations generously devoted time and funding to make this conference possible and worthwhile. As the Conference Director, I wish to express my gratitude to: Hofstra President Stuart Rabinowitz, Provost and Senior Vice-President for Academic Affairs, Herman A. Berliner, Senior Vice President for Planning and Administration, M. Patricia Adamski, Dean Bernard J.

Firestone of the College of Liberal Arts and Sciences, Dean Stephen Russell of Honors College, and all my colleagues and students in the Department of Economics and Geography, the Labor Studies Program, and the Latin American and Caribbean Studies Program. The talented staff of the Hofstra Cultural Center, led by Natalie Datloff and Athelene Collins, worked tirelessly to ensure the event's success. The principal organizer of the conference was the Center for the Study of Labor and Democracy (CLD), based at Hofstra. At CLD, Chanel Kwon was a model research aide, giving enthusiastic and skillful assistance with many aspects of the conference. The Center is an interdisciplinary research institute that conducts original research projects on important labor issues ranging in scope from the local New York Metropolitan Area to national and global economies. Information on the Center's activities and publications is available at www.hofstra.edu/cld.

At Edward Elgar, Alan Sturmer, David Fairclough, and their talented colleagues in the US and the UK have been most generous with their support and expertise, for which I am very grateful.

I would like to dedicate this book to my daughter and her generation of young people as they begin their own journey into the global economy.

1. Youth Employment: Crisis or Course Change? An Introduction

Gregory DeFreitas

A surprising decline in the economic status of young people is underway in the United States and many other high-income nations. It has taken varying forms, proceeded at different speeds, and provoked quite diverse responses in each country. In France, for example, a new youth labor law in 2006 sparked weeks of large-scale demonstrations across the country that nearly overturned a government, just months after widespread rioting by young underemployed immigrants. But at the same time in the United States, the news that the teenage employment rate had plunged to its lowest point in a half century went largely unnoticed by the public and policymakers alike. The fact that young Americans have simultaneously been experiencing shrinking real wages, occupational mobility rates, health insurance coverage, unionization and college affordability makes this only more remarkable.

With baby boomers nearing retirement and with some scholars predicting labor shortages soon, it would seem likely that the rising educational levels and computer skills of young people should translate into unusually bright career outcomes. While this is true of some countries, it now appears in doubt in the US and most others. Moreover, growing concerns among adults over rising immigration, strained public pension and health care systems, and the off-shoring of even high-skill tasks are driving millions to delay retirement and leading to warnings that a competitive 'generational storm' may be on the horizon. What are the causes and consequences of such trends? How does the US experience compare with those of other industrialized nations? What are the most promising policies for improving young peoples' future employment prospects?

Answers to these questions will not come easily. As veterans of our own individual youth experiences, we all know how complicated it can be. But today's youth will shape tomorrow's economy; their job problems and prospects have far-reaching social implications and deserve broader understanding and discussion.

YOUTH DEFINED

The main focus of our cross-country analysis in this volume is youth as currently defined by the United Nations: ages 15 to 24. However, 'youth' is not only a transitory stage in one's lifetime, but also a historically fluid and internationally variable socioeconomic category. It is recognized to start in most countries at the legal school-leaving age, ranging from 14 to 16. In the United States, no one is even counted in the official labor force statistics before 16, so that most US data on teenage employment covers only 16- to 19-year-olds. Increasingly, the broader age range from 15 to 34 has been adopted for much government and academic discussion of youth. This reflects in part the rising age of first marriage and childbearing and the increased popularity and costs of higher education. It also reflects the lengthening of average pre-marital residence with parents, which itself may be a cause or an effect of young people's delayed entry into full-time career employment. Commonplace convenience terms for the current younger cohorts are: 'Generation X', born 1965 to 1983 (ages 25 to 43 as of 2008) and 'Generation Y' or the 'Millennial Generation', born 1984 to 2002 (ages 24 and under in 2008). Frequent comparisons will be made here to the 'Baby Boom Generation', born 1946 to 1964 (ages 44 to 62 in 2008).

THE DECLINE IN YOUTH EMPLOYMENT RATES

The single most common measure of employment status for international comparisons is the employment–population ratio. It is calculated as the share of an age group's total population with a job during a specific period (typically the survey week). While intercountry differences in details of data collection must always be taken into account, these tend to be more insignificant today (at least in EuroStat, OECD and ILO data sets) than is true for other possible measures like the unemployment rate. The employment–population ratio (E/P) when expressed in percentage terms, is here referred to as the employment rate.

Among the selection of advanced economies whose young male employment rates in 1970 and 2003 are displayed in Figures 1.1 and 1.2, large international differences are evident, among both teenagers and 20- to 24-year-olds. In 2003, teenage male employment rates ranged from highs of 49 per cent in the United Kingdom and 43.4 per cent in Canada, to lows of just 5.4 per cent in the Netherlands and 12.6 per cent in Italy.

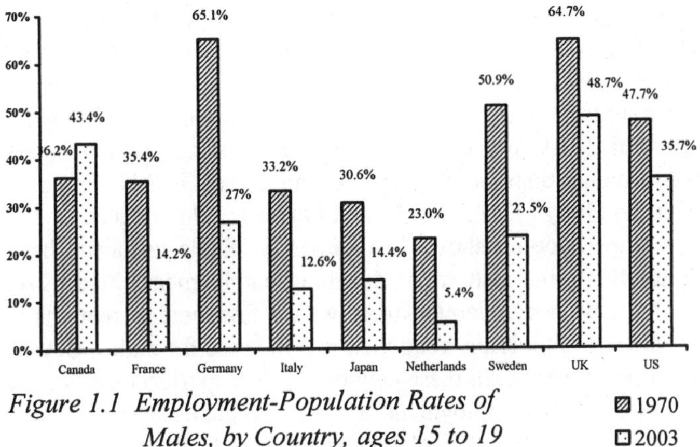

Figure 1.1 Employment-Population Rates of Males, by Country, ages 15 to 19

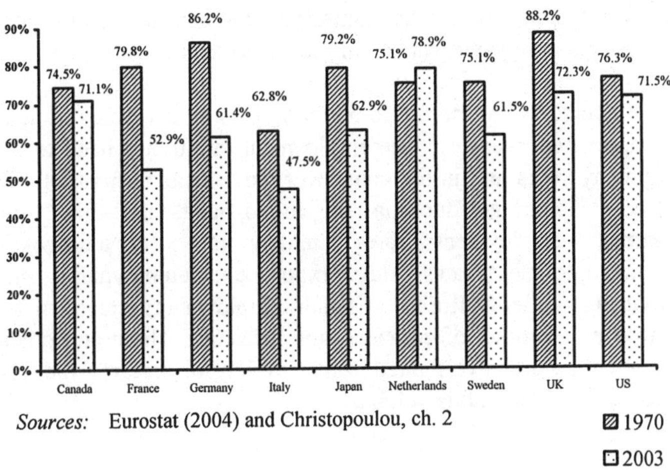

Sources: Eurostat (2004) and Christopoulou, ch. 2

Figure 1.2 Employment-Population Rates of Males, by Country, ages 20 to 24

But all countries except Canada experienced a decline in the fraction of teenagers with a job. In fact, the US employment rate in 2003 (35.7 per cent) was 12 percentage points lower than in 1970 and had dropped to its lowest level in 55 years of record keeping.

Among young people in their early twenties, Figure 1.2 shows a similar, if less marked, downward trend in employment for all but one country, the Netherlands. The countries with the highest employment rates for people in their early twenties — France, Germany and the UK — all experienced sharp declines. By 2003, the Netherlands had both the lowest teenage employment rate and, in sharp contrast, the highest rate of jobholding for slightly older youth (78.9 per cent). The Netherlands rate was over six percentage points higher than the US, the UK, and Canada in 2003 and over 25 points higher than Italy (47.5 per cent) and France (52.9 per cent).

As Rebekka Christopoulou shows in Chapter 2, female teenagers have displayed a roughly similar pattern of declining employment since 1970. Among women in their early twenties, there were a few more exceptions to the general downward jobholding trend than was the case for males. But for all youth of both sexes, nearly all these countries have experienced a decline in the ratio of youth to adult employment rates over recent decades.

Moreover, these employment declines cannot simply be explained by increased enrollment in higher education. As a number of studies in this volume show, declines in youth employment rates and in youth–adult employment ratios persist even after controlling for enrollment changes, though the explanatory significance of these changes varies across countries.

One must, of course be careful not to rely too much on two years of data for a single employment measure. The employment rate trends need to be explored over many years and in the context of movements in a variety of other indicators, including: duration of employment, part-time and temporary-contract employment rates, underground (off-the-books) employment, unemployment rates and duration, underemployment, and jobless inactivity (so-called 'NEETs' – not in employment, education or training), as well as a full set of compensation measures. These and other employment indicators are investigated with a variety of research models and the latest available data in this volume.

DOES YOUTH EMPLOYMENT REALLY MATTER TODAY?

However, the trends shown here in employment–population ratios appear consistent with patterns in a variety of other such measures that point to a broad, long-term, yet far from uniform decline in young people's jobholding since the early 1970s in many advanced economies. The dimensions, potential determinants and implications of this decline have been the subject of a number of major economic research collections since the early 1980s.[1] For many labor specialists, policymakers, and young people, these trends are fast approaching or have by now reached crisis proportions. But still others take quite a different view. From this alternative perspective, the fact that young people are less likely to be employed today, far from being a worrisome trend, may instead reflect fundamental, largely positive shifts of direction in high-income countries – a generational course change.

From this perspective, a number of demographic and socioeconomic phenomena have combined to make it both less essential and less advisable for most youth to enter the job market before about their late twenties. Among the possible arguments that supporters of such a view might make for a course change are:

1. Steadily rising educational demands of professional and other high-salary occupations today require completion of four years of college, plus an additional two years or more of graduate or professional school. The future payoff in steep upward economic mobility after graduation renders transitory youth unemployment problems unimportant.
2. Rising adult incomes have enabled increasing numbers of parents to support their children's higher education, thereby rendering youth jobs largely unnecessary. Most youth only seek jobs to finance luxuries and/or to socialize. Affluence in advanced economies has raised youth expectations about what pay and working conditions are acceptable. As a young person's 'reservation wage' level rises, she will not consider most of the low-wage work youth held in earlier eras.
3. An historic redistribution of jobs and incomes to the massive baby boom generation has created both unprecedented inequality and limits on their children's and grandchildren's current employment options unlike anything seen in the 1970s or earlier. In addition to filling top occupational positions, overqualified boomers have long since captured a disproportionate share of middle-level jobs, closing off job ladders to new young job candidates. As life expectancy lengthens and mandatory retirement laws are erased, boomers are discouraging young jobseekers for that much longer, the more that they delay retirement.
4. Government and business leaders have effectively decided to admit enough new immigrants to fill the low-wage jobs once reserved for youth.
5. Young people's lack of sustained widespread protest against their shrinking job options in most countries reflects their approval or at least acquiescence.

On the other hand, this 'course change' view must be questioned in the light of a variety of arguments that youth job trends today are approaching a crisis stage and threaten young people's long-term economic prospects. These counter-arguments include:

1. A college education today is a far less secure route to high-wage full employment than in years past. While youth with college degrees still average higher earnings than less-educated workers, their inflation-adjusted median wages have fallen in the US and elsewhere and are lower than in the early 1970s. And upward mobility of youth in the US appears to have fallen below that of many other nations, according to new research discussed below.
2. College-going costs have soared, even at public universities, straining the finances of increasing numbers of students and parents alike. The net cost of a public college education (after subtracting financial aid) in 2005 demanded 23 per cent of the income of a typical middle-income family and 73 per cent of the total income of the poorest fifth of families.[2] Reductions in government education grants in favor of mainly student loans have left the average American college graduate $20,000 or more in debt. This 'debt-for-diploma' system increasingly not only limits access by lower-income youth, it also forces even middle-income students to look for jobs during much of the year and appears to be lengthening the number of years it takes to graduate well beyond historic norms. Student employment can also affect academic performance, though research suggests that this effect is only significant for full-time jobholders.
3. Baby boomer parents and grandparents of today's youth are increasingly under pressure to work more hours and years to cope with the rising costs of their offspring's educations, child care and health insurance, as well as with the growing instability of job-based pensions. The fact that most of the adult workforce in the US is doing so with stagnant or declining real earnings makes it all the more helpful for family finances if teenage and older children find employment.
4. Immigration has soared in the US as in some Western European countries, sparking renewed controversy over whether its costs to host societies outweigh its benefits. Though the economic research in the past has not found its net costs to the native-born to be large, some low-wage workers and communities contend that it is a major threat to their livelihoods and increasingly demand much more restrictive admissions policies.
5. Youth's deteriorating economic prospects have reached the stage where some forms of active protest have taken place, particularly in France. In

> most other countries, there have not yet been mass protests of a sustained and visible sort. The longer that businesses and policymakers fail to make their own 'course change' toward giving high priority to youth job problems, the more serious those problems will become, the more young people will become aware of them, and the stronger and more widespread the response may be.

After reading the studies in this volume, one will have a much better ability to evaluate whether we are facing a true economic crisis or just a generational course change. Regardless of which perspective seems most persuasive, it is unquestionable that young people must at some point try to make the transition from school to full-time employment. The following chapters attempt to improve our understanding of that transition process, its economic outcomes, and policy alternatives for improving it. Here I sketch examples of some of the other dimensions of youth and adult labor markets besides employment rates alone, that must be part of such an evaluation.

EDUCATION AND EARNINGS MOBILITY

Youth is often said to be the most hopeful and optimistic period of life, and that is nowhere more evident than in the United States. International public opinion surveys have long shown American youth and their parents to be the world's most confident believers in the eventual returns to individual work effort. However, in recent years, these surveys have begun picking up growing signs of anxiety and even pessimism among adults questioned about whether young people will enjoy a better standard of living than their parent's generation – the so-called 'American Dream' of individual upward mobility. Half of adults surveyed nationwide in 2006 said that today's younger generation 'will be worse off than people are now.' Only one in three felt youth would be better off in the future, down from 41 per cent when the same question was asked in a 2002 survey.[3]

Table 1.1 shows inflation-adjusted (in 2004 dollars) annual wage movements since the early 1970s for youth aged 25 to 34, subdivided by sex and educational attainment. In order to avoid biased comparisons of recession years with business cycle peaks, these figures are all for the peak years. From 1973 to 1979, average real wages shrank for men and women, regardless of educational level. In fact, as large numbers of baby boomers began graduating from college, they suffered pay drops much steeper than those of the less-educated. In the 1980s, all groups except female college graduates had continuing pay declines. Those young men with no more than

Table 1.1. Annual real earnings (in $2004) of full-time, year-round US workers, ages 25 to 34, in economic peak years, 1973 to 2004

Median Real Wages ($2004)	MALES			FEMALES		
	High School Grad Only	**Some College**	**College Grad**	**High School Grad Only**	**Some College**	**College Grad**
1973	45,338	46,735	54,888	26,554	31,684	38,488
1979	41,753	43,728	48,152	25,819	29,181	33,949
1990	32,000	37,600	46,000	23,700	29,000	38,800
2000	32,300	38,000	50,900	23,500	27,800	39,900
2004	30,400	36,400	50,700	24,000	28,800	40,300
% Changes						
1973-79	-7.91	-6.44	-12.27	-2.77	-7.90	-11.79
1979-90	-23.36	-14.01	-4.47	-8.21	-0.62	14.29
1990-2000	0.94	1.06	10.65	-0.84	-4.14	2.84
2000-2004	-5.88	-4.21	-0.39	2.13	3.60	1.00
1973-2004	-32.95	-22.11	-7.63	-9.62	-9.10	4.71

Sources: Author's calculations from US Bureau of Labor Statistics data in US Department of Education (1996 & 2006).

a high school degree saw their real wages plummet by over 23 per cent. Only in the record-breaking full-employment boom of the late 1990s did most youth either manage to register some wage gains or at least keep pace with inflation. But even this was not nearly enough to recover their lost ground. By 2004, three years into a recovery from the brief 2001 recession, non-college male workers were still earning one-third less, and non-college women nearly ten per cent less than the 1973 non-college wage level.

Young college graduates were also hit by surprising wage declines, though not nearly as large as the less-educated members of their generation. Over the 1973 to 2004 period, average annual wages dropped 7.6 per cent (to $50,700) for male college graduates and rose a mere 4.7 per cent (to $40,300) for women. By 2004, the average young college graduate's annual wages were over $4,000 less than in 1973 for men and just $1,900 higher for women. This did mean that female college graduates made progress in reducing the gender pay gap. But their pay still averaged 20 per cent less than male college graduates – and was only $3,900 higher than the average male with only one to three years of college.

The fact that youth and non-college graduates have suffered steeper wage declines than older workers or the college educated has meant a sharp increase in wage inequality by age and education. Young high school graduates earned 70 per cent as much as older high school graduates in 1973, but only 65 per cent as much by 1999; among non-college females, the gap grew even wider: from an 87 per cent youth–adult wage ratio in 1973 to 73.7 per cent by 1999.

RISING BARRIERS TO EDUCATION AND MOBILITY

Though college graduation is no longer a guarantee of strong pay growth, it clearly tends to offer at least some protection to individuals from far more severe real wage cuts. Over the years 1973 to 2004, the educational wage differential between high school graduates without college and college graduates widened substantially for both sexes: young non-college male high school graduates in 1973 earned about 82 per cent as much as young male college graduates in 1973, but only 60 per cent as much by 2004. For young non-college women, the ratio dropped from 69 per cent to 60 per cent (Table 1.1).

But college-going costs are skyrocketing far faster than government and university financial aid. From 1980 to 2000, tuition and fees at public colleges and universities jumped 107 per cent, but average state expenditures per college student crept up just 13 per cent. Federal Pell grants, which covered 98 per cent of tuition at four-year public colleges in 1986, now cover just 57 per cent. And since 1980, Federal aid has shifted from mostly outright grants to students into a loan-based system that has left many lower- and working-class families fearful of assuming an unsustainable college debt burden.

The increasing disinvestment by Washington and many state governments is already having a discernible cost in skill acquisition relative to our global trading partners and competitors. A 2006 international comparative study found that the United States has been dropping fast behind other countries in college enrollment and completion. Among 27 countries studied, the US now ranks 16th in the fraction of youth who complete college degrees or certificate programs — behind even lower-income European nations like Poland and Portugal.[4]

As higher education has become much less affordable, class background of prospective students becomes more decisive in determining access.[5]

Among college-qualified high school graduates in the US, the proportion who enrolled in college within two years of graduation was 83 per cent of youth from high-income families, but only 62 per cent of middle-income and 52 per cent of low-income youth.[6] Lower-income students who manage to afford time in college are far more likely to be limited to a two-year program, often training them for no more than skilled working-class jobs.

The impact of these developments on youths' chances of future upward mobility is becoming evident in recent research. Intergenerational earnings mobility – defined as substantial earnings growth of children independently of their parents' earning level – appears to have fallen in the US and the UK well below the mobility rates of many advanced economies. A 2006 study by Canadian economist Miles Corak calculated intergenerational earnings

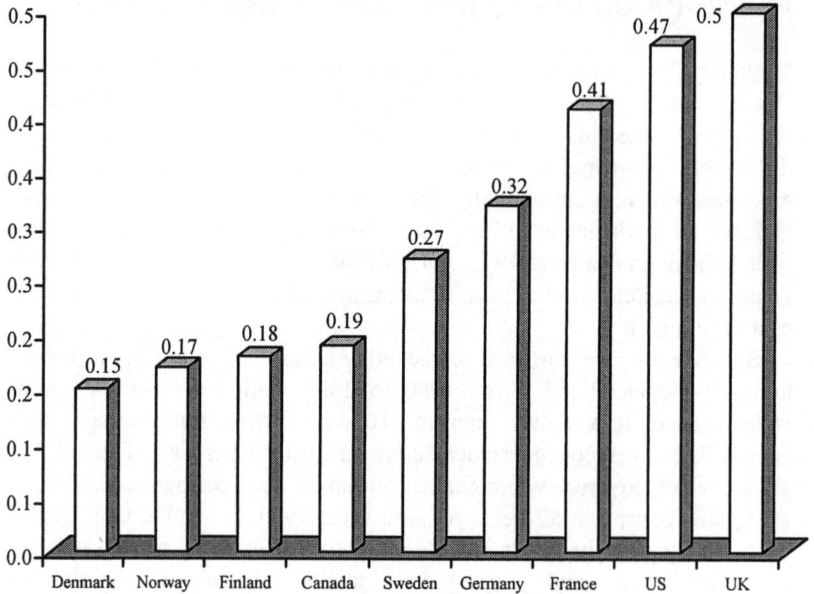

Note: The vertical scale is the percentage change in children's expected wages associated with a 1 per cent difference in parental wages.

Figure 1.3: Earnings Mobility is Lowest in US and UK

elasticities for nine countries.[7] This measure is defined as the percentage difference in children's expected earnings associated with a 1 per cent difference in parental earnings. The lower this elasticity, the higher children's independent mobility, since parental earnings differences are less important. Figure 1.3 charts the intergenerational income elasticities (vertical axis) for nine major developed nations. Its surprising result is that, compared with Canada, France, Germany and Nordic countries, the US and the UK are now the least mobile economies.

YOUNG PEOPLE'S RESPONSES TO ECONOMIC DECLINE

How are young people responding to these threats to their economic futures? The most active, sustained, nationwide protests have so far been in France. In March 2006, millions of French youth shook the government and captured world headlines with almost daily marches and rallies in over 150 cities and towns to protest against the government's new youth labor law. This new law, the First Employment Contract (CPE), would for the first time allow employers to dismiss without cause any worker aged 25 or younger. The CPE had been promoted by conservatives and their business allies as a 'modernizing' measure to increase 'labor market flexibility', by reducing an employer's risk of being stuck with unproductive new workers and thereby encouraging more new hires and, perhaps, lowering France's 23 per cent youth unemployment rate. That persistence of high youth joblessness, most virulently among racial and ethnic minorities, was a major spark in the Fall 2005 riots in the country's poor suburban areas.

But public opinion polls indicated widespread opposition to a more American-style 'employment at will' system. Employer promises that worker flexibility in sacrificing hard-won labor rights would translate into more, not fewer, decent job opportunities were not new and not widely persuasive. Even unemployed youth largely opposed the law and its throwaway 'Kleenex contracts' of employment as undermining hard-won job security and benefits. One parent was quoted: 'I'm sick and tired of these phony contracts and I want to protect my children's future.'[8] Students, supported by large numbers of teachers, workers, retirees, and labor union leaders, shut down most universities and threatened the conservative government. Their efforts forced the national government to backtrack within weeks, and the law was repealed. This was not the first time in recent years that French youth had built large and effective campaigns to protest perceived assaults on their educational and economic rights. They mounted national mobilizations against a government plan to impose a sub-minimum wage in 1995 and against declining school staffing and quality in 1998.

If French youth rank as the most activist group over employment issues, American youth today are often portrayed as falling at the opposite, passive extreme. The late 1990s witnessed the rise of the largest wave of youth activism in two decades. Unlike the anti-apartheid movement of the early 1980s or the antiwar demonstrations of the 1960s, the latest wave has been far more focused on three sets of related labor issues: 1) sweatshop wages and working conditions in the foreign factories that produce US college-name clothing; 2) global economic policies that threaten labor and environmental standards, without adequate debt relief for developing nations; and 3) 'living wage' campaigns to raise sharply minimum pay and benefit levels for low-wage youth and other workers.[9]

One reason for the lack of much American youth activism over their own economic problems is that they lack much bargaining power with employers. A mere 4.4 per cent of young workers aged 16 to 24 were union members by 2006, the lowest rate of any age group. The youth rate dropped by nearly half from 9.1 per cent in 1983, the first year in which the Bureau of Labor Statistics (BLS) began collecting annual membership rates by age group. At the same time, union density has fallen even more among older workers: it dropped among 25–34 year-olds from 19.6 per cent in 1983 to 10.6 per cent in 2004, and fell among 35–44 year-olds from 24.8 per cent to 13.7 per cent. The 1.034 million young workers under 25 who are now unionized (over 700,000 fewer than in 1983) account for just over 6 per cent of all union members.[10] Within these averages there are some striking interarea variations. For example, in the largest and most unionized metropolitan area, 13 per cent of employed New York City youth are union members – nearly three times the national rate. Still, this is half the city-wide membership density.[11]

Does the low rate of current union membership among young workers reflect weaker pro-union and/or stronger anti-union sentiments among youth? Not according to a number of public opinion surveys, old and new, that asked youth their attitudes toward unions. Nationwide, a growing majority of Americans, especially youth, tell pollsters that they side with labor unions against employers. In late August 2001, the Associated Press polled 1,010 Americans, aged 18 and over, asking them the question: 'In the labor disputes of the last two or three years, have your sympathies, in general, been on the side of the unions or on the side of the companies?' Of the respondents, 50 per cent said that their sympathies were on the side of unions, while just 27 per cent sided with companies. This represents a marked rise in pro-union sentiment from just a few years earlier.[12]

When the same question was asked in a nationwide Gallup poll in 1999, just 45 per cent responded that they sided with unions. The 2001 poll results show that women were more likely than men to express pro-union sympathies: 51 per cent to 48 per cent. But an especially large gap is evident between young and old. Nearly three out of every five young people aged 18 to 34 sided with unions, compared to less than two out of five older people over 65.

The findings from public opinion polls seem consistent with the research results from studies of actual National Labor Relations Board (NLRB) union elections.[13] If then, youth have relatively stronger pro-union attitudes than adults, what explains their far lower union membership rates? The nature of the jobs that most youth find and of the firms that hire them account for a large share of the explanation. First, their jobs are more likely to be entry-level, low-skill and often part time or temporary positions in small businesses – all characteristics long associated with low union density. Secondly, as Richard Freeman and James Medoff have argued, job creation in growing new firms tends to disproportionately favor youthful hires. Since job growth has increasingly been dominated by firms in the traditionally non-union service sector, youth have more and more only found entry jobs in such non-union industries.[14] Finally, large numbers of youth jobs today are with wealthy and notoriously anti-union employers.

Wal-Mart, the world's largest retailer with over $350 billion in annual sales revenue, is also the country's largest private non-union employer. Workers' anger over excess work hours, low pay and sometimes hazardous conditions at distribution centers did lead to organizing drives in Missouri in 1971 and in Arkansas in 1976 and 1981. But all were defeated by a combination of Sam Walton's personal threats to shut down the stores involved and his use of aggressive union-busting law firms to train store managers to identify and punish pro-union workers.[15] Most other retail chains and fast-food giants like McDonalds also have a very long history of devoting enormous resources to fighting off bitterly any employee efforts to seek union representation. Finally, unions themselves have too often neglected organizing young workers and/or advanced senior employees' interests at the expense of youth.[16] There are now increasing signs that some American unions are finally beginning to reach out in imaginative ways to young workers. These include new union organizing drives among young, low-paid graduate teaching assistants, who routinely teach classes and grade papers at many universities today. Other organizing has of late been supported by and sometimes led by young immigrant workers, as described in Chapter 10.

EXPLAINING YOUTH'S DECLINING STATUS

Mainstream economic theory has had a hard time explaining the deterioration of youth's economic status. Indeed many economists in the early 1980s were predicting the exact opposite. After all, they reasoned, the shrinking youth population share of the 'baby bust' cohort should improve their job and pay prospects over those of the crowded baby boomer labor market of the 1970s. Industrial shifts toward traditionally 'youth-intensive' services and retail trade sectors were also expected to raise employer demand for young workers. And Gen-Xers' longer average schooling levels and familiarity with computers compared to older workers seemed to be additional strong advantages.

Economists' research on these issues, including the new work in this volume, often find it useful to distinguish between a variety of possible explanatory factors on the side of employers' demand for labor and those on the side of workers' supply of labor. A short list of the most often emphasized labor demand and supply factors follows:

Demand

1. Aggregate employment fluctuations
2. Wage and benefit levels
3. Skill-biased technological change
4. Employers' discriminatory practices (by age, gender, race/ethnicity, and other characteristics)
5. Industrial restructuring
6. Global trade and employment flows
7. Employment protection institutions – government regulations on labor demand (for example, hiring/firing criteria, temporary employment contract regulations, minimum wages, health and safety).

Supply

1. Education and training completed
2. Work attitude, health
3. Family's income and employment
4. Nonmarket income incentives (for example, criminal behavior)
5. Reservation wage/benefits and minimal acceptable working conditions
6. Size of the youth labor force
7. Supply of complementary and substitute workers (for example, immigrants, adult women, older workers)
8. Labor unions
9. Government labor market policies (for example, unemployment benefits, training, job placement, school-to-work institutions).

CONTENTS

The book opens with a sweeping overview of youth job and pay trends in over a dozen advanced economies by Rebekka Christopoulou. After controlling for country differences in school enrollment, her findings show that country trends toward deteriorating youth status take the form, in the UK and US, of much larger declines in youth relative pay, than in relative employment. In contrast, France, Sweden (and Japan and Korea for males) have experienced large declines in youth relative employment, whereas changes in relative pay were not significant. Germany and the Netherlands appear to be the main exceptions to most pay or employment deterioration. Christopoulou finds that demand shifts, conditioned by particular labor market institutions, appear to account for intercountry differentials better than rival explanations.

The focus then narrows to take a detailed look at the most disadvantaged group of underemployed youth in New York City. The city's 'disconnected', out-of-school black youth suffer the lowest rates of jobholding in the city (42.7 per cent), but their level of jobholding has declined the most dramatically over time. In Chapter 3, Mark Levitan explores 1990–2000 census data that indicates that changes in the industry and occupational structure of the city's job market adversely affected employment in the kinds of jobs that Black male youth tend to hold. In at least one sector of the job market, blue-collar occupations in the goods producing and distribution industries, there is evidence that Black male youth lost share to adult immigrants. He concludes that the impact of this 'displacement' appears small relative to the overall decline in Black male youth employment.

Niall O'Higgins (Chapter 4) shows that young Italians today live with their parents longer, accumulate more schooling, and both get married and enter the labor force later than they did a decade ago. He looks for explanations in the relationships among schooling, marital and living arrangements, and labor force transitions of recent youth cohorts, through data in the Italian Labor Force Survey and the Household Survey of Income and Wealth. He finds that aggregate economic conditions seem to have played a significant explanatory role in these trends.

Among OECD countries, the Japanese youth labor market had shown relatively good performance until the bubble burst in the 1990's, as indicated by the low unemployment rate of young workers. In Chapter 5, Naoki Mitani shows that the main reason for the deterioration of the youth labor market is the sharp reduction in the labor demand for youth, especially the reduction in the number of full-time regular jobs caused by structural factors such as the increase in foreign investment to China, as well as cyclical factors. In addition, the employment adjustment behaviors under the relatively rigid employment protection legislation had negative effects on youth employment, together with the employment promotion policies for older workers, such as the extension of mandatory retirement age. He also finds that, along with young part-time workers, the number of unemployed, non-student NEETs has increased recently. Part-time young workers and NEETs are less likely to marry or have children, suggesting that better promotion of youth employment is needed as part of both economic and population policy in rapidly aging Japan.

Paul Ryan (Chapter 6) examines the extent to which the two national school-to-work institutions of Germany and Japan – the outstanding performers of the post-war era – have had their performance undermined by the recent decade-long economic stagnation in each country. He points out that, while youth cyclical sensitivity is among the most important determinants of their employment in a number of countries, its applicability may not be universal. Different nations show varying sensitivities of youth to adult employment cycles. And the youth employment decline in the US has occurred during many years of relative stability in aggregate employment.[17]

Lonnie Golden (Chapter 7) exploits both the new American Time Use Survey and a recent college student survey to reveal the characteristics and consequences of student employees on American campuses. He finds that a large share of students now work over 20 hours per week, with discernible impacts on various measures of school performance.

Many young people still feel compelled to take risky jobs in which too many are getting hurt at work. Across Europe, 18- to 24-year-olds are at least 50 per cent more likely to be injured in the workplace than more experienced workers.[18] The latest US job death statistics are discussed in Chapter 8 by Janice Windau, a US Labor Department epidemiologist. She shows that entry-level workers experience a disproportionately large share (one-third) of all work-related injuries. Although the young workers' death rate has moderated in the US since 1998, surprisingly large numbers continue to be killed on the job: an average of 560 per year through 2002.

Niev Duffy then documents in Chapter 9 the decline in employer-provided private health insurance coverage of young workers, the least protected of any age group. As the only advanced economy with mainly private, job-based insurance, the costly US system appears to leave its young increasingly vulnerable to crippling health costs. One in three persons under age 30 now lacks coverage. Her statistical analysis explores differences in rates of employer-provided health insurance coverage by age, while controlling for other individual and household demographic characteristics. She shows that the decline in private insurance coverage is likely to be most precipitous for the young. Moreover, federal and state cuts in the public Medicaid program have thinned its ability to help offset shrinking private insurance as much as it did in earlier recessions. The worrisome implication is that, with each economic downturn, millions more young adults and their children will lose their employer-provided insurance benefits, leading most to defer medical care, with potentially disastrous medical and financial effects.

Immigration is again the subject of furious debate in North America and Europe. The immigrant population of the US soared by over 80 per cent between 1990 and 2005. And immigrants entering the country since 1990 are notably younger on average than the native born. By 2006, nearly 12 million unauthorized migrants were among them. In Chapter 10, I evaluate recent research findings on the employment and wage impacts of recent immigration, including those from my own survey of New York employers. In the following chapter, Enrico Marcelli's empirical study of unauthorized Mexican immigrants finds that they have had negligible adverse or beneficial effects on youth and other workers' labor market outcomes in California during the 1990s.

A wide variety of implications for policy strategies to improve youth labor market outcomes can be found in most of this book's chapters. The concluding chapters are the most explicitly policy oriented. Harry Holzer (Chapter 12) reveals some unintended employment consequences of federal policies for low-wage African-American men, particularly the large share with criminal records. He explores several promising remedies, including: education and skills programs; improving access to employers and early work experience; raising the incentives of young men to accept low-wage jobs; and initiatives discouraging criminal behavior and early fatherhood, as well as reducing their negative consequences on employment over the longer term.

Arturo Gonzalez, Alfonso Flores-Lagunes and Todd Neumann evaluate the US Government's Job Corps program for disadvantaged youth in Chapter 13. They find evidence that Job-Corps-trained Hispanics tend to do relatively better in labor markets with high unemployment, especially in areas with less concentration of Hispanics. Spanish-speaking enclaves provided young Latinos not selected for Job Corps in the mid-1990s with employment opportunities that resulted in the relatively large accumulation of labor market experience that dominated the advantage that Job Corps training might have otherwise provided.

Finally, Michele Campolieti, Rafael Gomez and Morley Gunderson consider both the Canadian and US cases in their study of youth–adult differences in preferences for unionization and other forms of collective voice at the workplace. Compared to the US and a number of other countries, Canada has both relatively high youth employment and high rates of union membership. They discuss surprising evidence of youth-adult differences in the frustrated or unmet demand for unionization and non-union forms of voice, as well as the possible oversupply of unionization that may occur from union members who would prefer to be non-union. From their findings they conclude that unions which shift more of their attention and resources to helping youth meet their specific job challenges may find an important new source of growth.

NOTES

1. See in particular: Freeman and Wise (1982); OECD (1982); Freeman and Holzer (1986); Ryan, Garonna and Edwards (1991); OECD (1994); O'Higgins (1997, 2001); and Freeman and Blanchflower (2000a).
2. Draut (2005); National Center for Public Policy and Higher Education (2006): 19–22.
3. Pew Research Center (2006). The survey was conducted nationwide in March 2006 and covered 2,250 respondents.
4. Advisory Committee on Student Financial Assistance, 2002; National Center on Public Policy and Higher Education (2006); Kamenetz (2006).
5. McPherson and Shapiro (1998). See also National Center for Public Policy and Higher Education (2002).
6. Findings for 1992-94 from the National Education Longitudinal Survey, reported by Choy (1998).
7. Corak (2004a), as reported in Hertz (2006). See also Corak (2004b).
8. Sciolino (2006).
9. See the more detailed discussion of specific examples in DeFreitas and Duffy (2004).
10. US Bureau of Labor Statistics (1983–2007).
11. DeFreitas and Sengupta (2007).
12. For further analysis and sources, see DeFreitas and Duffy (2004).
13. Farber and Saks (1980).
14. Freeman and Medoff (1985).
15. Ortega (1998); Zellner (2002).
16. See, for example, the case studies in Tannock (2001).
17. See DeFreitas, Marsden and Ryan (1991).
18. Eurostat (2004).

PART ONE

Current Job Trends and Challenges

2. The Youth Labor Market Problem in Cross-Country Perspective

Rebekka Christopoulou[1]

The youth labor market problem came to the forefront of discussions among economic analysts in the 1980s as the bulk of the 'baby boom' generation entered the job market. The issue has not faded away through time, with the adverse trends in youth outcomes observed back then still persisting today. In fact, some leading labor economists argue that during the past 25 years the majority of the advanced countries experienced a deterioration in pay and employment for young workers so severe that it marks 'a constant scar rather than a temporary blemish'.[2] The persistence of the phenomenon is indeed surprising, given the decline in youth labor supply due to the positive demographic changes of the 1980s, in addition to the evident rise in school enrollments, the expansion of service industries that traditionally employ many youths, and the obvious trend towards computerization.

However, the post-1970s deterioration did not only affect youths; it was, in fact, a general phenomenon. Most of the advanced economies faced a sharp increase in the overall unemployment rate, except for the US, where the deterioration took the form of a severe increase in wage inequality. This might suggest to some that disaggregating by age is not necessary. Nevertheless, a valid reason to examine the youth labor market situation separately from and in comparison to that of adults would be if the deterioration has not affected both equally. Indeed, during the past three decades the traditional gap between youth and prime-age adults' labor market outcomes has risen considerably in many countries. More importantly, trends in relative outcomes have shown a substantial diversity between countries, with the deterioration taking the form of declines in either relative wages or relative employment or both.[3]

The youth labor market problem is not a simple one to explain. What makes young people strong candidates in the labor market in comparison to prime-age adults is their potential to be highly motivated and offer fresh ideas and insights in their work. On the other hand, their lack of experience (or tenure) and their tendency towards instability and experimentation with their professional orientation work against them. In addition, youths that participate in the labor market are less likely to have obtained education than older adults and are thus relatively less educated. Therefore, the fact that young people perform worse in the labor markets than older adults does not come as a surprise. However, as long as the skill gap by age does not widen through time one would expect relative labor outcomes not to increase as well. Therefore, given that the skill gap by age in terms of educational attainment has narrowed, observed trends suggest that there are forces in advanced labor markets that are biased against youths in particular (that is, against the experience dimension of skill). Changing technology and increasing international trade are the most obvious candidate explanations among many others that have been proposed.

However, most economic research attempting to explain the youth labor market problem has examined the influence of the candidate causal forces on relative employment and unemployment outcomes alone.[4] Thus, these studies share a common 'Achilles heel': they fail to provide the potentially critical link between trends in relative youth pay and employment, mostly because of limited available data on pay. Yet, the interconnected relationship of employment and earnings could be too important to be ignored.

The view adopted here is that a valid explanation for the youth labor market problem can only result from a cross-national time-series analysis, in which earnings and employment are taken as endogenously determined variables. This chapter attempts the first step in this direction. More specifically, the aims of this chapter are threefold: (a) to re-examine the youth labor market problem by presenting up-to-date evidence on youth labor market indicators and identifying patterns in their evolution between countries, by considering the pay and employment dimensions of youth labor outcomes simultaneously throughout the analysis; (b) to critically review the main explanations that have been proposed; and (c) to provide an insight into the workings of youth labor markets by addressing the problem within a micro-based analytical framework.

The chapter is structured as follows: section 1 examines changes in youth labor outcomes (both in absolute and in relative terms) by age and sex in 13 OECD countries; section 2 discusses the influences of supply-side and demand-side changes in interaction with institutional restrictions; section 3 addresses the potential role of labor market and school-to-work institutions in more detail; and section 4 presents the problem within the supply demand institutions (SDI) framework. The final section offers some concluding remarks.

RECENT LABOR OUTCOMES OF YOUTH AND ADULTS

In order to obtain a comprehensive picture of the relative position of youths in advanced labor markets, one should return to the original sources and re-examine the data. An updated description of data on employment, wage, unemployment and educational participation by age (in both absolute and relative terms) is provided in the sub-sections that follow. What becomes immediately apparent is the extent to which economic and econometric cross-group analysis is constrained by lack of data availability. Therefore, given the significant data limitations, the sample has been restricted to 13 OECD countries and although the time period of interest is from 1970 onwards, for which extensive employment and unemployment series are available for most countries (with the exception of Belgium, the Netherlands and Korea), the time series for pay and educational participation are far from complete, especially for teenagers. Still, the available data will suffice for the observation of general trends in most countries.

Young Adults versus Prime-Age Adults

Table 2.1 presents changes in employment-to-population ratios by age for males and females.[5] Evidently, as far as males are concerned, between 1970 and 2003 employment rates of both age groups fell in absolute levels for the majority of the countries under investigation. Young adults in the Netherlands and prime-age adults in Korea were the only exceptions. The picture is somewhat different for females. During the period 1970 to 2003, employment rates for prime-age adult women rose in all 13 countries, reflecting the large increase in their labor force participation over the last several decades. In Canada, Korea, the Netherlands, the UK and the US, employment actually increased for both age groups. However, the remaining countries experienced a fall in employment for the youth category of females and this followed a similar trend to that of males. More specifically, youth of both sexes have shown a bigger deterioration in employment than prime-age adults in countries of Continental Europe as opposed to the other countries. Computing the change in relative rather than absolute employment rates by age would make this pattern more apparent. Still, employment rates constitute only one side of the coin and changes in pay also need to be considered.

Regrettably, due to the limited pay data it becomes necessary to give up investigating the whole 1970 to 2003 period in order to allow for the simultaneous examination of pay and employment for the same time periods. Therefore, the investigation period for each country will be reduced

Table 2.1 Employment–Population Ratios by Age

Age	20–24			25–54		
Year	**1970**	**2003**	**Change**	**1970**	**2003**	**Change**
			Males			
Australia	91.1	75.5	-15.6	96.5	85.4	-11.1
Belgium	60.5	51.8	-8.7	88.5	84.4	-4.1
Canada	74.5	71.1	-3.4	91.6	85.6	-6.0
Finland	66.5	55.9	-10.6	91.3	83.3	-8.0
France	79.8	52.9	-26.9	97.1	89.3	-7.8
Germany	86.2	61.4	-24.8	96.9	84.2	-12.7
Italy	62.8	47.5	-15.3	92.4	86.5	-5.9
Japan	79.2	62.9	-16.3	96.4	92.0	-4.4
Korea	66.3	45.2	-21.1	92.4	92.7	0.3
Netherlands	75.1	78.9	3.8	90.6	90.1	-0.5
Sweden	75.1	61.5	-13.6	95.7	86.9	-8.8
UK	88.2	72.3	-15.9	95.7	87.6	-8.1
US	76.3	71.5	-4.8	93.2	85.9	-7.3
			Females			
Australia	61.3	68.7	7.4	42.5	68.6	26.1
Belgium	48.4	41.1	-7.3	45.8	67.7	21.9
Canada	55.8	69.9	14.1	38.6	75.7	37.1
Finland	63.6	54.7	-8.9	70.4	78.8	8.4
France	63.6	44.6	-19.0	47.1	74.4	27.3
Germany	67.3	59.1	-8.2	47.0	72.0	25.0
Italy	39.3	32.5	-6.8	27.9	54.9	27.0
Japan	69.1	63.4	-5.7	54.7	64.4	9.7
Korea	49.6	56.5	6.9	56.2	62.8	6.6
Netherlands	64.5	76.2	11.7	46.7	73.9	27.2
Sweden	63.7	57.3	-6.4	66.6	83.4	16.8
UK	59.4	64.2	4.8	52.8	74.1	21.3
US	53.1	64.2	11.1	47.8	72.0	24.2

Notes: Adult category for Sweden and France is 35–44 year olds and for Korea is 40–44 year olds. Start year for Belgium is 1983, for Korea 1980 and for the Netherlands 1977 for males (from Ryan (2001), table 4) and 1987 for females.

Source: OECD, Labour Force Statistics Indicators (Author's calculations)

Table 2.2 Mean Earnings, Ratio of 20– 24 to 25–54 Year-Olds' Pay

					%Change	
	Males	**Females**	**Males**	**Females**	**Males**	**Females**
<15 years						
Belgium	1985		1994			
(10 years)	77.2	78.9	76.9	76.3	-0.3	-2.6
Germany	1984		1998			
(15 years)	61.0	71.6	60.1	65.6	-0.9	-6.0
Italy	1987		1995			
(9 years)	72.8	83.0	66.2	79.0	-6.6	-4.0
Netherlands	1985		1996			
(12 years)	72.3	80.8	67.9	77.1	-4.4	-3.7
>15 years						
Australia	1975		2003			
(29 years)	81.3	95.1	63.5	73.5	-17.8	-21.6
Canada	1977		2001			
(25 years)	70.7	83.6	59.2	65.6	-11.5	-18.0
Finland	1980		2002			
(23 years)	67.5	76.1	62.2	65.1	-5.3	-11.0
France	1970		1998			
(29 years)	67.3	78.3	61.9	70.7	-5.4	-7.6
Japan	1973		2003			
(31 years)	60.8	88.8	55.5	75.9	-5.3	-12.9
Korea	1980		1996			
(17 years)	43.3	96.6	48.5	89.4	5.2	-7.2
Sweden	1975		2003			
(30 years)	67.1	76.6	60.3	71.0	-6.8	-5.6
UK	1976		1996			
(21 years)	74.7	85.7	62.4	71.0	-12.3	-14.7
US	1973		1998			
(26 years)	68.2	85.6	51.8	61.6	-16.4	-24.0

Notes: Data cover the longest available period for each country. Adults: 35–44 in Sweden and France; 40–44 in Korea and Netherlands. Youth 25–29 in the Netherlands. For Belgium we use median gross earnings.

Source: OECD,Labour Force Statistics (Author's calculations).

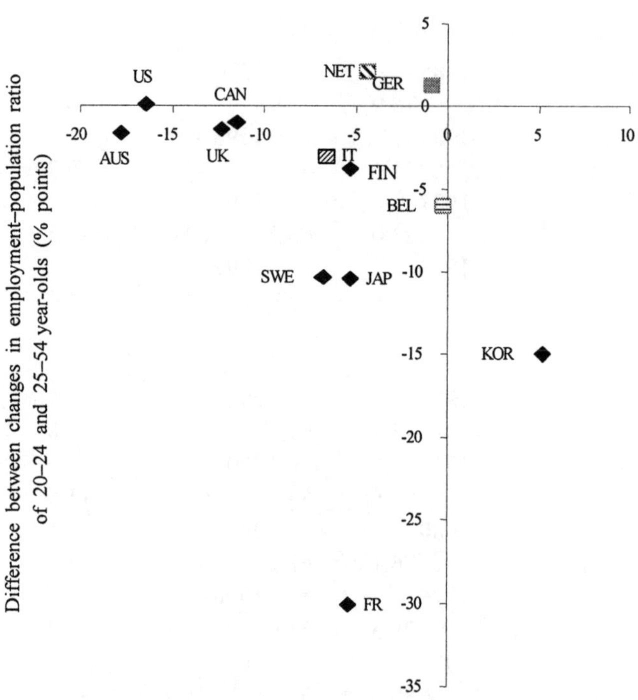

Notes: The time period per country is the longest available. Diamonds indicate period of change >15 years, squares indicate period of change <15 years.

Figure 2.1 Changes in Relative Pay and Employment of Young and Prime-Age Male Adults

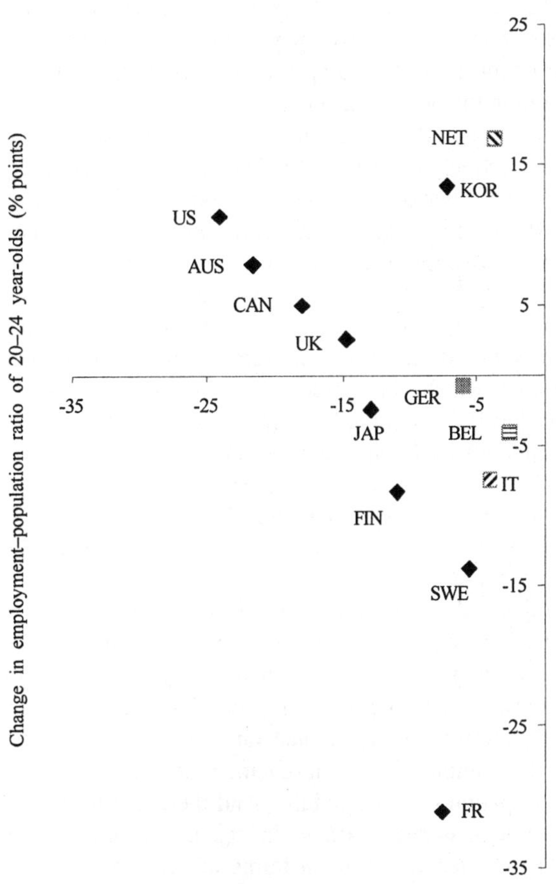

Notes: The time period per country is the longest available. Diamonds indicate period of change >15 years, squares indicate period of change <15 years.

Figure 2.2 Changes in Employment Ratios of Young Female Adults and in Relative Pay of Young and Prime-Age Female Adults

to the longest available time interval according to pay data availability. Unfortunately, this weakens cross-country comparability.[6]

Changes in relative earnings between 20 to 24 and 25 to 54 year-olds and the corresponding time periods per country are reported in Table 2.2. Except for the relative pay for young males in Korea which appears to increase, the experience of all the other countries shows deterioration. In most cases, the deterioration is higher for females than males. However, the pattern of deterioration in relative pay is similar for both sexes, with the Anglo-Saxon countries in the sample (Australia, Canada, the UK and the US) demonstrating the biggest decline.

In Figures 2.1 and 2.2 changes in relative pay and employment for men and women respectively are plotted against each other.[7] Although for some countries the time period available is too short to allow for valid conclusions, there are some points worth noting. In the case of male outcomes, countries appear to congregate around the axes, revealing an interesting trade-off between changes in relative pay and employment. In particular, there is a contradiction between the Anglo-Saxon countries, which mostly show deterioration in relative pay, and France, Sweden, Japan, and Korea, which mostly show a decline in relative employment. A similar pattern has been observed before in a sample of fewer countries and shorter time intervals by Ryan.[8] As in Ryan's analysis, a group of countries with 'successful' labor markets is also present, namely Germany and the Netherlands (and in bigger approximation Italy and Finland), situated close to the intersection of the axes. However, their 'success' is highly dependent on the time period under study.[9]

The same general lines are followed by the trends for females. In particular, where declines in relative outcomes take place, although often more severe than those observed for males, they show the same opposite experiences between the Anglo-Saxon countries and France and Sweden. However, this pattern is less clear than for males, as six out of the thirteen countries in the sample show improvement in employment, due to the increased participation of young adults. And there is a further difference in the observed trends between sexes: in Japan and Korea changes differ between males and females both in terms of relative employment and in relative pay. These differences are the basis for the view adopted here, that despite their similarities, male and female labor markets are strictly segregated.

The evidence in Figures 2.1 and 2.2, although strongly suggestive of a poor situation in youth labor markets, is not enough to define the problem. Two additional factors need to be taken into account – namely trends in schooling and youth inactivity – if one is to determine whether the position of young adults in advanced labor markets has shown a general deterioration compared to prime-age adults. In particular, low or falling levels of youth relative employment need not imply adverse experiences in youth labor markets if young people have voluntarily shifted into education or inactivity. Therefore ignoring these factors could lead to an overestimation of the youth labor market problem.

More specifically, educational participation and inactivity can affect the youth labor supply either exogenously to wage and employment trends, driven by voluntary choices, or as endogenous factors that are pushed by high youth unemployment and changes in relative pay. In the former case, declines in relative employment do not imply that youths are relatively worse off. On the contrary, by participating in education they increase their employment and wage prospects and by staying voluntarily inactive (for example, for leisure or travel) they show that they can afford to do so. It is only in the case of youths who have been forced by unfavorable labor market conditions to enroll in education or to give up searching for jobs and stay inactive that one can rightly infer deterioration. Unfortunately, the optimistic scenario of strict exogeneity of educational participation to labor market conditions seems groundless. If youths were restricting employment rates by willingly opting for alternative uses of time, then youth labor markets would signal supply constraints. Yet the evolution of unemployment rates across time for young adults suggests demand constraints instead, implying that some degree of endogeneity in the determination of educational participation is likely to be present.

Figures 2.3 and 2.4 illustrate the patterns of unemployment rates for young adult males and females respectively. Countries with similar experiences have been grouped together. It is obvious that in most cases the unemployment rates show a significant upward trend after the mid-1970s and, despite the multiple –and often sizable – variations, there appears to be no recovery. Finland, France, Italy and Sweden show the most sizable deterioration, especially for females. The US is the only country for which the complete series is available and no trend is apparent, with the unemployment rate fluctuating around 10 per cent. No trend (or even a negative trend) is also observed for Belgium, the Netherlands and Korea, but the time-series is incomplete for these countries, which implies that the trend could well be the reverse were earlier data available. In general, the evidence in Figures 2.3 and 2.4 indicate that there exists a strong non-clearing component in the nature of unemployment, signaling demand-constrained labor markets for the majority of the countries.[10]

As additional evidence, Figures 2.5 and 2.6 plot participation in tertiary education as a ratio of the 20 to 24 youth cohort size and the respective employment-to-population rates for males and females in ten out of the thirteen countries for which data are available.[11] Enrollment rates have risen for both sexes in all countries. Also, with the exception of the UK and the Netherlands –two countries with a high incidence of part-time and hence student employment[12] – educational participation and employment ratios appear to have generally moved in opposite directions. Although it is not true that educational participation simply reflects the reverse of youth employment, the negative association is evident. These trends complement those identified in an earlier study by Korenman and Neumark, where a negative relationship between enrollment in education and employment was also observed in Italy, Ireland, Spain, and Portugal.[13] Thus, even though determining the direction of the causality between the two variables is not straightforward, it is notable that there is no strong indication that educational participation is exogenous. Had educational participation been determined in complete independence from the labor market outcomes, one would expect simultaneous increases or falls in the two variables to occur more often and in more countries. The systematic negative association can therefore be taken as a suggestion of some endogenous interaction.

Naturally, whether educational participation is endogenous to labor market conditions and to what extent needs to be tested empirically as part of a formal examination. However, simple data description can form expectations, and in this case the possibility that educational participation is determined on a strictly voluntary basis is expected to be unlikely, especially since the declines in relative employment have often been too substantial to have left educational participation unaffected. Given this evidence, it is reasonable to claim that changes in relative employment–population ratios signal changes in relative labor demand. From this viewpoint, declines in relative employment imply deterioration, and the problem of young adults in the countries examined can be summarized as follows: youth labor outcomes have worsened in comparison to those of prime-age adults, with the deterioration taking the form of declines in either relative pay or relative employment or both.

Teenagers versus Prime-Age Adults

In the case of teenagers, the picture is less clear than for young adults aged 20 to 24, due to further data restrictions. This does not concern employment outcomes, for which complete time series are available, but involves shortfalls in pay data. In fact, the pay availability on female teenagers is too limited to be informative, and therefore only teenage males are considered here. Also, as there are no pay data available for Korea, the Netherlands, and Sweden, these countries are excluded from the analysis, while for many of the remaining countries data cover shorter time intervals than in the case of young adults.

Table 2.3 provides the changes in relative pay and employment rates between male 15 to 19 year olds and 25 to 54 year olds, referring to the respective time periods per country. These are then plotted against each other in Figure 2.7. It is evident that, like for young adults, the countries of Continental Europe show the most sizable declines in terms of teenage relative employment, whereas the group of Anglo-Saxon countries has experienced the biggest decrease in terms of teenage relative pay. Interestingly, in Belgium, Finland, Germany and Italy teenage pay has risen relative to that of prime-age adults and, especially in the case of Italy, the changes appear to suggest a general relative improvement. However, it is implausible that the changes in the time periods available for these countries are representative of the entire period of interest.[14] Thus, in sum, the general pattern of the changes in labor outcomes of male teenagers is similar to that of young adults.

The question again is whether the observed trends in terms of relative employment imply deterioration or not. Figure 2.8 illustrates the trends in unemployment rates of teenage males. Compared with the corresponding trends for young adults, relative unemployment rates of teenagers have generally fared more unfavorably, but in all other respects the observed trends are very similar. In particular, most countries have experienced deterioration in teenage unemployment that has persisted through time, indicating disequilibrium due to demand shortages.

Finally, the argument that educational participation is endogenous to employment and pay changes would be unsuitable in the case of teenagers, as enrollment in secondary schools is typically mandatory. In spite of this, participation in secondary education has also increased during the last three decades,[15] which may partly explain the positive changes in teenage relative wages observed in Germany, Finland, Italy, and Belgium, as the rise in teenage school enrollment reduces labor availability and also results in the average teenage worker becoming older. This is not the case in countries where students combine work and education by being employed part-time (for example, in the UK, the US, and the Netherlands).

REVIEWING THE PROPOSED CAUSAL FORCES

The explanations that have been suggested for the recent changes in youth relative labor outcomes originate from the aggregate literature and revolve around the idea of interactions between economic shocks and labor market institutions. What first shifted the research focus towards institutional

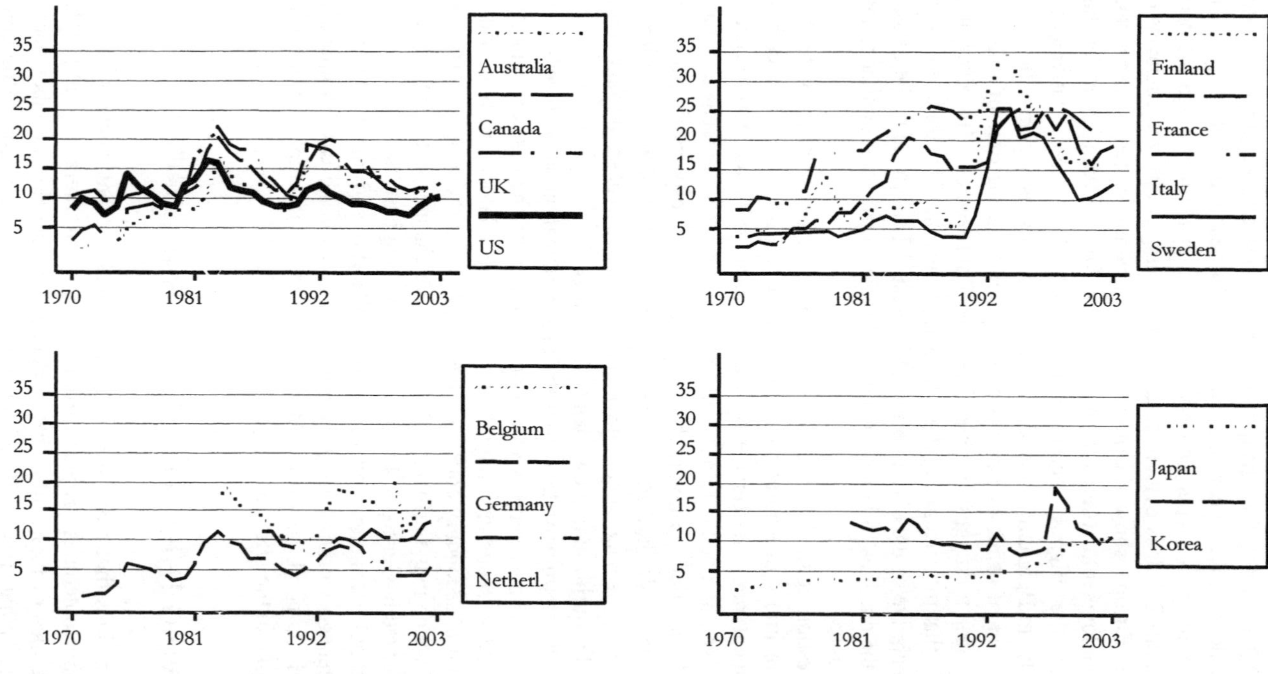

Source: OECD Labour Force Statistics-Indicators.

Figure 2.3 Unemployment Rates of 20 to 24 Year-Old Males

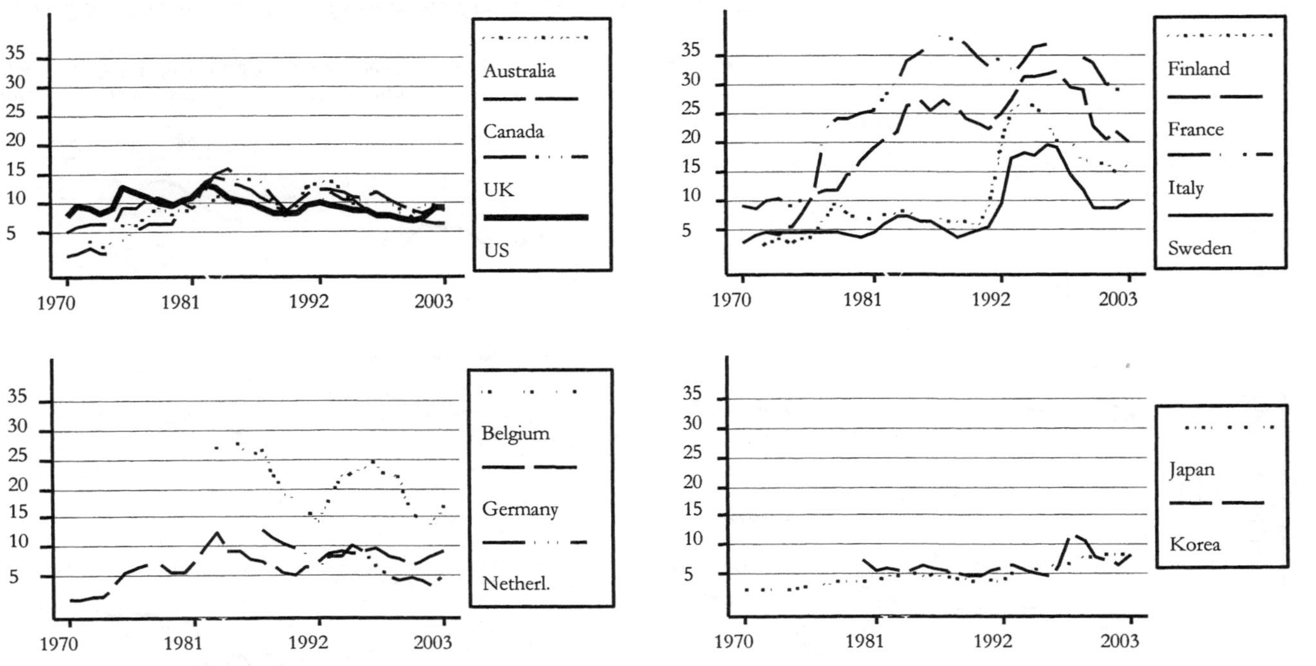

Source: OECD Labour Force Statistics-Indicators

Figure 2.4 Unemployment Rates of 20 to 24 Year-Old Females

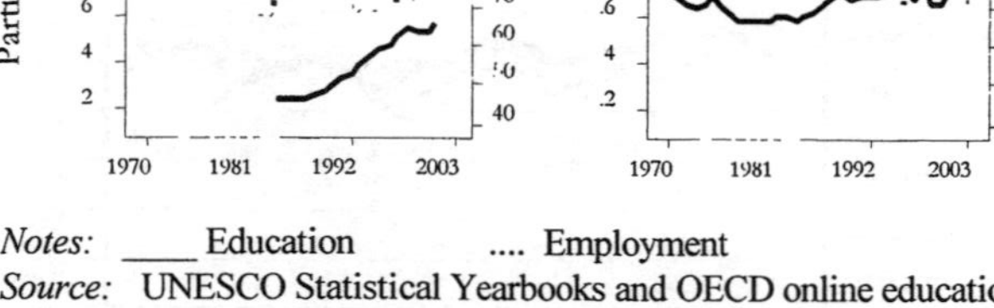

Notes: ____ Education .... Employment
Source: UNESCO Statistical Yearbooks and OECD online education database.

Figure 2.5 Educational Participation and Employment Ratios of Males

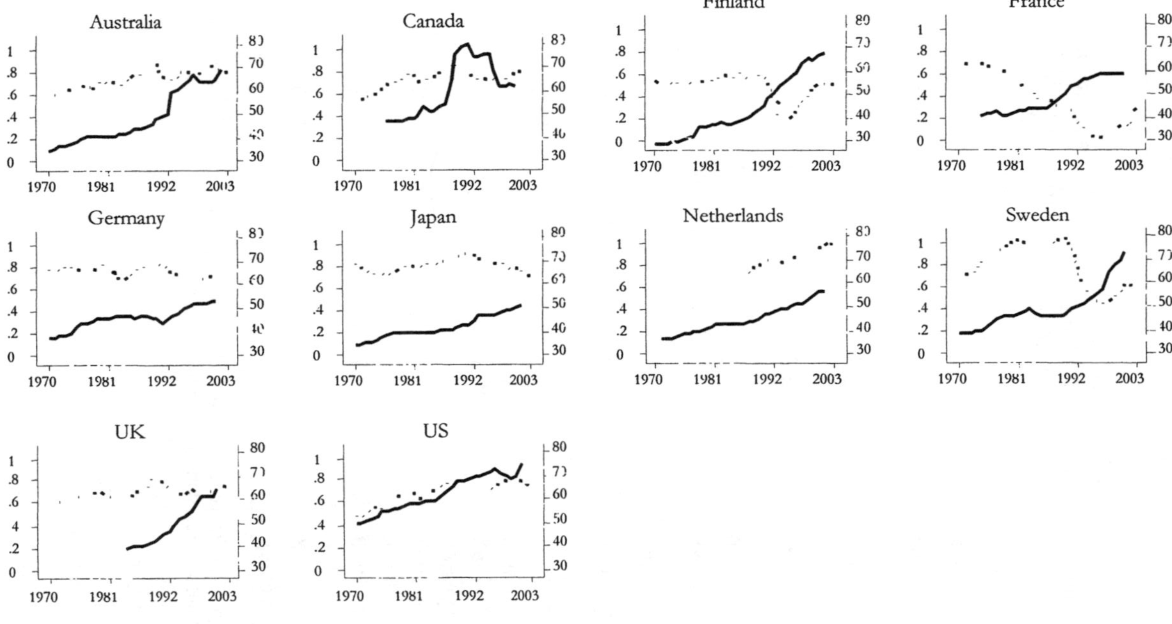

Notes: ____Education .....Employment
Source: OECD Labour Force Statistics-Indicators

Figure 2.6 Educational Participation and Employment Ratios of Females

Table 2.3 Changes in Relative Pay and Employment of Teenage and Prime-Age Adult Males

Country	Time Period	Difference between employment changes of 15–19 and 25–54 year olds	Changes in ratio of 15–19 to 25–54 year-olds' pay
	<15 years		
Belgium	1985–1994 (10 years)	-2.8	4.9
Germany	1984–1991 (8 years)	-3.8	1.1
Italy	1987–1995 (9 years)	3.2	2.1
Finland	1980–1990 (11 years)	-6.5	3.3
	>15 years		
Australia	1975–1998 (24 years)	-1.3	-9.9
Canada	1977–1995 (19 years)	1.9	-12.3
France	1970–1998 (29 years)	-19.1	-7.1
Japan	1973–1997 (25 years)	-5.7	-2.9
UK	1976–1996 (21 years)	-0.7	-9.8
US	1973–1998 (26 years)	-2.9	-11.9

Notes: Adult category for France is 35–44 year olds. For Belgium we use median earnings.
Source: OECD, Labour Force Statistics (Author's calculations).

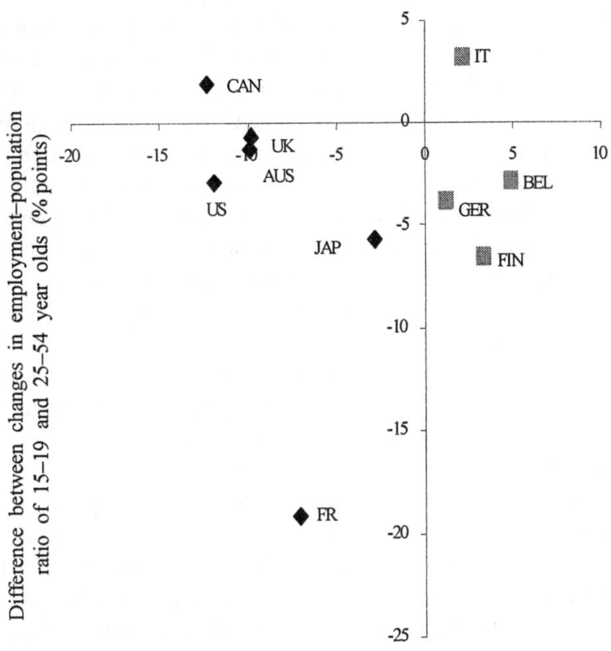

Notes: The time period per country is the longest available. Diamonds indicate period of change >15 years, squares indicate period of change <15 years.

Source: OECD Labour Force Statistics-Indicators.

Figure 2.7 Changes in Relative Pay and Employment of Teenage and Prime-Age Males

factors was the realization that since 1970 there has been a sharp divergence of economic performance within the OECD and, more specifically, the observed patterns of growing unemployment in Europe and growing wage inequality in the US.[16] These patterns gave rise to the so-called 'Krugman hypothesis,' according to which the root of differences in labor trends between skilled and unskilled workers is a combination of skill-biased demand shocks and institutions. The underlying principle is that pay-setting institutions in the labor market determine the flexibility of the wage mechanism and thus direct the effect of demand shifts either on pay or on employment. Therefore, skill-biased demand shifts when combined with rigid wages in Europe led to rising unemployment, while high wage flexibility in the US allowed their effect to fall on earnings differentials.

Nonetheless, Krugman defined skill as educational attainment only, ignoring its experience dimension, and as a consequence, the hypothesis failed to explain why amongst individual European countries a coincident increase in unemployment of both educated and uneducated cohorts was observed.[17] Moreover, it failed to explain why the declines were affecting mostly youth cohorts. Indeed, education-biased trends alone should have improved youth outcomes instead of worsening them, since the relative educational attainment of youths had risen strongly.

As expected, the Krugman hypothesis performs better when experience is added along with education as a skill component,[18] especially so if the aim is to explain the evolution of youth relative outcomes. In this case, it is more sensible to assume that demand shifts carry a 'double skill bias' (in Ryan's term) instead of an education bias alone; or in other words, that demand changes have been biased towards both education and experience, and the lack of experience of youths has outweighed the benefits of additional schooling.[19] Then, the double-skill-biased demand shifts in combination with the influence of labor market institutions may validly explain the deterioration in the situation of youth in advanced labor markets.

Naturally, the question to ask now is: what exactly are the forces that move relative labor demand against low-skilled workers? Internationalization factors and contemporary technological trends are the usual suspects. International trade can adversely affect the less-skilled through two distinctive channels. First, it can reduce the bargaining power of labor unions and the protectionist faculty of internal labor markets. Second, and more importantly, it can lead to the deindustrialization of advanced economies, as increased commercial with less developed countries and cheaper imported manufacturing goods cut low-value-added domestic manufacturing and the share of low-skilled employment. On the other hand, technological change can theoretically have an

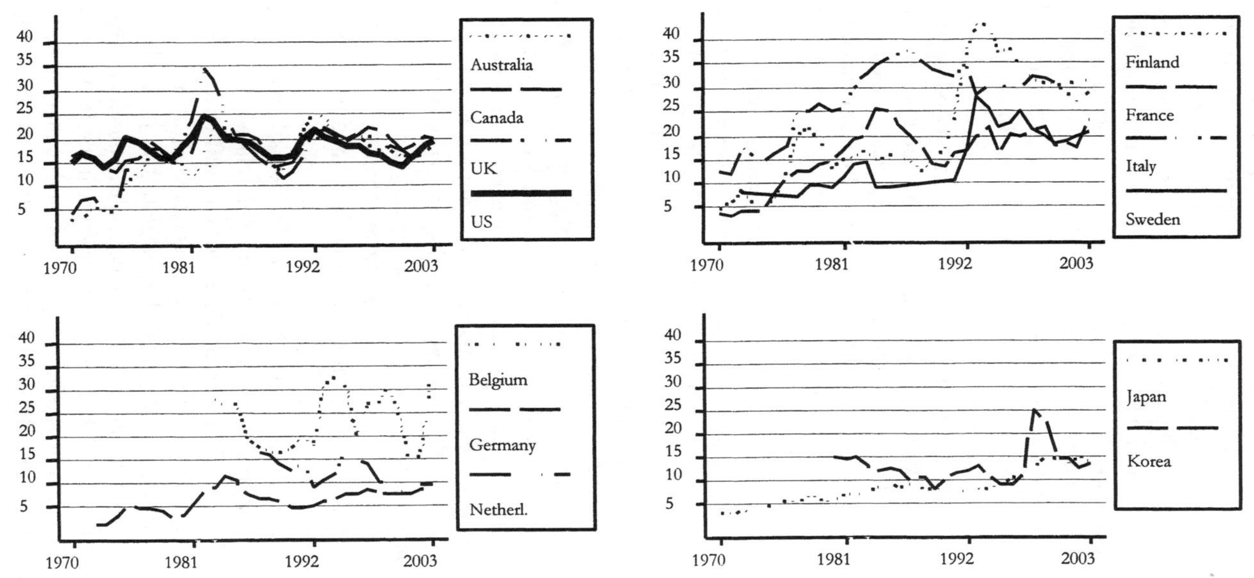

Source: OECD Labour Force Statistics-Indicators

Figure 2.8 Unemployment Rates of 15-19 Year Old Males

effect on labor demand either by substituting away from unskilled labor and towards skilled labor or by having the opposite effect. Computerization, for example, brings about the routinization of many simple repetitive tasks and the automation of many production procedures that would have been carried out by unskilled employees. It also provides skilled workers with more available information to be used creatively (Internet technology), and enables the development of new products and the tailoring of products and services to customer-specific needs. But the effect can also go in the opposite direction. Technology can substitute skilled labor by limiting very complicated tasks to the push of a button and – in the context of Marxian analysis – it can degrade, deskill and devalue work. In the latter case, skilled workers are the disfavored ones.

In most cases though, evidence from the modern period supports the former assumption. In fact, the skill-biased nature of both international trade and technology has been confirmed by empirical evidence (mostly from Canada and the US),[20] with the role of technological change on skill-relative outcomes proven more prominent,[21] although not sufficient to explain fully the observed trends on its own.[22]

Nonetheless, there is no obvious explanation why increasing international trade and changing technology would be experience-biased as well as education-biased. Computerization in particular should not work against youths as they tend to be more familiarized with computer usage and technology than older adults. A possibility is that technological change is education-biased in the short run but double skill-biased in the long run. More specifically, it is possible that technological change favors the educated during the transitional period when adaptation to new technology has to take place, after which it gradually becomes education-neutral as the diffusion of technologies leads to widespread familiarization.[23] So, if the ease of continuous adaptation to new technologies comes with experience, this could explain why in the long run an increasing rate of technological innovation disfavors youths even in those cases when they are equally as educated as older adults.[24] Still, more research is needed to shed light on this point.

Although it is not clear exactly how the double skill bias arises, the hypothesis is not contradicted by the trends in youth relative labor outcomes presented in section 1. However, neither does it suffice to explain the observed trends in all countries. If labor demand shifts tend to favor experience more as time passes, then they should also have affected the Netherlands and Germany in a direction dependent on their pay-setting institutions. Yet no major deterioration is apparent in these two countries. One reason for this could be the limited data availability that does not allow the examination of the trends during 1970 to 1985, which is when the bigger part of the deterioration took place for the rest of the European countries. Nevertheless, assuming that the story of success is true, a possible explanation could be given by the potentially youth-friendly influence of national school-to-work institutions, which are dominant in the two countries. With this in mind and aiming to form a more comprehensive explanatory scenario, Ryan assumed that double-skill-biased demand shifts interact both with labor market institutions as well as school-to-work institutions.

However, the explanation could be more straightforward. A different part of the literature on youth labor outcomes proposes economic cycles as their principal determining factor.[25] The supported assumption is that of 'youth super-cyclicality', which states that youth relative labor demand is more responsive to aggregate economic conditions than that of older adults. For example, under an adverse demand shock, a general break in hiring is expected to affect mostly youths, as they constitute the biggest part of inflows in the labor force. Super-cyclicality is expected to be present mainly in countries with rigid pay-setting institutions that deter market clearance and necessitate extra adjustment on the quantity-side. Moreover, super-cyclicality effects can also ensue via the 'first out, last in' practices prominent in internal labor markets. In other words, under a demand crisis in internal labor markets, youths are usually the first to be fired and the last to be hired, as less effort and time has been invested in their training in comparison to mature adults. In contrast, youth outcomes are less sensitive to shocks in occupational labor markets, where formal training systems provide young workers with transferable skills and recognizable qualifications and facilitate their mobility across employees.[26] The internal structures and the corresponding labor market experiences in Japan, France, and Sweden are consistent with this scenario.[27]

Evidently, most of the literature focuses on demand-side factors. However, supply-side changes were also present in advanced labor markets during the period of study and are potentially important. One of the most popular supply-side explanations for the youth labor market problem is the entry of the baby-boom generation in the job market during the 1970s. All else equal, an increase in relative youth cohort size implies a shift in relative labor supply, which should result in lower relative pay in countries with relatively flexible wages, and in higher youth unemployment in countries with relatively rigid wages. Indeed, the increase of the relative youth cohort has been a key factor of the initial deterioration in the youth relative outcomes during the 1970s. However, the trends did not recover after the youth proportion of the population declined during the 1980s in the US or the 1990s in Europe.[28] In other words, the labor outcomes did not follow the demographic cycles, implying that other forces must have played a more important role.

A more credible explanation on the supply side is provided by the changing quality of the labor force. In particular, if one assumes that those who enroll in school are the most able, as school enrollment rises, the quality of the youth labor force should fall. Yet the dramatic growth in the proportion of high school graduates going to college could also imply a decreasing selectivity of students on behalf of the colleges.[29] As a result, a portion of youths that would have been uneducated some years ago, has now shifted into the category of the educated, decreasing the average quality of the uneducated youths and resulting in a depreciation of college degrees. This should have decreased the relative competitiveness of youths in the labor market and most importantly, it should have decreased the importance of education relative to experience in the determination of youth labor outcomes.

A CLOSER LOOK AT INSTITUTIONS

It has been established so far that the influence of labor market institutions is potentially critical for the formation of youth labor outcomes. However, this influence varies among different sorts of institutions. To trace the channels through which institutions can affect youth outcomes, it is helpful to separate them into four categories: 1) employment protection (for example, laws regarding hiring and firing, the use of temporary contracts), which imposes direct restrictions on labor demand; 2) institutions that act on the supply side, namely the unemployment insurance system and the active labor market policies; 3) pay-setting institutions that mostly affect the rate of wage adjustment (for example, minimum wages, labor unions, the extent of centralization in wage-bargaining); and 4) school-to-work institutions (for example, school-employer recruitment networks, apprenticeships), which may have a positive impact on labor demand. The relevance of each to youth relative outcomes is addressed in turn. Finally, this section considers whether there are any connections between differences in institutions and youth relative labor outcomes.

Demand-Side Institutions

Employment protection institutions aim to increase job security by discouraging layoffs. However, they also entail the adverse effect of reducing hiring, since protection rules make dismissals costly and thus raise the bargaining power of the 'insiders', which in the case of a boost in demand increases their wages rather than employment.[30] Therefore, stricter legislation regarding employment protection is expected to be related to lower employment rates, and especially so for youths, as they constitute the biggest part of inflows into the labor force. This is very often confirmed by empirical evidence.[31]

Acknowledging the 'rigidity' arising from strict employment protection, and in an attempt to increase labor market flexibility in favor of the young, many European countries include age-specific provisions in the legislation: approvals of dismissals depends on social protection criteria like marital status, number of children, health, and seniority, thus leaving youths unprotected. Similarly, several countries allow the use of temporary work contracts, which cover youths more often than mature adults,[32] and for which no protection applies. In both cases, firing young workers is made less costly (or even entirely costless) and hiring young workers is encouraged but mostly temporary. As a result, both measures may actually have perverse effects, decreasing the welfare of youths, that is, of those they are supposed to help.[33]

The debate over the effectiveness of temporary contracts heated up after the 2006 labor law reform plans in France, which would have allowed employers to fire workers under age 26 without reason, notice, or severance.[34] After weeks of massive demonstrations led by students, the French government abandoned the proposed changes. However, the debate remains and is reinforced by the mixed empirical evidence. Some empirical studies find relatively adverse youth effects,[35] and others no youth effects at all.[36]

Supply-Side Institutions

On the supply side, high duration of unemployment benefits and easy access to them provide a disincentive to search for or accept work. This could be especially true for youths, as even when they are financially autonomous from their parents, they very often remain in the family home and are less likely than older adults to have dependents, like a spouse or children. As a result, youths could quit the labor force or stay unemployed for small increases in incomes from alternative sources more readily than mature adults. However, this is not expected with certainty. After all, young people have the longest working lives ahead of them and the least established reputations in the labor market, and stand to lose heavily in career terms from showing a willingness to remain on benefit. Moreover, the eligibility of youths as well as the replacement ratio they receive when eligible is lower on average than that of adults. This means that unemployment insurance policies could potentially leave youth outcomes unaffected or even increase youth relative employment prospects by providing a higher disincentive for older adults to participate in the labor force. Some empirical evidence suggests that youth relative unemployment rises as the generosity of the overall benefit system increases, yet the estimated effect is not always statistically significant.[37]

In addition to the generosity of the welfare system, youth labor supply is also affected by active labor market programs, specifically designed to help youths by offering job search assistance, work experience and job training. However, opposite to their intended effect, labor market programs may decrease youth employment prospects by stigmatizing the participants as 'disadvantaged' and 'low-quality' workers. Some programs do involve skill formation, but even so, if the training is work-based, participants are likely to displace regular youth employees, and in that case the programs are ineffective. According to available empirical results, active labor market programs seem to raise the well-being of participants in the short run,[38] but their long-run effects are poor, more so in the US than in Europe,[39] and more regarding youth relative pay than employment.[40]

Pay-Setting Institutions

Pay-setting institutions comprise two main forces: labor unions and minimum wage legislation. Considering minimum wages first, it is generally believed that they raise the bottom of the wage distribution, and thus they have a disproportionate employment effect on low-wage workers, including youth. However, empirical evidence does not always confirm this theory. In fact, although empirical research on the topic has been extensive, it has reached no consensus on whether higher minimum wages reduce employment for low-wage workers or have no effect at all.[41] Much of the disagreement comes from the US literature, climaxing in a dialogue between Card-Krueger and Neumark-Wascher over the effect of the increase in the minimum wage in New Jersey and Pennsylvania in 1992.[42] The latest paper by Neumark and Wascher constitutes an international minimum wage literature review; this highlights that 18 of the 19 studies with more reliable empirical methodology conclude that the minimum wage does have adverse employment effects, especially so for the low-skilled groups.[43]

Nevertheless, even if a general mandated minimum wage does not have any effect on youth employment, a youth sub-minimum wage — when used — is expected to have an impact on youth employment with certainty, as it gives rise to substitution between the relatively more expensive labor of prime-age adults and the relatively cheaper youth labor. Empirical evidence suggests a negative but moderate effect of the youth sub-minimum wage on youth employment, both in the Netherlands, where youth sub-minimum wages were sharply lowered between 1981 and 1983, and in Spain, where youth sub-minimum wages were raised in 1990.[44] Similarly, early research from Neumark and Wascher suggests that youth sub-minimum wage provisions in the US moderate the disemployment effects of minimum wages on teenagers.[45] However, as part of the ongoing debate, these results were challenged by Card, Katz and Krueger, on the basis that during the period of study sub-minimum wages in the states were not sufficiently used to be accountable for any adverse effect.[46]

As far as labour unions are concerned, their influence depends on the particular union aims and the microeconomic framework assumed. More specifically, in a framework where employment outcomes are always on the demand curve, such as in monopoly union or 'right-to-manage' models, labour outcomes will shift in opposite directions according to unions' aims. If unions pursue high wages, employment will deteriorate and vice versa. Then again, wages and employment can both shift in the same direction in models of efficient bargaining or employer monopsony, as equilibrium points are off labour demand curves.[47] Most aggregate empirical studies have found that unions compress the wage distribution but their effect on employment has been inconclusive, at least within the US and the UK.[48] Across the OECD, empirical research suggests a negative association between unions and employment,[49] but case studies in France, Germany, Canada and the US conclude against this result.[50]

Nevertheless, the focus here is on the trends in relative outcomes between age groups rather than absolute ones in either group, and relative outcomes depend mainly on the coverage of the youth cohorts from labour unions and the unions' priorities. More specifically, in unions dominated by prime-age adult membership where zero weight is given to interests of young workers, if elasticity of substitution in demand between age groups is high enough, the outcome pursued will be wage compression by age to restrict the competition that can drive down the wages of prime-age adult members. This strategy will be mainly pursued by unions with limited industrial power since strong unions are generally able to use durable direct controls on the use of youth labour instead.

However, in most cases unions are likely to give at least some weight to the interests of youths and then the policy of the union towards youth pay depends on the attitude of youths towards the union, the preferences of adults and the state of the market for unions. In particular, the union is expected to accept low youth wages under these circumstances: the less organized youths are in their representation within the union; the lower the levels of their activism and loyalty; the less sympathetic prime-age adults are towards youths; the lower the competition for youth membership between unions; and finally, the lower the importance of the existence of the union in the long term for the union leaders and members.[51] Then, given the direction towards which unions affect relative wages by age, the influence on relative employment outcomes will be in the same or opposite direction, depending on the microeconomic framework assumed, as explained above. Youth-specific empirical studies have found that labour unions tend to increase relative youth unemployment, but their statistical significance is uncertain.[52]

School-to-Work Institutions

Finally, school-to-work institutions, namely vocational training and school-employer networks, are also potentially important. Both aim to strengthen the links between education and the job market, the former by contextualizing learning and creating job-specific skills and the latter by accelerating employer–employee matching procedures and increasing the appeal of youths to employers. Therefore, school-to-work institutions are expected to affect relative youth outcomes by increasing relative labor demand. Indeed, country-specific studies have shown that vocationalism has a positive impact on employment,[53] mostly so on a part-time basis, with apprenticeships yielding superior results for youths than any of the other alternatives of regular employment, job training, unemployment and participation in labor market programs.[54]

However, this success is highly dependent on particular institutional support tailored according to country-specific needs and traditions. The German case provides a benchmark, by combining high integration between education and the labor market, and mutual commitments between employers and employees, facilitated in a collective bargaining system.[55] Most of the European countries where apprenticeship systems operate successfully follow the German paradigm, with their success stretching as far as the institutional support allows.[56]

Nevertheless, the German system is not without alternatives. Japan's internal labor market system eases school-to-work transition via a different route. It combines school-based hiring networks with employer-specific in-house training and a long-term employment system that provides job security and high promotion prospects,[57] all of which have fared well despite their notable decline under the 1990s stagnation.[58] Japan's 'internal route' is also followed by French training practices, although with little success.

Unfortunately, the lack of comparative and long-term data sets hurdles to cross-country empirical research, and therefore the effects of school-to-work institutions or networks on youth outcomes have been largely ignored by comparative youth-specific studies. However, in those rare cases that they have been accounted for, the estimated effects on youth outcomes have been positive and significant.[59]

Measuring Institutions

Having identified the ways in which institutions may affect youth labor outcomes, the next point to consider is whether and how much exactly institutions differ between countries, and more importantly, whether there is an evident connection between differences in institutions and youth relative labor outcomes by country. Table 2.4 presents newly reconstructed OECD indices of labor market institutions in the early 1980s and 2000s.

Considering demand-side institutions first, one can easily observe a dichotomy between the Anglo-Saxon countries that have relatively less strict employment protection rules and the countries of Continental Europe and Japan where protectionism is high. This pattern is apparent both for general employment protection legislation and for the legislation regarding temporary contracts only, which is more likely to influence youths. Even though in the 1980s and 1990s the labor law was 'softened' in many European countries, the dichotomy remained.

On the supply side, the situation is more complicated. In particular, the benefit system is not evidently more generous in Anglo-Saxon than Continental European countries; neither is Japan's benefit system similar to that of Continental European countries; and there is not even a generally observable decline in the generosity of the benefit system over time. More specifically, although the Anglo-Saxon countries offer relatively lower unemployment insurance, some of them, namely Australia and the UK, try to compensate for it with high benefit duration. These two countries also spend relatively more on policies than many of the Continental European countries. On the other hand, European countries experienced some notable changes in active policy spending. In 1982 Sweden's spending was impressively high, overshadowing the rest of the countries, but by 2001 it had decreased to less than one tenth of its initial value. In contrast, the respective figure for France rose almost as high as Sweden's was originally. Interestingly, the lowest spending on active policies was made by Japan (from 0 per cent of the GDP in 1982 to 0.15 per cent in 2001), which was also combined with very low replacement rates and benefit duration. In fact, Japan's supply-side institutions appear stingy overall. Presumably, the internal structure of the Japanese labor market offers sufficient job security to employees to make a generous formal benefit system redundant.

As far as wage-setting institutions are concerned, these are generally more powerful in the Continental European countries than in the Anglo-

Saxon ones, but the dichotomy is somewhat hazy, as the different measures of institutional strength contradict each other in many countries. For instance, French unions appear powerful if one looks at the union contract coverage and centralization and coordination indices, but the impression is quite the opposite if one considers the low (and decreasing) lever of union membership in the country. However, the level of union membership is the least reliable indicator of union strength. In fact, although a decline in union membership between 1982 and 2003 is evident in most countries, its effect for the Continental European countries is likely to be minimal, as with union coverage and bargaining centralization and coordination remaining at high levels, unions sustain their authority. Interestingly, as with the benefit system, Japan's pay setting institutions are weak overall (excluding the lever of centralization and coordination in bargaining which is moderate), thus following the Anglo-Saxon rather than the Continental European practice. Minimum wages in particular are lower in Japan than in any other country for which data is available; lower even than in the US.

Lastly, Table 2.5 provides registrations in apprenticeship in the late 1990s by country, as an indicator of school-to-work institutions. As this data is drawn from national sources, comparability between countries is imperfect. Naturally, no figure is given for Japan, as the Japanese school-to-work transition is based on informal networks and is difficult to quantify. Unsurprisingly then, the lead in school-to-work transition institutions is held by Germany, followed by the Netherlands. As these are two of the countries that — according to the restrictive amount of data available — avoided any significant deterioration in youth relative outcomes, the evidence tallies with Ryan's theory.[60] The Anglo-Saxon countries are the ones with the lowest figures. Unfortunately, due to a scarcity of earlier data, it is not possible to observe how apprenticeship has evolved over time.

On the whole, the evidence provided in Tables 2.4 and 2.5 is too complicated to allow for any inferences on the association between trends in relative labor outcomes by age and patterns of institutional restrictions. The fact that a general dichotomy is in many cases evident between the Anglo-Saxon and the Continental European countries gives confidence to the shocks–institutions scenario; nonetheless, there are a few cases in which this dichotomy is broken and the picture is made even more obscure when changes over time are taken into account.

THEORETICAL FRAMEWORK

In order to make better sense of all the information on youth relative labor outcomes and labor market institutions provided here, it is most helpful to

Table 2.4 Labor Market Institutions

	Regular empl. prot.		Temporary empl. prot.		Replac. rates		Benefit duration		Spending on youth ALMP		Youth min. wage		Union coverage		Coordinat./ centraliz.		Union density	
Years:	**1982**	**2003**	**1982**	**2003**	**1982**	**2003**	**1982**	**2003**	**1985**	**2001**	**1982**	**2003**	**1980**	**2000**	**1980**	**2000**	**1982**	**2003**
Australia	1.00	1.50	0.87	0.87	22.26	22.49	1.01	1.00	1.75	2.21	0.54	0.57	80	80	4.25	2.00	47.96	22.80
Belgium	1.68	1.73	4.62	2.62	44.12	42.15	0.86	0.90	0.29	0.11	0.55	0.46	90	90	3.50	3.75	52.11	55.76
Canada	1.32	1.32	0.25	0.25	18.60	15.11	0.33	0.33	0.60	0.50	0.42	0.41	37	32	1.00	1.00	35.84	27.43
Finland	2.78	2.17	1.87	1.87	24.45	35.60	0.77	0.65	1.97	3.80[a]			90	90	4.00	5.00	68.42	77.73
France	2.51	2.47	3.06	3.62	30.95	39.40	0.52	0.64	3.67	11.02	0.61	0.61[a]	80	90	2.00	2.00	17.00	8.20
Germany	2.58	2.02	3.75	2.02	29.17	27.20	0.75	0.72	0.83	2.50[a]			80	68	3.50	3.50	35.02	23.22
Italy	1.77	1.77	5.37	2.12	0.60	33.72	0.33	0.58	1.57[b]	5.34[a]			80	80	3.50	3.00	46.69	33.96
Japan	2.38	2.44	3.00	1.25	8.73	7.76	0.33	0.33	0.00[c]	0.15	0.30	0.31	25	15	2.50	2.50	19.70	32.78
Korea													15	10	1.00	1.00		
Netherl.	3.08	3.05	2.37	1.19	47.67	52.29	0.73	0.74	0.88	3.22[a]	0.57	0.48	70	80	3.75	3.50	32.78	22.26
Sweden	2.90	2.86	4.08	1.62	26.55	24.43	0.31	0.32	12.65	0.94[a]			80	90	4.00	3.00	78.00	48.72
UK	0.95	1.11	0.25	0.37	22.96	16.35	0.78	0.89	4.83	5.59			70	30	1.00	1.00	48.72	30.50
US	0.17	0.17	0.25	0.25	14.19	13.77	0.44	0.46	0.91	1.06	0.43	0.32	26	14	1.00	1.00	20.23	12.22

Definitions: Regular employment protection: OECD indicator of the stringency of regular employment protection legislation. Temporary employment: OECD indicator of the stringency of employment protection legislation for temporary contracts. Replacement rates: Average unemployment benefit replacement rate. Benefit duration: Years of unemployment benefits. Spending on youth ALMP: Ratio of spending on youth measures per unemployed to GDP per capita (%). Youth minimum wage: Youth minimum wage as a % of median wage (equals the adult minimum wage as a % of median wage for all countries except for the Netherlands and the UK). Union coverage: The share of workers covered by a collective agreement, in %. Coordination/centralization: Average of OECD centralization and coordination ordinal indicators. Ranges between a low 1 and a high 5. Union density: The share of workers affiliated to a trade union, in %.

Notes: (a)2002, (b)1991, (c)1987.

Sources: The Coordination/Centralization was derived from Table 3.5, OECD (2004a). For Korea, union coverage was also derived from OECD (2004a). The rest of the information was provided by Andrea Bassanini (used in Bassanini and Duval 2006).

Table 2.5 Apprenticeship Registration by Country

Country	Year	Number of registered apprentices	Apprentices as a % of the 20–24 year-old cohort
Australia	1998	124,500	9.3
Canada	1997	172,343	8.7
Finland	1997	36,289	11.6
France	1998	337,690	9.5
Germany	1997	1,622,000	36.7
Netherlands	1998	138,000	14.3
Sweden	2000	2,000	0.4
UK	1998	117,700	3.4
US	2000	360,511	2.0

Sources: Australia: ABS survey data; Canada: Sharpe (1999); Finland: European Training Village (1999a); France: European Training Village (1999b). (Data include overseas territories). Germany and the Netherlands: Table 1, Ryan (2000); Sweden: Lindell, and Abrahamsson (2002); UK: Work based training for young people: by type of training, in Office for National Statistics (2002). Modern Apprenticeships in England and Wales only; US: OATELS/BAT (2000). Source for population data is the online database of OECD Labour Market Statistics.

analyze it within the theoretical framework of the supply demand institutions (SDI) approach. This approach can be described in basic terms as follows: under the assumption of imperfect substitutability between skill-groups in demand and of no skill-group substitutability in supply, relative labor demand is considered as moderately elastic and relative labor supply as perfectly inelastic. Supply and demand are assumed to interact in a competitive setting in order to determine labor outcomes, and any deviations from the competitive equilibrium point are attributed to institutional or non-competitive forces that restrict wage setting (unions, minimum wages and so on). (Dis)Equilibrium outcomes can be altered by supply or demand shifts in different ways, depending on the existing institutional restrictions, or by institutional changes caused either exogenously or endogenously as responses to the shifts in demand and/or supply. Outcomes are assumed always to lie on the demand curve.[61]

Adjusted to explain the evolution of relative labor outcomes by age, the SDI framework assumes that youths and mature adults are under the influence of the same (country-specific) macroeconomic, technological, demographic and institutional changes, whose impact is channeled through the interacting forces of labor demand, labor supply and wage-adjustment under the given institutional restrictions. But as some forces and restrictions affect youths and mature adults in different ways, and as youths and mature adults are assumed to be imperfect substitutes in demand, the final effect on labor outcomes is different between age groups.

The extent of substitutability by age group in demand and supply, and thus their respective elasticities, are potentially crucial. Specifically, in a competitive setting, relative demand elasticity determines the effect of supply shifts on relative outcomes. Therefore, the assumption of imperfect demand substitutability (that is, of moderately elastic relative demand) entails that shifts in relative labor supply change both relative wage and relative employment outcomes. On the other hand, when considering labor demand shifts, the effects on labor outcomes are determined by the elasticity of relative labor supply. Since in the SDI framework it is typical to assume that relative supply is highly inelastic, shifts in relative demand are expected mostly to affect relative wages. However, this requires more careful consideration. Empirical studies have concluded that, when one aggregates across all workers, the labor supply curve is upward sloping and fairly steep. In disaggregated analysis though, this depends on the differences between the wage-responsiveness of the two age groups and the substitution possibilities on the supply side, which have been habitually ignored by the SDI approach. The wage responsiveness of youth labor supply is expected to be higher than that of older adults, as the former are in those stages of their life cycle when the alternative uses of time are highest (that is, education). Moreover, youths and prime-age adults may be members of the same households and youth participation may be largely affected by the relative wages or participation decisions of prime-age adults. Therefore a certain degree of flexibility in relative supply would not be surprising. In this case, potential shifts in relative labor demand would affect both relative wage and relative employment outcomes.

Using an enhanced version of the SDI framework, an attempt to understand the youth labor market experiences as observed since the 1970s is depicted in Figure 2.9. Both relative demand and supply are sketched as price-responsive, with either high or low elasticity, and all four possible combinations are considered. The competitive equilibrium outcomes are determined by the intersection of the relative demand and supply curves in each period. An adverse shift in demand (from D_0 to D_1), under perfectly competitive wage setting, moves the equilibrium from point A to B. The shift decreases both relative employment and relative wage outcomes. On the other extreme, under complete wage inflexibility the same change in relative demand shifts equilibrium from point A to point C, with relative

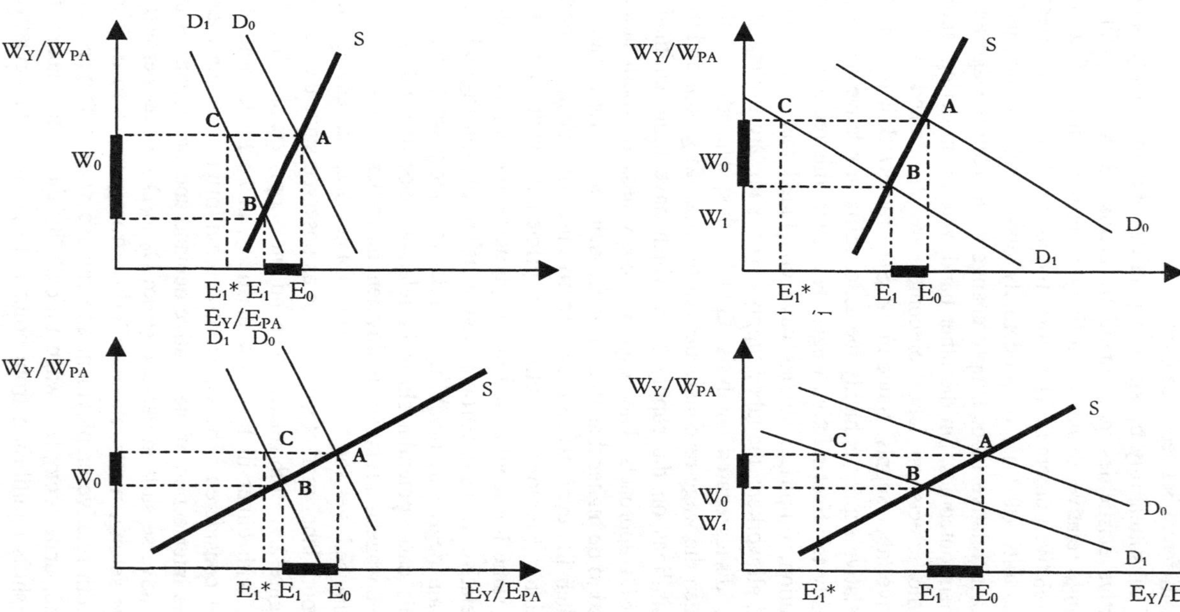

Notes: W = wages, E = employment, Y = youth and PA = prime-age adults. D = demand and S = supply. The horizontal axis represents relative outcomes at all times. The points indicated by W or E on the axes represent relative pay and employment respectively.

Figure 2.9 SDI Framework – Youths versus Prime-Age Adults

wages remaining unchanged but relative employment becoming much lower. Point C is still on the labor demand curve but it is technically a disequilibrium point as it is not at an intersection between demand and supply. This is attributed to the intervention of institutional factors, the effects of which are revealed by the divergence between competitive and actual levels of relative wages (W_0 - W_1).

As already mentioned, under perfectly competitive pay determination, the effect of the demand shift on relative outcomes depends on the elasticity of relative supply. Figure 2.9 shows that, indeed, the higher the elasticity of relative supply the bigger the effect on employment (E_0 - E_1) and the lower the effect on pay (W_0-W_1). However, under perfectly rigid pay-setting the supply elasticity plays no role. Instead, as relative employment outcomes are assumed always to lie on the demand curve, it is demand elasticity that matters. Thus, the higher the elasticity of relative demand the bigger the decrease in employment (E_0 - E_1*).

This analysis can be used in combination with the evidence provided in the previous section to provide an insight into the labor market situation in advanced economies. In particular, let us compare the labor market experiences of France and Sweden with those of Canada and the US, which – according to the evidence presented in Table 2.4 – have been on the two extremes of wage-setting regulation. Given that pay setting in France and Sweden is relative highly regulated, whereas in Canada and the US both union power and bargaining coordination are low, the two groups of countries should react to an adverse demand shift by moving towards points C and B, respectively. Considering now the changes in their relative labor outcomes, namely that Canada and the US have experienced mainly a decline in relative pay, whereas France and Sweden have experienced mainly a decline in relative employment, it is plausible to infer that the situation would be best described within the SDI framework by assuming a highly inelastic labor supply. Next, consider Japan. According to Table 2.4, Japan's wage-setting institutions are almost as powerless as those in the US, yet its labor market experience (for males) is similar to that of Sweden. So, Japan's story is consistent with a highly flexible relative supply schedule.

Thus, the SDI framework can explain how the shocks–institutions interaction is felt by each country given its specific characteristics. Although interesting, this analysis misses an important point. It only takes into account the influence of institutions that set wage restrictions, whereas, as explained in section 3, institutional restrictions may also arise on the quantity-side. In the case of Japan, for instance, low wage-setting regulation is combined with strict employment protection legislation, which – if taken into consideration – could completely change the story described above.[62]

However, the SDI framework draws together a number of desirable properties. Firstly, it is simple and intuitive. Secondly, it takes employment and wage outcomes to be simultaneously co-determined. Thirdly, it can assimilate all proposed explanations for the youth labor market problem: the 'double skill bias' and the 'super-cyclicality' hypotheses can be represented by a downward shift of the relative labor demand schedule, while demographic changes can be represented by a shift in the relative supply schedule. Even its drawback can be dealt with: the SDI framework can be extended to incorporate both supply-side and demand-side institutional interventions.

Note though that the discussion provides no more than a flavor of the workings of the labor markets in advanced countries. Cross-country heterogeneity both in changes in relative labor outcomes and in institutional mixtures is too substantial and the diagrammatic version of the SDI framework in Figure 2.9 is too basic, for this analysis to reach valid conclusions on the exact relationship between shocks, institutions, and relative labor outcomes by country. This is obviously a task for empirical research.[63]

CONCLUSION

The evolution of youth labor market outcomes in recent decades has attracted much attention, leading to the widely-held view that the position of youths across the OECD labor markets has deteriorated compared to that of adults since the early 1970s. However, there remains a need for more extensive research – involving more countries and longer time periods – in order to establish this assertion and to explain it effectively.

This chapter has re-examined the youth labor market problem and has presented up-to-date evidence on youth employment, unemployment, wages, and education participation. The observed trends have indeed suggested a general deterioration for youths, both absolutely, and most importantly, relatively to mature adults, with only a few exceptions. Consistent with previous evidence, relative deterioration between youths and prime-age adults has materialized as declines in either youth relative pay, or relative employment, or more rarely in both. Declines in relative employment have often been accompanied by increases in educational participation, but the general impression is that changes in educational participation were to some extent forced by adverse labor market conditions.

In addition, the declines in relative labor outcomes have formed patterns across countries. In the case of young male adults for instance, the Anglo-

Saxon countries in the sample have experienced large declines in youth relative pay whereas changes in relative employment were not significant. In contrast, France, Sweden, Japan, and Korea have experienced large declines in youth relative employment, whereas changes in relative pay were not significant. Germany and the Netherlands have been the only countries where the deterioration observed was minimal. However, Germany's success was found to be very sensitive to changes of the time period under consideration, and due to the lack of a full time series on pay the Dutch story remained inconclusive. Notably, these patterns change very little when young female adults or even male teenagers are examined instead.

According to the literature, the potential causes of the situation are numerous; one can count many candidate explanations for the youth labor market problem, as many forces or restrictions might be present in a labor market. However, the determining role is thought to be played by adverse demand shifts (changing technology, increasing international trade or general macroeconomic shocks) in combination with labor market institutions. To discuss this hypothesis, along with the evidence on changes in relative labor outcomes, this chapter has presented a set of new OECD institutional indicators. Then the evidence has been examined within the supply demand institutions framework to make the links between labor outcomes, shocks and institutions clearer.

Overall, the evidence provided in this chapter and the subsequent discussions have been far from sufficient to offer a conclusive assessment of the youth labor market problem. However, one should be reasonable enough to leave that to econometric research. The objective here has been to give a sense of the challenges that youths have been facing in the labor market during the recent decades, to identify the factors that are to blame, and to provide a basic understanding of the workings of youth labor markets in advanced economies.

NOTES

1. This work was undertaken as part of my PhD research under the supervision of Professor Paul Ryan and with the financial sponsorship of the Greek State Scholarship Foundation (IKY). I am grateful to Karin Doolan for her useful suggestions, comments and support. The provision of data on labor market institutions by Andrea Bassanini is also gratefully acknowledged.
2. Blanchflower and Freeman (2000a).
3. OECD (1999a); Blanchflower and Freeman (2000b); Ryan (2001).
4. See for example, the empirical work of Blanchflower and Freeman (2000c); Jimeno and Rodriquez-Palenzuela (2002); Bertola, Blau and Kahn (2002); OECD (2004a).
5. Data include part-time employment.

6. Relative changes between 20 to 24 and 25 to 54 year-olds reported for Belgium, Germany, Italy and the Netherlands refer to periods shorter than 15 years. Data for longer periods are available for the rest of the countries.
7. In order to remove the effect from the increased labor force participation of prime-age female adults, instead of using relative wages between youths and prime-age adults as is the case for males, changes in absolute youth employment rates are used. However, young adults also increased their labor force participation during the last decades and this remains present in the data.
8. Ryan (2001).
9. The picture of relative employment in Germany and Italy – as evidenced in Table 2.1 – is completely different when more years are included in the analysis. The same holds for changes in relative pay. In particular, Blanchflower and Freeman (2000b) present evidence of a 5 per cent deterioration in relative pay between 20 to 24 and 40 to 49 year olds (males and females together) in Germany for the period 1978–1990 and a 16 per cent deterioration in relative pay between 20 to 24 and 45 to 54 year old females in Italy between 1984 and 1993. This signals that both countries' position on the graph would be further away from the intersection of the axes if earlier data were available. Similarly, the lack of earlier data also leaves questionable the story of success for the Netherlands.
10. The trends may also suggest changes in job-search durations and costs. However, the observed fluctuations are too high to be strictly indicative of varying labour market frictions.
11. Data include all institutions (ISCED levels 5, 6, and 7) that require as a minimum condition of admission the successful completion of secondary education or evidence of the attainment of an equivalent level of knowledge. The series includes: (a) universities and equivalent degree-granting institutions; (b) distance-learning university institutions; (c) other tertiary educational institutions, such as teacher training colleges and technical colleges. The statistics refer to both public and private education. (Values missing between years have been inserted by linear interpolation, author's calculations.) Sources: *UNESCO Statistical Yearbooks* and OECD online education database. Note that the data on education make no distinction between part-time and full-time enrollment. Moreover, participation in tertiary education, given that it does not involve only 20 to 24 year-olds but also younger and older students, is not the same as educational participation of 20 to 24 year-olds. However, if the shares of <20 and >24 year-olds in tertiary education change little as enrollment rises, the data in hand may serve as a good proxy of changes in participation rates for young adults.
12. See Bowers, Sonnet and Bardone (1999).
13. In the Korenman and Neumark (2000) study, data on the youth category included teenagers and did not distinguish between sexes. The time period covered was 1970 to 1994, but for most countries data was unavailable before the mid-1980s.
14. At least regarding relative changes in employment rates in Germany, Finland and Italy, consideration of longer time periods yields evidence of sizable declines. Specifically, in the period 1970 to 2003 employment of teenage males decreased relative to that of mature male adults by 15.7 per cent in Germany, 28.9 per cent in Finland and 14.7 per cent in Italy.
15. Bowers, Sonnet and Bardone (1999).
16. See Freeman and Nickell (1988); Layard, Nickell and Jackman (1991); OECD (1994); Krugman (1994).
17. See Nickell and Bell (1996).
18. See for example, Card, Kramarz and Lemieux (1996).
19. See Ryan, Chapter 6, and the relevant references therein.
20. See Katz and Murphy (1992); Juhn, Murphy and Pierce (1993); Beaulieu (2000).
21. See for example, Berman, Bound and Griliches (1994); Wood (1994); Doms, Dunne and Troske (1997); Autor, Katz and Krueger (1998).
22. See Card and DiNardo (2002).

23. Katz and Autor (1999).
24. This could be more applicable to job-specific experience. Some evidence suggests that seniority premia vary more with technological change than with the technological level itself. See Hægeland (2001).
25. Clark and Summers (1982); OECD (1982, 1994, 1996); Blanchflower and Freeman (2000b); O' Higgins (1997, 2001).
26. Garonna and Ryan (1991); Marsden and Ryan (1991).
27. One would expect the effect of interaction of internal labour market structures and shocks to prove temporary. However, it is also plausible that employment does not recover in those terms, especially from the 1980s onwards.
28. Korenman and Neumark (2000).
29. Bishop (1991).
30. Van Long and Siebert (1983); Lindbeck and Snower (1986).
31. See Table 2.3 in OECD (2004b), for a summary of empirical findings.
32. Ryan (2001).
33. Blanchard and Landier (2002).
34. See the short discussion by Howell and Schmitt (2006).
35. See Scarpetta (1996); Jimeno and Rodriguez-Palenzuela (2002); Bertola, Blau and Kahn (2002); Djankov *et al.* (2003).
36. OECD (1999a).
37. See again Jimeno and Rodriguez-Palenzuela (2002) and Bertola, Blau and Kahn (2002).
38. Korpi (1997).
39. O'Higgins (1994); Grubb (1996).
40. Ackum (1991); Andrews, Bradley and Upward (1999).
41. Freeman (1994).
42. Card and Krueger (1994, 2000); Neumark and Wascher (2000).
43. Neumark and Wascher (2006).
44. Dolado *et al.* (1996).
45. Neumark and Wascher (1992, 1994).
46. Card, Katz and Krueger (1994).
47. Card and Krueger (1995); Manning (1996).
48. Boal and Pencavel (1994).
49. Nickell (1997).
50. Krueger and Pischke (1997); Card, Kramarz and Lemieux (1999).
51. Ryan (1987).
52. Jimeno and Rodriguez-Palenzuela (2002); Bertola, Blau and Kahn (2002); OECD (1998, 2004a); Bassanini and Duval (2006).
53. Payne (1995).
54. Ryan (1998); Abowd *et al.* (2000).
55. Steedman (1993); Oulton and Steedman (1994); Soskice (1994); Shackleton (1995).
56. The system operates well in Austria, Denmark, Ireland, Switzerland, and the Netherlands, but the UK's system has performed poorly. Its drawbacks include: lack of integration of the educational system with youth employment policy; lack of universally accepted qualifications; lack of involvement of trade unions and workers organisations and so forth (O'Higgins 1997). Still, the fact that Ireland could recently develop a solid apprenticeship system without heavy regulations and institutional development could be promising for the UK as well (Ryan 2000).
57. JIL (2002).
58. Nitta (1995).
59. OECD (1998) uses a dummy variable for whether or not countries have developed an apprenticeship system in youth employment and unemployment regressions and the estimated effect has been positive and significant.
60. See Ryan, Chapter 6.
61. For a detailed discussion on the SDI framework, see Katz and Autor (1999).

62. The SDI approach can also be criticized for two additional reasons. Firstly, it restricts labor market outcomes to lie on the labor demand schedule, and secondly, it does not account for labor market frictions. However, as post-1970 labor trends signal demand-constrained labor markets, and as labor market frictions in relative terms between groups are expected to stay roughly constant in time and thus leave relative labor outcomes unaffected, the two assumptions are not particularly restrictive – at least not for the purposes of the present study.
63. I undertake this task in my PhD thesis (Faculty of Economics, University of Cambridge). In particular, I use the SDI framework as a theoretical basis to build a structural disequilibrium labor market model for youths and estimate it given a panel database of 10 OECD countries (all countries discussed here except for Belgium, Italy, and Korea). For the typical country in the sample the estimation provides evidence in favor of all major explanatory scenarios; that is, of the super-cyclicality hypothesis and the double skill bias hypothesis as well as the significant wage-adjustment restrictions imposed by labor unions. As expected, cross-country heterogeneity in the results was also significant. The countries of Continental Europe showed bigger super-cyclicality effects and slower (not statistically different from zero) wage adjustment and the Anglo-Saxon countries showed a more 'flexible' rate of relative wage adjustment and lower super-cyclicality effects.

3. Out of School, Out of Work, Out of Luck? Black Male Youth Joblessness in New York City

Mark Levitan

In 2000, nearly one out of five of New York City's half million 16 through 24 year old males was neither in school nor at work. These nearly 100,000 young people were 'disconnected.'[1] To be disconnected – a large body of social science research informs us – is to be in danger. Youth with time on their hands are more likely than others to engage in activities (such as drug abuse and crime) that are destructive to themselves and their communities. Adults with large blank spaces in their résumés are more likely to be jobless and earn lower wages later in their lives than those who had been able to stay steadily connected in their teens and early twenties.[2]

The share of the city's male youth who were neither in school nor at work was nearly 1.5 times that for the nation at large (19 per cent compared to 13 per cent). The difference is due to the dramatically smaller share of the city's out-of-school youth who are employed (58 per cent versus 72 per cent). Lack of employment is a particularly acute and apparently growing problem for New York's out-of-school young Black males, just 43 per cent of whom were working in 2000.

This chapter focuses on the issue of joblessness among New York City's out-of-school male youth. Particular attention is paid to the plight of African American males. To explore the problem I use data from the 1990 and 2000 Census Public Use Micro Samples (PUMS) to analyze the sources of change in jobholding by race/ethnic group.[3] Gains or losses in employment are examined at two levels of aggregation: first, through the lens of 70 occupation by industry job cells and second, by three job tiers composed of groups of job cells.[4]

I find (via shift-share analysis) that, during the 1990s, White, Black, and Hispanic out-of-school male youth were in the wrong place at the wrong time; that is, changes in the industry and occupational mix of the city economy adversely impacted employment levels in the job cells that typically offer work to males in their late teens and early twenties. However, this 'structural change' was largely overshadowed by 'share change' – declines in the Black (and White) male youth share of all the employment available within the job cells. Other groups of labor market participants gained a larger share of employment in what had been areas of high Black male youth jobholding.

Which groups did Black male youth lose share to? Correlations between changes in various groups' share of employment by industry/occupation cell indicate a statistical association between the Black male youth loss of share and share gains by adult immigrants and single mothers, two groups who were becoming larger proportions of the New York City labor force during the 1990s. Pair-wise correlations provide no evidence that the Black youth share of employment fell because of competition from other groups of youth.

Further insight into the role of structural and share effects is obtained at the level of three job tiers: executive and professional; sales, support, and service; and blue collar. Black male youth are particularly dependent on employment in the sales, support, and service tier. The greatest decline in jobs held by out-of- school Black male youth from 1990 to 2000, however, was in the blue-collar tier. Almost all the job loss suffered by Black male youth in this sector was due to their declining share of employment in it. By contrast more adult immigrants were employed in the blue-collar tier in 2000 than in 1990. This suggests that in the area of the job market where 'typical immigrant' disadvantages, such as limited English or low educational attainment might be the least burdensome, immigrant labor was replacing Black labor.

A growing mismatch between the skills young Black males possess and the skills that employers seek in their employees is another and, perhaps, the most widely held explanation for rising Black male youth joblessness. The Census data do not provide a measure of the skills that workers use in their jobs, so researchers have used educational attainment as a proxy. Using this indicator I find a growing education gap between Black male youth and workers employed in New York City. The increasing gap offers an explanation why young Black males were not able to increase their presence in the sector of the city economy that enjoyed substantial job growth in the 1990s, the executive and professional tier.

A continued shift in the occupational and industrial mix in employment toward this tier will continue to threaten the ability of young Black males to secure work in the city, unless there are significant public policy initiatives. The need to address the high school dropout rate for 'minority' youth is one obvious policy implication of this study. Another implication is the need to create a comprehensive 'second chance' system for those youth who have already or will continue to leave high school without the credentials or connections to work and higher education that are necessary to make a successful transition to adulthood.

CONTEXT

A relatively large fraction of New York City's male youth is not connected to two institutions that are central to the process of becoming successful adults: school and work. Table 3.1 provides estimates derived from the 2000 Census to compare the distribution of the city's male youth with that of the nation by these activities. Nearly identical proportions of New York and US young males (16 through 24 years of age) are attending school (54 per cent). The city's high 'disconnected rate' is due, therefore, to the comparatively small fraction of its male youth who are out of school but are employed (merely 26.9 per cent in New York against 33.3 per cent in the nation). As a result nearly one in five (19.1 per cent) of New York's male youth were disconnected, while roughly one in eight (13.0 per cent) of male youth nationally were both out of school and jobless.

Table 3.1 Male Youth Population by School and Work Status

	US	**NYC**	**PP DIF**
In school	53.7%	54.0%	0.3
Out of school, at work	33.3%	26.9%	-6.4
Out of school, out of work	13.0%	19.1%	6.1

Notes: PP DIF: Percentage point difference

Source: This and all other tables: author's tabulations from 2000 Census PUMS.

These employment rate differences hold across the three largest race/ethnic groups in the national (and city) population. Table 3.2 provides employment–population ratios for out-of-school males. For all out-of-school youth, the New York City – US gap stood at nearly 14 percentage points. The disparity is not simply because New York has a higher proportion of race/ethnic groups who tend to have relatively low rates of jobholding. As the table indicates, the city suffers lower employment–population ratios within each group. These range from a nearly 12 percentage point gap for New York and national Hispanics to an almost 6 percentage point disparity between New York and national Blacks.

Table 3.2 Employment–Population Ratios for Out-of-School Males, 2000

	All	**NH White**	**NH Black**	**Hispanic**
US	71.9	79.4	48.4	68.3
NYC	58.4	73.0	42.7	56.6
PP DIF*	-13.5	-6.4	-5.7	-11.7

Notes: PP DIF: Percentage point difference.
NH = non-Hispanic
See Appendix 3.1 for a description of the race and ethnic categories.

Table 3.3 Change in Employment–Population Ratios, NYC Out- of-School Males, 1990 to 2000

	NH White	**NH Black**	**Hispanic**	**All**
1990	74.3	48.2	58.4	61.0
2000	73.0	42.7	56.6	58.4
PP DIF*	-1.2	-5.5	-1.8	-2.5

Notes: PP DIF: Percentage point difference.
NH = non-Hispanic
See Appendix 3.1 for a description of the race and ethnic categories.

Not only do New York's out-of-school Black youth suffer the lowest rates of jobholding in this comparison (42.7 per cent); their level of jobholding has declined the most dramatically over time. Table 3.3 reports the percentage point change in employment–population ratios from 1990 to 2000 for the city's out-of-school male youth. Citywide, the jobholding rate for out-of-school male youth declined by 2.5 percentage points. The drop for New York's Black youth was over twice as large: a 5.5 percentage point plunge. Why are New York City's Black male youth faring so poorly in the labor market?

Explanations of Joblessness

The issue of African American male youth joblessness is hardly new.[5] Explanations of it are part of a broader debate about declining employment and wage rates for a number of demographic groups over the past several decades. A review of a now immense body of work is beyond the scope of this chapter, yet it is worth sketching out some of the leading hypotheses so as to provide a context for this chapter's analysis. One way to organize these explanations is whether they are focused on the demand or supply side of the labor market. However, the reader will soon notice that, first, hypotheses that begin with one side of the labor market must make some reference to what is happening on the other and second, the contending ideas are not mutually exclusive.

Demand-side explanations of rising joblessness among Black male youth center on changes in the type of labor employers seek to hire. Perhaps the most widely accepted view is that technological change is shifting employer demand toward more skilled labor.[6] If the skills held by Black male youth are not increasing as rapidly as the increase in skill requirements, the growing 'mismatch' will either force them to accept lower wages or result in higher levels of joblessness. Another kind of mismatch, a spatial one, could adversely affect Black male employment. If the local employment mix is changing because of a shifting geographic distribution of economic activity, it may deprive urban areas of industries that once provided job opportunities for the less skilled.[7]

Another explanation that centers on the kinds of workers that employers want to hire is based on employer racial preferences. Employment discrimination based on race has a long history in the United States.[8] Employers may be reluctant to hire Blacks because of their own racial attitudes, judgments about the racial attitudes of their employees or customers, and/or a belief that 'on average' Blacks are inferior workers compared to other available sources of labor. If this were to be an important factor in increased Black male youth joblessness, there would need to be a reason why employer racial preferences had become a growing barrier to Black employment. One line of reasoning centers on the importance of 'soft' skills in the growing service sector. The shift from factory floor to sales counter makes having a 'pleasing manner' more important to job performance. But what is pleasing is so given to subjectivity that it is hard to demarcate where perception of skill ends and bias begins. The more employers value soft skills, the more room there is for bias to play a role in hiring.[9]

The conflation of skills and race provides a segue to supply-side explanations of why employers would be increasingly reluctant to hire young Black males. One possibility is that the quality of young Black male jobseekers has deteriorated because of pre-market factors such as the declining quality of inner-city schools or increasingly unstable family backgrounds. Another is that it has deteriorated relative to the increased availability of other sources of labor due to the rising labor force participation by women and the influx of immigrants.[10]

A second strand of supply-side explanations centers on a hypothesized decline in the willingness of Black male youth to accept the wages and working conditions of the jobs they could find work in given their level of skill.[11] In the light of the decline in real wages for workers in the low end of the labor market, there could be an ever-greater relative attraction for these young people to non-market activities or off-the-books employment.[12]

This chapter can only offer support for, or call into question, some of these contending hypotheses in the context of New York City over the period of ten years. The Census data provide a way to measure the impact of 'structural change' on Black male youth employment. Whether it is due to technology, changes in the international division of labor, shifts in regional specialization, or other factors, the data can be used to trace a shift in the industry and occupational mix of employment and to provide a measure of the extent to which that shift or 'structural effect' has adversely affected the kinds of jobs that have offered employment to young Black males.

The data can also be used to detect whether employment is shifting toward sectors of the economy that employ relatively more educated workers. A finding that would be consistent with the spatial mismatch hypothesis would be that there was a declining share of employment in sectors of the economy which employed less-educated workers. A finding consistent with the skills mismatch explanation would be that there is a growing gap between the educational attainment of young Black males and the educational attainment of persons who are employed in New York City, within the job tiers.

Another hypothesis the analysis can shed light on is the impact of increased competition for the kinds of jobs Black male youth have worked in by other groups of job seekers. New York City would seem a particularly apt case study in this regard because of both the large influx of immigrants into the city's labor market in the 1990s and the decade's impressive decline in the public assistance rolls and subsequent rise in jobholding by single mothers. The potential impact of these (or other) new sources of labor supply is assessed by measuring the extent to which losses in the share of employment that Black male youth held in specific sectors of the economy have adversely affected their overall level of employment. This will be referred to as the 'share effect.' The data allow an exploration of its magnitude, location in the industry occupation structure, and the identity of the groups that may have gained employment shares in areas where Black male youth have lost them. One mechanism by which an increase in competition would lead to declines in Black male youth employment is through the wage rate. A finding that would be consistent with the view that competition from immigrants, for example, was pushing young Black males out of the labor market would be that the wage rate had fallen in the part of the economy that experienced the greatest immigrant penetration.

ANALYSIS

To assess the extent to which male youth employment trends were adversely affected by structural change over the 1990 to 2000 period, I begin with a picture of where male youth were employed in 1990. Table 3.4 (Panel A) details the share of out-of-school youth that was employed in each of 70 industry/occupational cells constructed from industry and occupational classifications that were used in the 1990 Census.[13] Each cell in the table gives the percentage of total out-of-school male employment in that particular 'job' (such as executives and managers in the construction industry). Column totals give the total industry share of male youth employment. Row totals provide total occupation share. The other panels in the table provide the same information for each of the largest race/ethnic groups of out-of-school youth in the city.

The table identifies some interesting differences in the distribution of employment by race/ethnicity across the job cells, such as the importance of the service occupation in the food industry and the unskilled blue-collar occupation in the manufacturing industry for Hispanic male youth; the prominence of professional and technical occupation in the professional and public service industry for White male youth; and the magnitude of employment in the administrative occupation in the finance industry and the service occupation in the professional and public services industry for Black male youth.

A more general sense of the differences between these groups is difficult to establish across the 70 cells. This difficulty is compounded by the large number of cells in which estimates are derived from a fairly small number of observations. A more intuitive sense of interracial differences can be obtained when the 70 cells are (on an informal basis) grouped into three job

Table 3.4 Distribution of Out-of-School Male Youth Employment in 1990

A. All NYC	**Const**	**Mfg**	**TCU**	**Whlsl**	**Retail**	**Food**	**Finc**	**Busns**	**Persnl**	**Prf/Pub**	**Total**
Exec/Mgr	0.4	0.5	0.4	0.2	0.6	0.6	2.4	0.7	0.7	1.9	8.4
Prof/Tech	0.2	1.0	0.5	0.3	0.4	0.1	1.1	0.9	0.9	3.7	9.1
Sales	0.0	0.6	0.2	1.3	6.3	0.4	1.8	0.3	0.4	0.2	11.6
Admin.	0.2	1.5	2.9	1.0	1.6	0.1	4.2	1.5	0.5	3.3	16.8
Service	0.2	0.4	0.5	0.1	1.1	7.2	1.1	2.6	1.3	4.3	18.9
Skilled BC	5.4	2.0	1.7	0.6	1.7	0.1	0.1	1.6	0.2	0.5	14.1
Unskilled	2.7	5.1	4.1	2.1	3.7	0.3	0.4	1.3	0.8	0.6	21.2
Total	9.1	11.2	10.4	5.7	15.4	8.8	11.1	8.9	4.9	14.6	100.0
B. NH White											
Exec/Mgr	0.6	0.7	0.6	0.5	0.8	0.8	4.0	1.3	1.2	3.3	13.8
Prof /Tech	0.4	1.5	0.5	0.5	0.6	0.2	1.7	1.2	1.3	5.3	13.2
Sales	0.1	0.9	0.4	1.6	6.2	0.4	3.4	0.5	0.6	0.2	14.4
Admin.	0.1	1.2	2.3	0.5	1.5	0.0	4.1	1.3	0.6	1.9	13.7
Service	0.1	0.2	0.6	0.1	0.4	3.3	1.2	1.3	1.0	3.5	11.8
Skilled BC	8.1	2.1	2.1	0.7	2.3	0.0	0.1	1.9	0.4	0.5	18.2
Unskilled	3.4	1.6	4.0	1.4	2.4	0.1	0.4	0.7	0.6	0.3	15.0
Total	12.7	8.3	10.5	5.4	14.3	4.9	14.9	8.1	5.8	15.1	100.0

Table 3.4 (cont'd)

C. NH Black	**Const**	**Mfg**	**TCU**	**Whlsl**	**Retail**	**Food**	**Finc**	**Busns**	**Persnl**	**Prf/Pub**	**Total**
Exec & Mgr	0.2	0.0	0.0	0.0	0.4	0.6	1.2	0.1	0.4	1.5	4.4
Prof & Tech	0.3	0.8	0.6	0.1	0.2	0.1	0.5	0.3	1.0	3.4	7.3
Sales	0.0	0.3	0.1	0.9	4.5	0.1	1.3	0.1	0.2	0.3	7.8
Admin.	0.1	1.6	4.9	1.4	1.9	0.3	6.5	2.6	0.5	5.8	25.6
Service	0.2	0.5	0.8	0.3	1.9	4.1	0.7	4.7	1.2	7.6	22.0
Skilled BC	2.9	1.1	1.8	0.5	0.7	0.2	0.2	1.3	0.1	0.8	9.6
Unskilled	2.5	4.6	5.3	1.9	3.6	0.0	0.5	2.5	1.1	1.2	23.2
Total	6.2	9.0	13.5	5.1	13.3	5.4	10.8	11.6	4.5	20.6	100.0
D. Hispanic											
Exec & Mgr	0.3	0.4	0.4	0.1	0.5	0.3	1.2	0.2	0.5	0.6	4.4
Prof & Tech	0.0	0.6	0.4	0.2	0.1	0.0	0.6	0.8	0.4	1.7	4.9
Sales	0.0	0.5	0.2	1.1	7.1	0.4	0.3	0.1	0.2	0.1	10.1
Admin.	0.4	1.6	2.2	1.3	1.6	0.1	2.5	1.2	0.4	3.6	14.8
Service	0.4	0.7	0.4	0.1	1.3	13.2	1.3	2.8	1.8	3.6	25.6
Skilled BC	4.4	2.6	1.2	0.6	1.7	0.2	0.2	1.6	0.1	0.3	12.9
Unskilled	2.3	9.4	3.7	2.7	5.4	0.6	0.4	1.4	0.8	0.7	27.3
Total	7.7	15.8	8.5	6.1	17.8	14.8	6.5	7.9	4.4	10.5	100.0

Notes: See Appendix 3.1 for a detailed definition of the industry and occupation categories and the race/ethnic categories.

Table 3.5 Distribution of Employment by Job Tier

	Out-of -School Youth					
	NH White	NH Black	Hispanic	All	NYC	PP DIF
Executive & Professional	19.2	8.3	5.9	12.3	28.6	-16.3
Sales, Support, Service	37.2	52.7	46.9	44.3	41.5	2.8
Blue collar	28.1	24.9	34.0	29.2	14.8	14.4
Tiers' total	84.6	86.0	86.8	85.8	84.9	0.9

Notes: PP DIF: Percentage point difference between all youth and total NYC employment. NH = non-Hispanic.

'tiers', executive and professional occupations in the finance, business, personal, and professional and public service industries; sales, administrative support, and service occupations in the distribution and service industries; and blue-collar occupations in goods production and distributive industries. These three tiers, consisting of 42 jobs, together accounted for 86.5 per cent of youth employment.[14]

Comparing the proportion of out-of-school male youth who occupied these tiers for the three largest race/ethnic groups reveals that all of them were heavily reliant on employment in the sales, support, and service tier, but there are some noteworthy differences. As Table 3.5 details, Whites are relatively overrepresented in the executive and professional tier (19.2 per cent of their employment against 8.3 per cent for Blacks and 5.9 per cent for Hispanics). Blacks are disproportionately represented in the sales, support and service tier (52.7 per cent of their employment compared with 37.2 per cent for Whites and 46.9 per cent for Hispanics). Hispanics are the most dependent on employment in blue-collar jobs (34.0 per cent of their employment versus 28.1 per cent for Whites and 24.9 per cent for Blacks.

If out-of-school male youth were particularly vulnerable to structural change, the group's employment distribution should differ markedly from other labor market participants. Table 3.5 also compares the distribution of male youth employment to total New York City employment by job tier in 1990. These youth are underrepresented among the ranks of the executive and professional tier (by 16.3 percentage points), relatively over-reliant on jobs in the blue-collar tier (a 14.4 percentage point gap), while the shares of youth and employment for all those who work in New York City in sales, support, and service are fairly similar (a 2.8 percentage point difference).

In sum, it would seem that relative to all those who are employed in New York City, male out-of-school youth were particularly reliant on work in the blue-collar tier, and that among male youth, Hispanics would be particularly vulnerable to structural shifts such as a decline in manufacturing employment. Black male youth, by contrast, could be adversely impacted if factors such as technological change or an outsourcing of back office operations were eliminating employment in the less-skilled service industry jobs that make up the sales, service, and support tier.

Table 3.6 Percentage Point Change in Distribution of Total New York City Employment, 1990 to 2000

	Cons	Mfg	TCU	Whls	Retl	Food	Finc	Busn	Persl	Prf/ Pub.	Tot
Exec	0.0	-0.5	-0.2	-0.1	0.0	0.0	0.5	0.0	-0.1	0.5	0.1
Profsnl	-0.1	-0.1	0.0	-0.1	0.2	0.0	0.2	0.3	0.4	6.2	6.9
Sales	0.0	-0.2	0.2	-0.4	0.2	0.1	-0.1	0.0	0.0	0.1	-0.1
Admin.	0.0	-0.6	-0.7	-0.3	0.1	0.0	-1.6	-0.1	0.1	-0.5	-3.6
Service	-0.1	-0.1	-0.1	0.0	0.0	0.5	0.1	-0.6	0.4	-1.9	-1.7
Skilled BC	1.0	-1.2	-0.1	-0.2	-0.5	0.0	0.1	0.0	0.0	0.0	-1.0
Unskill BC	-0.6	-0.3	0.6	0.0	-0.1	0.1	-0.1	-0.3	0.2	0.0	-0.5
Total	0.2	-3.1	-0.4	-1.1	-0.1	0.8	-1.0	-0.8	1.2	4.4	

Change in New York's Employment Structure

Between 1990 and 2000 the composition of total New York City employment shifted toward the professional and technical worker occupation in the professional and public services industry. The growth in the share of total employment for this one industry/occupation cell was a remarkable 6.2 percentage points. All the other shifts in the share of employment by job were dwarfed by that change (see Table 3.6). Scanning the bottom row of the table, which gives total industry changes, reveals that all are small relative to the 3.1 percentage point decline in the share of manufacturing and the 4.4 percentage point increase in the proportion of total city employment in the professional and public services industry. The row totals, which provide total occupational change, indicate that there was a notable decline in administrative support (by 3.6 percentage points) and a jump (by 6.9 percentage points) in professional and technical employment.

Aggregating the small changes for the 70 jobs into changes by job tier provides a more general sense of how the structure of employment changed. Percentage point changes in the distribution of total New York City employment by job tier are provided in Table 3.7. The executive and professional tier's share of total employment rose by 8.0 percentage points. By contrast, the sales, support, and service tier shrank by 4.4 percentage points, and the blue-collar tier declined by 1.6 percentage points.

These shifts in the composition of employment would only have had a direct negative effect on the level of male youth employment if tiers that lost share were also suffering absolute, numeric declines. As the table indicates, while total employment in the city edged up by 18,000, employment levels fell in the blue-collar tier (by 55,000) and plummeted (by 156,000) in the sales, support, and service tier. Given the distribution of Black male jobholding in 1990, this would suggest that structural change might have driven a decline in Black male youth employment.

Table 3.7 Change in the Distribution of Total NYC Employment by Job Tier

	Percentage Distribution			**Numeric Change**
	1990	**2000**	**PPD**	**2000–1990**
Executive & professional	28.6	36.5	8.0	300,599
Sales, support, service	41.5	37.1	-4.4	-155,513
Blue collar	14.8	13.2	-1.6	-54,934
Citywide total	84.9	86.9	2.0	17,908

Notes: PPD: Percentage point difference. See text for the definition of the tiers.

How Did This Change Affect Male Youth Employment?

To measure the effect of the 1990 to 2000 change in citywide employment on male youth jobholding I employ shift share analysis. This technique is used to (first) compare the actual change in male youth employment against a situation in which the male youth share of employment in each industry/occupation cell's employment is held constant, but total employment in the cell undergoes its actual 1990–2000 change. By holding constant the youth

Table 3.8 Shift Share Analysis of Changes in Male Youth Employment

	NH White	NH Black	Hispanic
Actual Change	-12,556	-6,743	6,564
Change due to structural effect [a]	-1,392	-2,768	-2,068
Effect's share of change (%)	11.1	41.0	-31.5
Change due to share effect [b]	-13,090	-4,524	9,223
Effect's share of change (%)	104.2	67.1	140.5
Interactive effect [c]	1,925	548	-591
Effect's share of change (%)	-15.3	-8.1	-9.0

Notes: NH = non-Hispanic.

a. Change due to structural effect is the hypothetical change based on constant shares of job cell employment.

b. Change due to share effect is hypothetical change based on constant levels of job cell employment.

c. Interactive effect is a residual term that accounts for change due to combined effects.

share at its 1990 rate, the hypothetical case provides a measure of the extent to which structural change alone affected the level of male youth employment.[15]

The first row of Table 3.8 gives the actual numerical change from 1990 to 2000 in employment for New York City out-of-school males by race/ethnicity. It indicates that employment declined for Whites (by 12,600 jobs) and Blacks (by 6,700 jobs) but rose for Hispanics (by 6,600 jobs).[16] The table's second row indicates what the change in employment would have been had each group's share of total employment in each industry occupation cell remained at its 1990 rate. The change across the groups is negative, indicating that, given their place in the job structure in 1990, employment would have fallen because the total number of workers employed in the locations that mattered most to youth had declined. However, for each of the race/ethnic groups, this hypothetical decline is less than half of the actual decline in employment, 11.1 per cent for Whites, 41.0 per cent for Blacks and 31.5 per cent for Hispanics. The larger structural change effect for Blacks and Hispanics is consistent with the suggestion made above that these groups would be relatively more vulnerable to structural change. Yet, even for Blacks, it is clear that other factors were affecting their level of employment.

One factor that is readily identifiable in a shift-share analysis is whether these groups of youth were losing their respective shares of total employment by job cell. Thus I create another hypothetical, a 'share effect' that measures the effect that the change in each group's share of total employment in the cells had on its total change in employment.[16]

The results of this calculation are reported in the row labeled 'Change Due to Share Effect.' For each race/ethnic group this effect is much larger than the structural effect. The large and positive share effect explains how Hispanic out-of-school male youth were able to raise their level of employment despite the large declines in the number of jobs in the blue-collar tier (which was presumably picked up in the group's negative structural change effect); they gained an increasing share of what was still available. The relatively large (about two-thirds of the actual decline) and negative sign of the share effect for Black male youth indicates that their actual employment decline reflects more than their overrepresentation in the sales, support and service tier and that tier's total employment losses. Black male youth were also losing employment shares to others. To pursue this lead further, the next sections investigate who they lost employment to and the kind of jobs in which this employment was lost.

Who Gained the Jobs that Black Males Lost?

Which groups were filling in the space created by the declining share of job cell employment held by Black male youth? There are two obvious candidates. The 1990s saw a large influx of immigrants into New York City. Adult immigrants (persons 25 and older) increased their share of the city's working-age population from 27.7 per cent in 1990 to 37.1 per cent in 2000. Another possibility is single mothers who were leaving the welfare rolls. Although this group did not increase its share of the total working-age population, the second half of the 1990s saw a sharp rise in the employment–population ratios for this group, especially in New York City.[17] Another possibility is losses in employment shares to other groups of youth, such as those who are in school, female, White, Hispanic, or (non-Black) immigrant.

As a test of whether there is a general pattern of any of these groups gaining shares where Black male youth were losing them, I calculate correlation coefficients for the change in employment shares across the 70 job cells. If share gains for one group were located in the same job cell as share declines by Black male youth, there would necessarily be a (statistically significant) negative correlation between the patterns. Because Black male youth employment is unevenly distributed across the cells, it is

Table 3.9 Analysis of Change in Job Cell Employment

A. Correlations of Change in Job Cell Shares

Correlation of Black male youth with:	Correlation Coefficient
Adult immigrants	-0.4768**
Single Mothers	-0.2342*
In-school youth	0.4833**
Hispanic male youth	0.2258*
White male youth	-0.0289
Female youth	0.1003
Non-Black immigrant youth	0.2027*

B. Change in Groups' Share of Total Cell Employment

Black Male Youth and Adult Immigrants

Number of cells in which:	
Both gained share	17
Both lost share	3
BMY gain/AI loss	4
BMY loss/AI gain	46
Total	20

Black Male Youth and Single Mothers

Number of cells in which:	
Both gained share	10
Both Lost	19
BMY gain/SM loss	11
BMY loss/SM gain	30
Total	29

Notes: ** Correlation is significant at the 0.01 level (2-tailed).
* Correlation is significant at the 0.05 level (2-tailed).

possible that the correlation coefficients could be driven by changes in cells where there is very little employment and sample sizes are small. To adjust for that possibility, I weighted the observations by each cell's share of total Black male youth employment. The results are reported in Panel A, Table 3.9. There are two statistically significant correlations with the expected sign, those between Black male youth and adult immigrants and single mothers. The magnitude of the coefficient and the level of statistical significance for the correlation between Black male youth and single mothers, it should be noted, are smaller than the coefficient for the adult immigrants. The correlations between Black male youth and other groups of youth are either positive (in-school youth, Hispanic youth, and immigrant youth) or negative, but not statistically different from zero (White male youth). Hence the correlations offer no evidence of intra-youth substitution.

A negative correlation between changes in shares, though a necessary condition, is not sufficient to establish an association between share losses and gains. By construction the coefficients reflect the variation of each group's change of share around its respective mean change in share. It is possible therefore that a negative correlation could be driven by instances where relatively smaller but positive deviations for one group occur where there are relatively larger (and positive) deviations for the other. But this does not appear to be the case. As reported in Panel B of Table 3.9, in 46 of the 70 job cells, adult immigrant gains in employment shares were coincident with declines in Black male youth employment shares. The fit between single mother gains and Black male youth declines is somewhat weaker than this; it occurred in 30 out of the 70 job cells.

Changes in Employment by Job Tier

Further insight into the roles of structural and share changes in the decline of Black male youth employment can be gained by viewing it from the perspective of the change in employment by job tiers. Table 3.10 compares the change in employment by tier for Black male youth with that for adult immigrants and single mothers. To put these trends in context, the table provides for each group, data on total employment, group share of total city employment and group share of the city's working-age population (New York residents 16 through 64 years of age).

The table identifies what kinds of jobs Black male youth lost employment in. There was virtually no change in Black male youth's level or share of employment in the executive and professional tier. In the light of the impressive increase in citywide employment in the tier, this finding raises the issue, mentioned above, of whether there is a growing mismatch between skills demanded by employers and skills possessed by Black male youth. This will be taken up in a subsequent section.

Black male youth lost employment in the sales, support, and service, and blue-collar tiers. But the magnitude of the declines and the reasons for them differed in interesting ways. Although Black male youth were heavily reliant on employment in sales, support, and service work and despite the fact that this tier suffered the greatest overall job loss, Black males lost fewer jobs in the sales, support, and service tier than they did in the blue-collar tier (2,319 versus 3,021). Their employment decline in the sales, service, and support tier was driven by the structural change effect, which accounted for 1,605 of the 2,319 jobs loss. By contrast the Black male youth employment decline in the blue-collar sector was overwhelmingly a result of loss of employment share (2,522 of the total loss of 3,021). More than a third (37.4 per cent) of the 1990 to 2000 decline in Black male youth employment was a result of share losses in this one tier.[19]

In contrast to these employment declines, immigrant adults made strong employment gains in all three job tiers. This is especially noteworthy in that this group was able to increase its level of employment even in the tiers that were losing employment overall. This could only have happened if they were gaining share of what was left, and as the table indicates, the adult immigrant share of the sales, support, and service tier rose by 5.9 percentage points and their share of blue-collar employment jumped by 11.7 percentage points.

The numerical changes in employment by tier for single mothers are consistent with the citywide pattern. But the changes in their share of total tier employment run counter to what one might expect if welfare reform was driving the increased employment among single mothers. The group experienced a fall in its share of employment in the sales, support, and service, and the blue-collar sector, while it gained employment share in the executive and professional sectors. This is not the pattern one would have expected, if the increase in single-mother employment had been driven by relatively less-well-educated welfare leavers. The pattern of change also offers little further insight into what kind of jobs single mothers were gaining share in while Black male youth were losing share.

Immigrant–Black Male Youth Competition?

The coincidence of a share decline for Black male youth and share increases by adult immigrants in the blue-collar tier is consistent with one widely held explanation of rising Black male youth joblessness. That is, that the growing presence of immigrants in the job market has increased the supply of labor that is willing to work at low wages. This influx has in turn

Table 3.10 Change in Employment and Shares of Employment, 1990 to 2000

	Employment In Tier	**Group Share Change (%)**
Black Male Youth		
Executive & professional	590	0.0
Sales, support, service	-2,319	-0.1
Blue collar	-3,021	-0.5
Total employment	-6,743	N.A.
Adult Immigrants		
Executive & professional	179,605	9.2
Sales, support, service	38,431	5.9
Blue collar	35,213	11.7
Total employment	161,098	N.A.
Single Mothers		
Executive & professional	50,432	2.5
Sales, support, service	-19,431	-0.3
Blue collar	-4,883	-0.5
Total employment	28,792	N.A.

driven down the wage available to all workers with relatively lower skills. Given the declining attractiveness of the wage rates available to Black male youth, they have withdrawn from the labor market. There is clear evidence for two of the three links in this chain of reasoning. As we have seen, there has been an impressive increase in the immigrant presence in the New York City labor market. And the location of their largest share gains fits the story as well. The blue-collar tier would be the one where the need for English language fluency and formal educational credentials (disadvantages usually associated with immigrants) would matter least. New York City's manufacturing sector has always been an immigrant niche for just this set of reasons.[20] In addition, an increasing share of Black out-of-school male youth has, indeed, dropped out of the labor market. That is, a rising share of Black male out-of-school youth was neither employed nor actively seeking employment. From 1990 to 2000 the group's non-participation rate rose from 15.5 per cent to 18.0 per cent of the population.[21]

What about wage rates? Given the pattern of change in the composition of the tiers, one would expect that the clearest signal that wage rates were being depressed by the growing immigrant presence would be coming from the blue-collar tier. However, there was no dramatic decline in wages from 1989 to 1999 in either an absolute or relative sense for the tier.[22] As Table 3.11 illustrates, inflation-adjusted median hourly wages in the tier fell by 5.0 per cent from 1989 to 1999; this represents a fairly modest annual rate of change. Furthermore, the median wage in the tier did not fall much relative to the most important tier for Black male youth employment, the sales, support, and service tier. In 1989 the median wage in the blue-collar tier was slightly (2.5 per cent) higher than in the sales, support, and service tier. In 1999 the median wage rates were identical. These wage changes appear small relative to the magnitude of the decline in the Black male youth labor force participation rate. This is not to say that immigrants did not replace Black male youth in the blue-collar tier, but it does raise some doubt as to whether the substitution took place via the mechanism of a falling wage rate. It leaves open two other possibilities: one, that employers' racial preferences were playing an increasing role in their hiring decisions or, two, that young Black men were increasingly inclined to shun low-wage work.

Any judgment that immigrant competition played a major role in the Black youth employment decline must also be put in the context of group shares of the working-age population. From 1990 to 2000 the adult immigrant share of New York City's working-age population jumped by 9.3 percentage points, while the Black male youth share of the working-age population edged down by 0.3 percentage points.[23] Given those changes in the composition of the population, changes in the group shares of employment are to be expected. Unless the decline in the share of Black male youth in the population is seen as endogenous, that is, as a reaction to immigrant competition, some degree of share loss would be nothing more than a reflection of a shift in the demographic composition of the city. However, the Black male youth share decline in the blue-collar tier and the adult immigrant share increase in it exceeded their respective changes in their shares of the working-age population. If the share effect in the loss of blue-collar tier employment for Black male youth was adjusted to reflect only the impact of the 'excess' decline in employment, it would be reduced from 37.4 per cent to 15.0 per cent of the total 1990 to 2000 employment decline.

Table 3.11 Median Hourly Wage Rates, By Job Tier

	1989	1999	Change (%)
Executive & professional	$ 23.46	$ 22.12	-5.7
Sales, support, service	$ 14.82	$ 14.42	-2.7
Blue collar	$ 15.19	$ 14.42	-5.0

Note: Wages are stated in 1999 dollars.

Skills mismatch?

The failure of Black male youth to gain share in the burgeoning executive and professional tier is one of the several troubling findings in this study. Given the trends identified in this chapter, there is good reason to believe that future employment growth in the city will be heavily weighted toward this sector. The continued lack of Black male youth representation in the tier is consistent with a widely held demand-side explanation of their rising joblessness, that there is a growing gap between the skills employers seek and the skills that this group possesses. The Census data do not provide a way to measure the skills that workers use when they are on the job. Researchers typically use educational attainment as a proxy for job skills in their analyses.[24]

If the mismatch hypothesis for rising joblessness can be tested by trends in educational attainment, then there should be a growing gap between educational levels for Black male youth and the level of educational attainment in the city workforce. Table 3.12 provides an indicator of the level of educational attainment for Black, White, and Hispanic male out-of-school youth in 1990 and 2000. To simplify comparisons, these race/ethnic groups are divided into two categories, those with no more than a high school degree and those with some level of education beyond high school. There are stark disparities between the race/ethnic groups. In 2000, nearly six in ten (57.4 per cent) of White male youth had some education beyond high school, compared to less than one in four (22.2 per cent) of Black male youth and less than one in six (15.2 per cent) Hispanic male youth. The differences in trends are also dramatic; there was a 12.3 percentage point shift from the less to the more educated group for Whites, a much more modest 3.5 percentage point shift toward the more educated group for Blacks, and essentially no growth in educational attainment for Hispanic male youth.

Table 3.12 Educational Attainment for NYC Out of School Males (%)

	1990	2000	PP DIF*
NH White			
No more than HS	54.9	42.6	-12.3
Beyond HS	45.1	57.4	12.3
NH Black			
No more than HS	81.3	77.8	-3.5
Beyond HS	18.7	22.2	3.5
Hispanic			
No more than HS	84.4	84.8	0.4
Beyond HS	15.6	15.2	-0.4

Notes: NH = Non-Hispanic.
HS = High school.
PP DIF = Percentage point difference.

The lack of progress in levels of educational attainment for Black and Hispanic male youth also stands in sharp relief with the growing educational attainment for the city workforce, which saw a 7.3 percentage point shift from the less to the more educated category. This created a growing education gap between the Black and Hispanic male youth and jobholders in New York. By 2000 nearly two-thirds (65.3 per cent) of the people employed in the city have some education beyond high school (see Table 3.13).

Differences in levels of educational attainment by job tier offer no surprises. In 2000 the vast majority (86.7 per cent) of those employed in the executive and professional tier had some education beyond high school, compared to a bit over half (55.8 per cent) of those employed in the sales, support, and service tier and a third (32.8 per cent) of the blue-collar tier.

The changes within the sectors from 1990 to 2000 are more interesting. Educational attainment appears to have edged down in the executive and professional tier (a 2.5 percentage point shift away from the more educated category). By contrast, there was an 8.0 percentage point shift toward the more educated group in the sales, support, and service tier and a 6.2 percentage point shift toward the more educated group in the blue-collar job

Table 3.13 Educational Attainment by Job Tier (%)

	1990	2000	PP DIF*
Total Workforce			
No more than HS	42.0	34.7	-7.3
Beyond HS	58.0	65.3	7.3
Executive & professional			
No more than HS	10.8	13.3	2.5
Beyond HS	89.2	86.7	-2.5
Sales & service			
No more than HS	52.3	44.2	-8.0
Beyond HS	47.7	55.8	8.0
Blue collar			
No more than HS	73.4	67.2	-6.2
Beyond HS	26.6	32.8	6.2

Notes: HS = High school.
PP DIF = Percentage point difference.

tier. The rise in educational attainment in the blue-collar tier is notable given the large influx of immigrants into it. One possibility is that more workers in the skilled blue-collar occupations within that tier are entering employment through the route of two-year community colleges.

The sharply rising levels of educational attainment coupled with the decline in employment in the sales, support and service tier may be the finding that is most consistent with a technological change, rising skill demand story. In the 1990s the service sector saw the widespread introduction of computer-based technology, which in turn, lead to impressive rates of productivity growth. This pattern is also consistent with the spatial mismatch hypothesis, if firms in the service sector (such as finance or business services) were moving more routine tasks out of the city. If either dynamic carries into the future, it will continue to pose a significant barrier to gains in Black male employment.

To summarize the analytical sections of this study, it appears that Black male youth employment declined over the 1990s because of the loss of employment shares to immigrants in the blue-collar tier and the loss of employment due to structural change in the sales, support, and services tier.

A third factor played a role; the inability of young Black males to offset employment losses in declining tiers with gains in the executive and professional job tier that was experiencing all the New York City job growth.

IMPLICATIONS FOR LOCAL POLICY

This chapter, I believe, has two major implications for local policy making. The first is the need to close the growing educational attainment gap between New York's Black and Hispanic male youth and the city workforce. In the long run there can be no substitute for a serious effort to increase graduation rates and to raise the proportion of graduates who can successfully transition to work or higher levels of education. This need is widely recognized by the public and improving the schools has become a signature issue for Mayor Michael Bloomberg since he obtained mayoral control of the school system in 2002.

A second implication, which has yet to garner a commensurate level of priority, is the need to create a comprehensive 'second chance' system for the city's youth who have been poorly served by the city's schools. While it is essential that our schools do more to keep kids enrolled and that the educational system provides second (or more) chances for youth who have left school to reenter and complete high school, educational initiatives can do little for the 200,000 (male and female) youth who are currently out of school and out of work, or for those who will continue to join their ranks, even with the most ambitious of educational reforms. Practitioners who work with disconnected youth report that many have no desire, at this point in their lives, to return to the classroom. What they want is a job.[25] School-based programs must be complemented with an employment-based strategy focused on out-of-school youth.[26]

Specific Labor Market Initiatives

Increased job opportunities are essential to the prospects of New York's out-of-school youth. City-level policy making can foster the quantity and affect the quality of local job opportunities through its economic and workforce development programs, as well as its commitment to first-class infrastructure, high quality public schools and the world-famous public amenities that make New York an attractive place to do business and raise a family.[27] These investments, if well made, pay off in the long term for New Yorkers from all walks of life.

But the focus here is on actions that can yield immediate results. The proposals that follow suggest three ways that the city and the state can create employment opportunities for the most disadvantaged out-of-school youth. Specifically, New York's leaders can:

1. Continue to open apprenticeship opportunities in the construction industry.
2. Expand the apprenticeship model to new industries.
3. Establish a New York City Job Corps.

Open construction apprenticeship opportunities

A number of Western European nations have developed extensive apprenticeship systems as both a workforce development tool and as a mechanism to enable the transition of non-college bound young people from school to work.[28] In the United States, apprenticeships are largely confined to the unionized segment of the construction industry, where they successfully provide employers with a highly skilled workforce and offer participants a path toward a family-supporting career. The attraction of apprenticeships for out-of-school youth is that apprentices earn a wage while they are mastering a trade. Entry into building trades apprenticeships, however, is limited. The building trades unions are reluctant to bring more people into programs than they can provide jobs for. Another factor that limits access are entry requirements. Depending on the specific trade, admission into the program requires a high school degree or General Educational Development credential (GED) as well as satisfactory performance on physical and written examinations.[29]

Both of these factors are a significant barrier to many disconnected youth. But they are not immutable. First, more jobs, and therefore more apprenticeship slots, are in the offing. New York City is about to experience a construction boom. Massive projects from Lower Manhattan, the Far West Side, Columbia University, to Downtown Brooklyn, will be erecting office buildings, sports facilities, subway extensions, and new housing over the next decade. In addition, industry observers note that the ranks of the unionized construction workforce are aging. The impending retirement of the baby boom generation of skilled journeymen, along with these new projects, is creating a unique opportunity that the city has a responsibility to seize.

Mayor Bloomberg has established a Commission on Construction Opportunity for the purpose of ensuring 'opportunities for all.'[30] The Commission is composed of representatives from the industry, its unions, senior members of the administration, political leaders such as Congressman Charles Rangel and advocacy organizations, such as the Community Service Society. The Commission has created a 'pre-apprenticeship' program that is open to young people who have an interest in the building trades, but do not have the qualifications to enter apprenticeships directly.

Expand the apprenticeship model to new industries

Policymakers should also look beyond the confines of the construction industry to expand the apprenticeship model. Notwithstanding the decline in employment in the blue collar and sales, support, and service tiers, there are still jobs in New York that provide living wage careers, but do not require four-year college degrees to perform them.[31] For example, over 85,000 New Yorkers are employed in occupations classified as 'installation, maintenance, and repair.' Workers in these occupations keep the physical and technological infrastructure of our economy and our homes running. Everything from elevators, air-conditioning, and computer networks, to photocopying machines may be manufactured outside the city, but they usually need to be serviced here. Another example is 'transportation and material moving' occupations, which employ another 200,000 New Yorkers in the task of moving people and freight via subways, busses, taxis, aircraft and trucks.[32]

These jobs are blue collar in nature, and while some of them are manufacturing-related, they are also integral to the success of a service-based economy.[33] And they pay more than work in service occupations. The median wage for the installation, maintenance, and repair occupational group is $16.00 per hour. For transportation and moving occupations it is $12.00 per hour. These compare favorably to the median of $9.50 for service occupations.[34]

Unlike Western Europe, there is no overarching system for recruiting and training workers for these positions. Young people typically make their way to them via a patchwork of vocational high schools, the community colleges, or through social networks of family and friendship that provide the necessary connections. These routes exclude many disconnected youth because they lack the educational prerequisites or the connections to adults who are working in these fields. Apprenticeship-style programs in industries or occupations where they do not currently exist could offer disconnected youth an alternative path to these jobs.

As a start, the New York State Department of Labor (DOL) could use discretionary funds provided by the federal Workforce Investment Act to offer seed money and technical assistance to industry partners who want to establish apprenticeship programs in their industries. The DOL should issue a request for proposals from employer associations and trade unions that are interested in creating programs for their industry. As part of the criteria for awarding funds, proposals should be required to address the ways in which the programs will reach out and actively recruit disadvantaged youth.

Create a New York City Job Corps

Apprenticeship opportunities can be a good option for young people who are ready for a challenging situation. But one size will not fit all. For youth who have little or no work experience or have a difficult time getting hired because of specific barriers such as work-limiting disabilities or a criminal record, a different program model is more appropriate. One approach that offers participants work experience and a wage is publicly subsidized employment. This approach has a long history, dating back to the New Deal's Works Progress Administration and Civilian Conservation Corps. In the 1970s the federal government funded up to 750,000 public service employment positions through the Comprehensive Employment and Training Act. More recently New York City has created transitional job programs for welfare participants, such as the Parks Opportunity Program. Paid transitional employment can also be an important tool in job readiness programs for people returning from prison.[35]

What public service or transitional jobs programs offer is a time-limited, wage-paying job to people who do not yet have the capacity to secure employment in the unsubsidized labor market. Besides providing income and on-the-job training, these programs can offer remedial education and vocational training, as well as social services. An additional benefit to participants (and the broader community) is that they are performing real work that contributes to the well-being of the city. Typically participants in transitional jobs programs work for city agencies or nonprofit institutions. But opportunities in the for-profit sector should be considered as well. This is a relatively expensive model (depending on the wage rate and intensity of ancillary services, costs would range from $15,000 to $20,000 per participant per year), but it is one of the few approaches that has consistently shown positive outcomes for low-income youth in rigorous evaluations.[36] The city should initiate a New York Job Corps program that would provide 5,000 unemployed, out-of-school youth with a one-year publicly subsidized job.

These three suggestions are no cure-all. They are not large enough in scale. They do not meet every need or address all the barriers that stand between disconnected youth and steady work. They do illustrate, however, that meaningful steps can be taken to address the needs of out-of-school youth, if policy makers are willing to do so.

The costs of a more comprehensive effort, no doubt, would be considerable. But New York's political leadership and the public need to bear in mind the price of inaction. Each young person who ends up in prison rather than in a career is an enormous cost to society. The price of incarceration (at $20,000 to $30,000 per year) is just the most obvious expense. Wasted potential must also be weighed. Each young person who drops by the wayside is one less person who can contribute to the economy, pay taxes, provide love and sustenance to their children, and contribute to the life of the community.

APPENDIX 3.1

This appendix covers three technical topics: the race/ethnicity categories used in this study; the construction of the industry occupation job cells; and its source of data, the 1990 and 2000 Census Public Use Micro Sample.

Race/Ethnic Categories

The cross tabulations in this study make use of two different questions in the Census questionnaire. One asks respondents to provide their race, such as White, Black, Asian, etc. A separate question asks respondents if they are of Hispanic ethnicity. The study used these two variables to construct three mutually exclusive Race/Ethnic groups, Non-Hispanic Whites, Non-Hispanic Blacks, and Hispanics of any race. An issue in the construction of these categories is that, for the first time, the 2000 Census gave respondents the option of picking more than one race. For example, someone could say that they were both Black and Asian. Thus the racial categories in the 1990 and 2000 Census are not strictly comparable. For the purposes of this study, I created the White and Black categories using only those respondents who reported that they were White or Black alone. Because the Hispanic category includes persons of any race, it was unaffected by the change in racial categories.

Industry/Occupation Cells

The first step in creating the job cells was to construct a set of ten industries from the nearly 1,000 detailed industries listed in the 1990 Census industry classification system. Because of their negligible role in the city economy I excluded the agriculture, forestry and fisheries industries along with mining from my classification. In addition, I omitted the Census industries that reflected active military service. The remaining industries were grouped as described in the Technical Appendix Tables (available on request from the author).

The rationale for this classification was to strike a balance between providing enough detail to identify important differences within the industry mix and the need to create industries that did not have either too large or too small a share of male youth employment. For that reason, I created a separate industry for eating and drinking establishments, which have a unique role as a provider of male youth employment opportunities. The seven occupation categories that were created out of the over 800 Census occupations are also described in the separate Technical Appendix.

Creating a comparable schema using the 2000 Census posed some difficulties because in that year the Census moved from using an industrial classification code based on the Standard Industrial Classification System to one based on the North American Industrial Classification System. I used a 'cross walk' provided by the Census Bureau to match the 2000 Census industry code to the industries that I created from the 1990 Census codes. In those (relatively few) cases in which a detailed industry was split between two (or more) of those industries, I assigned it to the 1990 industry that had the largest share of the 2000 industry's employment. The translation from 2000 to 1990 occupation codes was more straightforward (see Technical Appendix).

Readers in search of definitions for these Census industry and occupation codes can find them at http://www.ipums.org.

The main abbreviations for industry and occupation groups used in the tables above are:

Industry abbreviations
Const = construction; Mfg = manufacturing; TCU = transportation, communications and utilities; Whlsl = wholesale trade; Retail = retail trade; Food = food and beverage services; Finc = finance, insurance and real estate; Busns = business services; Persnl = personal services; Prf/Pub = professional services and public administration.

Occupation abbreviations
Exec and mgr = executive and managerial; Prof and tech = professional and technical; Sales = sales; Admin = clerical and administrative; Service = services; Skilled BC = skilled blue collar; Unskilled BC = unskilled blue collar.

NOTES

1. These data are limited to the civilian, non-institutionalized residents of New York City. Therefore they do not include people in the military or the considerable number of male youth who are serving time in penal institutions.
2. See, for example, Besharov (1999).

3. All the data this study relies on are from the 1990 and 2000 Census public use micro samples. These data sets are comprised of a five per cent random sample of the US population, which is created by the Census Bureau from the long-form questionnaire that goes to one-in-five household across the nation. I extracted data from this sample for New York City residents and persons who work in the city (regardless of their residence) from: Ruggles, et al. (2005). The PUMS files can be obtained at http://www.ipums.org.
   The number of observations the PUMS provides is listed in the Technical Appendix (available on request from the author). These sample sizes suggest that the small changes that are reported by race/ethnic group should be treated with caution; they may not be statistically significant.
4. The data files and programs created to create the tabulations used in this report are available from the author upon request.
5. Freeman and Holzer (1986).
6. Johnson (1977).
7. Kasarda (1995).
8. Darity and Mason (1998).
9. Moss and Tilly (1995).
10. Blank and Gelbach (1998) and Borjas (1998).
11. Juhn (1992).
12. Freeman(1996).
13. See appendix 3.1 for a detailed description of how the industry occupational cells were constructed.
14. This approach and terminology is similar to one used by David Howell and several co-authors. Their approach to the construction of the jobs and tiers in this chapter is based on notions of labor market segmentation. See, for example, Gittleman and Howell (1995). The approach in this chapter is ad hoc.
15. To put this algebraically, the actual change in youth employment from 1990 to 2000 is expressed as the difference between the product of the youth share of total employment in each cell and the total number of workers employed in each cell summed across the 70 occupation by industry cells for each year:
   $$\sum Ys_{i00} * Te_{i00} - \sum Ys_{i90} * Te_{i90}$$
   where *Ys* is the youth share of total employment in job i and *Te* is the total number of workers employed in job i in either 2000 or 1990 and $\sum$ is an operator indicating the summation of the products.
   The structural change effect is then estimated as the change that would have occurred if the youth share of total employment in each cell had remained fixed at its 1990 rate, but total employment in each cell underwent its actual change. Algebraically:
   $$\sum Ys_{i90} * Te_{i00} - \sum Ys_{i90} * Te_{i90}$$
16. Readers will recall that the employment/population ratio for each of these groups declined from 1990 to 2000. From that perspective the analysis is focused solely on the numerator. The decline in the ratio for Hispanic male youth, despite the increase in the number of them who were employed, implies that the group's population was rising faster than its gain in employment.
17. The hypothetical 'share effect' indicates how employment would have changed if the level of employment in each cell held constant at its 1990 level, but the male youth share of employment underwent its actual change: $\sum Ys_{i00} * Te_{i90} - \sum Ys_{i90} * Te_{i90}$
18. Levitan and Gluck (2002).
19. These calculations were performed by the author in the same manner as those for the individual job cells.
20. Waldinger (1996).
21. Author's tabulation from the 1990 and 2000 Census PUMS.
22. The Census asks people about their wage and salary earnings in the prior year.
23. Author's tabulation from the 1990 and 2000 PUMS.

24. The issue of whether or the extent to which job skills can be adequately measured by educational attainment is beyond the scope of this chapter.
25. US Government Accounting Office (2004).
26. Labor market and education-based programs should not be seen as competing strategies. Employment-based programs in the schools can be a means toward dropout prevention. Work experience programs for out-of-school youth can provide remedial education and motivate youth to go back to school in the future.
27. Working Group on New York City's Low-Wage Labor Market (2000) provides a comprehensive array of job creation proposals.
28. Ryan (2001).
29. Another barrier, which some industry observers believe to be on the wane, is a history of racial exclusion.
30. Mayor Michael Bloomberg's *2005 State of the City* address, January 11, 2005.
31. This is not to say that the city should passively allow its remaining manufacturing sector to slip away. The Zoning for Jobs campaign advocates for policies that would foster New York City manufacturing. See www.nyirn.com/ZFJ/reports.php.
32. Author's tabulation from the 2003 Current Population Survey.
33. Although these jobs are not regarded as a high growth sector, the New York State Department of Labor projects that there will be an annual average of 5,030 and 2,620 job openings in the transportation and material moving, and installation, maintenance and repair occupational groups, respectively.
34. Author's tabulation from the 2003 Current Population Survey.
35. The Center for Employment Opportunities runs such a program in New York. See www.ceoworks.org for more information.
36. For an excellent summary of the literature on public service employment programs see Chapter 7 of Bartik (2001).

4. Still With Us After All of These Years: Youth Labor Market Entry, Home-Leaving and Human Capital Accumulation in Italy, 1993–2003

Niall O'Higgins

This chapter takes a look at developments in the youth labor market in Italy over the last decade or so. In doing so the approach taken is rather broader than is conventional in the recent literature. This is so in terms of the indicators examined: in addition to employment, unemployment (broadly defined), and educational participation, the chapter also looks at living arrangements and, briefly, marriage rates. The broader approach also applies to the definition of young people themselves. Rather than the conventional 15–24 year old age group, young people here are taken to include all those having completed between 15 and 34 years on this planet. This broader definition of young people is in line with the lengthening youth–adult transition process in general, and also with the generally longer transition period traditionally observable in Italy.[1] Indeed analyzing the process of the transition from the parental home to the establishment of an 'independent' residence over the last decade in Italy looking only at the under-25s would rather miss the point since almost all of the variation in the co-residence rate over the decade has occurred amongst those aged 25 and over.

Today, young people in Italy live with their parents longer, accumulate more years of education and both get married and enter the labor market significantly later than they did a decade ago. The analysis presented here is intended to further our understanding of why this is the case. The most studied of these phenomena is of course the transition from school to work. In recent times, however, attention has increasingly focused also on the transition from the parental home to an independent residence, or rather not – as is increasingly the case in Italy. I also briefly include consideration of the declining marriage rate given its intimate connection to the home-leaving decision of young people, particularly young women.

On this basis, youth transitions are analyzed in an effort to understand the extent to which aggregate economic factors contributed (or did not contribute) to the evolution of the transition processes. The approach adopted is similar in methodology to the study of Canadian and US youth labor markets undertaken by Card and Lemieux.[2]

Table 4.1 Employment, Educational Participation and Marriage Rates, by Living Arrangement, Age Group and Sex, Italy 2002–03

	Males		**Females**	
% who are:	**Living With Parents**	**Living in Separate Household**	**Living With Parents**	**Living in Separate Household**
Working				
15–19 years	11.1	57.4	6.5	20.8
20–24 years	43.7	68.9	32.8	33.4
25–29 years	66.7	87.4	53.9	55.9
30–34 years	78.4	92.8	64.3	54.3
Studying				
15–19 years	78.0	29.5	82.8	18.9
20–24 years	33.4	18.1	45.3	12.7
25–29 years	14.1	4.0	21.8	3.5
30–34 years	5.1	0.7	7.3	1.2
Married				
15–19 years	0.4	25.6	0.5	39.9
20–24 years	1.1	32.7	1.9	67.7
25–29 years	2.1	61.0	4.6	80.6
30–34 years	6.5	77.7	10.9	84.9

Source: ISTAT Labour Force Surveys, July and October 2002 and January and April 2003.

KEY TRENDS

The chapter is motivated by a series of general observations regarding the youth labor market. One concerns the intimate connection between the different types of transition. To some extent these are obvious – the transition between school and work, for example. Relatively few people in

Italy, even now, study and work at the same time.[3] Others are perhaps less immediately apparent.

Table 4.1 illustrates the interrelation between living arrangements and the other choices: working, studying, and getting married. The differences in behavior between those who live with their parents and those who have established their own residence are clear. Young men are much more likely to work if they are living away from their parents (although interestingly this is not true for young women over 20). Conversely, those living at home are much more likely to study. The decision of whether to study or work presumably has much to do with the explicit and implicit financial transfers implied by living with one's parents in addition to an individual's work–study preference or indeed different preferences regarding the urgency of establishing one's own household. The last part of the table illustrates the important role of marriage in living arrangements. Clearly, the forming of a long-term relationship (which in Italy still mostly means getting married) is the fundamental differentiator between living with one's parents and establishing one's own household, above all for young women.[4]

What then has been happening in Italy over the last decade or so? Figure 4.1 illustrates changes in the living arrangements of young men and young

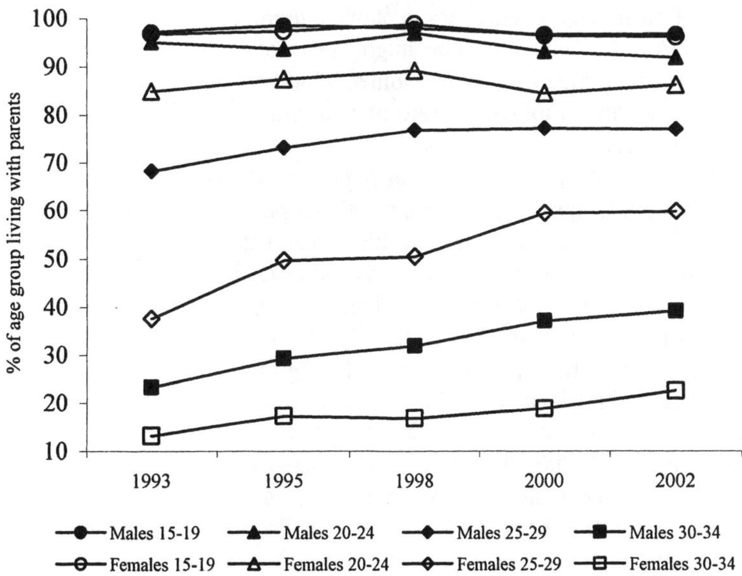

Source: Banca d'Italia, Survey on Household Income and Wealth

Figure 4.1 Percentage of Youth Living with their Parents, by Age, Italy 1993 to 2002

women between 1993 and 2002[5] for Italy as a whole. Evident from the figure is the fact that the increasing 'average' age at which young Italians leave the parental home is attributable to the rise in the proportion of 25–34 year olds who remain with their parents. There is a clear upward trend for young men and women young women in both the 25–29 and 30–34 year old age groups. In contrast, the traditional youth group (15–24) actually shows an, albeit very mild, negative trend, possibly depending to some extent on a greater tendency of young people to leave the household whilst still in education.[6] Also apparent is the difference between young men and young women, the latter being much more likely to leave the family earlier on. The gap between young men and young women seems to have narrowed for those in their late twenties and widened slightly for those in their thirties due to the different relative strengths of the positive trend amongst men and women in the two different groups.

Figure 4.2 shows a similar picture as regards trends in working arrangements. There is a clear downward trend in the proportions of teenage men and women working, largely reflecting a general trend towards greater educational participation. Young women in their late twenties and early thirties show a clear upward trend in labor force participation, albeit remaining well below the level of men, whilst the employment–population ratio of men over twenty has remained more or less constant over the period. At the same time, one might also notice the difference in levels between young men and young women which increases with age so that by their thirties the employment rate of young men is clearly above those of young women.

Figure 4.3 looks at the situation as regards educational participation. There is a perceptible upward trend in educational participation for young women from all the age groups. For men this is also true apart from those in their late twenties, who do not seem to have increased their participation to any significant degree. Not very surprisingly, the upward trend in participation is most marked amongst the under-25s of both sexes. Worthy of mention here is the late twenties age group. This group traditionally has a fairly substantial educational participation relative to other countries due to the low direct costs of university education in Italy (and in the high unemployment South, also the low opportunity costs) and the lack of limits on the time spent studying for a degree. In the late 1990s the Italian educational system began to be overhauled. Two of the consequences were progressive increases in university fees as well as in the costs and administrative barriers to prolonging one's studies indefinitely. This is a plausible explanation for the downward trend in educational participation observable particularly for males in their late twenties around the turn of the century.

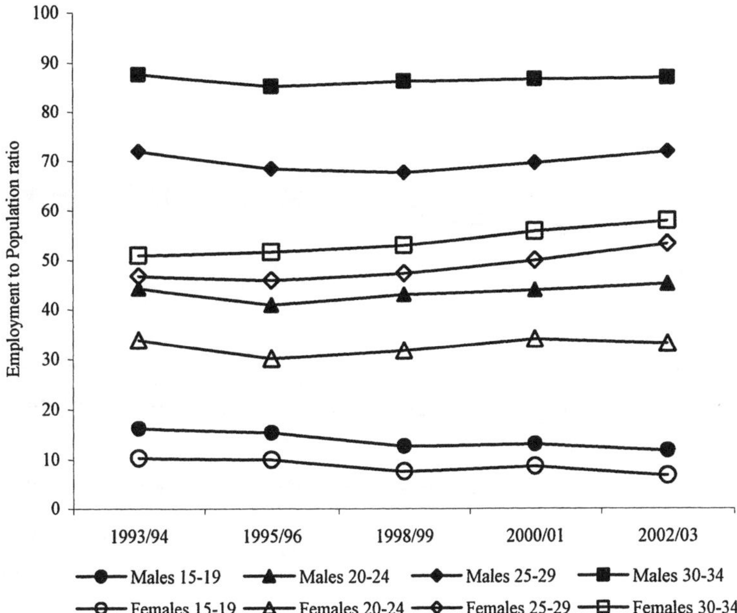

Source: ISTAT Labour Force Surveys, various years

Figure 4.2 Employment to Population Ratios by Age, Italy 1993/4 to 2002/3

Finally, Figure 4.4 presents information on the trend in 'marriage' rates. It might be observed that these figures report the proportion of the age group who are currently married (or cohabiting with a partner) and are thus influenced by divorce and separation as well as by the act of marriage per se. Notable from the graph are the higher rates of marriage amongst young women that reflect of course the tendency of women to get married younger than men. There is also a very clear downward trend in marriage rates, which is most marked for those over 25 for both men and women, particularly so for young women in their late twenties.

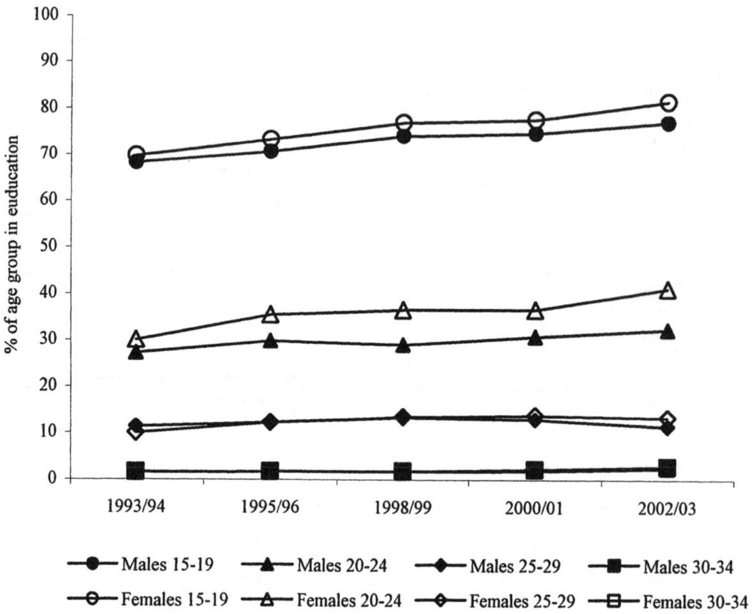

Source: ISTAT Labour Force Surveys, various years

Figure 4.3 Educational Participation by Age, Italy

RESEARCH STRATEGY

The model employed here looks at the relationship between the phenomena of interest – entering employment, participation in education, non-employment, remaining within the parental home and getting married – and two indicators of labor market conditions: a labor demand index and a wage index.[7] The purpose is to determine the extent to which changes in youth behavior were driven by these broad aggregates.

The demand index is intended to capture variations in local opportunities and is simply the region, gender and year-specific employment–population ratio of prime-age adults here defined as those aged 35–49 so as to avoid overlap with the age groups of interest. The index is derived from the same source as the dependent variables, namely the National Labor Force Surveys, 1993–2003. During the period under consideration, this was a quarterly rotating sample survey of Italian households (undertaken in January, April, July and October), covering around 200,000 per wave.

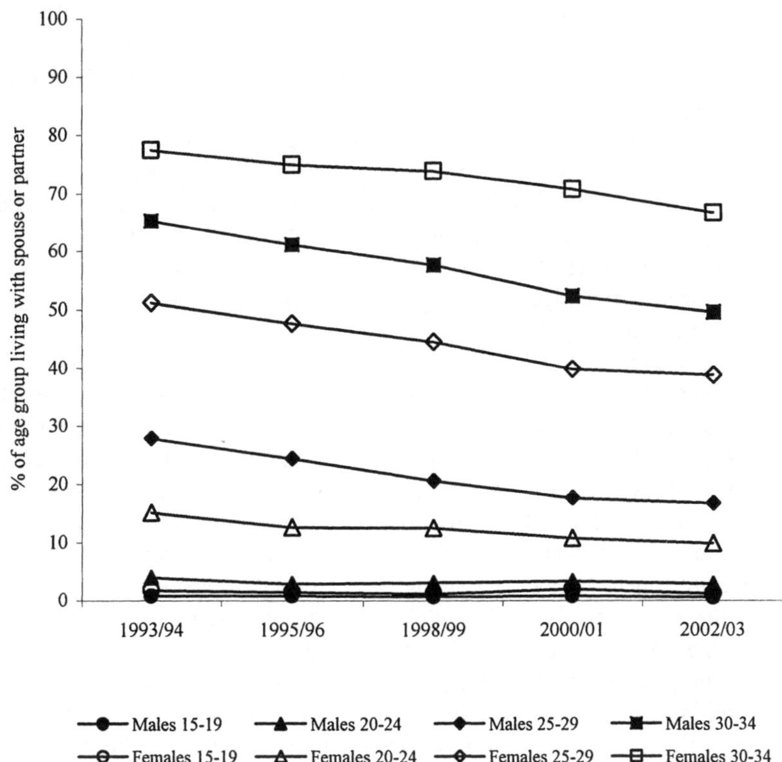

Source: ISTAT Labour Force Surveys, various years

Figure 4.4 Marriage Rates by Age, Italy 1993 to 2002

Each observation is based on annualized data from July of one year to April of the following year (corresponding to the academic year and therefore to the major shift points in young people's behavior) or around 800,000 individual observations.[8]

The wage index is intended to capture the attractiveness of available employment opportunities and is more problematic than the demand index. The Italian Labor Force Survey in this period contains no information on wages, so the Banca d'Italia's Survey on Household Income and Wealth (SHIW) was used. This is a much smaller and less frequent survey covering around 20,000 individuals every two or three years. The data points available for this variable determine the timing of the observations used in this study. Specifically, information is used for the years 1993, 1995, 1998, 2000 and 2002. The wage index is constructed as the natural logarithm of the regional 'youth' mean relative to the national mean of the hourly wage of employees aged 15–34. The index is potentially problematic for a number of reasons. Principal amongst these is the small sample size used for the construction of the individual observations and the notorious unreliability of self-reported income.[9] Different trials were also undertaken using different methods of calculating the 'average' regional youth wage. The estimation results do not differ greatly across the different wage indices employed, which gives some support to the use of this index.[10]

A second potential problem concerns the possible endogeneity of the wage index; in other words, the possibility that it is the behavioral 'dependent' variables which influence wages rather than vice versa. One basic assumption underlying the estimation of this model is that the youth wage is not affected by the supply of (youth) labor – this is of particular (but not exclusive) relevance in the estimation of the employment-rate. There are a number of reasons why one might suppose that youth wages are above their market clearing level, not least of which the very high unemployment rates facing young people in Italy.[11] Moreover, a simple test of the hypothesis is possible. Following the approach previously employed for the USA and Canada,[12] the regional youth wage variable was regressed on the proportion of young people in the working age population.[13] The resulting coefficient on the youth share of the population was positive albeit not statistically significant at conventional levels. This is of course contrary to the prediction of the market clearing model, where increases in labor supply should, *ceteris paribus*, reduce the prevailing wage, but consistent with a model with excess labor supply in which wages are determined exclusively by the demand side of the market.

In addition to single-year age-fixed effects, which allow for different propensities to, for example, remain in education for each single-year age group, the model also allows the effects of the economic variables to vary across each age group. Clearly it is to be expected that economic factors are likely to affect decisions differently at different points in one's life. Indeed, the results reported below very much reflect this.

Throughout, the dependent variables were lagged by six months. For example, for '1993', the employment–rate, educational participation and marriage rate variables were based on annualized LFS data from July of 1993 until April 1994. The purpose is:

1. to consider academic years – the decision to participate in education and consequently (to some extent) to participate in the labor market, particularly for the younger age groups, will largely be made in relation to the academic as opposed to the calendar year; and,
2. to further remove possible problems of endogeneity of the wage variable – it is reasonable to suppose that decisions affecting labor force participation, leaving home and so on will be dependent on current and past values of the explanatory variables; inclusion of the earlier period from the labor force survey would actually imply using future values of the wage variable to determine current behavior.[14]

EMPIRICAL FINDINGS

Tables 4.2–4.6 report the results of estimating the model for each of the dependent variables of interest. The two panels in each table report the results for young men and young women separately. For working behavior (Table 4.2), one can observe the very strong positive impact of the 'adult' employment rate on young people's likelihood of employment, particularly for young men.[15] Although the effect is also clearly statistically significant for young women, the coefficients are much smaller in size. This somewhat surprising result may be explained by the use of the female 'adult' employment rate as a regressor. Introducing the male employment rate as the explanatory variable into the regression for females removes this strong time trend from the demand index and produces coefficients which are similar to those of males. The implication is that the behavior of young women is less subject to the general upward time trend in the labor force participation rates of women and more influenced by variations in overall labor demand than are the participation rates of 'middle-aged' women.

Wage effects are also positive for those over 20; however, in this case the coefficients are, with the exception of young women in their early twenties, not statistically significant. Perhaps most interesting are the negative and (mostly) statistically significant coefficients on the demand and wage indices observable for teenagers of both sexes. One interpretation of this concerns the possibly positive impact of improvements in economic conditions on the expected long-run benefits of, and therefore demand for, education. The negative coefficient here may be taken to imply that these expected longer term benefits outweigh to some extent the positive direct effects of variations in demand per se.

Therefore, the effects of demand and wage variables on the decision to remain in education (Table 4.3) are less clear cut than for entry into employment. On the one hand, increases in demand and/or wages increase the opportunity cost of education[16] but at the same time may also raise the expected benefits of education in terms of improved employment prospects and/or higher wage returns.[17] The simple model employed here does not allow a distinction to be made between these two effects. For young women

Table 4.2 Effects of Demand and Wage Indices on Working Behaviour of Young People, Unified Age Groups

	Employment–Population Ratio, 35–49 year-old men	**Relative Regional Wage-rate, 15–34 year-old men**
Males		
15–19 year olds	-0.50**	-0.079**
20–24 year olds	1.10***	0.045
25–29 year olds	1.18***	0.093***
30–34 year olds	0.53**	0.009
	Employment–Population Ratio, 35–49 year-old women	**Relative Regional Wage-rate, 15–34 year-old women**
Females		
15–19 year olds	-0.74***	-0.082
20–24 year olds	0.36***	0.064**
25–29 year olds	0.73***	0.042
30–34 year olds	0.65***	0.004

Note: The table reports the results of estimating equation (4.1) given in note 7. For reporting purposes, the age varying coefficients on the demand and wage indices were restricted to be constant over five year age groups. This simplifies the table (rather than reporting 20 coefficients for each of the explanatory variables). In addition to the reported coefficients, each equation included unrestricted age, region and year dummies. Estimates were weighted by age specific regional population. Standard errors corrected for arbitrary heteroscedasticity and clustered for each region and year. Statistical significance at 10%, 5% and 1% are indicated by 1, 2 or 3 asterisks respectively. The number of observations in each equation is 1900 (19 regions x 5 years x 20 single-year age groups).

over twenty the effect of demand on educational participation is negative and statistically significant. Although the effect is weaker, the same can be said for young men over 25. Again however, the effect of demand and wages on teenagers appears to be positive, which supports the notion that employment and wage indices are being taken as indicators of employment and wage returns to education by this group, in other words, the expected benefits of education rather than its opportunity cost.

Non-employment is essentially a residual category. It may be interpreted as the broad unemployment–population ratio.[18] It will be

Table 4.3 Effects of Demand and Wage Indices on the Educational Participation of Young People, Unified Age Groups

	Employment–Population Ratio, 35–49 year old men	**Relative Regional Wage-rate, 15–34 year old men**
Males		
15–19 year olds	0.21	0.020
20–24 year olds	0.09	0.022
25–29 year olds	-0.11	-0.044**
30–34 year olds	0.01	-0.043
	Employment–Population Ratio, 35–49 year old women	**Relative Regional Wage-rate, 15–34 year old women**
Females		
15–19 year olds	0.22***	0.009
20–24 year olds	-0.08*	-0.049*
25–29 year olds	-0.17***	-0.028
30–34 year olds	-0.14***	0.047

Note: See note to Table 4.2.

observed that the coefficients on demand and wage indices in Table 4.4 are very similar, with changed signs, to the coefficients from the employment-ratio equation in Table 4.2. This suggests that the main response to worsening economic conditions was a move into inactivity rather than refuge in education and, in combination with the results from Table 4.3, to some extent calls into question the received wisdom on the Italian case, where education has traditionally been seen as a refuge for the unemployed. Given the increasing costs and difficulties associated with attending and above all remaining in university since the late 1990s, it would be interesting to see the extent to which the coefficients are stable over time or whether in fact the response to falls in labor demand in terms of increased demand for education has got smaller over the years in response to the institutional changes in Italy.

Turning to the determinants of co-residence with parents (Table 4.5), one finds strong negative effects of demand for all young women and for young men under 25. For young men, the effects of wages are also negative and declining with age, becoming statistically significant for those over 25. Also for women, the wage coefficient falls with age. These results are consistent with the models of family transfers and offsprings' residential decisions current in the literature.[19] Increased employment opportunities and/or higher wages in employment will tend to relax the financial constraint preventing young people from leaving the parental home. More prosaically, the family in Italy still seems to be playing the role of providing the social safety net not available from the State.

Table 4.4 Effects of Demand and Wage Indices on the Non-Employment of Young People, Unified Age Groups

	Employment–population Ratio, 35–49 year old men	**Relative Regional Wage-rate, 15–34 year old men**
Males		
15–19 year olds	0.35*	0.054
20–24 year olds	-1.18***	-0.065*
25–29 year olds	-1.07***	-0.048*
30–34 year olds	-0.55***	0.033*
	Employment–population Ratio, 35–49 year old women	**Relative Regional Wage-rate, 15–34 year old women**
Females		
15–19 year olds	0.55***	0.074
20–24 year olds	-0.24***	-0.012
25–29 year olds	-0.54***	-0.014
30–34 year olds	-0.49***	-0.053*

Note: See note to Table 4.2.

One of the main immediate determinants of leaving the parental home is marriage. As noted above, almost all young married couples live outside the parental home, although the extent to which this is because marriage provides a means to escape the parental home as opposed to the establishment of one's own residence being a natural but incidental consequence of marriage, remains open to question. In any event, since marriage and leaving the parental home are so closely connected, but without wishing to embark on a detailed discussion of the underlying issues,[20] Table 4.6 reports results on a similar equation estimated for marriage rates. To some extent at least the results support the maintained hypothesis. Particularly for the younger age groups, the demand indices (and, for young men, also the wage indices) exert a positive influence on the marriage rate of young people, confirming the notion of a relaxation of the financial constraint allowing the formation of separate two-person households.

Table 4.5 Effects of Demand and Wage Indices on Young People Remaining with Their Parents, Unified Age Groups

	Employment–population Ratio, 35–49 year old men	**Relative Regional Wage-rate, 15–34 year old men**
Males		
15–19 year olds	-0.50**	-0.030
20–24 year olds	-0.34**	-0.037
25–29 year olds	0.17	-0.084***
30–34 year olds	0.33*	-0.141***
	Employment–population Ratio, 35–49 year old women	**Relative Regional Wage-rate, 15–34 year old women**
Females		
15–19 year olds	-0.36***	0.077***
20–24 year olds	-0.21***	0.017
25–29 year olds	-0.14*	-0.102***
30–34 year olds	-0.32***	-0.006

Note: See note to Table 4.2, although note that the reference period in this case is 1998–99 to 2002–03 and the number of observations in each equation is consequently 1140 (19 regions x 3 years x 20 single year age groups).

Clearly however, differences between Tables 4.5 and 4.6 point to a more complex array of influences. Certainly it would be interesting to look separately at the evolution of the formation of single- and two-person households by young people.

*Table 4.6 Effects of Demand and Wage Indices on Marriage amongst Young People, Unified Age Groups**

	Employment–population Ratio, 35–49 year old men	Relative Regional Wage-rate, 15–34 year old men
Males		
15–19 year olds	0.47**	0.091*
20–24 year olds	0.36**	0.054*
25–29 year olds	-0.08	-0.034
30–34 year olds	-0.17	-0.039
	Employment–population Ratio, 35–49 year old women	**Relative Regional Wage-rate, 15–34 year old women**
Females		
15–19 year olds	0.35***	-0.007
20–24 year olds	0.02	0.001
25–29 year olds	-0.16***	0.048*
30–34 year olds	0.02	0.016

Note: See note to Table 4.2.

In order to get a sense of the extent to which aggregate economic changes have been driving changes in youth behavior, Table 4.7 reports the results of two exercises comparing estimated total changes in the behavioral variables over time with the changes over time in the behavioral variables explained by changes in labor market conditions. The first part of the table looks at the contribution of demand to total changes over time, whilst the second part looks at the extent to which macro-region-specific changes in labor market conditions have been behind divergent trends in young people's behavior in the less-developed South of the country compared to the North-Centre. The two comparisons are based essentially on the estimation of the models with and without the demand index.[21] In the first case, a model is estimated without demand and wage indices but with time-, region- and age-fixed effects. The difference in the fixed effects for the end year with respect to the base year provides an estimate of the total time trend in the phenomenon of interest. This is then compared to the time-fixed effects produced by estimating the model including the economic

Table 4.7 The Contribution of Labor Market Conditions to Changes in Young People's Behavior over Time and to Geographically Divergent Trends in Young People's Behaviour in Italy

a) Difference over time in Italy, 1995/6–2002/3

		Total change	Change Explained by labor market conditions	Unexplained change
Males	Working	1.8	0.9	0.9
	Studying	1.9	0.1	1.8
	Non-employed	-3.6	-1.0	-2.6
	Co-Residence	1.0	0.2	0.8
	Marriage	-5.6	0.1	-5.7
Females	Working	4.2	2.7	1.5
	Studying	3.6	-0.5	4.1
	Non-employed	-7.8	-2.2	-5.6
	Co-Residence	2.4	-1.3	3.7
	Marriage	-5.9	0.1	-6.0

b) Differences between the North-Centre and the South over time, 1993/4–2002/3

		Total change	Change Explained by Labor market conditions	Unexplained change
Males	Working	6.2	3.9	2.3
	Studying	10.0	12.6	-2.6
	Non-employed	-1.2	-1.5	0.3
	Co-Residence	0.0	-0.1	0.1
	Marriage	-2.6	1.1	-3.7
Females	Working	7.7	5.2	2.5
	Studying	7.4	12.2	-4.8
	Non-employed	-1.2	-1.5	0.3
	Co-Residence	-2.6	1.1	-3.7
	Marriage	-0.3	0.6	-0.9

Note: The table reports the resultant changes converted into percentage points. For co-residence with parents, changes refer to the period 1998/9–2002/3.

aggregates as explanatory variables. The time-fixed effects in this model correspond to the unexplained portion of the total time trend identified previously. The explained portion of the time trend is then simply the difference between the two. A similar procedure is adopted for the estimation of divergent trends between North-Centre and South. In this case, however, separate time-fixed effects are estimated for the North-Centre and South of the country for the two models (with and without explanatory labor market variables). The difference in the time-fixed effects between base year and end year for North-Centre and South in the restricted model (without explanatory labor market variables) provides the total time trend, whilst the same parameters from the unrestricted model provide the unexplained effects, and again, the total effect is the difference between them.

Looking at panel a) of the table, the first column reports the overall time trend in youth behavior. For example, overall, the employment rate of young men aged 15–34 rose by 1.8 percentage points between 1995–96 and 2002–03. Half of this change (0.9 percentage points) is attributable to changes in the demand index. Overall, the table suggests that labor market conditions were responsible for a substantial part of the time trends in the employment and non-employment rates, a modest portion of the time trend in the co-residence of young men, but very little of the change over time in educational participation or marriage rates. In several cases, in particular regarding the co-residence decisions of young women, the labor market variables worked against the overall time trend. For example, the model suggests that without the impact of labor demand, co-residence of young women would actually have increased significantly more than it did.

Turning to panel b), the table shows the impact of labor market variables on divergent (and occasionally convergent) time trends across the two macro-regions. Thus, for example, the table shows that on average, the gap between the North-Centre and the South of Italy in terms of young male employment rates increased by 6.2 percentage points. Of this increased divergence, a little under two-thirds (or 3.9 percentage points) is explained by differences in changes in the demand index. It is clear from the table that labor market variables made an important contribution to divergent time trends in youth behavior between the two macro-regions. One may note also that with respect to the strong difference in trends in educational participation between the North-Centre and the South, labor market factors more than completely account for the substantial difference over time in the trend. That is, the model suggests that differences in labor market conditions by themselves would have produced an even greater North–South divide in terms of educational participation than was actually observed. I would not wish to overemphasize the importance of this type of counterfactual exercise, but it does support the notion that labor market conditions played an important role in divergent North–South time trends in youth behavior.

CONCLUSIONS

In this chapter I have looked at a picture of changes in the Italian youth labor market, broadly defined. Applying a simple empirical model, I find that the strong influence of aggregate demand and wage indices on young people's behavior is clearly established. In particular, the analysis suggests that aggregate labor market factors played an important role in driving youth employment and non-employment rates as a whole over time. Moreover, such factors were very influential in driving divergent trends in employment and educational participation rates between the North, Centre and the South of Italy.

Beyond this, a number of other issues of interest also emerge. First, substantial differences are observable in the responses of young people of different ages. This suggests that analyses of issues such as leaving the parental home should take this into account. Leaving home at 20 is clearly a very different matter and influenced by different factors from leaving home at 30. Lumping together such groups is likely to produce a misleading picture. Second, the different timing of events and the differential influence of aggregate variables on them tends to bring into question the overly simplistic theoretical models underlying (although not usually being tested by) much of the research in this area. Third, although entry into a long-term relationship or marriage seems, particularly for young women, to be the key to escaping from the parental home, differences in the response of marriage and co-residence to economic aggregates, as well as the analysis of time trends, suggest that there is rather more to be investigated here. In particular, it may well be fruitful to look at exit from the parental home in order to form single-person households separately from the marriage-based exit. Finally, the analysis has raised the obvious question of the effects of changing university costs (and entry and exit mechanisms) which has characterized recent Italian history in the way that education is used as a refuge from unemployment.

NOTES

1. Indeed, active labor market policies for 'youth' in Italy typically apply to those aged up to 29, 32 or even 35 (depending on the policy). This contrasts with countries like the UK, for example, where typically 18 or 24 are the cut-off ages used for youth employment policy.

2. Card and Lemieux (2000).
3. This is also the reason why Table 4.1 does not include separately the non-employed category or 'activity'. Although studying and working are not necessarily mutually exclusive states in Italy, and given the way the studying is defined – including only those whose principal activity was studying, as opposed to all those undertaking some sort of off-the-job training or education – this is in practice the case. Only a little under 0.5 per cent of 15–34 year-olds reported studying and working in the academic year 2002/03. Thus 'not working' is essentially a residual category.
4. Interestingly, the table does not really support the three-state model employed in a recent study of the joint determination of working/educational participation and exit from the parental home in Italy by Giannelli and Monfardini (2003). That model posits three possible states: living in the parental home and either working or studying, or leaving the parental home and working. By contrast, the numbers of young people who actually leave home and continue studying is by no means insignificant, at least according to the LFS data.
5. In order to allow an analysis of trends over the full period, the figure is based on data from the Banca d'Italia's Survey on Household Income and Wealth (hereafter SHIW), which provides data on living arrangements over the whole period under study. The ISTAT Labor Force Survey Data which is used as a basis for the statistical analysis of living arrangements below (and for the other figures included here) has the advantage of a much larger sample size (each quarterly survey is roughly ten times the size of the bi- or tri-annual SHIW, but it does not, in the version which the author has, allow identification of living arrangements in 1993/4 and 1995/6.
6. In order to go to university outside their home town for example, an unusual but gradually increasing choice amongst young people.
7. More formally, the model is a three-way fixed-effects panel linear probability model for the different states of the form:

$$P_{irt} = \alpha_i + \alpha_r + \alpha_t + \beta_i(DEMAND)_{rt} + \gamma_i(WAGE)_{rt} + \varepsilon_{it} \qquad (4.1)$$

   where P is an age- (indexed by i), region- (indexed by r) and year- (indexed by t) specific probability; namely the employment rate, the educational participation rate, the non-employment rate, the proportion of young people living with their parents and the marriage rate. The model includes fixed effects for age, region and year (indicated by the α) and age-specific coefficients on the two main variables of interest, the demand and wage indices (indicated by β and γ). See also Card and Lemieux (2000).
8. Although, of course given the rotating nature of the sample, not 800,000 individuals.
9. See *inter alia*, Brandolini (1999) and Biancotti, D'Alessio and Neri (2004) for specific discussions of the reliability of the income variables in the SHIW. Note however, that employee wages are by far the most reliably reported income variables in the survey.
10. The small sample size also effectively excluded the possibility of using additional age (group) breakdowns of the regional wage rates. Trials were made using a five-year age breakdown on the wage variable combined with a larger geographical conglomeration. That is, rather than using the wage rate of 15–34 year-olds differentiated across 20 regions (and by year), a separate wage rate for 15–19 year olds, 20–24 year-olds, 25–29 year olds, 30–34 year olds was calculated separately for five (as opposed to 20) geographical areas. Interestingly, the results did not change greatly.
11. The youth (15–24) unemployment rate in Italy is amongst the highest in the EU, with only Poland and Slovakia having a worse situation facing young people. Moreover, the ratio of the youth (15–24) unemployment rate to the adult (25–54) unemployment rate in Italy is easily the highest in the EU. In 2002, the ratio stood at 3.5 compared to an EU average of 2.1. For a discussion of the issue, see for example, O'Higgins (2005).
12. Card and Lemieux (2000).
13. Including also time- and region-fixed effects and the prime-age adult employment rate.
14. Since the wage variable is based on annual income and the labor force variable on four time points during the year, using for example the April educational participation rates

would imply that the decision to stay on at (or return to) education in April of a year would depend on wage rates observable largely in the future.

15. The importance of demand to youth unemployment is of course a ubiquitous finding throughout the literature. See for example, Jimeno and Rodriguez-Palanzuela, (2002), on OECD countries and/or O'Higgins (2003) on the developing world.
16. This is the principal effect identified in the work of Card and Lemieux (2000), in their study of North American youth, where education acts as a refuge from unemployment.
17. For a discussion of this specific issue, see for example, O'Higgins (1992).
18. It includes of course the 'ILO' unemployed who are willing, able and actively seeking to work, but also all others who are not in employment or in education, and above all the so-called discouraged workers group. Following from the seminal work by Clark and Summers (1979), in recent years the usefulness of the distinction between those actively seeking work and those who are not (that is, the discouraged) has increasingly been the subject of debate. For a discussion of the issue in the Italian (as well as EU) context see, for example, Brandolini, Cipollone and Viviana (2006).
19. See in particular, Manacorda and Moretti (2006), Becker *et. al.* (2004) and Giannelli and Monfardini (2003) on Italy. Laferrière and Wolff (2006) provide a general review of microeconomic models of family transfers on which these empirical analyses are based.
20. Del Boca *et al.*, in a series of papers (for example, Del Boca *et. al.* (2000) on marriage and labor supply behavior amongst women), have looked at the issues related to marriage, fertility and employment amongst women. It is relevant to note that in Italy, in common with other southern European countries, the negative correlation between fertility and the employment rates of women has persisted to the present. In contrast, in most other OECD countries, the correlation has become positive since the 1980s (Del Boca, Pasqua and Pronzato 2004).
21. In practice this means the changes driven by the demand index, since the wage index is normalized to have mean zero in each time period there is no year-on-year change to impact on the fixed-year effects.

5. Youth Employment in Japan after the 1990s Bubble Burst

Naoki Mitani

Among advanced economies, the Japanese youth labor market was relatively strong until the economic 'bubble' burst in 1991. The main reasons widely suggested for this good performance were the smooth school-to-work transition, aided by close relationships between schools and firms (so-called *Jisseki Kankei*) as well as the long-term perspectives of Japanese employers willing to invest in training new school leavers.[1] Nonetheless, the youth labor market deteriorated sharply through the long recession after the Bubble Burst. This chapter investigates how and why the youth labor market deteriorated so much in Japan.

Undoubtedly, the main reason for the 1990s deterioration in the youth labor market was the reduction in labor demand for young workers due to the severe recession after the Bubble Burst, especially after 1997. Nonetheless, institutional factors, such as placement by schools and employment adjustment practices of Japanese firms, may also have played roles in the change in the youth labor market. We would like to investigate how they worked. Moreover, we should pay attention to the particular characteristics of the recession, such as the 'credit crunch' and deflation. Industrialized countries have never experienced such a deflation or 'liquidity trap' since World War II. We would like to investigate the effect of deflation on the employment of young workers. In addition, the demographic changes in this period should be taken into consideration. A massive generation of baby boomers has moved into the age group of the late 40s and early 50s. Given the high labor costs of these age groups, it may have significant effects on the employment of youth.

The next section surveys the recent developments in youth unemployment, with a simple international comparison. In section 3, we decompose the changes in (un)employment rates into those due to changing employment–population ratios and those due to changing labor force participation rates, to see how and to what extent the labor demand and labor supply forces contributed to the deterioration of employment rate. In section 4, we analyze how regular employment was reduced with expansion of non-regular employment for youth and the reasons for it. In section 5, we treat the issues of unemployment and educational attainment. In section 6, we investigate to what extent and how the inactive youth population has grown. The final section concludes the discussion.

RECENT TRENDS IN YOUTH UNEMPLOYMENT

The youth labor market in Japan showed relatively good performance, as indicated by its low unemployment rate, until the 1990s Bubble Burst. However, after the Bubble Burst in late 1991, the situation changed dramatically. National economic growth declined sharply: average annual growth in the 1980s was roughly 4 per cent, but it fell about 1 per cent from 1991 to 2002. The downturn was deeper in the latter half of the recession after 1997, when it was triggered by the rise of indirect taxes and the financial crisis. A severe credit crunch stemming from the accumulated bad loans persisted thereafter. Accordingly, the unemployment rate, especially for youth, soared. The overall unemployment rate reached its historical high of 5.4 per cent in 2002. The youth unemployment rate, which declined during the 'Bubble Boom' around 1990, increased more rapidly. Especially during the recession after 1997, the rise in the youth unemployment rate accelerated. It surpassed 10 per cent for young male adults aged 20–24 years old as well as for teenagers of both sexes. It reached 15 per cent for male teenagers (Figure 5.1).

The deterioration in the youth labor market is also indicated by the increase in the long-term unemployment rate among young workers. Long-term unemployment used to be more prevalent among older workers who have more difficulties finding jobs. However, recent developments show that the long-term unemployment rate rose more rapidly among youth and it surpassed that of older workers in the late 1990s. In 2004, the proportion of the male labor force aged 15–24 that was unemployed for more than one year was 3.3 per cent. That is, roughly one-third of the unemployed male young workers were unemployed for more than one year (Figure 5.2).

International comparisons shed some light on the extent to which the long recession has deteriorated the youth labor market in Japan. Figure 5.3 shows the unemployment rate of youth (less than 25 years old) for seven countries (France, Germany, Japan, Netherlands, Sweden, United Kingdom and the United States). Apparently, Japan is the only country that experienced a steady rise from 1990 to 2002, whereas in almost all the other countries youth unemployment decreased during the same period. In consequence, the gap in the youth employment rate between Japan and other countries has narrowed. It is even lower in the Netherlands than in Japan. Nonetheless, these trends reflect largely the differences in GDP growth rate across these countries. Figure 5.4 shows the relation between the average real GDP growth rate and the average unemployment rate for the 15–24 years old of both sexes for 1982–1991 and 1992–2002. According to this figure, we can observe that, first, whereas the other countries' economic growth rate was 2–3 percent on average and increased from the first period to the second period except for France, in Japan it decreased sharply from 4 per cent in 1982–1991 in 1992–2002. This suggests that the reduction in labor demand mainly accounts for the aggravation of youth unemployment in Japan after the Bubble Burst.

Second, apparently the cyclical elasticity of youth unemployment rates is larger in France, the Netherlands, the United Kingdom, and the United States than in Japan and Germany. This seems to have resulted in relatively small increases in the youth unemployment rate in the latter countries, in spite of the relatively large slumps of their economies. It may suggest that the smooth transition from school to work through the close relationship between schools and firms is still effectively working in Japan. Nonetheless, this relatively better performance many mask the severity of the recent youth unemployment/employment problems.

PLACEMENT BY SCHOOLS

The low unemployment of youth in Japan is often attributed to the relatively smooth transition from school to work based on a close relationship between senior high schools and firms (so-called *Jisseki Kankei*)[2]. Institutionally, some parts of the job placement activities for students are delegated to high schools. Employers must specify the conditions of the recruitment to the PESO (Public Employment Security Office): the number of offers to the school, job contents, wages, work-time and so on. Then, based on this information, each school recommends the students to employers, mainly based on their academic achievement. There is typically a close informal relationship between high schools and specific firms. Obviously, maintaining these relationships is important for schools in placing their graduates successfully and for firms in recruiting capable employees. The fact that the criteria to recommend students is mainly academic achievement gives a strong incentive for students to study at schools and is a good device for schools to control their students. This close relationship between schools and firms is considered to improve the matching quality of students and jobs. In fact, recent empirical analysis obtained results that are consistent with the hypothesis.[3] In addition, it is found that the quality of job matching of those younger workers who evaluate highly the vocational guidance by schools is likely to be better.[4] This suggests that schools play important roles in improving the efficiency of the placement of young workers at their graduation. Nonetheless, it is also known that the quality of job matching worsens in business cycle downturns as the number of good job offers to school decreases.[5]

Figure 5.5 shows the distribution of new high school leavers employed by the way they found their first jobs. As described above, institutional job offers are reported to or transmitted through the PESO to schools. The distinction between 'PESO' and 'School' shows simply which the respondents (new school leavers) considered more important. The sum of 'PESO' and 'School' is roughly constant, ranging between 80 per cent and 90 per cent from 1986 to 2002, although recently the proportions of 'Vacant advertisements' have increased somewhat. Thus it seems that the 'placement by schools' system for high schools still works, although the quality of job matching deteriorated because of the lack of good job offers.

DECOMPOSITION OF THE EMPLOYMENT RATE

The relatively low unemployment rate does not necessarily mean that relatively abundant employment opportunities are provided for young workers, because the decline in the labor supply may mitigate the rise in the unemployment rate.[6] A simple decomposition of the employment rate (=1-unemployment rate) shows that the 'discouraged worker effects' of young workers have played an important role in preventing the youth unemployment rate from rising dramatically.

We can decompose the changes in the logarithm of the employment rate as follows: [7]

$$\Delta \log(ER) = \Delta \log(EP) - \Delta \log(PR) \quad \ldots (5.1)$$

where

ER = employment rate = employment/ (labor force population of the relevant age group) = 1- unemployment rate

EP = employment–population ratio – employment/ (population of the relevant age group)

PR = labor force participation rate = labor force population/ (population of the relevant age group)

Δ = difference operator = (the value of the last period) – (the value of the first period).

Since the difference in the logarithm of an indicator is approximately equal to the growth rate of the indicator, equation (5.1) posits that:

Growth rate of the unemployment rate ≈
Growth rate of the employment–population ratio – growth rate
of the labor force participation rate ... (5.2)

If we postulate that the employment–population ratio indicates the extent to which an economy provides the relevant age group with employment opportunities and that the labor force participation rate indicates the extent to which the population of the relevant age group supplies the economy with their labor services, then equations (5.1) and (5.2) may be regarded as the decomposition of the (un)employment rate into the demand-side effect and the supply-side effect.

Table 5.1 shows the result of this decomposition for different groups. First, the labor market situation, as shown by the employment rate, worsened for all demographic groups after the Bubble Burst, but it deteriorated most severely for young workers, especially young adults. Second, the deterioration of the employment rate is mainly due to the decrease in the number of jobs for youth, as shown by the changes in the employment rate, especially for the period from 1997 onwards. The lack of employment opportunities for young workers induced a large 'discouraged workers effect', and this has prevented the youth unemployment rate from rising dramatically for this period.

Third, the reduction in employment opportunities is larger for the period 1997–2004. This reflects the fact that the downturn of the economy was deeper for the latter half of the recession after the Bubble Burst. In fact, the annual average growth rate of the real GDP was only 0.63 per cent for 1997–2002, far lower compared with 1.52 per cent for 1992–1996. The latter period of the recession was triggered by an increase in the consumption tax and the financial turmoil originating in several East Asian countries. The many bad loans of the Japanese banks caused a credit crunch. Small firms, the main source of job opportunities for youth in local areas, were severely affected, together with many larger firms.

Fourth, the reduction in employment opportunities was larger for young male workers. Structural changes such as the decline in the manufacturing sector and the rise in tertiary sectors have exerted relatively more adverse effects on males than females. In fact, male-dominated industries such as manufacturing and construction lost employment after the Bubble Burst, because of the transfer of factories to other lower-cost Asian countries like China, as well as reductions in public investment caused by the accumulated public debt. On the other hand, more traditionally female-oriented industries such as services were still growing in spite of the recession.

EMPLOYMENT

Non-Regular Employment

As shown above, employment opportunities declined sharply during the long recession after the Bubble Burst, especially after 1997. In addition, regular employment for youth shrank even further. Young workers were more likely to be employed as non-regular workers such as part-time workers, contract employees and dispatch employees. Smooth transition from school to work through close relations between schools and firms is associated with the fact that new school leavers were employed as regular workers upon their graduation. However this proportion for young workers aged 15–29 years old fell from 87.5 per cent in 1985 to 83.8 per cent in 1997.[8] It dropped more significantly for high school-leavers from 87.2 per cent to 79.8 per cent during the same period. It should also be noted that the smaller this proportion is, the lower the educational attainment. Although the comparable data are not available, this proportion seems to have dropped sharply during the severe recession after 1997. An econometric analysis using retrospective data from the Ministry of Labour Survey on Young Employees of 1997 showed that, controlling for gender, education, and trend term, a 1 per cent increase in the overall unemployment rate a year prior to leaving school decreased the probability of obtaining a full-time regular job upon leaving school by 7.9 per cent.[9]

Correspondingly, the increase in the ratio of part-time employment of young workers accelerated from 1997 (Figure 5.6). It is argued that the secular rise in the ratio of part-time workers[10] is caused by supply-side factors such as changes in the attitude of young workers. That is, more young workers prefer to work as part-time workers with less constraint at the workshop, having economic support from their parents during the prolonged period of living at home.[11] Nonetheless, the sharp increase in the ratio of part-time young workers after 1997 is considered to reflect more significantly the reduction in regular jobs for youth. Apparently, Figure 5.6 shows the countercyclical movement of this ratio. In addition, among the part-time workers who want to change employers, the proportion of those who want to change employers because they want more stable jobs is increasing.

Employment Protection Legislation and Aging

The reduction in regular jobs occurred disproportionately for young workers. This is partly accounted for by the employment adjustment behaviors of Japanese firms, especially large ones, which hire young workers and tend to invest in their human capital relatively intensively under long-term employment practices. Their training is both on-the-job and off-the-job. A significant part of the acquired skills is considered to be firm-specific. Thus, in economic downturns, firms tend to suppress the hiring of new workers then lay off incumbent workers, because of the high-risk sunk costs of firm-specific training.[12] In addition to the economic rationales, it is believed that 'rigid' employment protection legislation tends to protect the employment of incumbent workers. The Japanese Labour Standard Law stipulates that the employer must provide at least 30 days advance notice when it wants to dismiss a worker. An employer who does not give 30 days advance notice is required to pay the average wage for a period of not less than 30 days. However, the right of dismissal is virtually restricted by the doctrine of abusive dismissal established by the Supreme Court. It formalized the legal principles accumulated so far by declaring that 'even when an employer exercises its right of dismissal, it will be viewed as an abuse of the right if it is not based in objectively reasonable grounds so that it cannot receive general social approval as a proper act.'[13] Japan has been classified as one of the most rigid countries in employment protection legislation.[14]

Of course, these high employment protection practices do not prohibit Japanese firms from layoffs of incumbent workers when faced with severe economic difficulties. In the 'IT recession' in 2001, many large enterprises cut their workforces, but mainly by the recruitment of voluntary retirees with privileged severance payments. It is rare to dismiss workers for economic reasons. It is true that involuntary separation is concentrated disproportionately among older workers. Nonetheless, during the last recession, the burden of job destruction, especially that of regular jobs, was more concentrated on young workers than older workers, if we include those who were not hired as regular employees but who would have been if not for the recession.

Given these employment adjustment practices of Japanese firms, the aging of the labor force in combination with the extension of the mandatory retirement age resulted in a further reduction in regular jobs for youth. The proportion of older workers aged 50 years old increased from 33.3 per cent in 1997 to 37.1 per cent in 2004 as the baby boomers, who were born in 1947–1949, entered into this age group. In accordance with the aging of the labor force, the Japanese government had taken various measures to promote employment of older workers. As mentioned above, the most important measure in the last two decades was the rise in mandatory retirement age, which used to be 55, to 60 years-old. The law of promotion of employment for older workers prohibited the implementation of a mandatory retirement age under 60 years old in 1990. In effect, the proportion of firms whose mandatory retirement age was 60 years or older rose from 63.3 per cent in 1990 to 98.9 per cent in 2003. Nonetheless, in the recession, when the number of jobs was limited, the increase in older workers employed as regular workers had adverse effects on the regular employment of young workers. Various econometric analyses show results consistent with this hypothesis.[15]

Figure 5.7 shows the ratio of regular employees to the population by age group. According to this figure, employment opportunities as regular workers decreased for young workers under age 30 from 1991 to 2004. The decrease was most significant for the age group of 20–24 years-old.[16] However, surprisingly, jobs increased for those aged 30 or older under the recession. The ratio has increased most for 55–59 year olds. This figure suggests that regular employment of older workers has been maintained at the cost of fewer employment opportunities as regular workers for youth.

Wage Rigidity and Part-Time Employment

Under deflationary pressure, nominal wage growth had stagnated.[17] In addition, the rigidity of wages of regular workers may have contributed to reducing further regular jobs for youth. Figure 5.8 shows the relationship between the annual growth rate of nominal hourly wages for regular employees aged 15–24 years old of both sexes and the unemployment rate of the relevant sex-age group.[18] According to this figure, the wage growth rate declines as the unemployment rate rises. However, apparently it rarely declines to below zero and seems to stick to the zero line, even if the unemployment rate rises. The downward rigidity of nominal wages may be due to efficiency considerations of employers in recruiting good regular workers even in severe recessions and the transactions costs of changing the internal wage system. Nonetheless, combined with the recent flattening of age-wage profiles, the relative real hiring cost of regular workers remained high. Moreover, the wage differential between regular young workers and part-time workers aged 15–24 years old, measured as the percent ratio of the wages of part-time workers to those of regular workers, has widened steadily from 87.2 per cent in 1988 to 76.9 per cent in 2004. These increasing relative costs of regular workers might have reduced employment opportunities as regular workers for youth and contributed to the expansion of part-time employment for them.[19] If we include part-time young employees in the analysis, wages become more flexible to go lower in response to the rise in unemployment rates (Figure 5.9). This might have contributed to slowing the rise in unemployment rates due to the rigidity of nominal wages of regular employees. In Japan, it seems that the minimum wages do not bind the wages of low-wage workers, such as part-timers.[20] This view is consistent with the fact that the real wages of young part-time workers continue to decline persistently.

UNEMPLOYMENT AND EDUCATIONAL ATTAINMENT

In Japan, the burden of unemployment tends to be concentrated on young workers with lower educational attainment, as in other OECD countries (Figure 5.10). However, the differential between senior high school graduates and junior college graduates and above was small until the mid-1990s. This may reflect partly the efficient transition to jobs via school placement, common in senior high schools graduates and junior college graduates. It is not certain whether this is due to the decline of the quality of matching caused by the decrease in the number of good job offers or the decline in the average ability of senior high school graduates with the increasing enrollment in tertiary education.

Moreover, it is believed that drop-outs suffer disproportionately the burden of labor market slack. They are more likely to become jobless because, in addition to less human capital accumulation and its adverse signaling effect on employers, they tend to rely on private job-search means such as information from their family, relatives or friends, while graduates can benefit from the placement services of schools. In fact, the proportion of regular jobs among their first jobs for dropouts is much lower than for graduates.[21] The ratio of the number of high school dropouts to that of students increased slightly from around 2.0 per cent for 1990–1995 to around 2.5 per cent for 1996–2001 and then it has returned to the previous level thereafter. It is reported that the main reason for the rise during 1996–2001 was the increase in 'maladjustment to school or school life'.[22]

THE INACTIVE

As shown in section 4, the rise of the unemployment rate was mitigated significantly by the decline in the labor force participation rate. The severe recession made it difficult to get good jobs, and discouraged young workers from searching for them. This resulted in a decline in the labor force participation rate of young workers. In fact, the labor force participation rate of young workers aged 15–24 (of both sexes) fell from 47.2 per cent in 1993 to 44.2 per cent in 2004. This decline in labor force participation was partly due to the rise in higher education enrollment. The proportion of upper high school graduates who went to junior college or universities rose from 37.7 per cent in 1991 to 49.9 per cent in 2004, whereas it had been stable before the Bubble Burst. The rise in the enrollment rate to tertiary education may partly reflect the recent sharp decrease in the population aged 18, with a relatively stable prescribed number of entrant students. In addition, faced with the scarcity of good job offers, the number of students at college or universities who repeated the final year class and remained in school may have increased.

During the last decade, the fraction who are inactive has increased too.[23] According to the Labour Force Survey, the proportion of those aged 15–24 years old, who are neither in education nor in employment, has increased from 3.9 per cent in 1990 to 4.6 per cent in 2004. Further breakdown shows that it increased more for males, especially young male adults, and female teenagers. The increase is concentrated in the period of 1997 and onwards, except for female teenagers (Table 5.2).

The increase in the inactivity rate among youth suggests also the worsening of their employment situation. Their joblessness appears both as inactivity and as unemployment. The line between the two is blurred. Inactivity at an early stage of life deprives the opportunity for human capital accumulation, especially through on-the-job training, resulting in possible future low income or poverty. Recent research reveals that the inactivity is distributed disproportionately among youth of low-income households, and of low educational attainment.[24]

Path Dependency and Inequality

Path dependency or cohort-specific effects may affect the wages and the employment of young workers. The economic situation at the initial stage of professional life may have long-lasting effects on the wages and employment of the worker. During recessions, good employment opportunities are reduced and new school leavers are obliged to take worse jobs with poorer training opportunities within firms. In other words, the quality of the job matching tends to be lower. Given the limited chances to change jobs, this leaves scars on the professional careers of the generation that entered the labor market during recessions. Some empirical studies show that this generational effect is reflected in the lifelong earnings of workers. Firstly, wages of the cohort group that entered the labor market during the recession, *ceteris paribus*, tend to be lower over a long period of their professional life.[25] Secondly, the qualities of job matching of the first regular job as measured by the length of tenure tend to be worse for those young workers who entered during the recession.[26] Thus, they are more likely to change employers to seek for better matching, and the turnover rate of the cohort who entered the labor market during the period of high unemployment rate tends to be higher.[27] Thirdly, it is suggested that it will take a long time to catch up.[28]

Also, the cohort size or crowding effect may affect the wages and/or the employment of young workers. If we postulate that workers are not perfect substitutes across different cohort groups and that they foster their skills through their work experiences in the same manner, then the large size of the cohort results in lower wages. In fact, econometric studies show that the wages of generations of large size tend to be lower, other things being equal.[29] The results account partly for the recent flattening of age–wage profiles, or the rising relative wages of youth. The first baby boom generation has, by the 1990s, aged into their 40s and 50s, for which wages are typically the highest over the life cycle. After the Bubble Burst, the population size of youth was rather stable before the mid-1990 as the second baby boom generation (born in the early 1970s) entered the 15–24 age group. But thereafter it has been declining rapidly by over 1 per cent. However, although the decreasing numbers in current youth cohorts could have positive effects on employment of youth, they may be small.[30]

Long-lasting effects of the economic situation at the start of the professional life as well as the cohort size effects may alter the distribution of lifetime earnings.[31] Inequality within demographic groups has widened little so far. But it may widen in the future as the current young generation get older. Since it is known that part-time young workers and the inactive are less likely to be married or to have children,[32] the promotion of youth employment is needed not only as employment policy but also as population policy in a Japan faced with rapid aging and population decline.

CONCLUDING REMARKS

We have analyzed developments in Japan's youth labor market over the long recession since the Bubble Burst, especially during the severe recession after 1997. The unemployment rate of 15–24 year old soared to an historical high above 10 per cent and long-term youth unemployment increased significantly. However, a simple international comparison shows that the youth unemployment rates are still relatively low in Japan and Germany, after controlling for the economy's growth rate. The practices of placement by the school system and the lump sum hiring as regular workers on graduation still seem to work, although the quality as well as the quantity of matching has deteriorated as good job offers have been sharply reduced. Nonetheless, this relatively low unemployment rate masks the severity of the problems of youth employment and joblessness after 1997.

First, the employment–population ratio declined far more than the employment rate. This rise in unemployment rate, due to the large decrease in labor demand, would have been much worse had it not been hidden by the large decline in the participation rate or labor supply of youth. Second, regular employment for youth has sharply decreased, while non-regular employment such as part-time employment has grown. The uncertainty of economic circumstances in the future and increasing relative labor cost, partly due to the rigidity of nominal wages of regular workers, are considered to account for it, together with structural changes.

Third, the decrease in the number of regular employment slots for youth is also attributable to the growing number of older regular workers due to a rapidly aging population and the extension of the mandatory retirement age. The maintenance of regular employment for older workers under relatively strict employment protection legislation is likely to reduce the number of regular jobs for youth under the severe market slack.

Fourth, the number of the inactive who are not in the labor force and not in education has increased, although the majority of those not in the labor force appear to have been absorbed into schools. Fifth, the burden of the labor market slack is disproportionately concentrated on low-educated youth and dropouts, who are mostly out of the ordinary transition path from school to work. It is suggested that the dependency effects of the economic situation at the start of the professional life are long-lasting, so it is necessary to take measures to assist these people into employment.

Since 2000, the government has taken several real measures for youth for the first time. These include the establishment of new specialized placement institutions, like youth 'job spots' and job cafes that aim to attract young workers who never use PESO; trial employment; the Japanese Dual System or Japanese Job Corps; intensive job experience programs at junior high schools and so on. These measures are based on the experiences of similar efforts in other OECD countries. Some of these measures aim to assist those young workers who cannot benefit from placement by school systems. However, it is uncertain whether they are effective enough to cope with the current problems of youth employment and joblessness, as their budgets are very small, compared with other industrialized countries.[33] They should be strengthened based on the sufficient evaluation of individual measures.

The decade-long recession ended in 2002 and the Japanese economy began to recover. However, the youth unemployment rate may not decline rapidly, as those who had unsuitable jobs during the recession will begin to search for better jobs. But since youth employment is very sensitive to economic fluctuations, it is expected that the general youth labor market situation should improve soon. In addition, the impending retirement of the large baby-boom generation will begin in 2007, when they will reach their mandatory retirement age of 60. Combined with the decreasing relative size of the young population, this may improve regular employment opportunities for youth. The outcome depends upon the extent to which employers continued to hire regular workers with a long-term perspective of the future of the Japanese economy. In addition, it is urgently necessary to find ways to assist those young workers who were most severely affected by the recession and have a long way to go to catch up.

NOTES

1. For example, Mitani (1999).
2. In fact, according to the Japanese Cabinet Office (1998), the proportion of the workers whose opportunity to get the first job was 'placement by the school' (18–24 years old, both sexes, high school employed graduates) is much higher in Japan (33.3 per cent) than in other countries (Korea (12.6 per cent), France (8.8 per cent), Sweden (6.6 per cent), United Kingdom (6 per cent), Germany (4 per cent), United States (1.6 per cent)). For details of placement by school systems, see Kariya (1999).
3. Genda and Kurosawa (2001), Mitani (2001b).
4. Genda and Kurosawa (2001).
5. ibid.
6. Clark and Summers (1982).
7. Since $ER = E/L$, $EP = E/P$, $PR = L/P$, where E= employment, L= labor force population, P=population, we have the following equation: $EP=ER \cdot PR$ ... If we take the logarithm of both sides of this equation and take the difference, then we get equation (5.1).
8. Ministry of Labor (1985, 1997).
9. Genda and Kurosawa (2001), Table II.
10. A young part-time worker is often called a '*freeter,*' a Japanese word stemming from 'free' and 'arbeiters (part-time workers).'
11. For example, Yamada (1999). The phenomenon of the prolonged period of cohabitation of youth with their parents is common in OECD countries (Bowers *et al.* 1999).
12. Oi (1962).
13. Sugeno (1992). This doctrine became a substantive enactment in the Labor Standard Law in 2003.
14. OECD (1999a).
15. For example, Genda (2001) and Mitani(2001a).
16. This tendency does not change even if we take the effect of the rising enrollment in universities into consideration. The ratio of regular employees to the population minus students also decreased significantly from 75.2 per cent in 1991 to 61.4 per cent in 2004.
17. The annual average growth rate of CPI was 0.2 per cent, -0.3 per cent for 1992–2004 and –0.3 per cent for 1998–2004.
18. As hourly wages, we take the monthly contractual salary divided by the actual monthly contractual hours worked, excluding bonus and overtime payments for the following reasons: in the *Basic Survey on Wages*, there is only information on the amount of the bonus for the previous year; the information on the bonus of newly recruited workers is not available; and the hiring decision of the firm seems to be based on the contractual salary.

19. In addition to the differential in wage costs between regular and part-time workers, the increasing differential in other labor costs such as social security and training during the recession might have also contributed to the expansion of part-time workers.
20. Abe (2001) reported that only 16 per cent of part-time workers receive wages up to 10 per cent higher than the minimum wage and concluded that the minimum wages do not seem to support the wage level of part-time workers, especially in metropolitan areas. Thus the minimum wages do not seem to bind the wages of young workers or to reduce the employment of youth.
21. Mitani (1999).
22. Ministry of Education, Culture, Sports and Technology (2005).
23. Here we define for convenience the inactive as those who are not in employment and not in education. They have often been called 'NEET' (not in education, employment and training) recently in Japan.
24. Japan Cabinet Office (2005).
25. Inoki and Ohtake (1999). Genda (1997).
26. Genda and Kurosawa (2001).
27. Ohta (1999).
28. Genda (1997) showed that the age–wage profile is flatter for those university graduates who started their professional lives during recessions. Mitani (2001b) estimated that it would take some ten years for young workers who were not employed as regular workers upon their graduation to catch up in terms of wages or stability of employment, although there remains the econometric problem of selectivity. As state dependency effects are rather stronger and longer in Continental European countries than in the United States (Ryan 2001), it may be suggested that the Japanese labor market is more similar to those of the former countries.
29. Inoki and Ohtake (1999), Okamura (2000).
30. Korenman and Neumark (2000).
31. Ohtake (2005).
32. Sakai and Higuchi (2005).
33. According to Chart 1.5 of OECD (2002, p.29), the ratio of the budget of youth employment measures to GDP is on average about 0.1 per cent in OECD countries. But in Japan this ratio is less than 0.01 per cent in the budget of the fiscal year of 2005. It should be noted however, that the expenditures on the placement by schools are not included here.

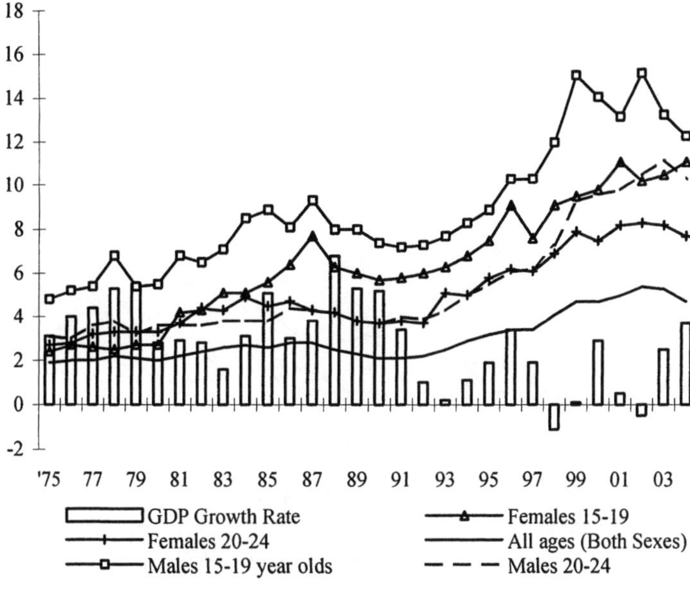

Source: Statistics Bureau (2005).

Figure 5.1 Growth Rate and Youth Unemployment Rate, Japan, 1975 to 2003 (%)

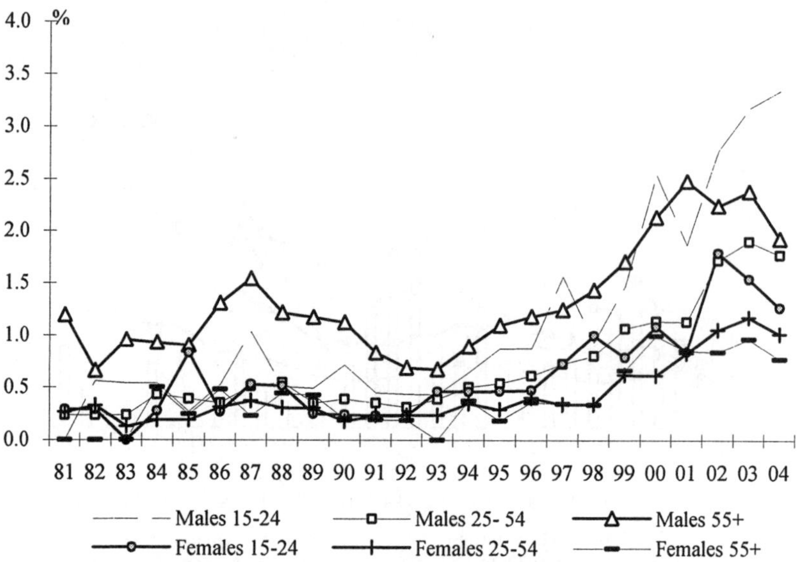

Source: OECD, CDE_LFS Database(www1.oecd.org/scripts/cde/)

Figure 5.2 Long-term Unemployed (1 year or more) as % of labor force, Japan, 1981 to 2004

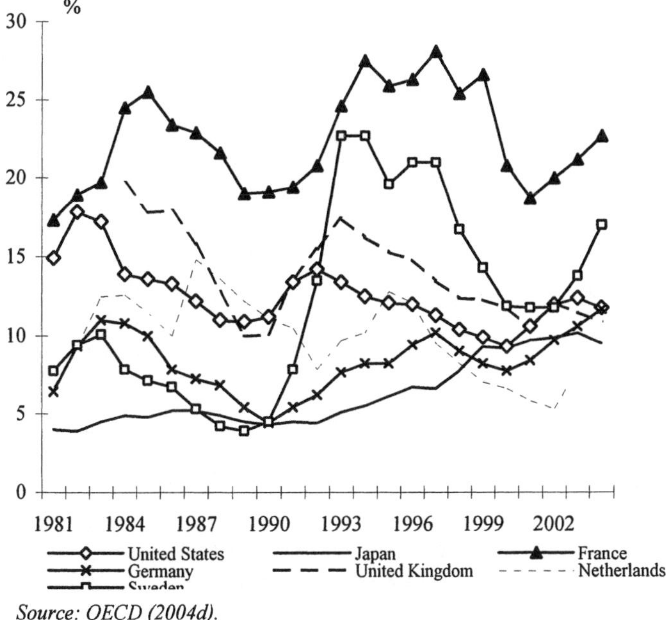

Source: *OECD (2004d).*

Figure 5.3 International Comparison of Youth (<25 years-old) Unemployment Rates

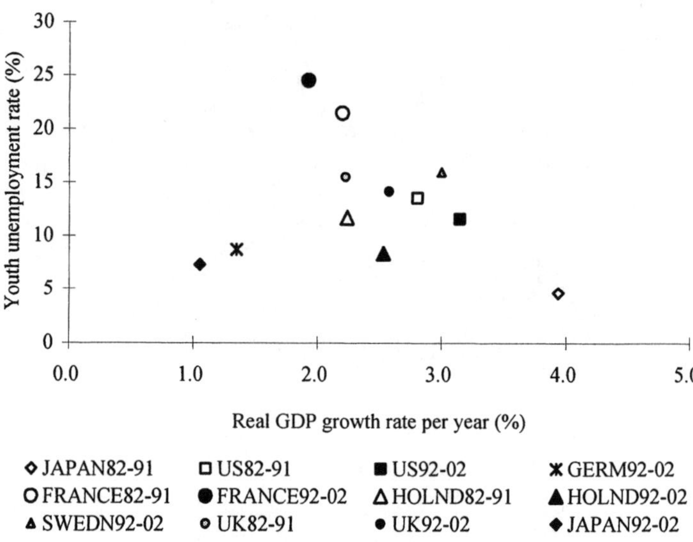

Source: OECD (2004d).

Figure 5.4 Real GDP Growth Rate and Youth (<25 years-old) Unemployment Rate, OECD Countries

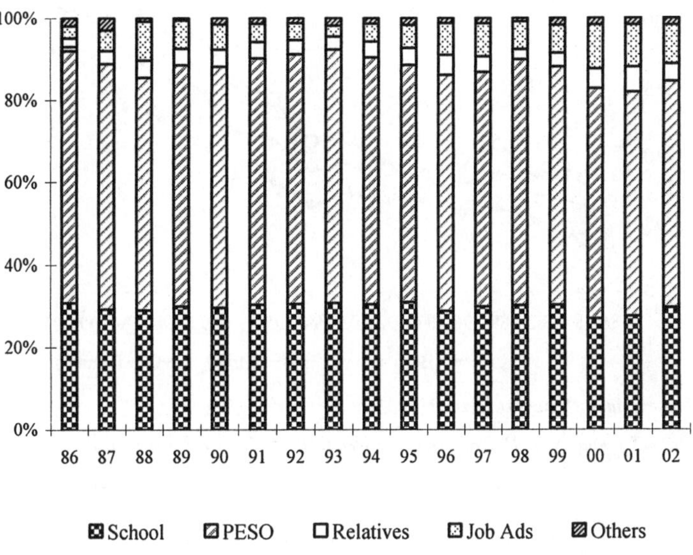

Source: Ministry of Labour and Welfare (2003).

Figure 5.5 Distribution of New Japanese Senior High School Leavers Employed, by How They Find their First Jobs

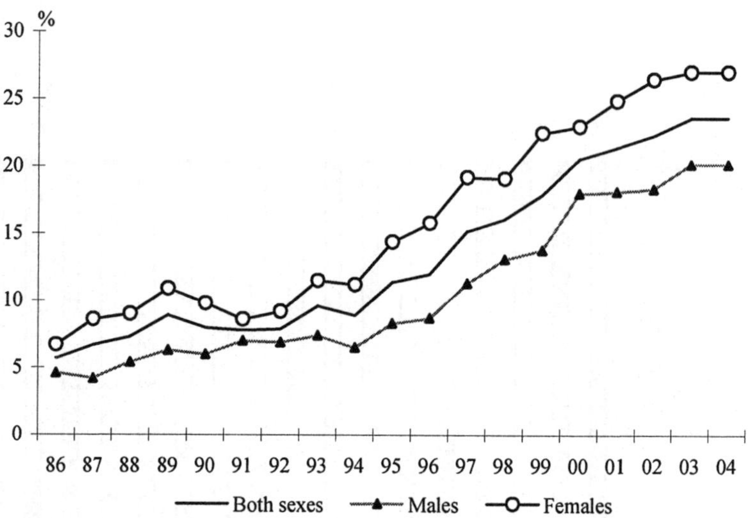

Source: Statistics Bureau (2005).

Figure 5.6 Proportion of Part-time Employment among Non-student Employees, ages 15 to 24, Japan

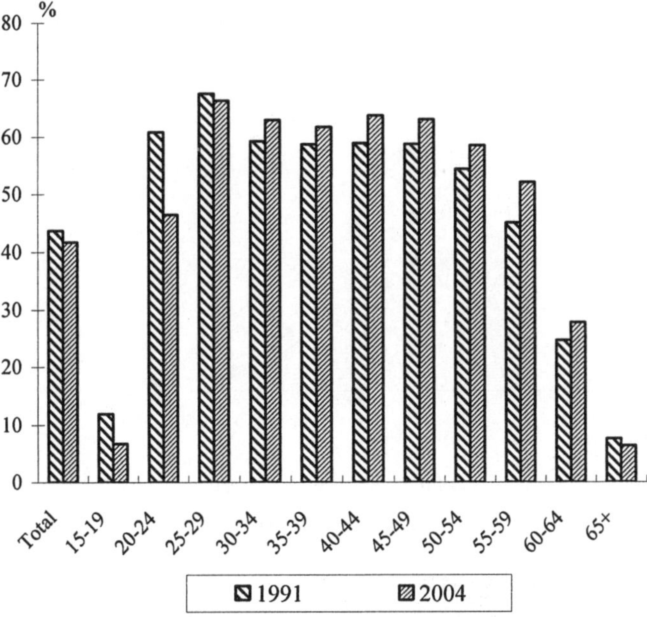

Note: Regular employees = those with employment term of 1 year or more, or not fixed

Figure 5.7 Regular Employees/Population Ratio, by Age, Japan

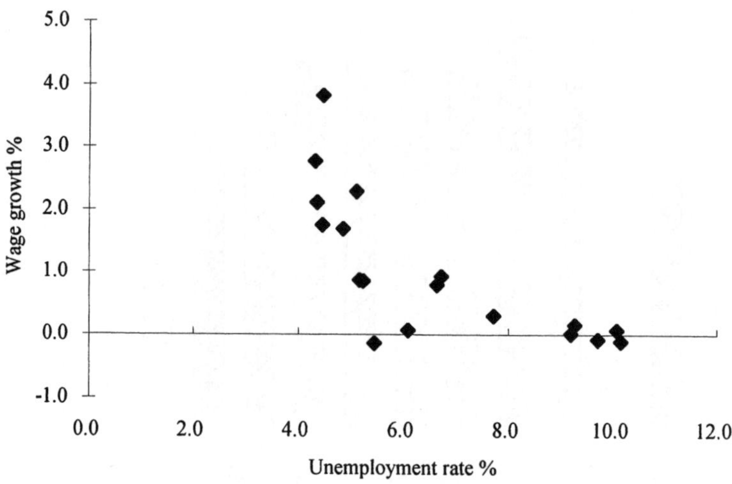

Source: Ministry of Labour and Welfare (2004).

Figure 5.8 Annual Growth Rates of Hourly Wages of Regular Employees and Unemployment Rates (ages 15 to 24), Japan, 1986 to 2003

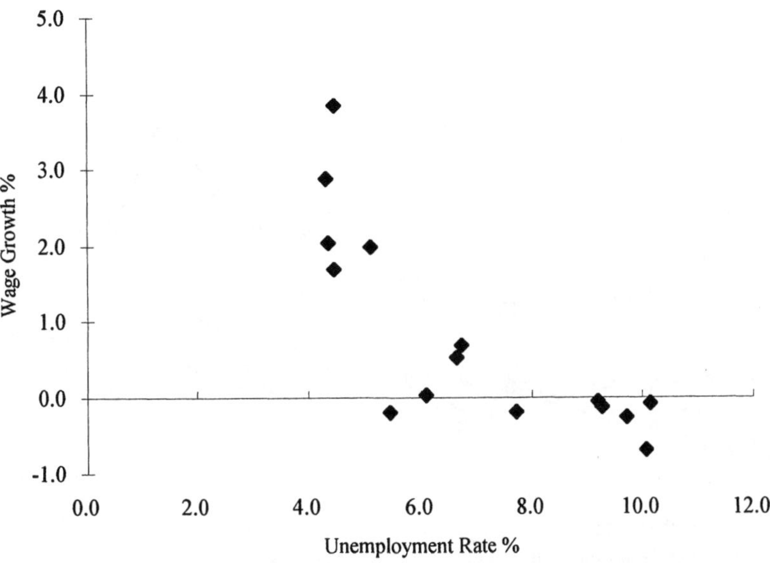

Source: Ministry of Labour and Welfare (2004).

Figure 5.9 Annual Growth Rates of Hourly Wages (Regular Employees + Part-timers) and Unemployment Rates (ages 15 to 24), Japan, 1986-2003

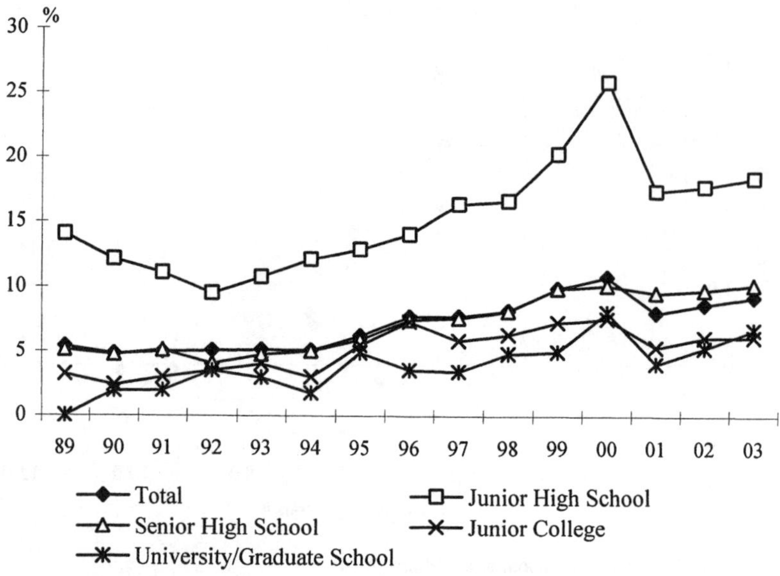

Source: Statistics Bureau (2005).

Figure 5.10 Youth Unemployment Rate by Education Attainment, Japan (15 to 24 year-old nonstudents)

Table 5.1 Employment Rate, Employment–population ratio and Labor Force Participation Rate, Japan (Annual average growth rate, in %)

Age group	Both Sexes			Males			Females		
	Emp. Rate	Emp. Pop. Ratio	LFP Rate	Emp. Rate	Emp. Pop. Ratio	LFP Rate	Emp. Rate	Emp. Pop. Ratio	LFP Rate
Ages 15–19									
1980–1991	-0.24	0.00	0.25	-0.17	0.69	0.85	-0.29	-0.63	-0.35
1991–2004	-0.43	-1.37	-0.93	-0.43	-1.64	-1.22	-0.45	-1.13	-0.68
1991–1997	-0.43	-0.90	-0.46	-0.57	-0.77	-0.18	-0.32	-1.24	-0.96
1997–2004	-0.43	-1.77	-1.34	-0.32	-2.39	-2.11	-0.55	-1.04	-0.43
Ages 20–24									
1980–1991	-0.05	0.50	0.54	-0.04	0.37	0.41	-0.05	0.65	0.70
1991–2004	-0.42	-1.00	-0.58	-0.52	-0.98	-0.47	-0.32	-1.03	-0.71
1991–1997	-0.40	-0.38	0.02	-0.39	0.10	0.50	-0.40	-0.89	-0.49
1997–2004	-0.43	-1.54	-1.10	-0.64	-1.91	-1.30	-0.25	-1.14	-0.90
Ages 25–54									
1980–1991	0.01	0.51	0.51	0.02	0.05	0.02	-0.01	1.25	1.24
1991–2004	-0.22	-0.13	0.09	-0.24	-0.32	-0.08	-0.19	0.16	0.36
1991–1997	-0.20	0.00	0.20	-0.20	-0.16	0.07	-0.19	0.23	0.43
1997–2004	-0.24	-0.23	0.00	-0.27	-0.46	-0.21	-0.19	0.09	0.30

Source: Statistics Bureau (2005).

Table 5.2 Not in Labor Force, In Education and the Inactive (% of population), Japan, 1990–2004

	Both Sexes			Males			Females		
	15–24	15–19	20–24	15–24	15–19	20–24	15–24	15–19	20–24
Not in Labor Force									
1990	55.5	81.8	25.8	56.1	81.5	27.4	54.8	82.0	24.2
1997	51.4	82.1	25.7	50.4	80.9	24.8	52.2	83.2	26.4
2004	55.6	83.6	31.1	55.7	83.4	31.2	55.6	83.7	30.9
In Education									
1990	51.7	80.1	19.7	54.6	80.4	25.7	48.6	79.9	13.4
1997	47.3	80.1	19.9	48.7	79.4	23.0	45.7	80.6	16.6
2004	51.0	81.2	24.4	53.1	81.4	28.0	48.8	81.0	20.6
Inactive									
1990	3.9	1.7	6.3	1.5	1.4	1.8	6.2	2.0	10.8
1997	4.1	2.0	5.8	1.7	1.5	1.8	6.5	2.3	10.0
2004	4.6	2.3	6.7	2.5	2.0	3.0	6.8	2.7	10.3

Source: Statistics Bureau (2005).

PART TWO

School-To-Work Transitions

6. Youth Employment Problems and School-To-Work Institutions in Advanced Economies

Paul Ryan

INTRODUCTION[1]

Young people around the world today face daunting employment-related problems – partly to find decent work, but often simply to find a job or, having done that, to retain it. The problems are represented in the first instance by unemployment. According to United Nations (ILO) estimates, about 88 million 15 to 24 year-olds were unemployed around the world in 2003, accounting for one in seven members of the global youth labor force (Table 6.1). Youth unemployment rates averaged 19 per cent in transition (ex-communist) economies, more than 20 per cent in sub-Saharan Africa, and more than 25 per cent in North Africa and the Middle East.

The incidence of unemployment at world level in 2003 was more than three times as high among young workers as among adult ones, with the ratio rising to five or more in South and South-East Asian countries. The previous ten years had seen increases in all these indicators, with both the number of unemployed youth and the rate of youth unemployment increasing by around one-quarter.

These statistics suggest that a generalization concerning advanced economies during the 1970s and 1980s applies also at the global level for the past decade: namely, youth labor market outcomes have deteriorated, both absolutely and relative to those of adults. Relative deterioration is shown in the increase in the ratio of youth to adult unemployment rates from 3.1 to 3.5 between 1993 and 2003. That increase is driven entirely by the increase in the developing world, which houses 74 million of the full 88 million young people unemployed worldwide – a share that reflects its large share of world population, the large share of youth in its own population, and high rates of labor force participation by young people.

Table 6.1 Youth Unemployment by Development Status of Country

Status	Number unemployed (m) 2003	Unemployment rate (%) 2003	Ratio of youth to adult rate (%) 2003	1993
Advanced	8.6	13.4	230	230
Transition	5.1	18.6	240	290
Developing	74.4	14.3	400	390
All (world)	88.2	14.4	350	310

Source: International Labour Organization (2004: table 4).

If unemployment represents only a first pass in any description of labor market dysfunctions, that applies particularly to young people, with their high quit rates and their exceptional needs for job search and matching. The indicator that responds most directly to the complication is long-term unemployment, which by definition excludes the 'frictional' component of unemployment. Although data are available only for developed economies, the situation of youth appears less severe on this indicator, which tends to be lower for young people than for adults. Nevertheless, in the mid-1990s, the long-term unemployment rate was similar to or higher than that of adults in five of the Group Seven (G7) advanced economies, with France and the UK standing out in this respect.[2]

A further dimension of youth outcomes in the labor market is under-employment, in the sense of involuntary confinement either to part-time employment, as typically in developed countries, or to low productivity, marginal activities, as typically in developing countries, where many young people cannot afford to turn down such activities and remain unemployed. The former phenomenon is particularly marked in Japan and France. In France, the share of youth employment that is involuntarily part-time is more than 14 per cent overall, and as much 32 per cent among the minority who suffer chronic unemployment after leaving formal schooling.[3]

Then there is the role of temporary and casual employment, whose prominence for youth in some countries contributes to high flows into and out of unemployment, and thereby to high youth unemployment rates. In France, 25 per cent of the jobs taken by the cohort of school leavers in 1999 involved a temporary employment contract.[4] In Japan, the share in male youth employment of non-regular contracts – a category that includes temporary, part-time, dispatched, contract, and entrusted contracts – rose from around one-fifth in 1987 to more than one-half by 2002.[5]

Last, but not least, comes youth inactivity: the absence of an active link to either formal learning or the labor market. These are the inactive jobless – often labeled the 'NEETs' (not in employment, education or training) – a group whose growth and size has caused concern in economies as diverse as the UK, Sweden and Japan. The category is actually highly heterogeneous, containing young parents and leisure seekers as well as low achievers and dropouts. The association of youth inactivity with social deprivation and personal pathology – in terms of parental unemployment and inactivity, low income, housing problems, mental health impairment, and drug abuse – has generated great policy concern. The growth of inactivity among young males was marked in the ten years following 1987 in the UK and Sweden, and while subsequent policy interventions may have contributed to its stabilization in the UK, they have not caused it to shrink.[6]

The social concern that youth inactivity can cause is dramatically illustrated by recent developments in Japan. Although youth inactivity rates have remained low and increased little in Japan, compared to other countries,[7] concern and frustration has been widely expressed over the phenomenon, as well as over particular aspects and related issues – including the so-called 'freeters', who do not possess full-time stable employment, and 'parasite singles', who remain dependent for food and board on their parents, rather than moving out and either holding down a stable job or raising a family, or both.[8] The fact that such youth life styles are generally regarded as acceptable in Italy[9] suggests that in Japan the problem has as much to do with social change and social control as with labor market pathology.[10]

Finally, the labor market problems of youth must be set in the wider socioeconomic context. The damage done by HIV/AIDS to youth, particularly in sub-Saharan Africa, is of a different order of magnitude from that done by lack of employment, and comparable instead to that caused by war and famine. There is the powerlessness that many young people must experience, and the anger they must feel, in the failing economies, societies and politics of some countries. And, comparatively banal, youth in advanced economies face the difficulty of developing an identity and a sense of place in an increasingly commercialized, style-dominated and consumerist environment – however much they may enjoy tasting its pleasures. The diagnosis is less gloomy, however, when education is brought into view. Youth educational participation and attainment have risen strongly in most countries – with most of Africa again as the exception – though this often does not bring the anticipated economic benefits until adulthood has been attained.

Nevertheless, taken as a whole, the economic problems facing youth are both pronounced and growing. This applies to the developed economies in comparison to their position in the post-war quarter century of full employment. It applies more acutely to developing economies, by comparison both to their past and to the superior opportunities available to young people in advanced economies.

This chapter focuses henceforth on youth employment and on advanced economies. The next section examines trends in the relative employment and pay of young workers, followed in section 3 by a discussion of the potential causes of those trends. Given the potentially influential role played by national school-to-work institutions in mitigating youth labor market problems, section 4 discusses the recent performance of the two that built up the most successful track record in the post-war decades: large-scale apprenticeship in Germany, and school-employer networks in Japan. The conclusions follow in section 5.

TRENDS IN YOUTH LABOR MARKET OUTCOMES IN ADVANCED ECONOMIES

Early in the last decade, Levy and Murnane highlighted the deterioration after 1970 in youth outcomes in the US labor market. At the turn of the present decade, Blanchflower and Freeman broadened the picture, pointing to a deterioration since the early 1970s in youth labor market outcomes in 'virtually all OECD countries'.[11] In my own work on this issue, I considered changes in relative pay as well as in relative employment. I focused on young male adults rather than youth as a whole, in order to reduce the distorting effects of supply-side changes – notably, increases in educational participation among teenagers and in labor force participation by adult females.[12]

The pattern that I found for seven advanced economies confirmed Blanchflower and Freeman's conclusions in some respects. No country showed any noticeable increase in youth outcomes, relative to those of adults, in either the pay or employment dimension, let alone in both. At the same time, the pattern of change proved more varied than Blanchflower and Freeman had suggested. Youth relative outcomes deteriorated after the mid-1970s in four advanced economies – France, Sweden, the UK, and the US – but not in three others – Germany, Japan, and the Netherlands (Figure 6.1). Moreover, in the four countries that saw a marked deterioration of outcomes, its content divided sharply between two in which the decline concerned relative pay (the UK and the US) and two in which it was relative employment (as a share of the population in the relevant age group) that fell sharply (France and Sweden). The patterns for teenagers and females (using for the latter changes in absolute rather than relative employment) proved broadly similar to that for young adult males, though with more widespread and marked deterioration for females than for males, particularly in France and Japan.

These attributes were consistent with an institutional interpretation of the pattern. Two types of institutional influence were suggested: first, in pay setting, as determining the extent to which deterioration shows up in pay as opposed to employment; second, in school-to-work transitions, as determining how severe the deterioration was in the first place. These issues are discussed in the next section.

The interpretation remained tentative. Its first weakness was lack of degrees of freedom: it depended on evidence for only a few countries, for which trends were measured across periods that varied from country to country according to data availability, and for which explicit controls for disturbing factors on both the demand-side and the supply-side factors had not been imposed. One response to that difficulty is to expand and improve the evidence by including more countries, and to measure the changes in youth outcomes over time periods that remove cyclical effects on youth outcomes. A second, more satisfactory, response, is to work with an entire panel of data organized by country-year, and to do so with a formal model that specifies the demand for and supply of youth labor, and the rate of adjustment of relative pay. The latter approach is being taken currently at Cambridge University.[13]

This chapter takes the former step only. Six additional countries for which relative pay and employment data can be matched across time (Australia, Belgium, Canada, Finland, Italy, and South Korea), are added to the original seven. The periods over which changes in both variables are measured are selected, country by country, so as to neutralize as far as possible any cyclical effects on youth outcomes, while maximizing the length of the period, so as to promote the visibility of any underlying youth-related trends.[14] The result is for each country the longest period, centered on the late 1980s, for which the rate of adult male unemployment – the widely used, if imperfect, indicator of the cyclical state of the aggregate labor market – was similar at both beginning and end. The periods in question vary between only seven years (for Italy) and twelve years (for Australia, Canada, and Japan).

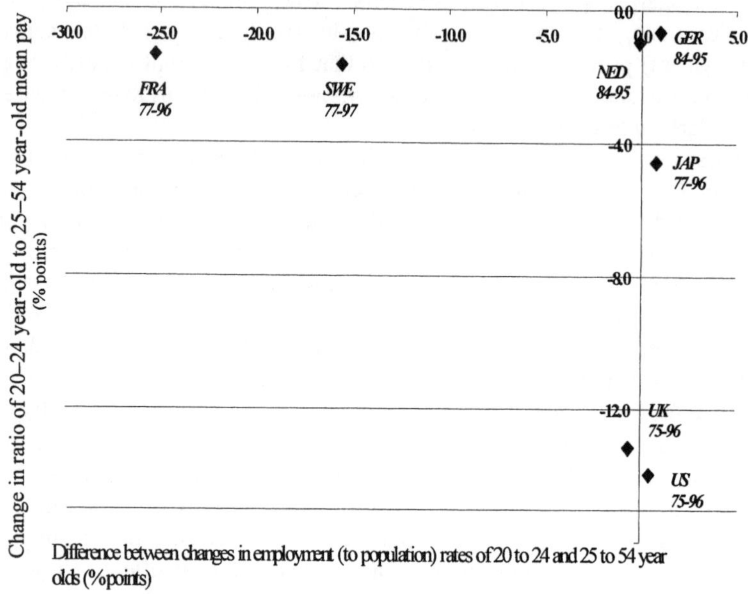

Source: Ryan (2001), Figure 2.

Figure 6.1 Changes in Relative Pay and Relative Employment of Young Adult Males by Country, Various Periods

The pattern in Figure 6.2 is similar in most respects to its predecessor in Figure 6.1. First, evidence of substantial youth-related deterioration now characterizes eight countries, not just four. Second, that deterioration again involves either relative employment (France, now joined by Belgium) or relative pay (the US and the UK now joined by Canada, Australia, Italy, and the Netherlands), but not both. Third, in some countries, again, no deterioration occurs – a category in which Germany and Japan are joined by Finland and South Korea among the additional countries, by Sweden from among the existing ones, and from which the Dutch depart.

The most striking contrast to Figure 6.1 is the absence for the two Nordic countries – Sweden and Finland – of any deterioration in periods that end before their employment crises of the early 1990s, which suggests that youth difficulties have been more cyclical than structural in those two countries at least. A further contrast is that a non-negligible, if modest, increase in youth relative pay is seen in one of the additional countries, South Korea.

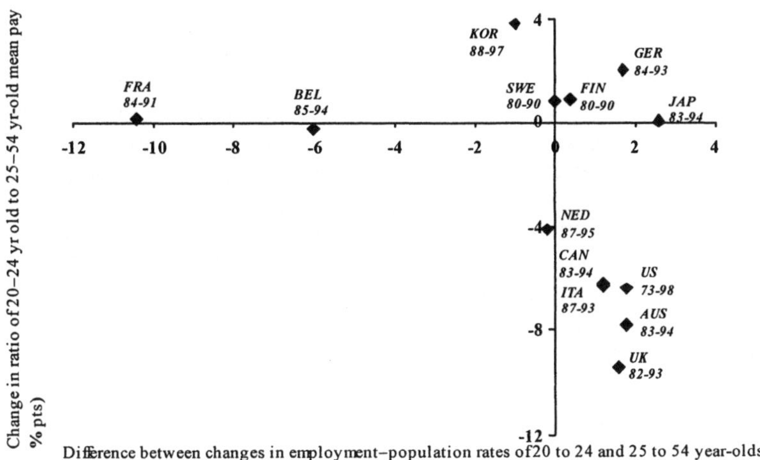

Source: Ryan (2001), Figure 2.

Figure 6.2 Changes in Relative Pay and Employment of Young Adult and Adult Males: More Countries and Cyclically-neutral Periods

The potential role of school-to-work institutions remains present. Germany and Japan again show no significant deterioration in either the pay or the employment dimension. The departure of the Netherlands from the 'no deterioration' category removes an anomalous aspect of Figure 6.1.

The pattern of changes in youth outcomes in Figures 6.1 and 6.2 is potentially distorted by three factors. The first concerns the time periods covered by the data, which are too short to permit any youth-related trend in labor demand to exert a cumulatively large effect on youth pay and employment.

Second, the picture may still be distorted by changes on the supply side. The effects of demographic fluctuations – the arrival in and departure from the labor market of successive baby boom cohorts – are in principle controlled in the above evidence by standardizing employment for the relative size of the population in the relevant age group. More problematic, however, is educational participation, insofar as it varies independently of conditions in the youth labor market. The large falls in relative employment in France and Belgium may reflect the growth – at least partly autonomous – of post-secondary participation. As however, educational participation grew more strongly still in Australia and Canada, it appears unlikely that changes in it can explain the comparative severity of the decline in youth employment in France and Belgium.[15]

Third, the validity of the pay and employment data may differ across countries and years. That possibility causes particular concern for Japan. The comparative stability of youth outcomes in Japan may be partly illusory, given that for Japan (i) annual data on pay and employment may both be confined to 'regular' employees, (ii) regular employment may involve higher pay than other categories of employment, and (iii) regular employment has fallen much more strongly among young than among adult employees (Table 6.2). The resulting distortion is potentially serious. It is likely that for youth employment as a whole relative pay fell by more, and relative employment fell by less, than is shown in Figures 6.1 and 6.2, but the extent of the distortion cannot be determined, nor can any remedy be proposed.

In sum, labor market outcomes for young people appear to have deteriorated on trend, relative to those for adults, in recent decades in many – but not all – advanced economies. The deterioration shows up in the English-speaking countries primarily in pay terms, but in Continental Europe and Japan primarily in employment terms. A degree of immunity appears however to have been present in Germany and Japan – which suggests potentially beneficial effects from national school-to-work institutions – but also in South Korea and, through the late 1980s at least, in Sweden and Finland. The validity of these patterns is however problematic, in view of the distorting effects of differences in measurement periods and

Table 6.2 Share of Regular Contracts in Employment by Age and Sex, Japan, 1992 to 2002 (Share of all Employees in Age-sex Category, %)

		15 to 19	**20 to 24**	**25+**
Male	1992	65.8	82.4	92.0
	1997	51.5	77.2	91.3
	2002	33.8	63.1	86.6
Female	1992	61.3	82.9	56.2
	1997	39.5	72.0	53.6
	2002	21.3	55.3	46.7

Notes: Excludes managers and directors (*yakuin*). Non-regular contracts include part-time, temporary (*arbeit*), dispatched (*haken*), contract (*keiyaku*), entrusted (*shokutaku*) and other sub-categories.
Source: Ministry of Internal Affairs and Communications, *Employment Status Survey*.

educational participation rates, and the limited validity of the pay and employment data themselves.

THE CAUSES OF NATIONAL TRENDS IN YOUTH RELATIVE OUTCOMES

The potential causes of the three leading attributes of Figures 6.1 and 6.2 are now considered in turn: first, the widespread deterioration in youth relative outcomes; second, differences in the part played by youth pay and youth employment within that deterioration; and, third, the absence or weakness of any deterioration in a minority of countries.

Youth-Unfriendly Economic Trends?

Two economic hypotheses have been advanced to account for a putative deterioration in the relative demand for youth labor: macroeconomic stagnation and skill-biased technical change. The former account, favored by Blanchflower and Freeman, sees inadequate aggregate demand in advanced economies, during a period of supply shocks and anti-inflationary macroeconomic policy, as causing the relative demand for youth labor to decline. The key mechanism is taken to be the 'last in, first out' status of youth employment, which makes it more cyclically sensitive than its adult counterpart. As a result youth relative unemployment rises in recessions and falls in recoveries.

Economic stagnation undoubtedly contributed significantly to the general change in the employment prospects for youth after the energy crisis of 1973–4, particularly in Europe during the 1980s and 1990s. It cannot however provide a complete explanation. First, the extent to which the unemployment of young people is more cyclical than that of adults varies from country to country, and appears to be negligible in some, including Germany.[16] Second, the theory cannot account for the marked deterioration in youth outcomes in the US itself, where the past three decades have seen no upward trend in indicators of spare capacity in the aggregate economy, such as the adult male unemployment rate.

The manifest weakness of any purely macroeconomic explanation has encouraged the exploration of a microeconomic alternative: skill-biased technical change. Analyses of the increase in pay inequality in the US by level of schooling have mostly attributed the trend to a re-composition of the demand for labor, favoring more skilled (educated) workers over less skilled ones. That re-composition is itself attributed to changes in technology – in particular, to employees' increasing use of information and communications technologies at work, on the assumption that skilled labor and ICT-based capital are complementary inputs to production – and also to changes in trade patterns – in particular, to growing specialization by developed economies in exports of high technology goods and services, which are intensive in skilled labor.[17]

Theories of skill-biased technical change have been elaborated primarily for the US, and primarily in relation to the schooling dimension of employee skills. They may apply also to the other principal dimension of skill: experience. If the demand for labor shifts, not only from less to more educated labor, but also from less to more experienced labor, the potential pro-youth effects of increased demand for more educated workers – given that young people have more and more recent schooling than adults – weaken, and may even be reversed. A 'double skill bias' view of the effects of changes in technology and trade, which emphasizes experience as well as education as the locus of skill bias, has found empirical support in an increase in the estimated gain in pay caused by increased labor market experience in the US and the UK.[18]

The quality of the evidence concerning experience-biased technical change does not however match its importance. Inferences in its support rely for the most part on indirect evidence, in which the schooling and experience dimensions of skill are not clearly separated, and on the empirical difficulties facing alternative explanations (for example, purely trade-based ones). Nor does it make obvious sense. Young people not only have more education, and more recent education than adults, but most have also become regular users of information technology, as a result of changes both in the curriculum and pedagogy of formal schooling and in the home lives of children, in which video games, personal computers, and the Internet now feature prominently. It may not be surprising that any skill-bias in technical change would hurt both low-achieving young people and displaced older workers, but it is less plausible that it would harm the average young worker.

More recent evidence on the issue is frustratingly mixed. One study finds a significantly positive association across sectors of the US economy between the wage return to experience (that is, the pay differential between young and adult employees) and employers' research and development spending as a percentage of sales (a proxy for high-technology products and processes), consistent with experience-biased technical change. The same study does not however find such associations for other potential proxies for technical change, including investment in fixed capital, the age of the capital stock, and the amount of capital that might be considered 'high tech'.[19] The share of employees who use a computer at work – another widely used proxy for skill-biased technical change – is only weakly related to age. Nor did that indicator become more related to age during 1984–97, a period when computer usage at work grew strongly in all age categories (Table 6.3).

Table 6.3 Use of Computers at Work by Age, US (% Employees)

	<30	30 to 39	40 to 49	50+
1984	24.7	29.5	24.6	17.6
1997	44.5	53.8	54.9	45.3

Source: Card and DiNardo (2002), Table 1.

The result is an abiding lack of certainty as to why the labor market should have moved so strongly against young people in most advanced economies in recent decades. Macroeconomic stagnation has contributed, and so probably has experience-biased technical change, but neither explanation, nor even the two taken together, provides a fully satisfactory account.

Institutions of Pay Determination

Whatever the cause of youth-unfriendly adverse developments in the labor market, the way in which those developments are manifested may be more amenable to explanation. There appears to be a clear difference between the content of deterioration between the 'coordinated' and the 'liberal' variants of advanced market economy: towards quantity adjustment in the former and price adjustment in the latter, in the shape of declines in relative employment and pay, respectively.[20]

A simple explanation of the difference uses a supply-and-demand model of relative pay and employment, in which a country experiences an adverse shift in the relative demand for youth labor. Under competitive pay setting, with an inelastic supply curve and an at least moderately elastic demand curve, the effects of a reduction in demand occur entirely in the price dimension.[21] Under centralized and coordinated pay setting by contrast – assuming that trade unions seek and achieve stable age-related differentials in pay – the burden of adjustment falls entirely in the quantity dimension.[22]

This interpretation represents the 'labor market flexibility' thesis associated with the work of Paul Krugman and the OECD *Jobs Study* on the aggregate labor market. Labor market institutions are seen as determining the relative importance of pay and employment in labor market adjustment to increased unemployment among unskilled workers. Countries with flexible pay setting saw a decline in the relative pay of unskilled workers; countries with inflexible pay setting, an increase in the relative unemployment of unskilled workers.[23]

The Krugman hypothesis has found little support for the schooling dimension of skills. It is however consistent with the evidence in Figure 6.2 on national changes in youth-related outcomes. The countries studied here differ considerably in the centralization and coordination of their institutions of pay setting, ranging from the highly decentralized (US) to the moderately centralized (Sweden). These institutional differences are broadly associated with the dimension in which youth outcomes deteriorated (in the countries that saw a substantial deterioration). Of the five economies in Figure 6.2 with the greatest downward relative wage falls for young people, four (Australia, Canada, the UK, the US) are liberal market economies, with the least centralized and coordinated institutions of pay setting. The decline in relative pay in Figure 6.2 averaged 7.5 per cent in those four English-speaking countries, but only 2.7 per cent in the other four economies with a marked deterioration in either dimension (Belgium, France, Italy, the Netherlands). Thus, although the Krugman thesis works poorly for the schooling dimension of skills, it may help explain its counterpart in the age-experience dimension of skills.[24]

School-to-Work Institutions

But what of the absence of any substantial youth-related deterioration in the other five countries: Germany, Finland, Japan, South Korea, and Sweden? The evidence in Figure 6.1, which concerned fewer countries and longer periods, without controls for cyclical effects, suggested a role for national school-to-work institutions. Of the three countries that showed no substantial deterioration in youth outcomes, Germany and Japan possess distinctive and widely praised national institutions to smooth the transition of young people from schooling to employment: mass apprenticeship and school–employer hiring networks, respectively. Those institutions potentially increase youth employment by improving information flows, job–worker matching and work-relevant skills. Were those benefits for youth employment to persist through early adulthood, the same institutions might explain the exemption of the two countries from the otherwise general adverse change in youth outcomes.

The problem with that line of explanation is not only the paucity of observations, but also the difficulty of explaining along such lines the lack of any deterioration in the Netherlands, a country not endowed with any distinctive institutions in the school-to-work area. That difficulty disappears in Figure 6.2, which shows for the Netherlands a moderate deterioration in youth relative pay. The same difficulty re-emerges, however, in the absence of prominent school-to-work institutions in Finland, South Korea and Sweden, the three other countries that in Figure 6.2. show no deterioration in youth labor market outcomes.

A potential explanation of this anomaly is that the role of school-to-work institutions in promoting youth outcomes was not put under strain in any of the three countries during the periods used for Figure 6.2. The last year for both Finland and Sweden is 1990, which saw the start of the sharp economic downturn that followed the collapse of the Soviet Union. The havoc wreaked on youth relative employment by that recession in both countries is consistent with limited ameliorative powers for their school-to-work institutions. Similarly, the favorable trend in youth outcomes in South Korea during 1988 to 1997 may be interpreted simply as a result of strong economic growth, interrupted by the financial crisis of 1997, rather than of any particularly favorable variant of national school-to-work institutions.[25]

The interpretation is speculative, and again based on a small number of observations. It does not explain how these three countries might have avoided the widespread adverse trend in youth outcomes visible in the other countries during the periods studied in Figure 6.2. But it is at least consistent with a distinctive contribution for national school-to-work institutions to the buoyancy of labor market outcomes for young adult males in Germany and Japan – only.

In sum, the facts available extend the evidence of a widespread but not universal deterioration in youth outcome in advanced economies since the 1970s. The widespread nature of the deterioration probably reflects nationally specific combinations of macroeconomic stagnation and changes in technology and trade. Differences between countries in the extent to which any youth-related deterioration showed up in relative pay or employment may plausibly be attributed to differences in pay-setting institutions. Finally, during the periods covered in Figure 6.2, national school-to-work institutions appear in both Germany and Japan to have neutralized any adverse trend in the relative demand for youth labor.

SCHOOL-TO-WORK INSTITUTIONS UNDER STRAIN

The preceding evidence that school-to-work institutions may have ameliorated an adverse trend in outcomes for young workers in Japan and Germany during the late 1980s and early 1990s suggests a direct examination of the performance of those national systems, whose performance proved so impressive from the 1960s onwards. Since the early 1990s, however, both have come under pressure from protracted economic stagnation. Between 1993 and 2005 the German economy grew only modestly, at an average rate of 2.2 per cent per annum, while the Japanese economy hardly grew at all, at 0.3 per cent per annum[26] The result in both countries was a trend increase in labor market slack. The open unemployment rate for 25 to 54 year-old adult males rose in Germany from 6.5 to 9.9 per cent, and in Japan from 2.0 to 4.3 per cent, between 1994 and 2004 – during which period the average rate for OECD countries as a whole fell slightly, from 6.1 to 5.7 per cent.[27] The power of the two countries' school-to-work institutions to maintain the labor market position of young people has been tested severely as a result.

Germany: Mass Apprenticeship

The German approach to vocational education centers around work-based learning. Apprenticeship programs, which typically last three years, comprise part-time classroom instruction and workshop activity at a public college, and training and work experience at a workplace. The resulting qualification is generally recognized as evidence of occupational competence. The employer is responsible for the apprentices whom it sponsors, but the rules within which the employer and the apprentice contract with each other are regulated externally by a combination of law and social partnership – the latter involving both sectoral employers' associations and district chambers of commerce, along with representatives of both employees and educators.[28]

Apprenticeship functions along similar lines in some other countries, including Germany's smaller neighbors. What distinguishes German apprenticeship, in addition to its elaborate regulatory apparatus, is its scale of operation. In recent decades between one-half and two-thirds of young Germans have undertaken an apprenticeship. This scale of operation, combined with high training quality, is widely taken to account for the superior performance of the youth labor market in Germany, as compared to other advanced economies. The youth unemployment rate, which lies in many countries between twice and three times its adult counterpart, is rarely far from it in Germany. The links between apprenticeship and the good performance of the youth labor market in Germany are complex, but generally interpreted by economists in terms of some mix of exceptional skills in the youth labor force and information-matching benefits to employers.[29]

The German apprenticeship system has come under strain at particular historical junctures, including notably the labor market debut in the mid-1980s of the second baby boom cohort of the post-war years. An even more strenuous episode has resulted from the macroeconomic stagnation that has lasted since the reunification boom of the early 1990s. In the labor market as a whole, between three and five million people have been unemployed at any one time. In the eastern, ex-GDR, federal states, not only has unemployment been persistently high, but also the scarcity of private sector employment has meant a dearth of apprentice places in the private sector. More recently, the rapid expansion of higher education has reduced the number of young people – and particularly more able young people – seeking an apprenticeship. The growing liberalization of economic institutions has weakened the willingness of employers to offer apprenticeships.

How has German apprenticeship fared under such unpromising conditions? Evidence of strain is immediately apparent. As Figure 6.3 shows, starting from 1990, the number of apprentices fell, relative to the youth population, and the substantial surplus of apprentice places offered by employers over places demanded by young people disappeared. A corollary of the latter development is that the share of young people not receiving an offer in their first choice training occupation has risen. Moreover, the supply of places in the eastern provinces has been sustained only by extensive public intervention, in terms of both provision and subsidy. These developments all reflect the stresses that face mass apprenticeship in conditions of protracted stagnation and industrial restructuring.

Looked at from another angle, however, German apprenticeship shows a high degree of continuity. The share of young people entering apprenticeship, which fell from nearly 70 per cent in 1990 to around 60 per cent by 1995, has since remained broadly stable at that level (Figure 6.3). The decline in the number of places in the early part of this decade, which outstripped the fall in the youth population, was reversed in 2004. Its reversal did indeed require a major mobilization of employers in support of apprenticeship, as in the early 1980s, as well as unprecedented public spending on apprenticeship in the eastern provinces, but such measures constitute the conjunctural foundation of the remarkable stability of German apprenticeship in the face of serious economic difficulties.

Japan: School–Employer Hiring Networks

The responsibility for matching school leavers and employers in Japan has since the 1960s fallen to high schools themselves. In those hiring networks that link particular schools and employers, the employer is called upon to offer career employment only to final year students – as opposed to hires direct from the labor market – and to select among applicants largely according to teachers' recommendations; the student is required to apply

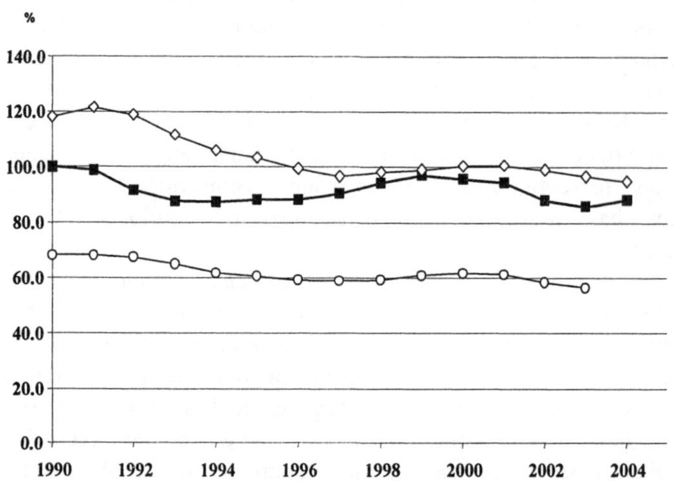

Source: Bundesministerium für Bildung und Forschung (BMBF): *Berufsbildungsbericht 2005*, übersicht 1, 32 (pp. 7, 110); *Grund- und Strukturdaten*, 2004, Tables 1.1, 1.2, 2.1.

Figure 6.3 Indicators of Apprenticeship Activity, Germany, 1990–2004

only to one employer at a time. Employers respond to schools that provide them with good candidates by offering more places in subsequent recruitment rounds. In the system's heyday, from the 1960s through the early 1990s, one-half of school leavers found employment through such recruitment networks.[30]

The result was an annual mass transition from school to work that left few young people behind. Thus, during 1990 to 1992, at the end of the 'bubble economy' boom, fully 99 per cent of final year students in high schools had received a job offer before graduating (at the end of March; Figure 6.4).

The workings of the Japanese school-to-work 'superhighway' remain a matter of debate. Interpretations of its effectiveness emphasize variously: skill creation, in terms not so much of the vocational contribution of the education system, as of the high academic attainments and trainability of high school graduates, and the willingness of employers to invest in their training at work; information; the trustworthiness of teachers' evaluations of student attributes; and motivation – the willingness of young people to accept low starting pay in return for the promise of career employment.

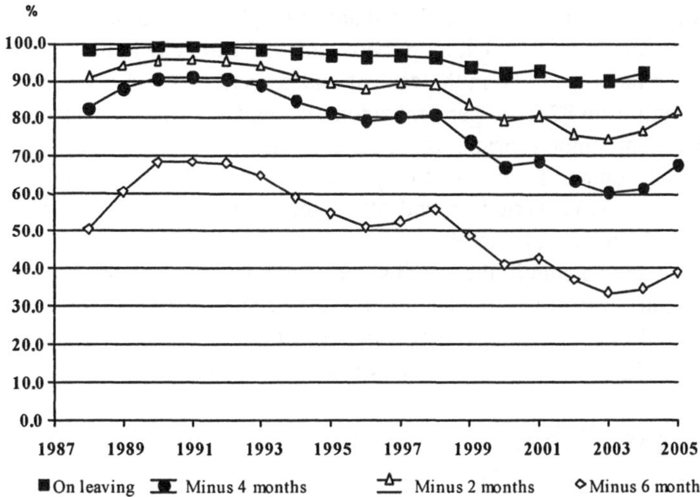

Note: Employment offers obtained through the school and public employment office (PESO) only; the Japanese school year ends in March.
Source: Ministry of Health, Labour and Welfare, *Survey of Situation of Job Seekers Who Received a Job Offer in Secondary School* (Tokyo, annual).

Figure 6.4 Share of Final-year High School Students Seeking Work who Received a Job Offer by Stage During the School Year, Japan, 1988–2005 (%).

How well have these recruitment networks coped with a prolonged macroeconomic setback, which has been deeper than its German counterpart? Evidence of strain is again clearly visible. One symptom is the fall in job offers received before graduation. The share of final-year high school students who had a job offer half way through their final year fell from more than two-thirds in the early 1990s to one-third by 2003–2004 (figure 6.4). The decline provoked official concern well before the nadir was reached.

A further symptom is the increase in the rate of withdrawal from labor market entry during the last year of high school. In the early 1990s, the share of final year students looking for a job fell by less than 1 per cent during their last six months in school; by 2004, the decline amounted to fully 11 per cent. Most of the change concerned the final two months of the school year (Figure 6.5). The increase in last minute withdrawal from labor market entry also suggests a fall in the availability of employment to graduating students, whether in terms of quantity, quality, or both.[31]

A third feature is the change in the attributes of employment among the young people who do find work. The share of employees holding a regular employment contract fell much more between 1992 and 2002 among young workers than among adults: in the case of males, from 66 to 34 per cent for teenagers, and from 82 to 63 per cent among young adults, but only from 92 to 87 per cent among prime-age adults.[32] The share of school-leaver recruitment accounted for by large employers, whose entry jobs involve the best career prospects, varied around 40 per cent during 1975–85, but had fallen below 30 per cent by 1995.[33]

Similarly, the decline in the youth share of regular employment between 1992 and 2003 was much greater in large organizations than in small and medium-sized ones.[34] The increasing number of young 'freeters' – that is, non-regular employees, whether with a casual, a part-time, or a temporary

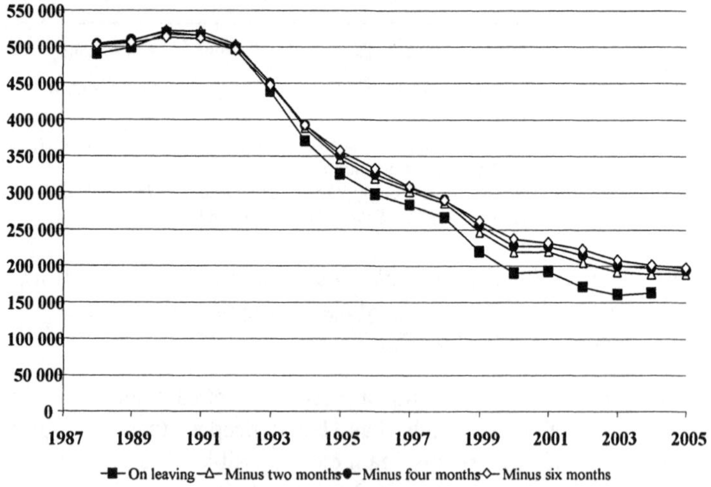

Source: Figure 6.4

Figure 6.5 Number of Final-year High School Graduates Seeking Employment by Stage During the School Year, Japan, 1988–2005

employment contract – have generated great controversy in Japan. Some interpretations emphasize the decline of the traditional work ethic and the growth of individualism; others, the growing scarcity of employment opportunities, particularly those carrying a good career prospect with a single employer. The former interpretation also involves particular values. High job turnover among young workers, which is widely viewed in the US in terms of job search and experimentation, and extensive youth dependence on parental support, which is viewed in Italy as a normal part of life, tend to be interpreted in Japan in terms of youth self-indulgence and irresponsibility. However, whatever the importance of changes in preferences and values among young people, the demand side has clearly played a part as well. The growth of labor market slack has contributed to the growth of freeter numbers, particularly in big cities, where familial and social controls on youth tend to be weaker than elsewhere.[35] These symptoms reflect the well-known deterioration in Japanese school-to-work institutions – one that helps to explain the less favorable position of changes in youth outcomes in Japan when recent years are included.[36]

The changes are even to some extent to be welcomed. The performance of Japan's school-to-work institutions was always more impressive in quantitative than in qualitative terms. They took little account of individual interests in matching school leavers to job vacancies. The Japanese government has for some time welcomed increased turnover in youth employment as a contribution to improved job–worker matching.

Table 6.4 Share of Two Cohorts of School Leavers in Employment, France (% Cohort Members)

Cohort of leavers[a]	**Contract type**	**At leaving**	**3 months later**	**15 months later**
1998	All	54	62	74
	Indefinite[b]	22	25	39
2001	All	69	77	79
	Indefinite[b]	30	35	45

Notes:
a. School leavers at all levels of attainment
b. Unlimited duration (*Contrat á Durée Indéterminée*)

Sources : *CEREQ (2002, p. 36) ; CEREQ (2004, p. 4)*

The central point here lies, however, elsewhere: the same institutions have not been reduced to rubble. The share of high school graduates receiving a job offer by the time they graduate has remained high: it dipped below 90 per cent in 2002, but only marginally and briefly (Figure 6.4). The number of job offers received by graduation presumably represents the acid test, not the number received six months beforehand, however reassuring it may be for students to have a job lined up well in advance of leaving school.

The institutional buoyancy suggested by this attribute is indeed limited: ninety per cent of school leavers holding a job offer is markedly less than ninety-nine per cent, and a lower proportion of those job offers contain the direct prospect of career employment. Nevertheless, viewed from a comparative perspective, the Japanese school-to-work system is seen still to perform reasonably well – for males at least. That applies particularly in relation to France, a country to which Japan is often compared, in view of similarities in the organization and ethos of their school systems and in the prominence of career employment in the internal labour markets operated by large employers.[37] Table 6.4 shows that in 1998 only 54 per cent of young people leaving the education system went straight into a job, and only 22 per cent into the French equivalent of regular employment (that is, a contract of indefinite duration). The equivalent shares were markedly higher for the 2001 entrants cohort, who benefited from an economic recovery, but the improvement in youth shares proved as ephemeral as the recovery itself.

This comparison between Japan and France is imprecise, given differences in legal definitions of employment, the timing of the surveys, and the levels of educational attainment involved.[38] Even so, it suggests that Japan's school-to-work institutions continue to perform reasonably well. Some countries, notably southern European ones, might well be pleased to exchange their school-to-work performance for Japan's.[39]

CONCLUSIONS

This chapter has reviewed the employment-related problems that face young people around the world nowadays. The problems assume different forms in richer and poorer countries. The most acute needs prevail in the poorer countries. The problems facing youth in developed economies vary considerably from country to country. The evidence suggests that the key issues are, firstly, whether the national labor market is organized more along liberal or coordinated lines, and, secondly, whether an effective set of school-to-work institutions is present.

Contemporary changes in the relative pay and employment of young people in advanced economies are only partly consistent with the hypothesis of a universal experience-biased trend in the demand for labor, whose effects are mediated through national pay setting and school-to-work institutions. Institutions of pay determination do appear to determine how resistant differences in pay by age and experience are to any adverse trend in the relative demand for youth labor, and thereby whether such trends manifest themselves in adverse changes in relative pay or in relative employment.

School-to-work institutions appear to have protected young people from the consequence of that painful choice in Germany and, to a lesser extent, in Japan. The performance of those two countries' institutions has been visibly eroded since the early 1990s by protracted macroeconomic stagnation. Viewed from a comparative perspective, however, both sets of institutions show a striking resilience, with the share of young people entering apprenticeship remaining high in Germany, and the share of school leavers receiving a job offer remaining high in Japan.

NOTES

1. I would like to thank Hofstra University for inviting me to give the keynote speech at the 2005 youth employment conference, on which this chapter is based, Rebekka Christopoulou and Dai Miyamoto for providing data, and Gregory DeFreitas for encouragement and assistance.
2. Ryan (2001), 34–92; OECD (1995), Tables 1.8, 1.9.
3. Mora (2005), p.3. In Japan, 27 per cent of 15 to 24 year old employees worked without a regular employment contract in 2004; Japan Institute for Labour Policy and Training (2006), Table II–15.
4. Loc.cit.
5. Ministry of Internal Affairs and Communications, *Employment Status Survey*, various years; Ryan, P. and Miyamoto, D., 'The pay and employment of young workers in Japan, 1986–2003', unpublished paper, Department of Management, King's College London.
6. Ryan (2001), Table 1. The share of the 16–18 year old English population that is inactive jobless (NEET) rose slightly, from 10 to 11 per cent, between 2001 and 2005; Department for Education and Skills (2003, 2006), Table 3.
7. The number of 15–35 year old Japanese people who were NEETs fluctuated between 1985 and 2001 between 360,000 and 500,000, with only a slight upward trend; JILPT (2006), Figure 1–5.
8. Genda (2005).
9. O'Higgins, Niall, Chapter 4 in this volume.
10. A journalist for an Osaka newspaper in May 2004 distinguished four categories of inactive youth: 'gangster' ('antisocial hedonist, caring only for the present'), 'withdrawn' ('remains indoors, socially withdrawn'), 'paralyzed' ('stalled before finding a job, as a result of thinking too much') and 'set back' ('loss of confidence after an early quit in first job'). I am grateful to Megumi Hirose for providing and translating the article.
11. Levy and Murnane (1992); Blanchflower and Freeman (2000c).
12. Ryan (2001), section 5.1.

13. Rebekka Christopoulou, *Youth Unemployment in Advanced Economies*, doctoral dissertation in progress, Faculty of Economics, Cambridge University; an introduction to her project is provided in Chapter 2 in this volume.
14. The effects of maximizing the length of the measurement period, irrespective of cyclical effects, are shown by Christopolou in Figure 2.1 in Chapter 2 of this volume.
15. Ryan (2007).
16. Blanchflower and Freeman (2000c), Table 1.11.
17. For example, Katz and Autor, in Ashenfelter and Card, ed. (1999).
18. For example, Levy and Murnane, op. cit.; Gregg and Machin, in Barrell, ed., 1994).
19. Allen (2001), 440–83.
20. Hall and Soskice (2001).
21. These assumptions are not necessarily innocuous. The relative supply of youth labor might be expected to be responsive to relative pay, given the greater potential importance of alternative activities (schooling, leisure) for young than for adult workers. Moreover, if substitutability in production between young and adult employees is low, the elasticity of the demand curve will also be low. Some reassurance is provided on these issues by econometric evidence, based on panel data for nine advanced economies, that relative price effects are insignificantly different from zero in relative supply, and significantly non-zero and moderately large in relative demand (Christopoulou, 2005, Table 1).
22. Although it is often assumed that trade unions automatically bargain for low and stable pay differentials, that cannot be taken for granted when it comes to the pay of young workers. Trade unions may seek low or high relative pay for young workers according to a variety of factors, including their bargaining power, the ease of youth–adult substitution in production, and the share of young workers in the membership (for example, P. Ryan,1987).
23. Krugman (1994).
24. Ryan(2001), pp. 53–4. Other evidence on the links between institutions of pay setting and the youth labor market, notably OECD (2004a), chapter 3, proves mixed. On the one hand, countries and periods with greater trade union membership and bargaining coverage, as well as more centralized and coordinated pay setting, tend to have higher relative youth pay (Table 3.8); on the other hand, trade union membership excepted, the same variables are not negatively associated with relative youth employment (Tables 3.9, 3.10). In contrast to the approach taken here, the OECD's analysis focuses on levels of rather than changes in youth outcomes, and it does not analyze pay and employment simultaneously.
25. Real national income (GDP), which had grown during 1980–90 (the period covered in Figure 6.2) by 35 and 24 per cent in Norway and Sweden respectively, fell during 1990–5 by 4 per cent in Finland, and rose by only 3 per cent in Sweden. Similarly, it rose by 90 per cent during 1988–97 in South Korea, but by 23 per cent during 1997–2002 (OECD Statistical database, http://stats.oecd.org/wbos/default.aspx?datasetcode=SNA_TABLE1), accessed on January 20, 2007. Korean school-to-work institutions resemble those of Japan in terms of the organization and performance of the school system, but they lack an equivalent of Japan's elaborate school–employer networks; Park et al. (2001).
26. Source: as for note 25, above.
27. OECD, 2006, Statistical Appendix, Table C (accessed on January 20, 2007 at http://www.oecd.org/dataoecd/53/15/36900060.pdf).
28. Ryan (2000).
29. For example, Büchtemann, Schupp and Soloff (1993), 97–111.
30. Kariya (1999).

31. Student responses to poor employment prospects tend to concentrate on staying on (entering higher education), particularly outside large cities (Japan Institute of Labour, 2003).
32. Ministry of Internal Affairs and Communications, *Employment Status Survey*, various years. The fall was greater still for young females.
33. Mitani (1999), Figure 6. Large employers remain more prone to hiring high school graduates than are smaller ones: in 2004, 44 per cent of employers with at least 5,000 employees did that, as compared to only 21 per cent of those with between 100 and 300 employees; JILPT (2006), Table III-3.
34. Among male senior high school graduates in regular employment, the number of 18-19 year olds as a percentage of that of 25–59 year olds fell between 1992 and 2003 by 5.4 percentage points (from 6.5 to 1.1 per cent) in firms with more than 1,000 employees, but by only 1.4 points (from 3.2 to 1.8 per cent) in those with less than 100 employees; Ryan and Miyamoto (2005), Figure 5.
35. Japan Institute of Labour, op. cit.; Genda, op. cit.
36. Christopoulou, chapter 2 in this volume: Figure 2.1.
37. Nohara (1999), 59–71.
38. Breakdowns of aspects of early employment by level of attainment in France suggest that the situation for high school graduates (that is, holders of the *Baccalauréate*) is likely to be similar to that for 'all levels of attainment': for example, the share of the first 2.5 years after leaving school spent in employment by the 1998 cohort was the same (77 per cent) for high school graduates as for all leavers (*CEREQ Bref*, op. cit., p.5). The similarity is not surprising, given that job finding rates increase with level of attainment and the high school graduate stands around the middle rungs of the ladder of attainment.
39. Rates of youth employment one year after leaving school in Italy, Spain and Greece in the mid-1990s, at between 29 and 37 per cent, were much lower than those in France (57 per cent) and the US (70 per cent (OECD 1999, Figure 3.4)).

7. Work and Non-Work Time Use of US College Students

Lonnie M. Golden

How much do youth enrolled in school tend to work – and why does it matter? In the United States, perhaps more than in most comparable countries, an increasing proportion of youth are attempting to combine both paid work and schooling activities. A new annual national survey conducted by the US Bureau of Labor Statistics, the American Time Use Study (ATUS) creates an exciting new opportunity for researchers to address questions regarding youth employment issues in ways not possible with earlier data sets. The large ATUS sample of over 20,000 individuals contains extremely fine detail regarding the specific uses of time among the employed. It provides 17 broad categories of 'first tier' potential uses of time over the course of a day, breaking it down to 452 specific uses of time. These data provide four new opportunities for research, yielding new insights into the employment, pay and work schedules of enrolled college students. One is that it allows a contrast between students and non-students in the same age cohort regarding their time devoted to various activities of interest, such as work and several non-work time uses. A second is that it permits a contrast in time use between enrolled students who are employed full-time, part-time or not at all. A third is that uses of time may be observed that were heretofore not available in the same data set as work hours, such as studying time and sleep time. Finally, the new data are contrasted to the patterns of time use that I found in surveying first-year students at a commuter campus of a large East Coast public university.

HOW ECONOMISTS LOOK AT COLLEGE JOBHOLDING

The conventional economic model of labor supply predicts that individuals will seek employment if their going market wage rate per hour is expected to surpass the value of an hour of their 'leisure' or 'non-work time.' Youth will thus choose to participate in the paid work force and desire more hours if their potential market wage rate opportunities are rising (a 'substitution effect'), their non-wage sources of income are depleting (an income effect) and/or their preferences for earnings vis-à-vis preferences for time are growing.

However, virtually all theoretical and empirical analyses of labor supply behavior treat the time allocation decision as a sequential one. It is presumed that those choosing to enroll in college do so to postpone going on the job market. Others may 'choose' to move from school to work directly from high school. Higher education is portrayed as a human capital investment of both time and money in skills development, credentials or other benefits that is expected to yield higher net returns in income over one's lifetime. Very little research explores theoretically or empirically the potential effect, either on the quality of human capital attained while in college or on the future earnings trajectory, of attempting simultaneously the activities of work (particularly when unrelated to career plans) and college enrollment. Performing paid work while enrolled in college may sustain one's enrollment and minimize subsequent debt. However, it may come at the expense of performance in school and knowledge gained to the extent that work time crowds out class time or studying time, particularly when the paid work hours are either long or taxing.

Conventional models of household labor supply decisions typically identify no more than three categories of time use: work, leisure time and household production. Sometimes the household production time is broken down by housework and parenting or caregiving time. The latter use of time is to produce 'child quality.'[1] However, the standard model is ill-equipped to account directly for the various, distinct uses of 'leisure' time, which include attending classes and studying. The conventional model, as modified by Gary Becker, does recognize the substitutability between uses of time, in terms of both hours and energy. For example, time and energy spent in paid work may be a zero-sum with unpaid household production activities. Thus, for our purposes, the uses of time other than paid work can be further subdivided to create six classifications in total: 1) productive leisure; 2) recuperative leisure; 3) social reproductive leisure; 4) consumptive leisure; 5) non-productive 'pure' leisure; and (6) non-productive work-related leisure. Each subcategory of non-market time has a unique economic and social impact. Productive leisure enhances human capital development, such as studying time in formal education or career-relevant reading. Recuperative leisure includes rest and recreation activities that in the longer run facilitate achievement of one's productive potential. Social reproduction refers to child rearing and household chores, as well as civic and volunteer work – activities that build future human and social capital. Consumptive leisure encompasses activities such as shopping, which drives much of consumption spending. Non-productive 'pure' leisure includes personal care or activities that disengage the mind and body (for example, 'relaxing, thinking' in the ATUS). Non-productive work-related leisure reflects inactivity, such as commuting time (not directly accounted for in the ATUS, unfortunately). How individuals or groups differ in the allocation of their time among these distinct categories has bearing on their own well-being. For our purposes here, I highlight only the first three categories and focus mainly on enrolled students.

PROS AND CONS OF YOUTH JOBS: A MATTER OF HOURS

Occupational safety and health research has been fairly thoroughly documenting the various consequences of long work hours on individuals, such as the added risks—primarily via fatigue or stress—to health, injury, well-being and work-family imbalance.[2] In addition, there are spillover costs on children, family and community life and on the quality and quantity of leisure time.[3] However, spillover economic consequences of long work hours on non-work uses of time, such as the quantity and quality of academic pursuits and achievement, have not been explored as much.[4] A high and growing proportion of high school and college students engage in paid work in the US, with a remarkably high proportion working quite lengthy hours.[5] About half of all full-time working students work 25 or more hours per week. Three-quarters of working undergraduates average over 25 hours per week.[6]

There are several potentially positive long-term results of youth employment in the labor market: not only the additional current earnings, but also the formation of human capital and thus future earnings capacity and higher employment probability.[7] However, a burgeoning research literature finds some negative associations between the hours commitment of students toward paid work with their current and future academic performance as well as their well-being generally.[8] For example, 10 additional hours of work per week reduce math test performance scores.[9] Even part-time jobs were associated with reduced math and science achievement or course taking.[10] Recent longitudinal data reveal that the working behavior of high school students during the school year and/or summer affects their tendency to graduate or drop out.[11] The research shows that paid hours of work, once exceeding some moderate threshold, typically in the range of 20 or more hours per week, may prove detrimental to various indicators of students' academic performance. Generally speaking, full-time hours are far more likely to lead to negative effects than part-time hours.[12] Long hours often translate into relatively lower grade point averages (GPA) achieved.[13] This probably occurs either directly, by reduced time and energy for class time, time studying alone or with peers and assignment work, or indirectly via its effect on sleep time and other physiological restorative activities. There is some correlation between additional hours studying and higher GPA. For every extra hour of work per week, GPA decreases by 0.16.[14]

The consequences of youth employment, on balance, are more about the hours commitment than employment itself. However, documenting the isolated effect of work hours on student performance and well-being has been challenging and generalizations are elusive. In no small part this is because the effects on school behavior and grade performance may be moderated and mediated by the student's family environment.[15] Moreover, students whose work is limited to the 10–19 hours per week range actually seem to perform better than all other students, working and non-working. Thus, there appear to be advantages to time management, organization and efficiency when working, say, just two days per week or a few hours per day. However, even hours this long come at the expense of increased stress and reduced time for socializing. Finally, the safety and health effects of youth labor depend not only on hours worked, but on the conditions of the work climate and the degree of compliance and enforcement of protective safety and health regulations.[16] Thus, it is tricky to draw direct policy inferences for regulating youth hours of work directly.

Among the nation's 16- to 17-year-old high school students, over 40 per cent hold jobs during the school year.[17] There is a marked gender gap: overall, boys are twice as likely to work twenty hours or more than girls. About 25 per cent of those holding jobs worked 20 hours or more per week. Twenty per cent of Black males work twenty hours or more, compared to just 4 per cent of Black females. The findings reveal little negative association between school engagement and work. In fact, among the lowest income families, high work intensity goes along with more school engagement and better schoolwork performance, as long as hours per week were moderate. Teens who worked long hours were also more likely to be suspended and to do less homework. Girls who worked long hours were more likely to do better in school than girls working fewer than twenty hours or not at all. There was little difference regarding low engagement between males working long hours and males not working. Teens in families considered welfare leavers were most likely to work twenty hours a week or more and were more likely to do better in school. Teenagers in families who were once on welfare but currently are not are most likely to work long hours. Teens of current welfare families are more likely to work fewer than twenty hours or not hold jobs at all and do worse overall in school, with behavioral and emotional problems. Overall, working hours among high schoolers thus does not necessarily translate into negative school-related performance outcomes, if hours are not long.

When only looking at teens who work long hours, the results point to diminished engagement in school, lower school performance, increased psychological distress, higher drug and alcohol use, higher rates of delinquency, and greater autonomy from parental control.[18] However, when looking at the prior history in school of teens who work long hours, these teens were less academically inclined to begin with. The students most likely to find a job working twenty hours or more are those with low GPAs and no aspirations for the future.

Working students who eventually graduated often had worked 21 or more hours per week. Nearly 24 per cent of working freshmen worked 21 or more hours per week during the school year, as did 56 per cent of working seniors.[19] Working students who eventually graduated from high school spent a large amount of time at work while also juggling their academic requirements. More than half of freshmen who worked during the school year worked more than 50 per cent of the school weeks, although most worked 10 hours or less per week. By their sophomore year in high school, 54 per cent of students who worked during the school year worked more than half of their school weeks, with 18 per cent of them averaging 21 or more hours per week. By their senior year, three-quarters of employed students worked more than half of school weeks. Moreover, 25 per cent of seniors worked over half of the school year and averaged between 21 and 30 hours a week, while an additional 20 per cent worked more than half of the school year and averaged 31 or more hours a week. Of the 75 per cent of seniors who worked during the school year, over three-fourths had worked more than 50 per cent of school weeks. About one in five employed seniors worked more than 50 per cent of school weeks and averaged 31 or more hours of work per week. Having an allowance at home generally reduces the amount of work hours during high school years.[20]

The working behavior during the school year of students who later drop out differs from the working behavior of students who eventually graduate. Youths who eventually dropped out of high school were less likely than their peers to have worked more than half of the school year prior to the one in which they dropped out. For example, 52 per cent of working youths who dropped out of high school during their senior year worked more than half of the school weeks during their junior year. By comparison, among youths who eventually graduated from high school, 70 per cent of those who worked during their junior year worked more than half the weeks of that school year. Eventual dropouts who worked more than half of the school weeks tended to work more hours per week than did their counterparts who eventually graduated. For example, students who dropped out as sophomores and worked more than half the school weeks during their freshman year were nearly twice as likely as their freshmen counterparts who eventually graduated to average 21 or more hours of work per week. This pattern continued for youths who dropped out in later years. Among students who dropped out as seniors and worked more than half the school weeks during their junior year, 33 per cent averaged 21 or more hours of work per week. By comparison, 29 per cent of juniors who worked more than half the school year and eventually graduated averaged 21 or more work hours per week.

Working during high school reduces academic success also by reducing the probability of being an honors student.[21] There are documented adverse effects on study in the form of missed lectures, and students' perceptions are that coursework grades are lower than they would have been had they not been working.[22] Nevertheless, students highlight the benefits of working, which are not only monetary but include the development of skills, greater understanding of the world of business and an increase in confidence, all of which are advantageous to their studies, both at the present time and in the future.

Most students – up to 74 per cent of those in school full time – work while enrolled in college. Nearly half (46 per cent) of all such full-time working students tend to work 25 hours or more a week; they often do so because they cannot afford to go to college if they work any less.[23] Federal financial aid for higher education has not been keeping up with increasing college tuition costs. About 42 per cent report that working this many hours has hurt their grades, limited their class schedule, and has limited their class choice. Students recognize that working full time not only compromises their academic studies, but also limits their ability to engage in civic learning, community service, and other extracurricular activities. While evidence shows that many students are working at levels that are likely to impact negatively their academic achievement and the quality of their education, they often cannot afford to cut back their work hours. About 84 per cent identified themselves primarily as students working to meet college expenses. Students of low-income families often find themselves working long hours to finance their way through college; they were much more likely to work than wealthy students to pay for tuition, fees, or living expenses, rather than to earn spending money or to gain job experience. However, this conflicts with recent findings for high school students: higher employment rates and hours among those with relatively higher family income levels.[24] This is also in contrast to Hannah and Baum's finding that the primary reason for teens working is to purchase and maintain a car.[25]

INITIAL FINDINGS FROM THE AMERICAN TIME USE SURVEY

The ATUS asked participants to track the use of all blocks of time in the previous 24-hour period. It creates 17 'first tier' activities, and coded 452 total categories of detailed activities. The chief categories of concern here are paid work, sleep, education (class time, studying time), socializing, household work and commuting (traveling time). The ATUS permits an empirical contrast between those who are enrolled as students who are employed, enrolled but not employed and not enrolled (of comparable age). To observe which precise uses of time are reduced when hours of work increase, the ideal data would be longitudinal. However, the ATUS could be used to approximate the reduction in hours devoted to various types of non-work activities with, for example, a one-hour climb in paid work hours, and perhaps bifurcating the sample into longer versus shorter hours individuals. For example, we could observe whether longer hours of work come at the expense of sleep time generally and specifically among students.

The relevant key findings from the 2003 ATUS are:

1. Those in the 15 to 49 age range who are not enrolled in school work about twice as many hours per day in the labor market. This suggests that the typical enrolled students are employed for about half as many hours as their employed age cohorts. Men work longer on average per day than women. This holds for both just those only working in part-time jobs as well.
2. Among those enrolled who are also employed part-time, men average slightly over and women slightly under one hour of work per day.
3. The time that enrolled students spend on their education averages 2.84 hours a day.
4. Those who are enrolled in school actually get slightly more sleep per day than those who are not enrolled, perhaps surprisingly. Men employed part-time or not enrolled get more sleep than men who are employed full-time. Among those employed part-time, women and men get the exact same amount of sleep time. Among the non-enrolled, women appear to get more sleep than men.
5. The non-enrolled spend a longer amount of time engaged in paid work and household activities. Non-enrolled people spend on average 2.4 hours a day more at work and 0.4 hours a day more on household activities than do enrolled students.
6. Those who are enrolled spend no less time socializing then those who are not enrolled.
7. The enrolled do spend less time on housework.
8. The non-enrolled have a considerably greater total amount of free time.

They spend this mostly with family members and friends. They participate in almost double the amount of time in recreational activity than do enrolled students.

9. Those who are employed full time average just under 6 hours of work per day. They spend only a negligible amount of time in school or studying activities. Those who are employed at a part-time job, however, study or attend school for an average of an hour and a quarter per day. They work an average 3 hours on a given day.

A NEW SURVEY OF FIRST-YEAR COLLEGE STUDENTS

In order to obtain more detail on the possible relationships between work status and academic performance than is available in the ATUS, I organized a survey of freshman, first-year seminar (FYS) students in 2004 at a large, non-elite public university (largely commuter) campus on the East Coast. We queried students regarding their weekly hours typically devoted to various work, educational, and social activities. We also asked them the perceived effect they expect this to have on their own academic performance indicators.[26]

The key results from the FYS campus survey are:

1. 69 per cent of FYS students are employed. This is consistent with previous surveys, although somewhat on the relatively high side.
2. The remaining 31 per cent of FYS students are without paid jobs, although half of them are seeking work or prefer only seasonal work.
3. About 43 per cent of employed students work between 13 and 20 hours per week (Figure 7.1).
4. About 32 per cent of employed students work between 21 and 34 hours per week. This is similar although somewhat on the low side compared to other samples of college students and paid work (Figure 7.1).
5. About 70 per cent of such FYS students hold jobs that are not relevant to major and career plans.
6. Employed students tend to devote in total more hours to studying than non-employed students (with the exception of the limited few who study very long hours) (see Figure 7.2).
7. Most employed students perceive that their jobs have low to moderate interference with school performance (Figure 7.3).
8. Employed students earn slightly better grades than their non-employed classmates: among student workers, 13 per cent report a grade point average in the previous semester of 3.0–3.4, and 17 per cent are at 3.5 or higher. Only 4 per cent of non-employed students earn 3.0–3.4, and 16 per cent were at 3.5 or above (Figure 7.4).

9. The sampled students hold relatively low paying jobs and many in the sample, like the bulk of this college's students, come from households with quite modest income levels.
10. About one in every six employed first-year students would be prepared to reduce income in order to get reduced work hours. This is less than a third of the proportion that would choose more income despite longer hours. However, this proportion is surprisingly high given their low pay and income levels. It is twice the rate found in the latest national census survey among all workers.[27]

CONCLUSIONS FROM BOTH SURVEYS

In summary, American college students appear to be working a substantial and growing number of paid work hours from freshman year on. However, there is considerable variation among students, in terms of how many hours they work and study, and how they use the remainder of their time generally. Students spend most of their free time on campus waiting for their next class or working at their part-time jobs. The enrolled also spend much of their non-class time at their part-time jobs. Social time is almost strictly kept to the weekend and is a small amount of time even then. The non-enrolled spend their non-work time mostly with family members and friends, and participate in almost double the time in recreational activities than enrolled students.

Most importantly, however, there appears to be no clear, direct linear relationship between hours of work and non-work time uses, including hours devoted to studying or schoolwork. Nor does work seems to influence reported academic performance, such as freshman's expected effect on their GPA, with the exception of those that have a relatively high GPA. Thus, it is not entirely clear whether or not students, at least by their own perceptions, are able to cope effectively with the pressure of having both work and educational demands on their time. Working does not appear to hamper most students who are employed less than full-time hours relative to those who are not employed while in college. However, it is impossible to observe with this and any available survey whether their own performance would have been improved had they not been working at all.

Deriving implications for policies to promote academic achievement as well as enhance employment options will require more precise estimation of the effect of working hours, holding other influences constant, a task beyond the scope of this study. Thus, future research should attempt to identify the precise tipping point where paid work hours begin to threaten not only the health and safety of young workers juggling school and work, but also the point at which their school performance becomes impaired. This should instruct and guide future thinking and policy proposals on college and career guidance, government financial aid, school-to-work institutions, and youth employment regulations.[28]

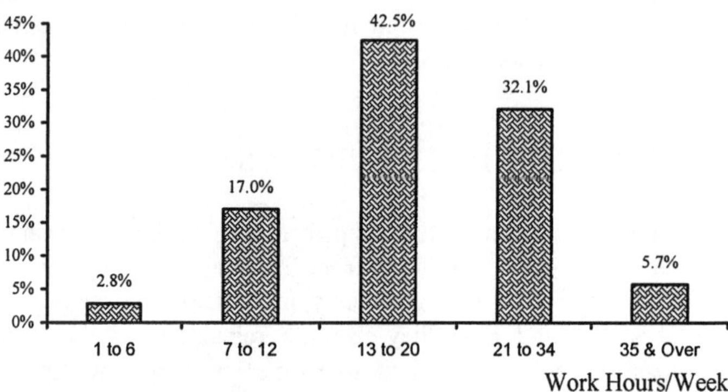

Figure 7.1 Employed Students by Hours Worked

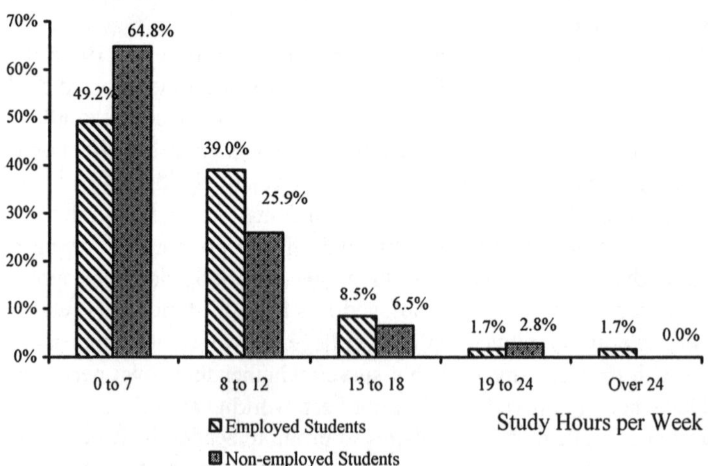

Figure 7.2 Hours of Study per Week, by Student Job Status

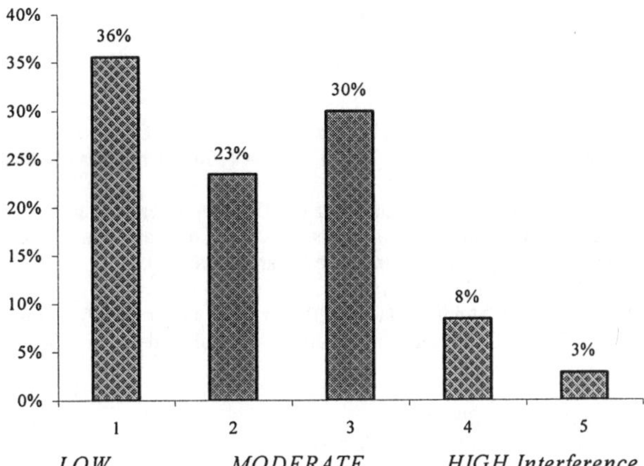

Figure 7.3 Percent of Employed Students whose Job Interferes with their Schooling

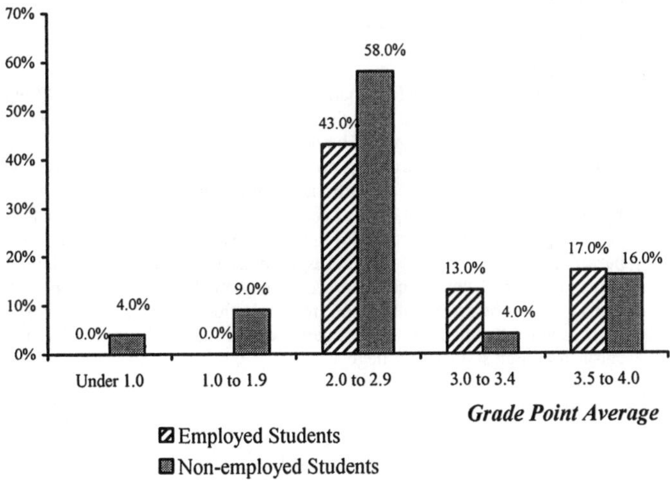

Figure 7.4 College Grades Last Term by Job Status

NOTES

1. See Paley (2005).
2. See Fenwick and Tausig (2001); Sparks *et. al.* (2001); Dembe (2005).
3. For example, Galinsky *et. al.* (2001); Pocock (2001); Crouter and McHale (2005) and Sullivan and Gershuny (2001).
4. With the notable exceptions of Merz (2002) and Hamermesh and Lee (2002).
5. See Bailey and Mallier (1999); Lerman (2000); Curtis and Shani (2002).
6. King and Bannon (2002); Dundes and Marx (2006–07).
7. See Rich (1996) and Ruhm (1997).
8. Lillydahl (1990); Steinberg (1996); Bailey and Mallier (1999); Lerman (2000); Rau and Durand (2000); Curtis and Shani (2002); Hannah and Baum (2002); Stinebrickner and Stinebrickner (2003).
9. Tyler (2003).
10. Singh and Ozturk (2000).
11. US Bureau of Labor Statistics (2005).
12. Orszag, Orszag and Whitmore (2001).
13. Ehrenberg and Sherman (1987); Crawford, Johnson and Summers (1997); Dundes and Marx (2006–07).
14. Stinebrickner and Stinebrickner (2004).
15. Roisman (2002).
16. National Academy of Sciences (1998).
17. Lerman (2000).
18. Kelly (1998).
19. US Bureau of Labor Statistics (2005).
20. Hannah and Baum (2002).
21. *Ibid.*
22. Curtis and Shani (2002).
23. King and Bannon (2002).
24. Lerman (2000) and Brown (2001).
25. Hannah and Baum (2002).
26. Survey respondents =156, response rate = 67 per cent, 54 per cent males and 46 per cent females.
27. See Golden (2005).
28. The National Institute for Occupational Safety and Health, in its 1998 report, *Protecting Youth at Work* concluded that the US Department of Labor should be extended the authority to limit the number of hours students can work per day and regulate the times when they start and stop working on school nights (Chaplin, 1999; National Academy of Sciences, 1998). However, exceptions should be made for school-to-work programs and for students who must work out of economic necessity. Current regulations exist only for youths aged 14 and 15 years old, who may work outside school hours in various non-hazardous jobs under these conditions: no more than 3 hours on a school day, 18 hours in a school week, 8 hours on a non-school day, or 40 hours in a non-school week. Also, work may not begin before 7 a.m., nor end after 7 p.m. (except during summer). Such limits could be expanded to the hours worked for youth up to 18 years old if they are enrolled in high school or college.

PART THREE

Dying for a Job

8. Occupational Fatalities among Young Workers

Janice Windau

How dangerous are the jobs that young workers hold today? This chapter examines recent occupational fatality data for American workers ages 24 and under. These workers comprise a sizable portion of the workforce. In 2005, almost 20 million workers were between the ages of 16 and 24 – about 14 per cent of the total employed. Because younger workers have little experience on the job, they may be at increased risk of being injured. Bureau of Labor Statistics data from the Survey of Occupational Injuries and Illnesses show that workers with less than one year with the employer comprise one-third of the injured, but only one-fourth of those employed.

The findings here indicate that, as with fatalities of workers of all ages, fatalities among workers 24 years-old and younger have declined in recent years. Fatal work injuries declined 9 per cent among these workers when comparing the two five-year periods 1993–97 and 1998–2002, slightly better than the 7 per cent decline seen in the all worker fatality count. Similarly, fatal work injury *rates* fell among workers aged 15–24. Fatality rates allow one to compare the number of fatalities in various worker groups, or the same group over time, relative to the number of workers in the group. These rates fell among civilian workers aged 15–24 from 3.9 per 100,000 full-time equivalents in 1994–98 to 3.4 in 1999–2003, a decline of 13 per cent. The overall fatality rate for civilian workers 15 and over experienced a similar drop from 4.9 in 1994–98 to 4.3 in 1999–2003, a 12 per cent decline.[1]

WHERE THE NUMBERS COME FROM

Because the population of workers 24 and under is so diverse, it was split into two separate cohorts: those under 18 and those aged 18–24. These age groups were chosen because Federal and State child labor laws typically apply to workers under 18; furthermore, persons 18 and over are generally considered adults. To distinguish between the two groups, the chapter will sometimes refer to workers under 18 as 'youths' and workers aged 18–24 as 'young adult workers.'

Data from the Bureau of Labor Statistics (BLS) Census of Fatal Occupational Injuries were used in the analysis. These data cover workers of all ages and all types of employment, including public sector, self-employment, and unpaid work for a family farm or business. Much of the analysis compares fatalities for workers under 18 and those 18–24 in two different 5–year periods – 1993–97 and 1998–2002. Although fatality data for 2003 and 2004 were available at the time this chapter was prepared, those data were compiled using a different industrial classification system from data for previous years. Industries in the 2003–2004 data were classified according to the 2002 North American Industry Classification System (NAICS), while those in the 1992–2002 data are based on the 1987 Standard Industrial Classification (SIC) System. The classification schemes are not comparable. Data presented in this article exclude fatalities related to the events of September 11, 2001 as well as those that occurred to workers while outside the US.

FATAL INJURIES BY EVENT

Transportation incidents accounted for more than half the fatalities among workers under 18 in 1998–2002 and a little over two-fifths of the fatalities among workers 18–24 during the same period (see Table 8.1). Transportation incidents rose from the previous five-year period for both groups. For workers under 18, the increase resulted mainly from an increase in vehicle- and equipment-related incidents on farms and other off roadway areas—and to a lesser extent from highway traffic crashes and from being struck by vehicles. For workers aged 18–24, the increase resulted mainly from a rise in highway fatalities and being struck by vehicles.

Fatal falls also increased for both age groups, particularly among young adult workers. Falls among young adults increased by one-third between the two five-year periods. Almost 30 per cent of the falls among workers aged 24 and under during 1998–2002 were from roofs.

Another major portion of fatalities for both groups resulted from workplace homicides, accounting for 10 per cent of young worker fatalities in 1998–2002. Compared with the previous five-year period, the number of workplace homicides dropped dramatically (by 45 per cent) for the two groups, as they did for workers of all ages combined. The worker fatality total resulting from contacts with objects and equipment also declined for the two age groups, primarily due to a drop in fatal injuries from workers being struck by objects. Electrocutions and other exposures to harmful substances and environments declined slightly for both groups. About half the electrocutions among young adult workers resulted from contacts with overhead power lines.

FATAL INJURIES BY INDUSTRY

Agriculture, Forestry, and Fishing

The agriculture, forestry, and fishing industry has one of the highest fatality rates of any industry division. It typically has a fatality rate four times that of all industries combined and is a major contributor of work fatalities among youths. During 1998–2002, it accounted for 41 per cent of the fatalities among workers under age 18. Fatalities in this industry dropped slightly among this age group from 134 during 1993–97 to 125 during 1998–2002. About half the fatalities in the latter five-year period occurred in crop production. Another one-fourth of the fatalities were in livestock production, half of which involved dairy farms. Landscaping and other agricultural services and commercial fishing accounted for most of the rest of the fatalities in this industry division.

Workers on family farms are at particular risk of suffering a fatal injury. They comprised about 60 per cent of the 125 fatally injured youths in this industry and about one-fourth of the fatal work injury victims among all youths during 1998–2002. Almost two-thirds of the youths who were fatally injured while working in agriculture, forestry, and fishing were under age 16.[2]

Many of the deaths among youths working in these industries resulted from vehicle- or tractor-related incidents. These types of incident comprised about two-thirds of the industry total for the 1998–2002 period. Half of the incidents occurred on farmland and other private property, and another third on public roadways. Transportation-related incidents rose by 17 per cent among youths working in the industry between the two five-year periods – 1993–97 and 1998–2002. Much of the increase occurred among workers riding as a passenger in a truck or on a tractor, operating an all-terrain vehicle, or riding on or driving a horse-drawn vehicle. Overall, tractors were involved in about one-fourth of the youth fatalities in agriculture, forestry, and fishing between 1993 and 2002. Incidents involving tractors included overturnings—both on and off public roadways, collisions with other vehicles, falls from tractors, and being struck by the tractor. Fatalities occurring while operating or using tractors or other machinery declined by half between the two five-year periods.

Many of the youths killed while working on farms were performing activities prohibited by the Department of Labor's Hazardous Orders for

Table 8.1 Fatal Occupational Injuries among Workers 24 and under, by Age and Selected Event, 1993–2002

Event	Under 18		18 – 24	
	1993–97	1998–2002	1993–97	1998–2002
Total	335	304	3,070	2,795
Transportation incidents	138	157	1,175	1,195
Highway	63	67	641	688
Nonhighway	35	54	168	156
Worker struck by vehicle	21	27	155	176
Assaults and violent acts	66	44	615	376
Homicides	57	32	501	274
Suicides*		6	108	97
Contact with objects or equipment	68	50	538	466
Struck by object	30	16	280	227
Caught in equip. or obj.	20	22	169	151
Caught in collapsing materials	15	12	79	77
Falls	21	25	232	308
Fall from roof	9	9	72	88
Harmful substances or environments	34	24	400	346
Electrocutions	17	15	252	229
Fires and explosions	7	3	106	100

Note: A dash indicates that data do not meet publication criteria.

Agriculture. These orders restrict workers under age 16 from operating many types of farm machinery except if they do so for family farms or after completing a bona fide training program. Yet one-fifth of the fatalities to agricultural wage earners under age 16 occurred while the youth was operating machinery. Another fifth occurred while riding as a passenger on a farm vehicle, another regulated activity.[3]

Among workers aged 18–24, agriculture, forestry, and fishing accounted for 334 fatalities during 1998–2002 – an increase of 16 per cent over the previous five-year period. Most of the increase was due to a rise in the number of fatalities among landscape and horticultural service workers, who comprised almost one-third of the fatality victims in this industry division for the age group. Fatalities among 18–24 year-olds in this industry rose from 62 in 1993–97 to 105 in 1998–2002, a 69 per cent increase. Their deaths resulted from highway vehicle crashes, being struck by a vehicle, falls from trees, being struck by a tree or branch, non-highway vehicle incidents (such as a mower or tractor overturning), and electrocutions from contact with overhead power lines.[4] A rise in fatalities among workers on dairy farms also contributed to the increase among young adult workers in agriculture, forestry, and fishing.

Over half of the fatalities to young adult workers in the overall agriculture, forestry, and fishing industry resulted from various types of transportation incidents. Highway fatalities among young adult agricultural workers almost doubled between 1993–97 and 1998–2002, rising from 39 to 74. Non-highway incidents accounted for over 12 per cent of the fatalities in the industry, and water vehicle incidents among fishers such as falls from boats and capsizing boats, accounted for 11 per cent of the industry total.

Construction

In the US overall, the construction industry reports more job-related deaths each year than any other industry and typically has fatality rates three times the all-industry average. During 1998–2002, construction had the highest fatality total among workers aged 18–24 and accounted for 27 per cent of their fatalities. During the same period, the industry ranked second in fatalities among workers under 18, accounting for 18 per cent of the total.

Among young workers under 18, fatalities in construction rose 12 per cent, from 48 to 54, between the two five-year periods. Falls and transportation incidents accounted for about two-thirds of the fatalities among construction workers under 18 during the 1998–2002 period. Similar to the youths who were killed while working in agriculture, many of those killed while working in construction appeared to have been performing activities prohibited by the Hazardous Occupations Order, including installing or repairing roofs, driving a vehicle, and performing excavation work.[5] Ten of the 54 fatally injured youths in construction were under 16, although workers under 16 are only allowed to perform office or sales work away from the actual construction site while working in the industry.

Fatalities among workers 18–24 years-old working in construction increased from 593 during 1993–97 to 748 in 1998–2002, an increase of 26 per cent. Much of the increase resulted from a 54 per cent rise in falls. Overall, falls accounted for 29 per cent of the fatalities during 1998–2002 among construction workers in this age group. Eighty of the 219 falls were from or through roofs. Falls from scaffolds and building girders or structural steel each accounted for 32 of the fatal falls.

Transportation incidents accounted for 28 per cent of the deaths among the young adult construction workers. About half of the deaths resulted from highway traffic incidents, and another third resulted from the worker being struck by a vehicle. Electrocutions, half of which involved overhead power lines, accounted for 18 per cent of the fatalities among young adults working in construction. Being struck by objects or equipment and being caught in collapsing structures or in cave-ins resulted in another 15 per cent of the deaths.

Service Industries

Service industries accounted for 13 per cent of fatalities in both the under 18 and 18–24 age groups during 1998–2002. Fatalities among service industry workers under 18 years-old increased from 25 in 1993–97 to 38 in the 1998–2002 period. Business services (which includes building maintenance) and amusement and recreational services accounted for over one-fourth of the fatalities in the services industry. Fatalities more than doubled among youths in these two industries between the two periods. Transportation incidents, assaults and violent acts, contact with objects and equipment and falls all increased during 1998–2002 over the previous five-year period. In over half of the transportation-related incidents during 1998–2002, the youth was operating a vehicle, many of which were golf carts or other off-road vehicles.

Fatalities among 18–24 year-old service industry workers fell 14 per cent from 415 in 1993–97 to 358 in 1998–2002. Much of the decrease was in business services, which accounted for 102 (28 per cent) of the service industry total in the latter five-year period. Many of the fatalities among 18–24 year-olds working in the business services industry were in building services, equipment rental and leasing, personnel supply services, and detective and armored car services. Other service industries with notable numbers of fatalities among young adult workers were automotive repair, services, and parking (57 fatalities); amusement and recreation services (56 fatalities); health services (21 fatalities); and engineering and management services (22 fatalities). About 45 per cent of the fatalities in service industries resulted from various types of transportation incidents—a little over half of which were traffic fatalities. Thirteen per cent of the fatalities in this industry resulted from homicides; suicides accounted for another 7 per cent of the industry total.

Retail Trade

During 1998–2002, retail trade accounted for 13 and 11 per cent of the fatalities among workers under 18 and 18–24 years-old, respectively. The number of fatalities among youths under 18 working in retail trade declined from 72 in 1993–97 to 40 in 1998–2002, a decrease of 44 per cent. Much of the decline resulted from a 51 per cent decrease in homicides among these workers, but fatalities resulting from other types of events fell as well. The decline in homicides was evident throughout various retail trade industries, including food stores, eating and drinking places, and miscellaneous retail establishments. Still, homicides comprised about half the fatalities among youths working in the retail trade sector during the 1998–2002 period. Transportation-related incidents accounted for about a third of the total. In about half of these incidents, the youth was driving the vehicle involved.

Retail trade fatalities also declined among workers 18–24 years-old. These fatalities dropped 39 per cent from 499 recorded in the previous five-year period to 303 in 1998–2002. Food stores and eating and drinking places each saw a 43 per cent decline in fatalities among 18–24 year-olds, while automotive dealer and service station workers saw an even greater percentage decline (61 per cent). As with the younger worker fatalities, much of the decline in retail trade fatalities among workers aged 18–24 resulted from a decrease in homicides, which fell from 303 in 1993–97 to 143 in 1998–2002, and comprised almost half of the total fatality count for young adult workers in retail trade. Highway fatalities also fell among these workers, going from 101 in the 1993–97 period to 88 in the latter period. These events accounted for almost 30 per cent of the total for 1998–2002.

Manufacturing

Manufacturing accounted for 11 per cent of the fatal injury total among all workers between 1998 and 2002, compared with 9 per cent of the fatalities among workers aged 24 and under. Manufacturing accounted for a smaller proportion of fatalities among workers under 18—about 6 per cent of the

1998–2002 total. Certain manufacturing work is prohibited for youths under 18, including most work with power-driven machines, logging and sawmilling, and explosives manufacturing. Fatalities among youths working in manufacturing in 1998–2002 occurred in lumber and wood products (which includes logging and sawmilling); stone, clay, glass, and concrete products; and printing and publishing (which includes carriers delivering newspapers). While Federal labor laws exempt most newspaper carriers from child labor regulations, some State labor laws do cover these workers. Most of the newspaper carrier fatalities occurred as a result of traffic incidents in which the youth was a passenger in a vehicle.

Manufacturing comprised 10 per cent of the total fatality count for workers 18–24 years-old during 1998–2002. These fatalities dropped by one-fourth from the previous five-year period (from 361 to 268). Lumber and wood products accounted for 29 per cent of the manufacturing fatalities in this age group during 1998–2002. These workers were most often killed from being struck by falling trees and branches and from various vehicle-related incidents. The manufacture of food and kindred products – which includes meatpacking, poultry slaughtering and processing, and grain mill products – accounted for another 14 per cent of the manufacturing fatality total for workers 18–24 years-old. The major hazards resulting in worker fatalities in this industry included highway crashes, falls, and running equipment and machinery.

Transportation and Public Utilities

Over the years 1998 to 2002, transportation and public utilities comprised 16 per cent of the fatalities among all age groups combined, 9 per cent of the total for workers 18–24 years-old, and 2 per cent of the total for workers under 18. Federal child labor laws prohibit workers under 18 from performing many of the tasks associated with working in the transportation and public utility industries. Workers under 16 are prohibited from driving a motor vehicle or working as an outside helper on a motor vehicle, transporting people or property, working in warehousing and storage, and working in communications and public utilities. In addition, many States and individual companies require an individual to be at least 18 to drive for the purpose of transporting people or goods, although Federal labor laws permit 17 year-olds to drive at work on an occasional basis and under certain conditions.

During 1998–2002, there were five fatalities among youths under 18 in the transportation and public utilities industries – a drop from the 1993–97 total. Four of the five decedents were either self-employed or working in the family business at the time of the fatal incident.

Young adult workers are also subject to minimum-age requirements with regard to driving. Federal Department of Transportation regulations require drivers of certain types of vehicles and drivers who transport certain passengers or hazardous cargo in interstate commerce to be 21 or older to obtain a commercial drivers' license. During 1998–2002, there were 258 fatalities among workers 18–24 years-old in the transportation and public utilities industries—roughly the same number as in the previous five-year period (265 fatalities). Almost 60 per cent of these workers were employed in trucking and warehousing. Other fatalities in the industry division occurred in air and water transportation, taxicab services, communications, and electric, gas, and sanitary services.

The fatalities involving young adult transportation workers primarily resulted from vehicle-related incidents, with the exception of taxicab drivers, who were more likely to die as a result of homicide. Fatalities in trucking and warehousing primarily resulted from highway collisions, rollovers, and being struck by a vehicle, and fatalities involving air and water transport primarily resulted from incidents involving the respective mode of transport. Transportation incidents were also an important factor in fatalities among public utility workers. Over half of the fatalities among communications industry workers aged 18–24 resulted from transport-related incidents, and over half of the fatalities among refuse industry workers resulted from the worker falling from the garbage truck or being struck by a vehicle.

Wholesale Trade

Federal child labor laws prohibit certain activities associated with working in the wholesale trade sector. Workers under 16 are barred from working in warehouses, and workers under 18 are forbidden from operating forklifts and other power-driven hoisting apparatus. During 1998–2002, wholesale trade comprised 4 per cent of fatalities among workers of all ages, and 3 per cent of fatalities among workers 18–24 years-old. While the exact fatality count for wholesale trade workers under 18 for 1998–2002 was not reportable, there was a substantial drop in fatalities among these workers, compared with the 1993–97 total. The 12 fatalities that occurred in the 1993–97 period were primarily in wholesale motor vehicle parts and supplies and farm products. During 1998–2002, there were 93 fatalities among 18–24 year-olds in wholesale trade—a decrease of about one-fourth from the previous five-year period. There were 10 or more fatalities among 18–24 year-olds in the following wholesale industries: groceries and related products, motor vehicle parts and supplies, and farm supplies. Over half (52 per cent) of the fatalities resulted from highway crashes.

Government

Government agencies accounted for 10 per cent of all fatal work injuries during 1998–2002, and 6 per cent of the fatalities among workers under 18. Many of the youths were volunteers or trainees in firefighting, the military, or social services. Over the 1993–2002 period, two-thirds of the fatalities among youths working in the public sector resulted from various types of transportation-related incidents.

The public sector also accounted for 339 (12 per cent) of the fatalities among 18–24 year-old workers during 1998–2002, compared with 366 deaths during 1993–97. Most of the decline resulted from a reduction in fatalities among military personnel within the US.[6] These fatalities declined by 15 per cent from 208 in 1993–97 to 176 in 1998–2002 and made up slightly over half the fatalities among young adults working in the government sector.

Transportation-related incidents accounted for 103 (59 per cent) of the deaths among military personnel in this age group during the second five-year period. Highway crashes resulted in 39 of these deaths, and 37 were due to aircraft crashes. Incidents involving vehicles or mobile equipment occurring off public roadways resulted in another 16 deaths. Also of note

Table 8.2 Fatal Occupational Injuries of Workers Aged 17 and under by Selected Industry, 1993–2002

Industry	**1993–97**	**1998–2002**
Total	335	304
Private sector	325	287
Agriculture, forestry, and fishing	134	125
Construction	48	54
Manufacturing	17	19
Transportation and public utilities	9	5
Wholesale trade	12	–
Retail trade	72	40
Services	25	38
Government	10	17

Note: A dash indicates that data do not meet publication criteria.

Table 8.3 Fatal Occupational Injury Totals among Workers 18–24 Years-Old by Selected Industry, 1993–2002

Industry	1993–97	1998–2002
Total	3,070	2,795
Private sector	2,704	2,456
Agriculture, forestry, and fishing	287	334
Mining	106	64
Construction	593	748
Manufacturing	361	268
Transportation and public utilities	265	258
Wholesale trade	126	93
Retail trade	499	303
Services	415	358
Government	366	339

Note: Mining includes 75 fatalities in oil and gas extraction in 1993–97 and 51 fatalities during 1998–2002.

were the 22 suicides (12 per cent) among the military personnel in the age group, compared to the 4 per cent of fatalities among all workers during 1998–2002. Accidental gunshot and shrapnel wounds resulted in nine deaths, and five deaths resulted from homicide.

Another major portion of the fatalities among young adult workers in government occurred among protective service workers. There were 36 fatal injuries in police protection among 18–24 year-olds in 1998–2002—17 of which resulted from highway vehicle crashes, 13 resulted from homicide, and 3 resulted from the worker being struck by a vehicle. Fire protection accounted for another 26 fatalities among government workers 18–24 years-old—9 of which resulted from fires and 7 resulted from highway crashes.

Another 17 of the young adult government workers were killed while working in educational institutions, including elementary and secondary schools and colleges and universities. Various vehicle-related incidents and suicides were the major contributors of fatalities among these workers. The transportation and public utility industries accounted for another 16 fatalities among young adult government workers—9 of which were in electric, gas, and sanitary services. Half of the fatalities among transportation and public utility workers resulted from vehicle-related incidents.

CONCLUSION

Transportation incidents comprised the largest portion of fatalities among the two age groups studied. Between 1998 and 2002, these incidents accounted for 52 per cent of the fatalities among workers under 18, and 43 per cent of the fatalities among workers aged 18 to 24, the same percentage as fatalities among workers of all ages. Homicides, which accounted for about one-sixth of the fatalities among workers aged 24 and under during 1993–97, fell during 1998–2002, accounting for one-tenth of the fatalities during the latter period. Fatal falls increased between the two five-year periods, particularly among young adult workers.

Agriculture, forestry, and fishing industries accounted for about two-fifths of the fatalities among workers under 18 between 1998 and 2002. The family farm was particularly hazardous for these youths, accounting for about 60 per cent of their fatalities. Although relatively small in numbers, work fatalities among youths increased between the two five-year periods in construction, services, and government (see Table 8.2). For workers aged 18–24, the construction industry comprised over one-fourth of the fatality total between 1998–2002 and sustained a notable increase between the two five-year periods (see Table 8.3). The fatality total among landscape and horticultural service workers also increased during the study period. Industries with notable decreases in fatalities among young adult workers included mining, manufacturing, retail trade, and services.

ACKNOWLEDGMENTS

The author gratefully acknowledges the contributions of Greg Fayard, Mike Martell, Sam Meyer, and Steve Pegula in the preparation of this chapter.

NOTES

1. Fatality rates were calculated for civilian workers aged 15 and older, using fatality counts from the Census of Fatal Occupational Injuries (CFOI) and hours worked from the Current Population Survey (CPS), which are converted to full-time equivalent workers. The fatality rate calculation used here differs from that used to create rates shown in CFOI's production releases. Those rates are based on CPS annual average employment.
2. Youths working on farms owned or operated by their parents fall outside the scope of Federal child labor laws. Other regulations covering agricultural work are generally less restrictive than rules covering other industries. Youths in agriculture may perform tasks deemed hazardous at a younger age than in non-agricultural industries and may work during school hours at age 16 or if employed on the parents' farm.
3. Because the fatality census does not have information on whether or not the worker

had completed a certified training program on equipment involved in the fatal incident, some of the youths may have been operating the machinery legally. In addition, about 60 per cent of the young worker fatalities in agriculture – those working on the family farm – fell outside the scope of Federal child labor laws. These fatalities may have been covered under State laws. Additional information on youths' activities resulting in fatal injuries can be found in Windau and Meyer (2005). Information on Federal child labor regulations is available on the Internet at www.osha.gov.

4. Additional information on injuries among landscape and horticultural workers and groundskeepers can be found in Wiatrowski (2005) and Pegula (2005).
5. Windau and Meyer (2005).
6. Fatalities among the military are only included if they occurred in the United States or in surrounding waters or airspace.

9. Falling Private Health Insurance Coverage Among Young Workers in the United States

Niev J. Duffy

Private health insurance coverage among both adults and children in the United States has been in decline since the 1970s. Though some of the sharpest declines in coverage occurred as a result of the 1990–92 recession, during the economic recovery that followed – the longest boom ever – private health insurance coverage rates continued to drop.[1] The decline in coverage during this period of economic growth has been attributed to a loss of employer-sponsored benefits among middle- and upper-income households.[2] By the year 2000, only slightly over two-thirds (67.4 per cent) of Americans under the age of 62 were covered by an employer-sponsored plan. The economic downturn starting in 2000 led to even more precipitous declines in rates of coverage so that, by 2003, an additional seven million Americans were without employer-sponsored coverage and the share had fallen by another four percentage points, to 63 per cent.

Overall rates of health insurance coverage have decreased more rapidly for young adults than they have for mature adults, contributing to a growing gap in access to care between the two groups. One explanation is that young workers are more likely to be among the working poor, a group that has much lower rates of employer-provided health insurance coverage both for themselves and their families.[3] Evidence also shows that, in the United States between 1987 and 1996, the share of young workers that were offered health insurance by an employer declined, while it was stable for older workers.[4]

To date, little research has been performed to measure and/or explain disparities in private health insurance coverage between young working adults and older cohorts. This study explores a variety of factors that may contribute to growing age-related disparities in rates of private health insurance coverage in the United States.[5]

DATA

Data were obtained from March Supplements of the United States Current Population Survey, an annual cross-sectional survey of roughly 65,000–75,000 households compiled by the Census Bureau and the Bureau of Labor Statistics. Weighting of the data provides a representative sample for the United States. The dataset contains demographic and health insurance information on all individuals within a household. Subjects between the ages of 19 and 64 were chosen for the analysis leaving 93,579 individuals in 1989 and 79,462 in 1999.

Subjects were classified as young adults if they were between 19 and 29 years of age (n=26,359 in 1989, n=18,985 in 1999), and mature adults if they were between 30 and 64 (n=67,220 in 1989, n=60,477 in 1999). Subjects that reported having private health insurance were divided into three categories, reflecting the source of their health insurance coverage:

1. Own employer-provided coverage – coverage in a subject's own name, obtained through that worker's union or employer;
2. Family Coverage – employer or individual "non-group" coverage provided through another family member. Roughly 90 per cent of family coverage is employer-based; and
3. Own individual "non-group" coverage – "non-group" coverage in a subject's own name purchased individually.

Subjects were also considered to have private health insurance if they reported having both private insurance and public health insurance such as Medicare or Medicaid.

RESEARCH METHODS

Bivariate analyses were performed to compare rates of health insurance coverage at the beginning and end of the ten-year period between 1989 and 1999, for each of the age groups. Bivariate comparisons of young and mature adults were also performed in order to identify statistically significant ($p<0.01$) gaps in rates of insurance coverage between age groups, both in 1989 and 1999. T tests were then used to compare the gap in rates of coverage between young and mature adults in 1989 with the corresponding gap in coverage in 1999, in order to identify significant increases in disparities in coverage between young and mature adults ($p<0.01$).

Multivariate logistic regression analysis was used to explore differences in rates of employer-provided health insurance coverage by age while controlling for other individual and household demographic characteristics. The analysis adjusted for work status, education, sex, race/ethnicity, disability, region, metropolitan status, and school enrollment.

FINDINGS

Of the three main sources of private health insurance – employer, and family and individual "non-group" coverage – the first is by far the most important source of health insurance among all adults under the age of 64. The recession of 1990–92 led to dramatic declines in all three types of private coverage for both young and mature adults. However, during the economic recovery that followed, these two age groups experienced very different rates of recovery in the three types of health insurance coverage. These differences, and their combined impact on overall rates of private health insurance coverage across age groups are discussed below.

Declining Own Employer-Provided Health Insurance

In general, the proportion of the population with own employer-provided health insurance increases steadily with age before tapering off after the age of 60. Only 15 per cent of adolescents aged 19–21 had own employer-provided health insurance in 1999, while rates of coverage peaked at 54.5 per cent among individuals in their 50s.

Since 1989, own employer-provided health care coverage has declined dramatically for young adults, particularly for those under the age of 25, with most of the decline occurring between 1989 and 1992 (Figure 9.1). The chances that a young adult had employer-provided health insurance in 1999 was far lower than in 1989. The resulting odds ratio comparing the rate of coverage in 1999 with the rate in 1989 is 0.85, with a confidence interval of (0.82–0.89), showing a significant decline in the likelihood of coverage, ($p<.0001$), (Table 9.1). Though the decline in employer-provided health insurance coverage is often blamed on a rise in part-time and temporary employment, particularly among young people, the bulk of the decline in benefits among young adult workers resulted from declining coverage among full time year-round workers, for whom the odds ratio comparing 1999 with 1989 was 0.73(0.69–0.78), ($p<0.0001$), (Table 9.1).

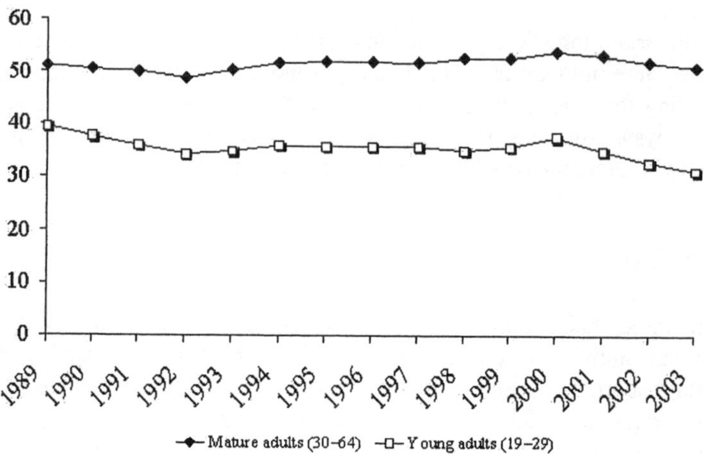

Figure 9.1 Percentage Enrolled in Own Employer-Provided Health Insurance, 1989–1999, Young (19–29) and Mature (30–64) Adults

The decline in the odds ratio is slightly greater after compensating for a variety of demographic factors.

In contrast, rates of own employer-provided health coverage actually rose on average among mature adults aged 30–64, between 1989 and 1999. The odds ratio comparing the likelihood of a mature adult having employer-provided health insurance in 1999 with the likelihood of having employer-provided coverage in 1989 was 1.06 (1.04–1.09) showing a significant rise in the likelihood of coverage, ($p<0.0001$) (Table 9.1). This increase was entirely a reflection of rising incomes and higher full-time labor force participation rates among mature adults, which rose from 63.6 per cent in 1989 to 67.3 per cent in 1999. Though the rate of employer-provided coverage rose overall among mature adults, the coverage rate actually fell among full-time year-round workers in that age group. The odds ratio comparing coverage in 1999 with coverage in 1989 was 0.87 (0.84–0.90) among full-time year-round workers, ($p<0.0001$) (Table 9.1). The decline in the odds ratio is slightly greater after accounting for demographic factors.

During the 1990s, the gap in own employer-provided health care coverage between young and mature adults widened dramatically ($p<0.0001$). This wider gap is reflected in the drop in odds ratios comparing rates of employer-provided coverage across the two age groups from 0.63 (0.61–0.64) in 1989 to 0.50 (0.48–0.52) in 1999 (Table 9.2).

Rates of own employer-provided health insurance coverage fell most rapidly for young employees working full-time year-round (Table 9.3). As a consequence, the gap in coverage between young and mature adult employees who work full-time year-round also grew significantly ($p<0.0001$), leading to a decline in relative odds ratios from 0.81 (0.77–0.85) in 1989, to 0.68 (0.65–0.71) in 1999 (Table 9.2). This gap widened significantly even after accounting for a variety of demographic factors ($p<0.0001$). The odds ratio, adjusted for demographic characteristics, declined from 0.83 (0.80–0.87) in 1989, to 0.74 (0.71–0.78) in 1999 (Table 9.2).

Table 9.1 Odds Ratios Comparing Rates of Private Health Insurance Coverage in 1989 and 1999, by Type of Insurance Coverage

Type of Coverage	**Young Adult OR(CI)**	**Mature Adult OR(CI)**
All Private insurance coverage	0.80(0.77–0.83)§	0.86(0.84–0.88)§
Own employer coverage	0.85(0.82–0.89)§	1.06(1.04–1.09)§
Family coverage	1.01(0.97–1.05)	0.85(0.83–0.87)§
Own individual non-group coverage	0.62(0.56–0.69)§	0.76(0.72–0.80)§
Own employer coverage, full-time year-round	0.73(0.69–0.78)§	0.87(0.84–0.90)§
Own employer cov, full-time year-round, adjusted†	0.74(0.69–0.79)§	0.86(0.83–0.89)§
Own employer cov, currently employed, adjusted‡	0.78(0.75–0.82)§	0.92(0.89–0.94)§

Notes:
† Adjusted for education, sex, ethnicity/race, disability, region, metropolitan status, and school enrollment.
‡ Adjusted for full-time work status, education, sex, ethnicity/race, disability, region, metropolitan status, and school enrollment.
§ $P\leq0.0001$

Table 9.2 Odds Ratios Comparing Rates of Private Health Insurance Coverage between Young and Mature Adults, in 1989 and 1999

Type of Coverage	1989 OR(CI)	1999 OR(CI)
All Private insurance coverage	0.55 (0.53–0.56)§	0.51 (0.49–0.53)§
Own employer coverage	0.63 (0.61–0.64)§	0.50 (0.48–0.52)§
Family coverage	1.11 (1.07–1.14)§	1.32 (1.27–1.37)§
Own individual non-group coverage	0.69 (0.64–0.73)§	0.56 (0.51–0.62)§
Own employer coverage, full-time Year-Round	0.81 (0.77–0.85)§	0.68 (0.65–0.71)§
Own employer cov, full-time year-round, adjusted†	0.83 (0.80–0.87§	0.74 (0.71–0.78)§
Own employer cov, currently employed, adjusted‡	0.71 (0.69–0.74)§	0.63 (0.60–0.66)§

Notes:
† Adjusted for education, sex, ethnicity/race, disability, region, metropolitan status, and school enrollment.
‡ Adjusted for full-time work status, education, sex, ethnicity/race, disability, region, metropolitan status, and school enrollment.
§ $P \leq 0.0001$

Declining Coverage Through Family Members

On average, rates of family coverage are higher for young adults than they are for mature adults: 25 per cent and 20 per cent, respectively (Figure 9.2). However, the higher rate among young adults is entirely due to older adolescents aged 19–21, some of whom still have coverage through a parent. In 1999, the rate of insurance coverage obtained through a family member was highest for older adolescents aged 19–21, at 46.5 per cent, but fell to its lowest point, 13.3 per cent for adults aged 25–29.

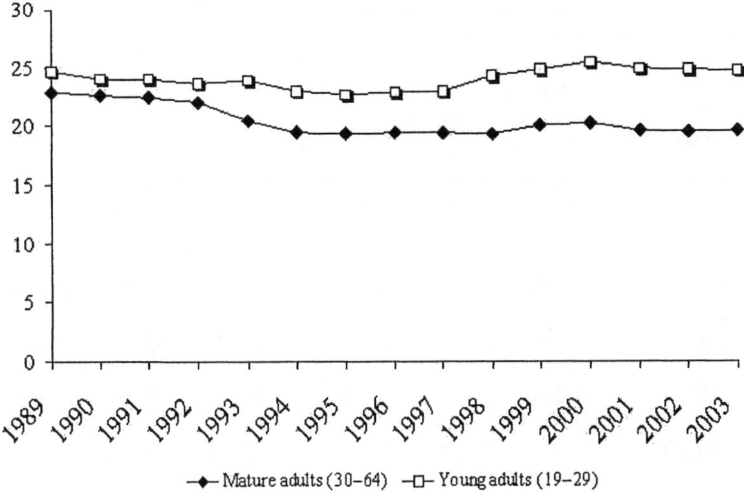

Figure 9.2 Percentage Enrolled in Private Health Insurance Obtained Through a Family Member, 1989–1999, Young (19–29) and Mature (30–64) Adults

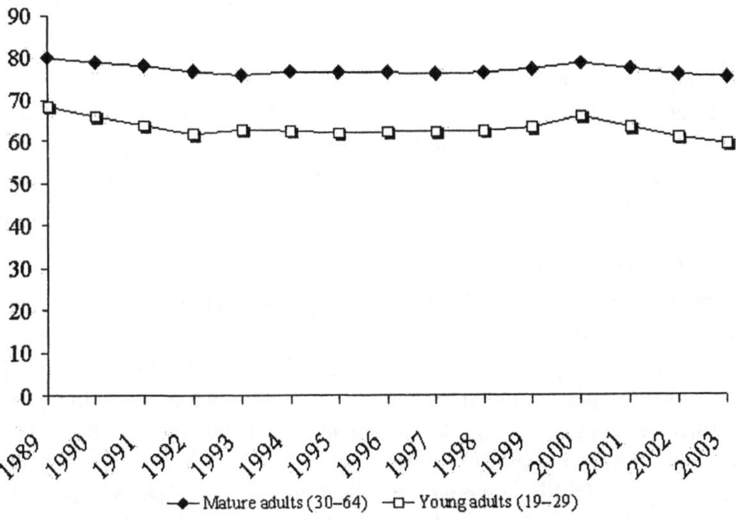

Figure 9.3 Percentage Enrolled in Private Health Insurance from all Sources, 1989–1999, Young (19–29) and Mature (30–64) Adults

Table 9.3 Change in Rates of Employer-Provided Health Insurance Coverage among Full-time Year-round Employees and All Workers by Age, 1989 and 1999

Age	Full-time Year-round Own Employer Coverage			All Workers Own Employer Coverage		
	1989	1999	%CHG	1989	1999	%CHG
19–21	50.1%	39.4%	-21.4%	27.7%	21.7%	-21.5%
22–24	66.0%	57.9%	-2.3%	50.1%	42.1%	-16.1%
25–29	74.1%	69.2%	-6.7%	62.1%	59.2%	-4.7%
30–39	73.5%	68.8%	-6.4%	62.7%	60.6%	-3.4%
40–49	73.3%	70.8%	-3.4%	64.4%	62.9%	-2.2%
50–59	73.0%	72.6%	-0.4%	63.9%	65.9%	3.2%
60–64	73.5%	71.5%	-2.7%	62.6%	63.5%	1.5%

Though young adults under the age of 30 experienced a decline in the rate of private insurance coverage obtained through a family member during the early- to mid-1990s, on average, they appeared to experience a full recovery of benefits during the economic recovery that followed. However, this trend masks the fact that the subgroup of young adults aged 25–29 experienced a strong decline in family coverage from 16.4 per cent in 1989 to 13.3 per cent in 1999.

Among mature adults 30 years of age and above, rates of family coverage declined during the recession of the early 1990s and experienced little or no recovery during the remainder of the 1990s (Figure 9.2). The odds ratio comparing the likelihood of a mature adult obtaining private insurance coverage through a family member in 1999 with that in 1989 was 0.85 (0.83–0.87), ($p<0.0001$) (Table 9.1).

The gap in family coverage between young and mature adults rose significantly between 1989 and 1999 in favor of young adults ($p<0.0001$). As a consequence, the odds ratio comparing coverage between the two age groups rose from 1.11 (1.07–1.14) in 1989, to 1.32 (1.27–1.37) in 1999 (Table 9.2).

Declining Individual "Non-Group" Coverage

Individual "non-group" coverage declined steadily for all age groups throughout the 1990s. Odds ratios comparing 1999 with 1989 were 0.62 (0.56–0.69) for young adults and 0.76 (0.72–0.80) for mature adults, ($p<0.0001$) (Table 9.1). The gap between young and mature adults also widened significantly, ($p<0.0001$) to the detriment of young people, with the odds ratio comparing young and mature adults dropping from 0.69 (0.64–0.73) in 1989 to 0.56 (0.51–0.62) in 1999, ($p<0.0001$) (Table 9.2).

Overall Private Health Insurance Coverage

Rates of overall private health insurance coverage are significantly lower for young adults than for mature adults ($p<0.0001$), 63 per cent versus 77 per cent, respectively in 1999. The odds ratio comparing rates of coverage between these two age groups was 0.51(0.49–0.53) in 1999, ($p<0.0001$), meaning that the relative odds of a person between the ages of 19 and 29 having private health insurance was half what it was for a person between 30 and 64 (Table 9.2).

Declines in overall private health insurance coverage between 1989 and 1999 have been highly significant for all age groups ($p<0.0001$) (Figure 9.3). The odds ratio comparing rates of overall private health insurance coverage among young adults in 1999 with those in 1989 was 0.80 (0.77–0.83), ($p<0.0001$), (Table 9.1). The corresponding odds ratio for mature adults was 0.86 (0.84–0.88), ($p<0.0001$).

Rates of decline have been most rapid for young adults between the ages of 19 and 29, increasing the gap in overall private insurance coverage between young and mature adults since 1989 ($p<0.0001$). The growing disparity is reflected in a decline in the odds ratios comparing the rates of coverage between the two groups from 0.55 (0.53–0.56) in 1989, to 0.51 (0.49–0.53) in 1999 (Table 9.2).

The loss of own employer-provided health insurance coverage was responsible for the vast majority of the decline in overall private health insurance among young adults in the US. In contrast, among mature adults, a rise in employer-provided coverage, largely due to increased labor force participation, has helped to offset the decline in family coverage that accounted for roughly half or more of the decline in private insurance coverage within that age group.

Though rates of individual "non-group" coverage are very low, their steady rate of decline during the 1990s accounts for between 25–35 per cent of the decline in private health insurance coverage among those aged 19–50, and a considerably larger share for those over 50.

DISCUSSION

The net result of recent changes in employer, family and individual "non-group" health insurance coverage has been a significant decline in private health insurance among all age groups between 1989 and 1999. Most of the decline in private coverage occurred during the economic recession of the early 1990s. Young adults in their peak childbearing years experienced the sharpest declines in private insurance coverage. The principal cause of the decline in private insurance within this age group has been the loss of employer-provided health care benefits.

Current estimates of expected future growth in numbers of uninsured people will be overly optimistic if they do not take into consideration the fact that unusually high rates of economic growth and labor force participation in the US during the second half of the 1990s, helped to offset declines in employer-sponsored health insurance among full-time year-round employees.

In addition to very high labor force participation rates and rising incomes, the stabilization of health care costs during the transition to managed care in the 1990s helped to limit temporarily the decline in rates of private health insurance coverage. However, health care costs have recently resumed their double-digit inflation, and the declines in employer-provided coverage that continued among working Americans during the 1990s are likely to accelerate as a result.

As in the early 1990s, the decline in insurance coverage in the US is likely to be most precipitous for young workers and their families. And since Medicaid expansions that helped to offset the declines in private insurance during the late 1980s to mid-1990s are no longer a source of growth in insurance coverage, another recession could lead to unprecedented increases in rates of uninsurance among the children of young adults.

Two important limitations of the Current Population Survey data have some relevance for the analysis presented here. Beginning with the 1995 March Supplement, the order of the survey questions concerning health insurance was changed in a way that may limit the comparability of data leading up to 1993 and following 1994. The most significant result of the change is that reporting of private insurance among children rose considerably. Holahan and Kim derive an innovative two-period approach to cope with the discrepancy, when young dependents are an important part of the analysis.[6] However, the change appears to have little or no consistent impact among adults in overall private insurance coverage and changes in family and employer-provided health insurance trends were smooth and consistent with employment trends. A one-period model was used in the analysis since a two-period model did not significantly alter any of the conclusions.

An extra question was added to the 2000 March Supplement (corresponding to 1999 data) in order to verify a lack of health insurance among those not identifying a source of coverage. This tended to boost the reporting of private insurance, and thus limits the comparability of data up to and following 1998. However, the evidence supporting the conclusions of the paper is only strengthened by removing 1999 from the analysis. The data for this year was included in order to demonstrate that the results presented here are still applicable, despite recently reported improvements in rates of private health insurance coverage (possibly resulting from misinterpretations of recoded data).

Despite these limitations, this study raises important concerns regarding the health of young adults and their families. Since young adults are far more likely to be among the working poor, especially if they have children, they are less able to afford out-of-pocket expenses for doctor's visits and medications for themselves and their children. Studies clearly show that the uninsured, particularly those among the working poor, are more likely to sacrifice needed care and to have less access to services.[7] They are also less able to afford reproductive health care services that would allow them to limit unwanted pregnancies or to obtain pre- and post-natal care.

Though young adults are often perceived to be at lower risk for a variety of morbidities, their high rates of uninsurance have very serious implications for the health status of young adults as well as for the health care facilities attempting to meet the needs of this vulnerable population. A lack of access to reproductive health care among young adults contributes to high rates of unintended pregnancies among young people in the US and the rapid spread of sexually transmitted diseases among young adults that have reached epidemic proportions. In addition, the rapid decline in private health insurance among young adults in their peak childbearing years (19–29) has led to rapidly declining rates of private insurance among young children during much of the 1990s.

These trends also have very important implications for the level of demand on the resources of public programs that seek to provide health care to uninsured children – particularly among the working poor – such as Medicaid expansion programs and Child Health Plus (CHIP). In the future, rapid declines in employer-provided health insurance among young adults, many in their peak child-bearing years, could greatly increase the numbers of children eligible for such programs.

NOTES

1. Holahan and Kim (2000).
2. Ibid.
3. Guendelman and Pearl (2001).
4. Cooper and Schone (1997).
5. This analysis builds on my earlier detailed studies of New York youth in Duffy (2002a, 2002b).
6. Holahan and Kim (2000).
7. Holl *et. al.* (1995); Newacheck *et. al.* (1998); Weinick, Weigers, and Cohen (1998); Klein *et. al.* (1999); Newacheck *et. al.* (1999); McCormick *et. al.* (2000); Guendelman and Pearl (2001).

PART FOUR

How Does Immigration Affect American Youth?

10. Immigration and Youth Employment: Recent Debates and Research Findings

Gregory DeFreitas

Unprecedented inflows of new immigrants into the weak job markets of the United States and Western Europe in recent years have re-ignited passionate economic and political controversies over the impacts of immigration. The US recorded more immigrant arrivals in the 1990s than in any decade before. Likewise, between 1990 and 2004, the non-national populations of Italy and Spain expanded by five to six times. Since 2004, migration by Eastern European jobseekers within the European Union has grown well beyond the predicted volume. In 2005 alone, the UK recorded its largest population increase in over a half-century, thanks largely to more than one-half million Polish, Czech and other immigrants – a far cry from the 15,000 new entrants predicted by the government just a year earlier.[1]

The fact that immigration levels have jumped in the same time span that youth employment prospects have deteriorated in the US and much of Europe raises the troubling question whether the foreign born may be competing for jobs with and/or dampening the wage growth of the native-born. Coupled with mounting economic anxiety and heightened security concerns after the September 2001 attacks, these trends have led European Union countries to curtail in-migration from non-EU nations, as well as to rethink full implementation of the policy of free inter-country mobility within the EU (the Schengen Accord). In fact, since the inclusion of ten Eastern European countries into the EU in May 2004, most of the original 15 nations have delayed granting their citizens full immigration rights, out of concern over both sizable new flows from the newest EU countries and the weak external border controls against unauthorized migrants in poorer member states.[2]

In the US by 2006, public opinion polls found that a majority believed that immigration was a burden, taking jobs, housing, and health care from native-born Americans. The rising political temperature over the issue led to deployment of National Guard troops along the Mexican border, civilian border patrols by self-appointed Minutemen, and the most sweeping Congressional reform proposals in two decades. The latter included both hundreds of miles of new border walls and criminalization of unauthorized immigrants and of any citizens assisting them. This, in turn, sparked unprecedented mass protest demonstrations around the country by millions of immigrants and their allies.

This chapter first summarizes the latest measures of key dimensions of immigration to the US, before discussing recent findings by the author and others on the wage and employment impacts of immigration on native-born youth and older workers. It concludes with an outline of the implications of these findings for ongoing debates about immigration policy.

NEW IMMIGRATION FLOWS AND FEATURES

How many immigrants are in the United States today, who are they, and where are they? Answering such basic questions requires first having a clear sense of who exactly are counted as 'immigrants.' Government statisticians, independent demographers, and much of the public have often differed in their preferred definitions.

Three broad legal immigration categories are the focus of most of the federal government's records:

1. Legal Permanent Resident Immigrants (LPRs) – Commonly known as 'green-card' holders (though the actual card has long been different colors) or 'legal aliens,' LPRs are foreign-born non-citizens who have most of the same non-voting legal rights as American citizens. Those seeking full rights must pursue the path to naturalization as US citizens. Government figures on the number of new LPRs admitted annually are a misleading measure of the actual influx of foreign-born persons. In recent years, over one-half of them were already in the US for a time before the year in which they won 'adjusted status' to LPR. Sharp swings in the official counts of LPRs have been common over the years, more reflective of shifts in staffing at immigration offices and backlogs of applicants than of actual inflows from abroad.
2. Temporary Legal Nonimmigrants (TLNs) – Persons granted short-term admission to the country without any permanent legal right of settlement are officially known as 'non-immigrants.' These include the 30 million or more foreign tourists visiting each year, as well as students (F visas and M visas), skilled guest workers (H-1B visas), and intracompany transfers of foreign employees to US workplaces (L visas).[3] Federal government

recordkeeping on the numbers and whereabouts of nonimmigrants, long criticized by independent studies, became subject to much public questioning after September 2001. The subsequent creation of the new Bureau of Citizenship and Immigration Services (BCIS) to replace the former Immigration and Naturalization Service (INS) was designed in part to correct these information gaps.

3. Unauthorized Migrants – Undocumented or unauthorized migrants either enter the country bearing fraudulent documents or none at all, or they enter with legal visas and then overstay their visa period. Government records on INS border arrests were until recent years the main, highly inaccurate basis for guesstimates of unauthorized inflows.

A broader definition of immigrants as all foreign-born US residents (not born abroad of US citizen parents) is favored by most demographic and social science researchers. This measure includes non-citizens as well as naturalized citizens, plus legal and unauthorized immigrants, but excludes American citizens born abroad or in Puerto Rico. The most complete, regularly available data sources for estimates of the current stock of foreign-born residents are the US Census Bureau's annual Current Population Survey, the American Community Survey, and the decennial census. All ask respondents for their country of birth, US citizenship status (native-born citizen, naturalized citizen, or non-citizen), their state or country of residence the previous year, and year of arrival in the US. The latter is determined from a question – 'When did you come to live in the US' – whose wording, while meant to omit foreign tourists by implying longer-term residence in a permanent dwelling unit, could be ambiguous for some respondents. In order to estimate net changes in the flow of immigration each year, census and survey data on the number of new arrivals must be merged with estimates of the other two sources of changes in the immigrant stock: number of foreign-born deaths and number of foreign-born residents emigrating out of the country. Since there are no regular government data sources on emigration, current estimates (commonly around 275,000 per year) may be subject to sizable error.

One in eight Americans is foreign born today, according to the US Census Bureau's latest estimates. The foreign-born population jumped by over 80 per cent between 1990 and 2005 (from 19.8 to 35.7 million), rising at a rate over five times faster than the native population. The 11.3 million influx of the 1990s – the most numerous of any immigration decade in US history – was followed by another 4.6 million arriving during 2000–05. The foreign-born share of the total population in 2005 (12.4 per cent) was still below the 14.7 per cent share a century ago. But it is now over 2.5 times higher than in 1970, when the US recorded only 9.6 million immigrants who

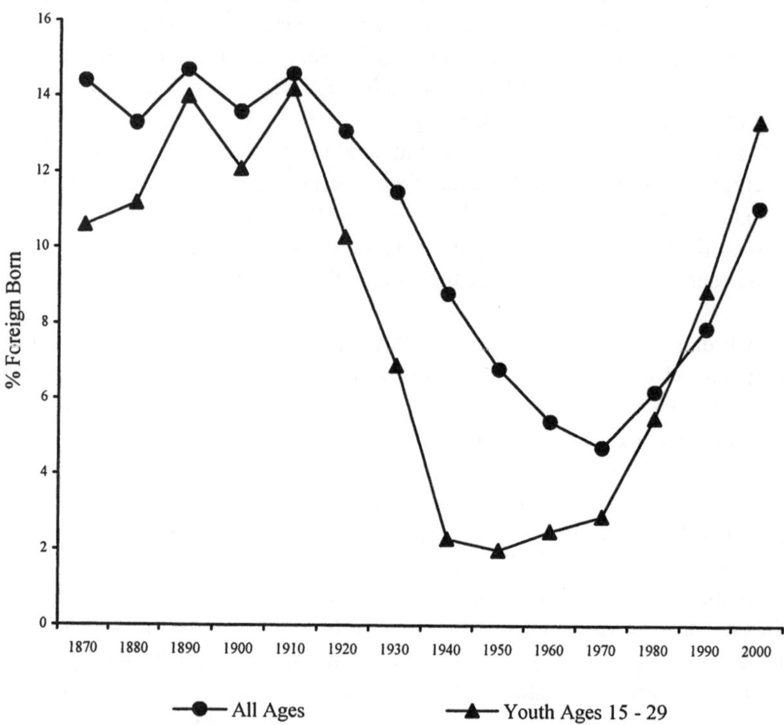

Figure 10.1 Immigrant Share of US Population by Age, 1870 to 2000

accounted for just 4.7 per cent of the country's population.[4] Annual immigration flows have not increased steadily: they spiked from the early 1990s to a peak in 1999–2000 of 1.5 million.[5] Thereafter, the annual influx fell by 25 per cent to 1.1 million by 2004, the same level as in the early 1990s.

As immigration has expanded, it has become far more diverse in terms of race, ethnicity and national origins. In 1960, Europeans still accounted for three-fourths of all foreign-born residents in the US, while Latin Americans were only 9.4 per cent and Asians 5.1 per cent. But by 2000, the European share had dropped to 15 per cent as the shares of Latin Americans jumped to 51 per cent and of Asians to 25 .5 per cent.

Young immigrants now account for a larger share of the country's youth population than in nearly a century. Figure 10.1 traces decennial census figures on the proportion of foreign-born youth aged 15 to 29 in the US population of that age group from 1870 to 2000.[6] From the early twentieth century until 1990, young people were consistently underrepresented among successive immigrant cohorts. But by 2000, when immigrants represented 11.1 per cent of all Americans, the 7.8 million foreign-born youth accounted for 13.4 per cent of all youth. Immigrants entering the country since 1990 are notably younger on average than the native born. Over one in five recent immigrants is aged 15 to 24 today, compared to just 14.2 per cent of the native population. The gap is far wider among young adults aged 25 to 34: they account for 31.9 per cent of recent immigrants, but only 15.5 per cent of the aging native population (Figure 10.2).

What explains these patterns? First, major legislative changes over the last four decades have markedly altered immigrant admission criteria. In 1965 Congress finally repealed the European-biased national origins quota system in effect since the 1920s.[7] This was widely viewed as another victory for the national Civil Rights movement, but was expected to have far smaller impacts than the 1964 Civil Rights Act. However, once the immigration law went into effect in 1967, it led to a surge of new migration by Asians and others long excluded, many taking advantage of greatly expanded admissions for family reunification. The effect has been to shift dramatically the racial/ethnic composition of immigration. Then the end of the Vietnam War in 1975 generated massive refugee flows from Southeast Asia, which have been supplemented since then by smaller but still significant numbers from Cuba and the former Soviet Union.

Another key legal change came under the Reagan Administration in the late 1980s, with amnesty granted to 3 million undocumented migrants under the Immigration Reform and Control Act (IRCA). By the early 1990s, this had led to an increase in the number of their immediate relatives subsequently granted legal residence status. This temporary bulge in admissions shrank over the decade. The Immigration Act of 1990 was another principal cause of more entrants, since it greatly increased the number of LPRs admitted each year to 675,000. This was to be a 'flexible ceiling' which could be exceeded (as it regularly has been) whenever more visas for immediate relatives of US citizens were needed, while still allowing at least 226,000 slots for other family-based claims.

As these migration 'pull factors' were taking effect, economic 'push factors' were adding new pressures at the southern border. Once NAFTA was approved in 1994, ending Mexican farmers' import protections from US agribusiness, more rural unemployed were added to migration streams. Then the severe 1995 economic crisis in Mexico saw GDP drop over 6 per cent and unemployment soar, driving more to seek employment up north. The record-breaking US jobs boom of the late 1990s fueled added demand

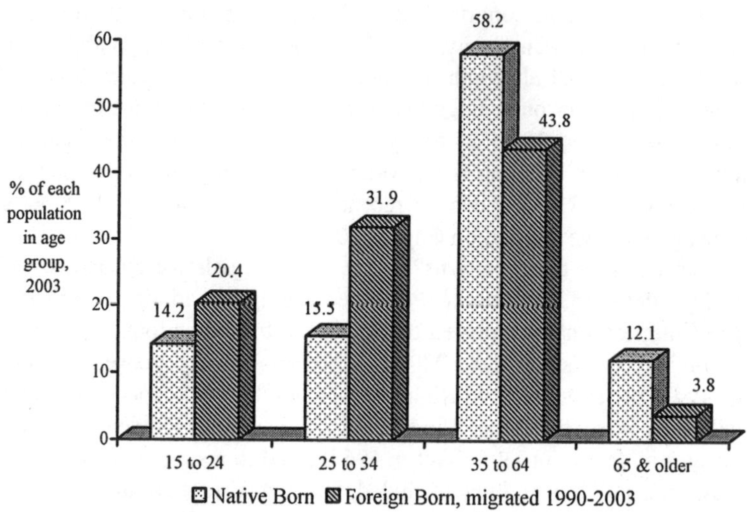

Figure 10.2 Recent Immigrants are Much Younger than the US-Born Population

by both low-wage employers, particularly in construction, for cheap, often undocumented labor and by Microsoft and other high-tech employers seeking more H-1B temporary visas for higher-skill migrants. But the US recession of March to November 2001 slowed job creation markedly. And the heightened border security, visa processing delays, and lowered refugee entry ceilings after September 11th ended the sharp immigration spike.

Unauthorized immigrants appear to have increased their share of foreign inflows rapidly in the past decade, according to the best available demographic estimates. As recently as 1996, the undocumented population in the US was widely thought to be no more than about four million. But it had more than doubled to 10.3 million just eight years later.[8] As Figure 10.3 illustrates, unauthorized migrants today account for a sizable minority, at 29 per cent, of the total foreign-born population. Research on the demographic characteristics of the undocumented sketch a youthful population (over one-third aged 18 to 29), dominated by Mexican-origin migrants (57 per cent of the total) and Central and South Americans (24 per cent).

Both legal and unauthorized immigrants have for some years now been dispersing geographically across the country well beyond the traditional

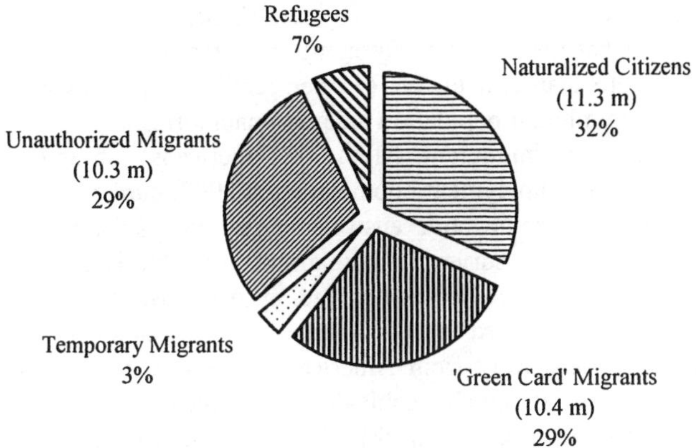

Figure 10.3 Legal Status of Immigrants in US, 2004

gateway states – California, New York, New Jersey, Texas, Florida, and Illinois. While these 'Big Six' continue to hold about three-fifths of the foreign born, a group of some two dozen other 'new immigration states' have attracted a steadily rising share of new arrivals. Between the 1990 and 2000 censuses, North Carolina had the fastest percentage growth in immigrants of any state– 278 per cent – as the size of its foreign-born population exploded to 377,000 by the decade's close. Georgia and Nevada each experienced over 200 per cent increases. And within these and other states, immigrants increasingly move directly to new suburban destinations, rather than concentrating only in major cities.

LABOR MARKET IMPACTS

As growing numbers of immigrants have spread throughout the United States, more and more Americans have become aware of and increasingly concerned about their presence. According to a 2006 nationwide opinion survey, 62 per cent of respondents said that they had 'many' immigrants living in their area, compared to just 39 per cent in a similar 1997 survey.[9] The latest survey revealed a public holding often exaggerated views of the size and composition of the immigrant population. When asked what percentage of today's population is foreign born, one-fourth of respondents said 25 per cent, and another 28 per cent thought it was higher than that. Only one in three came close to the correct, 12 per cent figure. Another question asked what fraction of all foreign-born persons were here illegally. Surprisingly, more than two in five (44 per cent) wrongly thought that at least half of the immigrant population today is unauthorized.

What impacts are immigrants having on Americans' job and earnings prospects? Since the employment boom ended in 2000, public opinion polls have found increasingly negative answers to that long-standing question. When asked in the 2006 survey if 'immigrants are a burden, taking jobs, housing and health care,' 52 per cent agreed, up from just 38 per cent when the same question was asked in 2000. Nearly one in four today think that immigrants 'take jobs away from American citizens.' At the same time, there seems to be as much ambivalence as there is anxiety about immigration. After all, a near majority of those surveyed did not consider them a 'burden,' over three-fourths did not agree that immigrants take citizens' jobs, and only 16 per cent responded affirmatively to a more precise question: whether they or a family member 'has either lost a job or not gotten a job because the employer hired an immigrant instead.' More people felt that legal immigration levels should stay the same or be increased than favored decreases. In fact, four out of five people surveyed expressed positive views about Latin American immigrants, agreeing that they 'work very hard' and have 'strong family values.'

Young people today appear to have the most positive attitudes toward immigrants of any age group. Among survey respondents aged 18 to 29, only 34 per cent viewed immigrants as a 'big problem' and just 43 per cent felt immigration was a 'burden,' well below the fractions of older Americans holding such views.[10]

The Basic Economic Model

Economic research on immigration's impacts has proliferated in recent years. It takes as its starting point the basic demand-supply framework that is commonly applied in mainstream economics to both product and labor markets. Foreign- and native-born labor forces are typically modeled as separate productive factors that may be either complements or substitutes. If complementary, then increases in immigration will raise the productivity of and rate of return on both inputs, which may also expand employment opportunities. But, if they are substitutes, then immigration threatens to intensify competition for jobs and to lower – or at least slow the growth of – native wage rates. Undergraduates are told in the most widely used textbooks that more immigration pushes the labor supply curve downward to the right, tracing out lower wage equilibria. The falling wage may, in turn, result in more native workers dropping out of the labor force or being replaced by immigrants.

But there is another possibility, too often given less, if any textbook space. If immigration also increases productivity, expands consumer demand for employers' products and services, and/or increases the absolute number of employers, then it is also possible that the downward-sloping employer demand curve for labor could be shifted upward to the right. That is, simultaneous shifts in both the labor supply and demand curves may result from immigration, leaving the net effects on equilibrium wage and employment levels uncertain: it is theoretically possible that more immigrants could end up raising, lowering, or not changing the market wage and native-born employment level at all. Moreover, the magnitude of such shifts on wages and employment also depends on the relative elasticities of each curve. So, with the net impacts indeterminate from theory alone, the only way to settle the question is to look at empirical research to see what statistical analysis of labor market data can tell us about how much, in different times and places, immigration-induced shifts in labor supply and demand curves affect the wage and employment of different groups of workers.

Impacts on Wages: Empirical Findings

The earliest attempts to test empirically immigration's effects on domestic wage levels relied on single-year national cross-sections of 1970 or 1980 census microdata. For a set of cities or metropolitan areas, the wage of local native workers was regressed on the number or proportion of labor force participants who were immigrants, plus a variety of control variables.

A comprehensive National Research Council survey of the economic studies completed by the mid-1990s concluded that:[11]

> Comparisons of geographic areas with different levels of immigration show only a weak relationship between native wages and the number of immigrants in a city or state. Furthermore, in these studies the numerically weak relationship between native wages and immigration is observed across all types of native workers, skilled and unskilled, male and female, minority and nonminority. The one group that appears to suffer substantially from new waves of immigrants are immigrants from earlier waves, for whom the recent immigrants are close substitutes in the labor market.

The 'interarea' comparative studies that yielded most of these early findings were later said to be subject to several biases. First, since they looked only at aggregate native wages, any negative immigration impact on low-skilled natives may have been offset by positive effects on the high skilled. Likewise, different immigrant cohorts may have had different effects, which need to be distinguished empirically. Another possible weakening influence on immigration impact estimates may have been the exodus from high-immigration labor markets of those natives whose jobs were most threatened by immigrant labor. If they were in fact being displaced by immigrants, this negative effect could be missed by researchers. Still another consideration is that foreign inflows to the lower-wage jobs of largely non-college-educated workers in the industrial periphery may have quite different effects from inflows to largely primary jobs in core industries.

In fact, some of the earliest studies had taken into account most of these potential sources of bias. For example, DeFreitas tested census wage data in a multi-equation econometric model that controlled for both immigration and native workers' interarea migration. The main results for 1980 were: recent Hispanic immigration had insignificant wage effects for native White women, African American men, and Hispanics, regardless of the sector of employment. The only group experiencing statistically significant (though small) negative effects was African American women. In contrast, low-skill White male natives actually appeared to gain significantly from higher immigration.[12]

Once 1990 census data became available to researchers in the early 1990s, some studies questioned whether the earlier findings were still applicable to more recent migrant waves. George Borjas argued in a book and a number of papers that US immigrants' 'quality' has steadily deteriorated, rendering them increasingly substitutable with low-wage natives.[13] He theorized that less-skilled immigrants are more attracted than the high skilled by a destination offering a narrower earnings distribution and better options for welfare and unemployment benefits than in their homeland. This, together with the greater legal access to visas for non-Europeans created by the 1965 legal reforms, widened the education gap between natives and recent immigrant cohorts. For example, in 1970, 40 per cent of the native born and 48 per cent of the foreign born had not attained a high school degree. But by 1990 the gap had widened to 22 percentage points (15 per cent of natives, 37 per cent of immigrants). The clear implication is that larger numbers of less-educated immigrants may have intensified the competition for jobs and wages with non-college natives and thereby lowered the latter's relative and absolute living standards.

This view has been challenged by a growing number of studies. For example, Lalonde and Topel show that there have been increases, not declines, in the average years of schooling of most nationalities. The fact that the native–immigrant schooling gap has widened is entirely explained by the post-1965 shift in the national origins mix toward non-European countries. Relative to natives' of similar race and ethnicity, recent immigrants' educational background is no weaker than in the past.[14]

Past generalizations about immigrant quality have also missed the important fact that most of the decline in mean years of immigrant education is the fault of illegal entrants: three-fourths of those from the main source countries of the undocumented lack a high school diploma, compared to only one-fourth of recent legal migrants. Moreover, one-third of recent legal entrants hold a college degree, compared with only one-fifth of US natives. One in five doctors and computer specialists in the country today is foreign born. And the secular fall in immigrants' average education and wage levels relative to natives appears to have halted in the early 1990s, and begun a modest reversal.[15]

But claims that much of the new immigration was little-educated and/or undocumented seemed to some labor specialists to provide a reasonable explanation for the sharp ongoing decline in labor union membership and bargaining power. Vernon Briggs has argued that millions of the undocumented live in such fear of deportation that they are too intimidated to complain about poor wages or working conditions, much less support unions.[16] Since decades of economic research have documented that unions tend to raise wages for their less-skilled members even more than for the higher skilled, shrinking union membership and leverage is especially harmful to less-educated workers.

In 2003, Borjas exploited 2000 Census data for a new study that concluded that immigration between 1980 and 2000 lowered the average annual wages of native-born men by 3.2 per cent overall, but by far more for less-educated men. The wage declines ranged from 2.6 per cent among those with only a high school degree to 4.9 per cent for college graduates to 8.9 per cent for high school dropouts. Results showing a negative effect of immigration on college graduates, yet no significant impact on those with no more than one to three years of college, appeared inconsistent with his theory. But the claim that immigration might have cut dropouts' wages by nearly nine per cent prompted new concerns and new research.

Most economic studies to date have found smaller, if any, negative associations between immigration and native workers' wages, regardless of schooling level. In a wide-ranging review by researchers at the Federal Reserve Banks of Dallas and Atlanta, Pia Orrenius and Madeline Zavodny concluded that new immigrants have had slightly positive effects on service and professional employees' wages, and no statistically significant effects on manual laborers. There may be a negative immigration impact on the annual wages of the low-skilled native born, but they put it at 2.4 per cent – nearly three-fourths lower than the Borjas estimate.[17]

In fact, more recent studies dispute the claim that immigration has played much of a role in wage declines among the lowest educated. In a 2005 paper, Ottaviano and Peri tested 1970–2000 metro-level data on a model quite similar to that used by Borjas.[18] They looked at the wages of native- and foreign-born workers subdivided into eight work-experience groups that were, in turn, divided into four education levels. To make certain that any negative immigration effects are not obscured by the out-migration of affected natives from those cities, the authors' model assumes perfect geographic mobility of workers and firms. However, in contrast to Borjas's work, Ottaviano and Peri add the more realistic assumption that capital stock may not be fixed. That is if, say, immigration helped a city's businesses expand sales and they then responded by investing in new equipment and/or buildings, this effect would be captured by their estimates, but not by those of Borjas. In their findings for the 1990s, Ottaviano and Peri reported that, for every 10 per cent rise in an area's immigration, the average native-born worker's wage increased by 2.7 per cent. Immigration was also associated with positive wage effects for each native education group except high school dropouts. But their estimate of the impact of immigration on native dropouts' average wage (-2.4 per cent) was markedly smaller than that of Borjas.

Impacts on Employment: Empirical Findings

Do immigrants worsen the job prospects of the native born? Most studies suggest that – whether measured by the unemployment rate, employment–population rate, or weeks worked per year – natives' employment does not appear to have been harmed substantially by higher immigration. In an all-too-rare study attempting to gauge the specific effects on youth unemployment, Winegarden and Khor examined state-level figures from the 1980 census.[19] They estimated that a 10 per cent larger share of undocumented immigrants in a state's population was on average associated with 1.3 per cent higher unemployment rate for Whites aged 16 to 24. But this means that it would take a huge 75 per cent jump in the relative size of the local undocumented population to raise Whites' average unemployment rate by 1 percentage point. No displacement effects were found for minority youth, for whom the estimated immigration impact was very small in magnitude and statistically insignificant. The authors checked to see if the lack of any effect on their unemployment rates simply reflected labor force withdrawals, but the relative size of the immigrant population also lacked any significant relationships with either non-participation rates or employment–population ratios.

The lack of sizable adverse employment effects could be (as noted above for wages) simply reflecting a tendency for job displacement to take the form of greater out-migration from high-immigration areas by natives more vulnerable to immigrant competition. But contrary to Filer's findings for the 1970s, Kristin Butcher and David Card show that the dominant 1979–89 pattern was a strong positive correlation between in-migration rates of natives and recent immigration to major metropolitan areas.[20] That is, rapidly growing cities in California, Florida, and Texas drew larger numbers of both native- and foreign-born movers. William Frey recently found a similar pattern among Whites, Asians and Latinos in the 1990s – results at variance with his earlier work which, like Filer, focused on indigenous White workers fleeing high-immigration cities.[21]

More recent census data for 1990, 2000, and 2004 was examined by Rakesh Kochhar to look at what relationship, if any, exists between interstate differences in immigration growth rates since 1990 and changes in each state's employment rates of US-born youth aged 25 to 34.[22] He concluded that there was no consistent relationship between high immigration growth and native youth employment levels. For example, 13 states with above-average immigration in the 1990s also had employment rates of native-born young workers that were above the national average in 2000 (Table 10.1). Those high-growth and high- employment states included Colorado, Georgia, and North Carolina. On the other hand, ten states (including Arizona, Nevada, and Washington) with above-average immigration growth had below-average youth employment rates. In the other set of 27 states with below-average immigration: 13 had above-average native youth employment rates (including Florida, New Jersey, and Texas), but 14 states had below-average youth employment (including California, Ohio, and Pennsylvania). Similar results were found for the full population aged 16 and over, for low- and higher-education natives, and for the years 2000 to 2004. These findings are based on simple correlations that future research should investigate more deeply through regression analysis. But the fact that one-fourth of the workforce is in states with both high immigration and high native employment rates illustrates the need for caution in making strong claims about immigration's negative impacts.

Of course, the fact that most national studies have not found strong negative effects on native jobholding does not mean that individual native workers are never passed over in hiring or displaced from current jobs in favor of immigrants. Some criticize the national studies for operating at too aggregate a level to detect the real consequences of immigration in specific labor markets and industries. A number of case studies of apparel, construction, restaurants, and other industries have shown how successive waves of immigrants can establish their own niches.[23] They then expand and insulate their jobs from competition with natives through ethnic networks that fill nearly all job vacancies. New arrivals from abroad are channelled by

Table 10.1 Immigration Population Growth and Native Youth Employment–Population Rates, by State, 1990–2000

	Foreign-Born Population Growth, 1990–2000	
Native-born Youth (ages 25–34) Employment Rate, 2000:	**BELOW AVERAGE Immigrant Growth**	**ABOVE AVERAGE Immigrant Growth**
ABOVE AVERAGE	CT DC FL HI IL MA MD ME ND NH NJ RI TX VA	CO DE GA IA IN KS MD MN MO MC NE SC WI
BELOW AVERAGE	AK CA LA MI MS MT NM NY OH OK PA VT WV WY	AL AR AZ ID KY NV OR TN UT WA

Source: US Census Bureau PUMS data, 1990–2000; Kochhar (2006).

long-settled friends and relatives to work opportunities in immigrant-owned businesses or in other firms with sizable migrant concentrations. Employers, immigrant or not, come to prefer these networks as low-cost recruitment and screening devices, but this effectively excludes native jobseekers.

In order to look at the rarely studied labor demand side of this issue, I recently directed the New York City Youth Employment Survey. Nowhere in the US are youth employment issues more current than in New York City. With nearly a million young people aged 16 to 24, the city's youth outnumber the total populations of seven states and of every city in the country except the top ten. But New York has another, very troubling distinction: for some years now, barely one-fifth of its teenagers have held jobs in any given week, a rate far below that of the 1960s and well below the national average today. The fact that immigration levels have climbed in the same time span that youth employment has dropped raises the question whether the foreign born may be taking jobs that would otherwise have gone to native-born youth. Long the destination of more immigrants than any other American city, New York saw the foreign-born portion of its population jump from 18.2 per cent in 1970 to 28.4 per cent in 1990, then rising to 36 per cent by 2000 (2.9 million people).

The New York City Youth Employment Survey was a confidential telephone survey funded by the U.S Department of Labor on a probability sample of 424 private sector employers (of 10 or more paid employees). It included a wide array of information on hiring practices, employment changes over the past year, current employment by age, sex, and nativity, and expectations of future hiring.[24]

Among my survey's principal findings were the following. First, statistical analysis found little evidence that immigration plays a major role in lowering the youth employment rate. In order to take into account the variety of different possible influences on youth employment in such a way as to isolate the independent influence of immigration, a multivariate regression model was developed and estimated separately for two dependent variables: 1) the employment share in each establishment of native youth aged 16–19; and 2) the employment share in each establishment of youth aged 20–24. The principal explanatory variables that I tested were:

1. the employment share in each establishment of immigrant workers;
2. business sales or service revenue growth;
3. the minimum number of years of completed schooling required for entry-level positions;
4. minimum number of years of work experience required for entry-level positions;
5. relative importance of soft skills and technical/computer skills in the hiring decision;
6. employer's reliance on informal or formal methods of searching for new workers;
7. employer's recent use of any government programs aimed at improving youth employment;
8. 14 industry control variables were also included in each regression.

The regression analysis produced no large or statistically significant negative relationships between higher immigrant employment shares in each establishment and the fractions of jobs held by either teenagers or older youth. Changes in employment over the past year were also examined, but there were few signs of direct displacement. Downsizing firms were about equally likely to cut the number of immigrants as they were to lay off young workers. Among growing establishments recording new immigrant hires, one-fifth also hired more teens and nearly two-thirds hired more workers in their early twenties. Our survey findings that far fewer expanding firms plan to fill upcoming vacancies with teenagers than with older youth and adults is consistent with this.

Evidence is emerging of similar patterns even among employers like McDonald's. In a study of two Harlem fast-food restaurants, Katherine Newman and Chauncy Lennon found that, out of a sample of 418 jobseekers, 35.8 per cent were youth aged 15 to 18. Over 90 per cent were turned down for the jobs. Those aged 19 to 22 fared much better: they were 27.4 per cent of applicants and 26.4 per cent of hires. And the 37 per cent of applicant aged 23 and over accounted for some 55 per cent of new hires.[25] They concluded that: 'Older workers have been pushed down into a labor market niche that was, not long ago, a youth job.'[26]

Also, my survey findings strongly indicated that the New York economy's weak job growth and structural shifts have been far more important than immigration to young people's labor market problems. The city fell into deep recession early in 1989, over a year ahead of the rest of the country. By 1995, when all but one other major city (Los Angeles) had long since regained at least as many jobs as the recession had erased, New York had still only recovered one-third of all jobs lost. Insofar as firms usually treat youth as a marginal labor pool to make adjustments to demand fluctuations, their hiring will tend to be more sensitive than that of older workers to swings of the business cycle. This has been verified in national time-series studies.[27] New York's sharper and more prolonged economic contractions might thus be expected to exact an especially high toll on its youngest workers. Young jobseekers increasingly find themselves in competition with displaced older youth and adult workers. The latter have seen their full-time jobs threatened if not eliminated by the mergers of large banks, the shrinkage of hospitals reeling from Medicaid cuts and Health Maintenance Organization (HMO) competitors, and public sector cutbacks forced by the city's current fiscal crisis. Most national studies of employer demand have concluded that young workers tend to be more labor substitutes than complements with adults.[28]

EXPLAINING THE FINDINGS

What then explains the fact that such a large body of national studies shows little or no net impact of immigration on natives' wages or employment? First, immigration does not just expand the supply of labor, it also increases demand. Immigrant expenditures on consumer goods, cars, and houses generate multiplier effects rippling through the economy to spur job growth for natives as well. A growing volume of studies by economists, sociologists, and geographers have attested to the importance of new immigrants to urban commerce and housing markets.[29] For example, in New York City in the 1990s, in-migration exceeded the city's out-migration by about 36,000, raising the population to over 8 million, its highest ever. But this growth was solely due to immigration replenishing a city losing its native-born older people. One of every two newborn children in New York has immigrant parents and foreign-born homebuyers account for nearly half of all newly occupied housing. Even the lowest-educated migrant group from Mexico has an average household income 85 per cent that of the citywide norm, thanks largely to more and longer-working earners per household.[30]

Immigration can also expand natives' consumer demand insofar as it helps lower prices or restrain price hikes on the goods and services that immigrant workers produce. And the growth of immigrant concentrations in cities like New York, Los Angeles, and Miami draws foreign capital here, as businesses in their homelands seek to become part of these expanding markets. Industry case studies are too narrow to capture these broader effects.[31]

Immigrants also average higher self-employment rates, creating their own business demand for related business services and materials, often from non-immigrant suppliers. While this increases labor market segmentation, immigrant niches absorb workers who might otherwise have to compete with natives for jobs elsewhere. New research by Jonathan Schwabish and Jane Lynch has found that, 'between 1990 and 2000, the number of self-employed workers in New York City grew by 2.9 per cent. In the first period of analysis—between 1985 and 1990—over 28,000 of workers moving to New York City were self-employed, accounting for 6 per cent of migrants to the city.'[32] Between 1995 and 2000, this number had risen by 13 per cent – that is, self-employed immigrants increased at over four times the rate of non-immigrants. Clearly, not all national-origin groups are as prone to self-employment as the Chinese, Cubans, Iranians, and Koreans.[33] But research that has compared native- and foreign-born persons of any particular ethno-racial group indicates that foreign-born persons of the same group tend to display higher self-employment rates.[34] Additional research has found that Cubans and Koreans experienced an improvement in annual earnings tied to self-employment, while no such improvement was experienced by Chinese or Blacks.[35]

Higher immigrant self-employment may also act to partially mitigate the impacts that low educational and language attainment might otherwise have on both immigrant workers and non-immigrants in the same labor market. Pyong Gap Min's research has shown how small business ownership provides a means for well-educated Korean immigrants who are limited by their lack of English language ability to reproduce their middle class status.[36] According to the Schwabish-Lynch study:

> For those who arrive with relatively little education and few financial assets, self-employment can play an invaluable role in creating broader economic opportunities by helping individuals to overcome labor force disadvantages, including exclusion from professional networks, lack of American diplomas,

> and limited English proficiency. Within the context of enclaves, in which a relatively high number of co-nationals reside, self-employment provides international migrants with the opportunity to provide certain goods or services to their co-nationals at a comparative advantage relative to natives or other migrants.[37]

Still another explanation is that many of the most recent immigrants are imperfect substitutes with native workers, or even complements, since they take the harshest, low-status work that even low-wage natives tend to spurn. This is apparently a view widely shared by the public. In the Pew Center's 2006 nationwide opinion survey, 65 per cent said that immigrants take jobs that Americans don't want – compared to just 24 per cent who thought that they 'take jobs away from American citizens.'[38]

Finally, there is mounting evidence that many immigrants – far from being a uniformly docile, anti-union workforce ripe for endless employer abuse – are at least as willing as the native born to take collective action for better wages and working conditions. The number of foreign-born union members increased by 48 per cent, to 1.8 million, between 1996 and 2003.[39] In sharp contrast, native-born union membership declined by 5.7 per cent in this same period. It is indicative of their rapid labor force growth (as well as the stiff obstacles to union organizing) that immigrants' union density still fell, from 12.1 per cent unionized in 1996 to 10.2 per cent seven years later. Many immigrants, including the undocumented, have played leading roles in a number of major recent organizing drives, including the successful campaigns to unionize office building cleaners ('Justice for Janitors'), health care aides, limousine drivers and food service workers.[40]

Many labor unions are increasingly recognizing the crucial importance to their future of overcoming their past practices of indifference, and often hostility, toward migrant workers. In the fall of 2000, the AFL-CIO formally shifted its support to a new federal amnesty program for qualified undocumented immigrants and demanded that they be guaranteed 'full workplace rights.' At the same time, it supported more effective border enforcement and new policies of skill upgrading for native-born workers. In so doing, the AFL-CIO has also criticized the IRCA law's employer sanctions as the worst of both worlds: posing no serious deterrent to employer violators, but enabling too many employers to use the mandatory I-9 forms as a means to discriminate against some job candidates and threaten employees who seek union representation.

Those unions committed to active organizing and member mobilization are reaching out as seldom before to the foreign-born worker. For example, while the building trades unions have historically been among the least receptive to the undocumented, they have increasingly sought Spanish-speaking organizers to improve their outreach efforts. According to Tony

Martinez, a Salvadoran organizer hired by a New York local of the Carpenters Union: 'A lot of these concrete contractors were hiring undocumented workers. We don't have anything against undocumented workers; I'm an immigrant myself. Neither does our council nor the international. Our mission is to organize all the carpenters, to elevate the standard of living for all carpenters.' [41]

Racial, ethnic and gender divisions persist in unions as in society at large, and few immigrants have as yet moved into union leadership positions. For some undocumented workers, an increasingly important complement to (or occasionally, substitute for) traditional labor unions have been community-based 'worker centers.' Over one hundred worker centers are now in operation across the country. Among the more established in the New York City metropolitan area are the Chinese Staff and Workers Association and Restaurant Opportunities Center of New York, and Long Island's Workplace Project. These and others typically combine job placement, legal assistance and language training with activism over worker rights, fair hiring practices and labor law violations. They have been especially active among lightly unionized workers like landscaping day laborers, taxi drivers and household cleaners. And they have played a major role in a few major local and statewide legislative victories, like New York State's Unpaid Wages Prohibition Act, setting substantial penalties against employers who refuse to pay for all hours worked, regardless of the laborer's immigration status.[42] In August 2006, the AFL-CIO clearly recognized the importance of such organizations by signing a partnership agreement with the National Day Laborer Organizing Network (NDLON).[43] The agreement gives NDLON, the nation's largest day laborer organization, non-voting representation on AFL-CIO Central Labor Councils and greater voice in union efforts to represent the lowest-paid migrant workers.

CONCLUDING REMARKS

American public attitudes on whether to ease or restrict immigration have fluctuated sharply over time. After the 1990–91 US recession and the conservative Congressional victories of 1994, a more restrictive period began. New legislation was passed in 1996 to strip most immigrants of important legal protections, exclude them from public assistance programs, impose higher income tests on Americans wishing to sponsor them, and limit claims for political asylum. The record-breaking economic boom of the late 1990s muted demands for further restrictions and drew larger undocumented inflows into a larger number of communities, urban and suburban, than ever before. The fact that record-breaking immigration occurred at the same time as the wage growth and low unemployment of the 1990s boom seemed for a time powerful evidence against immigration's critics. But once the boom ended in early 2001, and the subsequent slow recovery proved the weakest in decades, immigration came in for renewed criticism. While many blamed the weak economy on a national fiscal policy more focused on tax cuts for high incomes and high-tech military contracts than on job creation, others decried the country's porous borders.

Even five years into a slow economic recovery, most Americans in 2006 felt high anxiety about their own standard of living. A national opinion survey found that 56 per cent worried that 'jobs are difficult to find in this community.'[44] Even those with full-time work were affected. Average wages dropped by two per cent, after inflation adjustment, between 2003 and 2006 – only the third span of prolonged real wage decline since World War II. Moreover, unlike the 1970s and 1980s wage slumps, most workers now have added concerns about the rising costs and eroding coverage of their health insurance and pension plans. It is understandable, then, that many might look with concern on record-setting volumes of immigration so large that they account for one-half of recent labor force growth.

Economists have in recent years directed increasing research efforts to evaluating the economic implications of immigration for native-born workers. A lively debate continues among them about the precise costs and benefits of current immigration for different age and skill sectors of the country's workforce. But to date, most systematic research has found that there do not appear to be large net negative impacts of immigration on either the average wages or employment of the native born. Of course, these findings only refer to current levels of immigration; there are no guarantees that immigration's benefits would always offset its costs at dramatically higher levels.

This is by no means to deny that there may be some negative effects today on some groups, particularly high school dropouts, who account for about 9 per cent of today's workforce. Anything harming the prospects of this most vulnerable group warrants serious concern and prompt remedies, even if the estimated effect is relatively small (about 2.4 per cent lower annual native wages).[45]

Even if immigration law was better designed and enforced, it appears to offer false hope of making a qualitative difference to the declining fortunes of much of the low-wage workforce. But a host of policy options may offer far more realistic prospects of long-term benefits to non-college workers, young and old. I have written in detail elsewhere about some policy alternatives for a more progressive immigration approach.[46] At a minimum, rather than either highly liberalized or highly restrictive policies, a realistic progressive approach would combine a humanitarian admissions system with adequate protections of labor and living standards both here and abroad. The federal government, which alone controls immigration policy, could provide the states in which new arrivals concentrate the financial aid needed to expand their services accordingly; it could also provide generous job and training assistance to any native-born workers found to be harmed by past immigration flows.

Improved border controls will never be enough to slow illegal migration markedly from desperately poor nations. That will probably require new efforts to influence the American demand and the foreign supply. The fairest and most efficient way to curtail US employers' preferences for the undocumented may be to start aggressively enforcing health, safety, and other workplace labor standards, raise the minimum wage above its present poverty level, and change labor laws to encourage greater unionization. This will reduce the competitive advantage of many firms relying on exploited migrants at the same time that it betters the lot of both native- and legal foreign-born workers.

On the supply side, to reduce the need of so many Third World workers to emigrate, a frank reassessment is needed of the historic role of the United States's foreign military and financial policies in themselves creating large displaced populations. The US could begin leading other rich nations in funding projects that foster sustainable development and job growth in poor nations that are leading sources of immigration today.[47] This could be partially financed by imposing 'social tariffs' on the products of multinational companies whose labor and environmental standards are below acceptable levels.[48] Renegotiation of NAFTA and CAFTA to establish serious penalties against employers violating such standards might be an optimal starting point. Likewise, aggressive debt relief to aid developing countries now burdened by billions in foreign debt could have important long-term benefits to the donors and the recipients alike.

NOTES

1. Batty (2006), 1.
2. Papademetriou (2006).
3. For program details and recent policy debates see DeFreitas (2006a).
4. US Bureau of the Census (2003, August 2006).
5. Passel and Suro, (2005).
6. Author's calculations from census data in Gibson and Lennon (1999) and US Bureau of the Census (2003).

7. For a summary of the major recent changes in immigration law, see DeFreitas (2002).
8. Passel (2005a). See his description here and in his references to the data and methods used in estimating the unauthorized population.
9. Pew Hispanic Center conducted the survey in February–March 2006 among a nationwide sample of 2000 adults, supplemented by another 800 sampled in five large metropolitan areas. For details, see Pew Hispanic Center (2006).
10. Ibid.
11. National Research Council (1997), 6.
12. See DeFreitas (1988, 1991). Altonji and Card's (1991) study of less-skilled workers yielded mostly insignificant coefficient estimates for the effect of immigrant population share on natives' weekly wages, whether in 1970 and 1980 cross-sections or in a simple 1970–80 first-difference model. The notable exception was a significant elasticity estimate of -.086 in an instrumental variables model. However, the instrument they chose for the decadal change in the local immigrant density was the immigrant density in 1970. Given the highly dubious value of this instrument, the resulting elasticity estimate should probably be taken as a questionable upper bound.
13. Borjas (1999, 2003).
14. Lalonde and Topel (1991), 297.
15. Fix and Passel (1994); Funkhauser and Trejo (1995).
16. Briggs (2001).
17. Orrenius and Zavodny (2003).
18. Ottaviano and Peri (2005).
19. Winegarden and Khor (1991).
20. Butcher and Card (1991).
21. Frey (2005).
22. Kochhar (2006).
23. Waldinger (1985); Bailey (1987); Grenier, *et al.* (1992). See also Levitan, Chapter 3, this volume.
24. For survey details and full regression results and analysis, see DeFreitas (1996).
25. Similarly high acceptance rates were enjoyed by immigrant Blacks, only 11 per cent of applicants but 26 per cent of hires.
26. Newman and Lennon (1995).
27. See Freeman (1992) and DeFreitas (1991).
28. See, for example, Hamermesh (1985) and Costrell *et al.* (1986).
29. See, for example, Aldrich and Waldinger (1990); Myers (1999); Gober (2000); and Lofstrom (2002).
30. New York City Planning Dept. (2004).
31. Cross-industry studies of individual cities suffer fewer disadvantages, but have so far been rare. Perhaps the most influential has been Card's (1990) paper on the impacts of the sudden influx of 125,000 Cubans from the port of Mariel in May–September 1980. He found virtually no effect on the wages or unemployment rates of less-skilled workers, even among Cubans who had immigrated earlier.'
32. Schwabish and Lynch (2005).
33. Tarry Hum's (2005) study of New York City found that the self-employment rate among all New Yorkers in 2000 was 9 per cent. But for foreign-born Blacks, it was notably lower at only 6 per cent while for Asians, it was higher, especially for Korean immigrants, where nearly one in four (21 per cent) was self-employed. The immigrant self-employed were also concentrated in specific industries. For example, a little more than half of the Korean self-employed were in one of six industries – dry cleaning and laundry, grocery stores, nail salons, construction, taxi and limousine service, and restaurants. Self-employed Asian Indian immigrants were similarly concentrated in a handful of industries, including restaurants, newspaper distribution, and hotels. See also Light and Gold (2000).
34. Light (2000); Lofstrom (2002).

35. Portes and Min (1996).
36. Min (1996).
37. Schwabish and Lynch (2005).
38. Pew Hispanic Center (2006).
39. Migration Policy Institute (2004). For economic research showing similar unionization propensities among immigrant and native youth, see DeFreitas (1993).
40. See, for example, the accounts in Delgado (2000) and Ness (2005).
41. Antonio Martinez, quoted in DeFreitas (2006).
42. See the account of this legislative campaign by Jennifer Gordon, first director of the Workplace Project (now a Fordham University Law School professor), in Gordon (2005).
42. Greenhouse (2006).
44. Pew Hispanic Center (2006).
45. DeFreitas (1991).
46. DeFreitas (1998).
47. See, for example, the papers in Bohning and Schloeter-Pareded (1994).
48. Of course, this and other policy proposals are highly controversial and require far more careful and lengthy discussion than the space limitations of this paper permit.

11. Unauthorized Mexican Immigration and Youth Labor Market Outcomes in California in the 1990s

Enrico A. Marcelli

Our present political preoccupation with the putative adverse fiscal and labor market effects of unauthorized immigration is neither new nor accompanied by much empirical evidence. This statement is perhaps surprising to those unfamiliar with how demographer-economists and sociologists estimate such effects and requires some elaboration. In this chapter, after first providing some background to our immigration debates, I then investigate both US census data and a recent large California immigration survey to estimate the decadal trends in educational attainment, occupation distribution, industry distribution, and hourly earnings of unauthorized Mexican immigrant male and other workers. By looking separately at different age groups and major ethno-racial-nativity groups, as well as estimating statistically their wage impacts, the findings may help clarify immigration's current implications for young Californians' future employment. Overall, the findings suggest that unauthorized Mexican male workers do not appear to have significantly lowered the wages of younger workers in California in recent years.

BACKGROUND

The earliest example of how residents of what would eventually become the United States of America embraced newcomers selectively is found in the colonial response to the decision of the British imperial government to export convicts and paupers, many of whom were youthful males. The colonists resented England's generally restrictive position toward European immigration to the colonies during the 17th and 18th centuries, that is, its effort to rid itself of less desirable residents was viewed suspiciously on this side of the Atlantic. In short, and contrary to conventional wisdom that US immigration policy has consistently moved linearly in the liberal direction, local and regional efforts by colonists to resist imperial immigration laws may be interpreted as the first contemporary example of how this is not the case.[1]

The nation's founders, for instance, actively sought to secure those who were more likely to help build a new nation or at least advance colonial economic interests, and convicted criminals and the poor were understandably not high on their preference list. The usual story we tell ourselves is that selective immigration policy did not emerge until the late 19th and early 20th centuries with the exclusion of Chinese immigrants upon completion of the transcontinental railroad, and the instituting of strict national quotas based on the widely held yet flimsy belief that eastern and southern Europeans were less intelligent than 'Nordic' types. However, this historical interpretation of US immigration policy is highly questionable.[2] Elsewhere I have argued that what is alternatively termed illegal, undocumented, or unauthorized immigration is an institution established by US policy rather than an unintended consequence of failed US policies or simply the sum of all individual unauthorized immigrants.[3] This distinction is important for immigration and immigrant policy formation, even when trying to estimate how an influx of a certain number of 'illegal aliens' influences the employment and wage outcomes of other US-resident workers.[4] Adverse fiscal or labor market effects of unauthorized immigrants, should any be detected, in other words, may partly reflect decades of immigration and other policies rather than simply the number, or some innate undesirable characteristic, of immigrants.

In any event, another century would pass before, in the late 1970s, the United States began to distinguish legal from unauthorized immigrants explicitly (for example, not by ethno-racial or national origin) in its national-level immigration policy discussions. And it was not until 1986 and 1996 that the first two immigration laws in US history were passed that directly articulated methods of and reasons for restricting illegal immigration. It is generally agreed that the methods of the former – penalties on employers that knowingly hire unauthorized immigrant workers, legalization of 2.7 million unauthorized immigrants, and more resources for border enforcement were not effective at slowing illegal immigration.

CURRENT DEMOGRAPHIC AND ECONOMIC CONTEXT

Thus, by the early 1990s arguments for restricting illegal immigration slowly but not completely shifted away from the labor market competition and labor productivity stories and toward the idea that unauthorized immigrants drain the United States, or at least particular locales such as California, fiscally. Rather than replacing the labor market competition/productivity version of the argument against illegal immigration however, the negative fiscal impact version was and remains complementary – immigrants not only steal jobs and drive down wages, but when they are employed they are still poor and take more in public services than they contribute through culture, entrepreneurship, or income taxes.[5]

And yet our two most sophisticated demographic estimation methodologies (to be outlined below) intimate that the fiscal approach has been no more effective than the labor market approach (at least in terms of how these policies have been implemented) at reducing the number of unauthorized immigrants entering and remaining in the United States during the past decade. The number of unauthorized immigrants residing in the United States, for instance, is estimated to have risen from about 4 million in 1990 to 5–6 million by the mid-1990s, to 12 million in the mid-2000s.[6] Within the leading recipient state of California and focusing on Latino immigrants only, I have estimated that the number of unauthorized Mexican immigrants (UMI) and other Latino immigrants (ULI) has risen steadily despite several highly selective state-level immigration initiatives and federal-level policy changes during the previous decade. While it appears that there was a three-year downward trend beginning in 1996, it is uncertain what proportions of this are attributable to policy changes and worsening macroeconomic conditions, and this only lasted until 1999.

The overall rise in the number of UMI and ULI in California is estimated to have been between 61 and 75 per cent, or from about 1.1 to 2.3 million. The precise figure depends on whether one applies legal status predictors obtained from logistic regression analysis of the 1994 or the 2001 Los Angeles County Mexican Immigrant Residency Status Survey (LAC-MIRSS) data to US census data since 1996. This date is significant as it marks the passage of the Illegal Immigration Reform and Immigrant Responsibility Act (IIRIRA) in August and the Personal Responsibility and Work Opportunity Reconciliation Act (PRWORA) in September. Should some version of President George W. Bush's proposed legalization/guestworker program become law, a similar number of UMI who were legalized in the US via the Immigration Reform and Control Act (IRCA) of 1986 (about two million) would be eligible and in California this time around.

The search for the negative labor market effects of 'immigrants' has shifted somewhat during the past two decades from a consideration of how all foreign-born resident workers (including naturalized US citizens) in certain regions or states within the United States impact the job and wage outcomes of other workers by educational attainment or occupation, to analyses of how particular immigrant groups (for example, Mexican immigrants) affect others' (young non-Latino Black, other Latino, high school dropouts) labor market outcomes.[7] Most recently, partly because the bulk of evidence indicates that specific immigrant groups or all immigrants taken together have only negligible labor market effects, some researchers have begun to analyze immigrant worker effects in the entire US labor market rather than in particular metropolitan areas or states.

In the light of policy debates concerning illegal immigration that began in the late 1970s during the Carter administration, which produced the 1986 IRCA and the 1996 illegal immigrant and welfare acts cited above, there have only been a handful of studies that have used credible estimation methodologies to investigate the labor market effects of unauthorized immigrants, and none have targeted one group of workers one would expect to be substitutes – young workers.[8] Given that younger workers are less educated and have less labor market experience than older workers on average, and that the geographic concentration of unauthorized Mexican immigrants is estimated to have risen in California during the past decade, in this study we focus exclusively on UMI and other California residents' human capital.[9] For instance, the proportional concentration of UMI male workers in the San Francisco Bay Area increased considerably between 1990 and 2000. This pattern is more prominent in this area as well as the Los Angeles and San Diego metropolitan areas, but is also observed throughout the state. There are thus good reasons to suspect that UMIs compete with other California residents for jobs or wages.

DATA AND METHODS

Below I apply demographic predictors (age, gender, education, years residing in the United States) of unauthorized residency status obtained from the 1994 and 2001 Los Angeles County Mexican Immigrant Legal Status Surveys (LAC-MIRSS) to foreign-born Mexican males enumerated in the 1990 and 2000 US Public Use Microdata Samples (PUMS) to estimate the decadal trends in 1) educational attainment, 2) occupation distribution, 3) industry distribution, and 4) hourly earnings of unauthorized Mexican immigrant male and other workers (aged 16–24, 25–44, and 45–64 years) by major ethno-racial-nativity group (other immigrant, US-born Latino, non-Latino US-born Asian, non-Latino US-born Black, and non-Latino US-born White). Motivated by previous work on how authorized and unauthorized immigrants influence others' labor market outcomes, a second stage of the analysis estimates the relationship between the inflow of UMI workers between 1990 and 2000 and hourly wages among workers aged

16–24 years in California using ordinary least squares (OLS).[10] The take-home message is that the immigration of UMI into California during the 1990s is estimated to have had trivial effects on the wages of males aged 16–24 years in 2000 – both collectively and by ethno-racial group.

Although a more detailed description of the 1994 and 2001 LAC-MIRSS data is provided in several recent publications, I will briefly outline how these were collected and how we employ the survey-based estimation methodology developed by demographer David M. Heer and colleagues during the 1990s.[11] The more commonly employed residual or composite estimation methodology enables researchers to generate estimates of the number of unauthorized immigrants by nation of origin and US state of residence, but does not provide information beyond numbers and location. Alternatively, a relative new technique soon to be called the 'grouped answers approach' and still being validated is similar to the survey-based method in its effort to measure individual unauthorized immigrant status by asking a serious of indirect questions about legal status in large surveys such as the 2004 General Social Survey.[12]

The 1994 and 2001 LAC-MIRSS data were collected randomly from households within approximately 100 census blocks that were randomly selected from census tracts in which it was estimated that at least 25 per cent of the population was foreign-born Mexican. One advantage of the 2001 data was that questions concerning participation in the 2000 Census could be asked and analyzed to help government researchers in their most recent report on illegal immigration to correct for the underenumeration of unauthorized immigrants in the United States.[13]

Once inside households with at least one foreign-born Mexican adult, interviewers asked questions concerning migration experience (including whether the interviewee was a naturalized citizen, legal permanent resident, or non-immigrant visa holder), labor market experience, social networks, and access to health insurance and medical care.[14] Authorized or unauthorized immigrant residency status predictors were then estimated for each female and male adult separately by regressing reported legal status in the LAC-MIRSS data on four demographic variables that are also included in the 1990 and 2000 PUMS data. Importantly, all four demographic explanatory variables were obtained from questions worded almost identically to those in the 1990 and 2000 censuses. The next step in this methodology involved ranking each foreign-born Mexican female and male adult enumerated in the 1990 and 2000 PUMS data separately in descending order by the estimated probability of having been unauthorized, and then tagging each individual as legal or unauthorized. Probabilities were obtained by applying the demographic legal status predictors generated from the 1994 and 2001 LAC-MIRSS data to foreign-born Mexican adults enumerated in the 1990 and 2000 PUMS data. Rather than arbitrarily selecting some probability threshold (for example, 60 per cent) for tagging an individual as unauthorized, we assigned unauthorized status, beginning at the top of our ranked probabilities and moving downward, to the number of Mexican immigrants, who came closest to the sum of all probabilities by gender. In other words, the estimated numbers of adult Mexican female and male immigrants tagged as unauthorized in our weighted PUMS data approximate the number estimated directly from our weighted LAC-MIRSS samples as well as the sum of the probabilities of having been unauthorized in the PUMS data.[15]

The final step of our analysis uses this information to compare UMI and other California male workers descriptively and to estimate econometrically whether male UMI workers were more likely to have been substitutes or complements with their legal resident co-workers in California.

EMPIRICAL FINDINGS

Workers in Different Occupational Groups

Not only are increasing numbers of UMI males aged 16–64 years estimated to have been coming to and settling in California during the 1990s, but they also appear to have surpassed the number of relatively young male workers (16–24 years) in the state. The approximate number of UMI males rose from over 300,000 in 1990 to nearly 570,000 by 2000 (Table 11.1). Meanwhile, the number of non-UMI male workers aged 16–24 years decreased over the decade by about 50,000, to an estimated total of 550,000 by 2000). The only other ethno-racial-nativity group to have experienced a substantial increase was US-born Latinos. While such population estimates are provocative, they tell us almost nothing about whether male UMI have been displacing or replacing relatively young California workers.

Of course, workers from members of various other foreign- and US-born groups entered and left California during the 1990s. Though Table 11.1 cannot fully reflect this, it does provide some additional information about those non-UMI male workers who remained and may have competed directly with UMI males. These descriptive data suggest that UMI males aged 16 to 64 were most similar to US-born Latino and other immigrant workers in terms of hourly earnings and demographic characteristics. In 2000, for example, UMI males earned 39 per cent of the wages of US-born Non-Latino Whites and US-born Latinos earned 63 per cent. Other immigrants earned 75 per cent, US-born non-Latino Asians earned 96 per cent, and US-born non-Latino Blacks earned 71 per cent of the US-born non-Latino White mean wage. UMI were also most similar to US-born Latinos in terms of their age profile and fell in between US-born Latinos and US-born non-Latino Whites in marriage rate. UMI male workers had a very high proportion with at most a middle-school education (74 per cent in 2000). The next worse outcome on education was for other immigrants, 34 per cent of whom did not have any high school experience.

Lastly, although there were very small differences in the percentage working full time between the groups, UMI and other immigrant males were much less likely to have held 'white collar' jobs and more likely to have had 'other collar' jobs – those best characterized as agricultural, service-oriented, or operators, fabricators, and laborers. These results suggest that it is with US-born Latinos and non-Latino immigrant workers that UMI males are most likely to have been competing in the labor market. Additional analysis by country of birth (not shown here) reveals that UMI male workers were most similar to other Latino immigrants – a result that is consistent with previous research for Los Angeles County in 1990.[16]

Figure 11.2 provides more detailed information about occupational distribution for 2000 than table 11.1, which simply reported occupational distribution by 'collar' (that is, white, blue, other). UMI males appear to have been overrepresented compared to other youth workers in Agriculture (43 per cent versus 2.5 per cent), Service (22 per cent versus 17 per cent), Precision-Craft-Repair (23 per cent versus 18 per cent), and Laborer (31 per cent versus 23 per cent) occupations, but underrepresented in Technical Sales and Administrative Support occupations (9 per cent versus 31 per cent) as well as Managerial and Professional positions (3 per cent versus 10 per cent). The small percentage of UMI males in management is explained by their disproportionately high representation in agricultural management (Figure 11.2). We also see from this figure results that are unsurprising given what ethnographic research has taught us about occupational segregation among unauthorized Mexican immigrants in California. Among the 33 occupations ranked in descending order of UMI representation, we observe that there were higher proportions of UMI in eight (that is, farming, food and service, cleaning and maintenance, material moving, production, construction trades, agricultural management, motor vehicle operator and production).

In general, these results suggest that UMI male workers have jobs that are typically more physically demanding and socially less desirable compared to non-UMI youth workers in California. But once more, whether UMI male workers are competing with other relatively young male California workers or simply filling jobs that are deemed culturally undesirable is not discernible here. All we may conclude from the results so far is that these two groups of workers have quite different levels of human

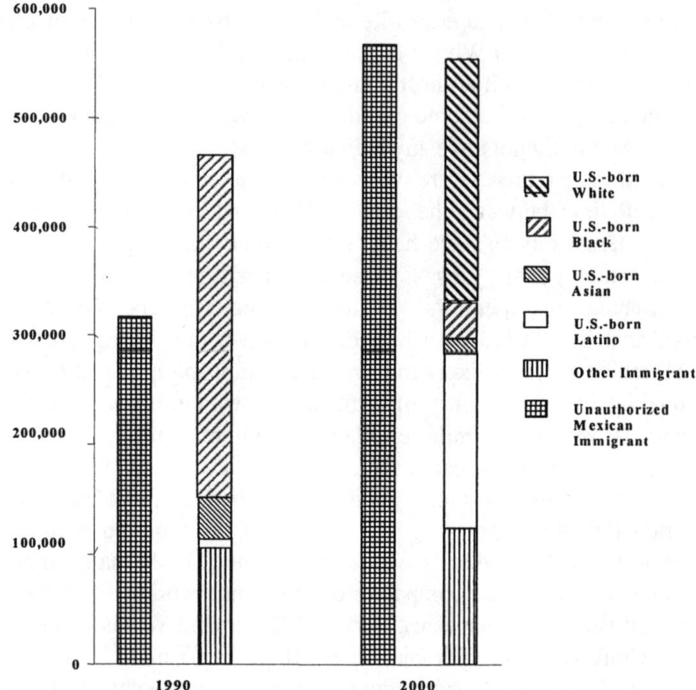

Figure 11.1 Number of Unauthorized Mexican Immigrant Male (aged 16–64 years) and Other Young Male (aged 16–24 years) Workers in California, 1990–2000

capital and are employed in quite different occupations. It is not a foregone conclusion however, that human capital 'endowments' are driving the apparent labor market segmentation.[17] Structural barriers to and opportunities for employment for UMI workers (for example, phenotype, lax enforcement of employer sanctions, disproportionate power of employers given UMI fear of deportation) may also be at work.

A final graph (Figure 11.3) suggests that the relationship between the influx of recent UMI males to California and the change in inflation-adjusted mean wages by selected occupations from 1990 to 2000 was inverse. Specifically, the proportional representation of recent UMI males (X axis) appears to have been negatively associated with the percentage change in mean wages (Y axis) by major occupational category. However, the only decline in real wages is estimated to have occurred in farming, forestry, and fishing – an occupational group where more than one in four were UMI male. The more UMI males in an occupation who arrived during the 1990s, the lower the rise in the inflation-adjusted mean hourly earnings among other youthful males. The same conclusion regarding causation discussed above is warranted once again. Whether UMI males are driving down wages in certain occupations, thus contributing to their lower social status and replacing young California male workers, is questionable. It may be that as younger workers' educational opportunities, cultural conditioning, and labor market opportunities improve, they are less inclined to perform low-paying manual labor that UMI males willingly accept.

Wage Rate Comparisons

The last step of our analysis investigates econometrically whether the flow of UMI males during the 1990s was negatively related to other workers' hourly earnings in 2000. Although we do not employ instruments for the number of UMI who entered various occupations during the 1990s in an effort to suggest causal direction as past studies have, our results are consistent with their finding of negligible wage effects.[18]

Our sample includes all UMI males estimated to have been in the 2000 California labor market and young workers (16–24 years-old). Although UMI males represented a mere 8 per cent of all employed males in California in 2000, once we restrict our sample to other workers between the ages of 16 and 24 years, a larger proportion (52 per cent) of the sample is UMI. Partly a consequence of this sample's young age, only 39 per cent were married, but fully 52 per cent had not earned a high school degree. Before collapsing wholesale and resale trades into one industry category, manufacturing had the highest proportion of workers (18 per cent). Alternatively, information industries, finance, insurance and real estate (FIRE), and health and social services had the smallest representation. Most relevant to this study, the mean number of UMI males who entered California's labor market(s) during the 1990s was 18,209. Furthermore, the numbers entering the six major non-military occupation groups during 1990s were ranked as follows – 5,600 in management, 17,800 in technical, 30,000 in agricultural, 47,200 in craft, 57,500 in service, and 63,500 in laborer occupations.

We first report results of regressing the hourly wages of all males aged 16–24 years in 2000 on the number of UMI having entered during the 1990s controlling for various individual characteristics (age, ethno-racial group, marital status, education, and industry) in the first column of Table 11.2. Although a very small amount of the variation in wages is explained by this model, we see that several demographic characteristics (being older, Asian, and married) as well human capital characteristics (education) were positively related to hourly wages. But most importantly for our purposes, we estimate that UMI males who entered California's labor market during the 1990s had a very small negative effect on others' hourly earnings. As mentioned in the introduction to this chapter, this finding is consistent with past studies that have employed instrumental variable techniques.[19] By observing the results reported in columns 2 through 6, we further see that although the adverse effects of UMI on others' wages is greatest among US-born Black male workers aged 16–24 years, even this effect is miniscule and its statistical significance is relatively low compared to the parameters estimated for other groups. So while we are able to detect a negative relationship between wages and the number of UMI who entered California to work by major occupation during the 1990s, this relation is trivial. Unauthorized Mexican male workers do not appear to have driven down the wages of younger workers in California during the intercensal years.

DISCUSSION

There is a clear picture of the human capital characteristics and labor market outcomes of unauthorized Mexican immigrant (UMI) male workers in California during the 1990s compared to other non-UMI young workers. And there are two competing hypotheses that remain unanswered in this chapter. First, in general UMI males and other males have very different age profiles, levels of educational attainment, and occupational distributions. UMI males were younger, had lower levels of education, and filled less socially esteemed jobs compared to other young male workers in California. Second, average earnings in the major occupational categories were negatively related to the occupational concentration of UMI males.

Third, whether this segmented labor market story is best understood as emanating from a neoclassical economic analytical framework – that is, one that sees such segmentation as a direct result of different human capital endowments – or a more institutional analytical framework which sees such segmentation as the result of both human capital endowments and various structural barriers and opportunities, requires a more econometrically sophisticated design than we have attempted above. But these findings are consistent with studies that adopted such designs in the past. Most importantly, there have been too few systematic studies of unauthorized immigrants' impacts on earnings and employment in the United States. Part of the explanation rests in the paucity of relevant data. These shortages, combined with the illegal immigration policy debates in the US Congress since 2006, suggest that this will be fertile ground for future research.

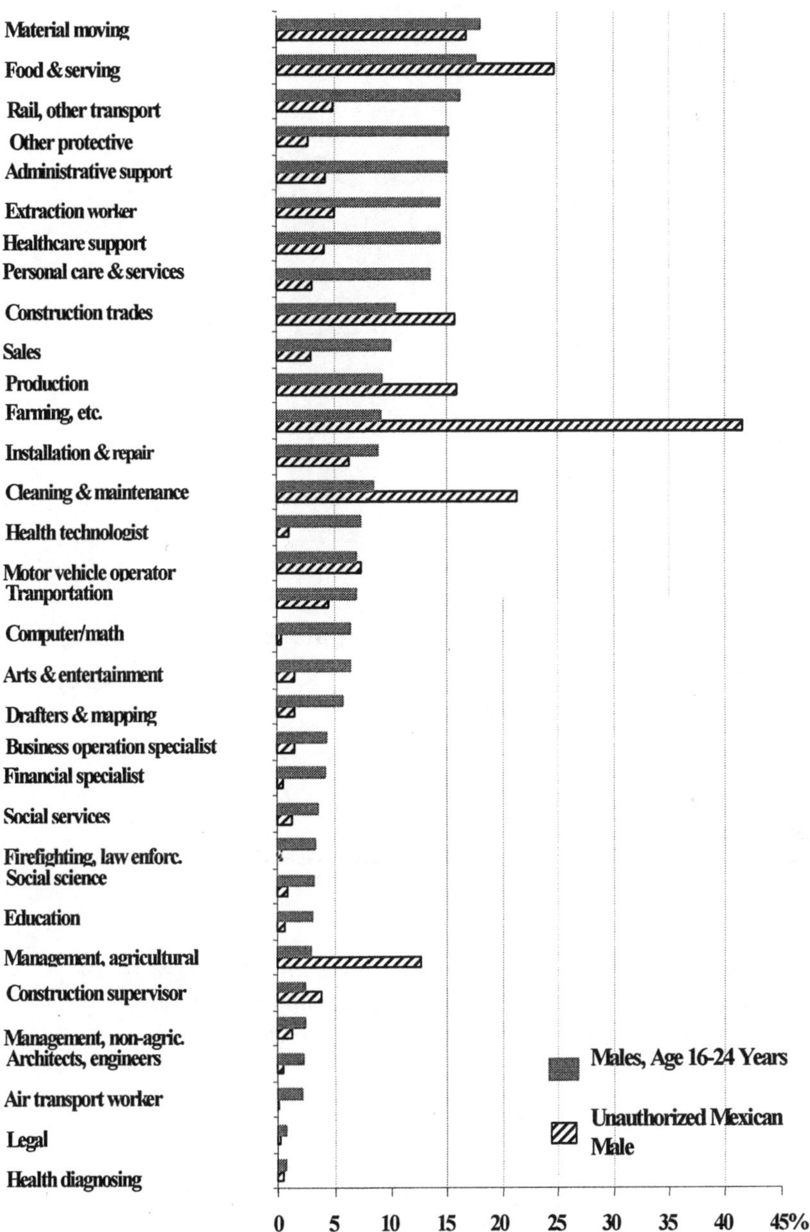

Figure 11.2 Unauthorized Mexican Immigrant Male and Other Workers by Detailed Occupational Category, California, 2000 (%)

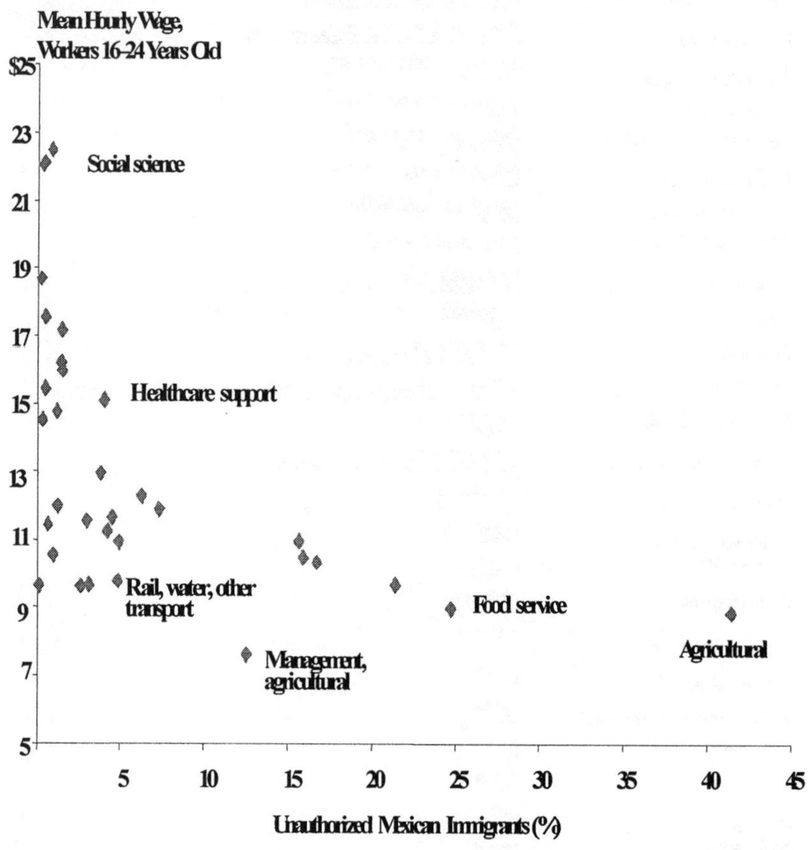

Figure 11.3 *Mean Hourly Earnings of Male Workers Aged 16–24 Years and Per cent Male Unauthorized Mexican Immigrant Workers, by Selected Occupational Category, California, 2000*

Table 11.1 Demographic and Labor Market Characteristics of Unauthorized Mexican Immigrant Male (aged 16–64 years) and Other Male (aged 16–24 years) Workers in California, 1990–2000

	Unauthorized Mexican Immigrant		Other Immigrant		US-born Latino		US-born Asian		US-born Black		US-born White	
	1990	2000	1990	2000	1990	2000	1990	2000	1990	2000	1990	2000
WAGE	$7.53	$11.36	$14.61	$21.60	$13.94	$17.97	$18.15	$27.40	$14.60	$20.23	$19.63	$28.78
Age												
16-24	41.7%	27.1%	9.2%	6.6%	17.9%	22.6%	9.1%	11.6%	11.5%	10.0%	8.4%	6.5%
25-44	52.9	66.5	63.5	58.9	59.8	56.1%	62.0	59.0%	59.5%	56.5%	59.9%	51.4%
45-64	5.4	6.4	27.3	34.5	22.3	21.3%	28.9	29.4%	28.9%	33.5%	31.8%	42.0%
Married	50.4%	57.7%	69.6%	69.6%	56.5%	49.6%	56.8%	50.2%	49.5%	47.7%	62.2%	60.7%
Education												
Middle School	79.5%	74.5%	40.0%	35.2%	27.9%	24.8%	6.8%	4.5%	14.6%	12.6%	8.9%	6.7%
High School	11.9	16.3	15.7	15.6	31.1	31.6	17.6	10.3%	27.3	27.5	22.3	19.8
College	8.6	9.2	44.3	49.2	41.0	43.6	75.7	85.1%	58.1	59.9	68.8	73.5
Occupation												
White Collar	3.1%	4.4%	25.6%	29.9%	18.4%	19.9%	45.0%	55.3%	23.8%	24.9%	38.9%	43.2%
Blue Collar	5.4	31.1	17.0	29.1	20.6	34.4	23.0	28.4%	27.3	41.3	22.3	27.4
Other Collar	91.4	64.5	57.5	41.0	61.0	45.7	32.0	16.4%	48.9	33.9	38.7	29.3
Population, 16–24	132,249	153,726	129,500	123,130	104,735	162,285	10,200	13,830	37,800	32,975	313,375	220,360
Population, 16–64	317,145	567,255	1,407,625	1,865,627	585,109	718,077	112,128	119,253	328,695	329,753	3,730,661	3,390,192

Table 11.2 OLS Regression Analysis of Male (Age 16–24) Hourly Wages in 2000 on the Number of Unauthorized Mexican Immigrant Males Who Entered California's Job Market in 1990s

	(1) All Males	(2) Other FB	(3) USB Latino	(4) USB Asian	(5) USB Black	(6) USB White
Explanatory Variables:	β	β	β	β	β	β
Age (years)	0.557[a]	0 681[a]	0.334[a]	1.138[a]	0.462	0.592[a]
Other Foreign-born	-0.019					
Latino, U.S -born	-0 319					
Non-Latino Black, U S -born	-0.036					
Non-Latino Asian, U S.-born	2.188[b]					
Married	0.698[b]	0.141	0.561	-3.025	-1 307	1.659[a]
High School	1.133[a]	1.206[c]	1.853[a]	-0.737	-2.486	0 680[c]
College	2 954[a]	4 063[a]	2.160[a]	3.922[c]	0 681	2.593[a]
Industry						
Agriculture, Forestry, & Mining	-1.804[b]	-2 034[b]	-0.932	-7.129[c]	1 010	-0.963
Construction	0.028	0.221	0.206	-0.523	-1 062	-0.413
Wholesale and Retail Trade	-1.69[a]	-1 358[c]	0 275	-3.029	-4 453[a]	-3 102[a]
Transport, Warehousing, & Utilities	0.716	-5.411[b]	0.845	-1.665	25 775	-1.586
Information	1.073	1 153	2 271	1 629	0.863	-0.191
FIRE	-0.162	2 834[a]	0.300	13.673	-3 880	-1.231
Professional, Management, Admin.	0.377	2 191	0.244	0 108	-2 828	-0.528
Education, Health, Social Services	-0.987	-1 513[c]	1 569	- 1.199	4 036	-4.036[a]
Arts, Entertainment, Food Services	-1.712[a]	-1 628[b]	- 0.848	-3.283[b]	-0 324	- 2.704[a]
Other Services (except Public Admin.)	-1 448[a]	-0 263	-1.085[c]	-3.220	-0 468	-2.641[a]
Public Administration	-0.848	1.248	1.099	-3.446[c]	-2 452	-2 029
Recent Unauthorized Mex. Immigrants	-0 00005	-0.00005[b]	-0.00001	0.00000	-0.00011[c]	-0.00006
Intercept	0 537	-2 594	2.585	-12 280	8 713	1 441
Number of Obs (Unweighted Sample):	20,609	4,677	5,869	522	923	8,618
Adjusted R-Squared:	0 03	0 04	0 01	0.09	0 04	0.04

NOTES

1. See Zolberg (2006).
2. Heer (1996); Ridley (2000): 78–79.
3. Marcelli (2004a).
4. Fix and Passel (1994).
5. Marcelli and Heer (1998).
6. Warren (2003); Passel (2005).
7. Smith and Edmonston (1997, 1998); Bean and Hammermesh (2000); Borjas (2004).
8. Bean *et al.* (1988); Marcelli and Heer (1997); Marcelli et al. (1999); Winegarden and Khor, (1991).
9. Pastor and Marcelli (2001).
10. See the 1990s studies by DeFreitas (1991); Marcelli and Heer (1997); Marcelli (1999).
11. Heer *et al.* (1992); Marcelli and Heer (1997); Marcelli (2004a, 2004b); and Marcelli and Lowell (2005).
12. US Government Accounting Office (1998).
13. Van Hook and Bean (1998); Pastor and Marcelli (2003).
14. Marcelli (2004).
15. Marcelli (1999); Heer and Passel (1987).
16. Marcelli and Heer (1997); Marcelli (1999).
17. Marcelli, Pastor and Joassart (1999).
18. DeFreitas (1991); Marcelli, Pastor and Joassart (1999).
19. Marcelli, Pastor and Joassart (1999); Marcelli (2004b).

PART FIVE

Strategies for Improving Future Job Prospects

12. How Can We Improve Employment Outcomes for Young Black Men?

Harry J. Holzer

During the economic boom of the 1990s, employment rates improved dramatically for less-educated young women – especially among African-Americans who were also single mothers. These improvements have been widely attributed to three developments: 1) the very strong economy of that period; 2) welfare reform, which generated pressures on young mothers to leave welfare and find jobs; and 3) the growth of supports for low-income working parents, such as the Earned Income Tax Credit (EITC) and expansion of child care subsidies.

In contrast, employment rates of less-educated young men were largely unchanged over the 1990s (after adjusting for business cycle effects); and those among young Black men continued their long-term decline. Indeed, the trend for Black men during the 1990s was more negative than during the 1980s, after controlling for the strength of the economy and trends in education.[1]

What accounts for the deteriorating employment situation of less-educated young men and especially young Black men? What policy steps might help improve this situation? We address these questions in this paper. We begin by reviewing some data on employment trends over time for less-educated young men, and what we know about their causes. Then we consider a range of possible policy remedies, before drawing some conclusions below.

TRENDS IN EMPLOYMENT

In Figures 12.1–12.4 we present data on the trends in employment and labor force participation among less-educated young men. The first two figures present employment–population ratios for those aged 16–24 and 25–34, respectively; the next two present labor force participation rates. The data

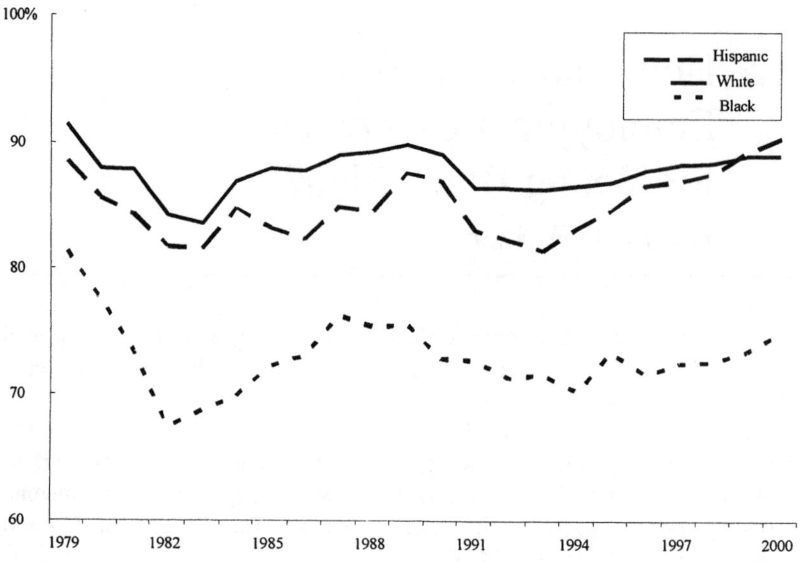

Source: Current Population Surveys, Outgoing Rotation Groups

Figure 12.1 Employment–Population Rate, Males Aged 16–24, 1979–2000

cover the period 1979–2000, and include only those with a high school diploma or less education.[2]

The data in Figures 12.1 and 12.2 clearly show that employment rates among young men respond to the ups and downs of the business cycle. Also, young Black men have lower employment rates at all points in time than do young Hispanics or Whites. The data show mild declines over time in employment activity for the latter groups.[3] But the long-term declines for young Black men are even more stark. The data in Figures 12.3 and 12.4 on labor force participation are less affected by cyclical economic factors, and show clearer patterns of mild declines in activity among less-educated young White and Hispanic men along with sharper declines for young Black men. The latter figures also indicate that the secular decline in labor force activity was even stronger in the 1990s than the 1980s, despite the stronger economy of the former period. A few other factors are noteworthy before we move on. The data for the years 2001–04 show declining employment activity for all of these groups, due to the prolonged labor market downturn of the past few years. Since our focus here is on long-term

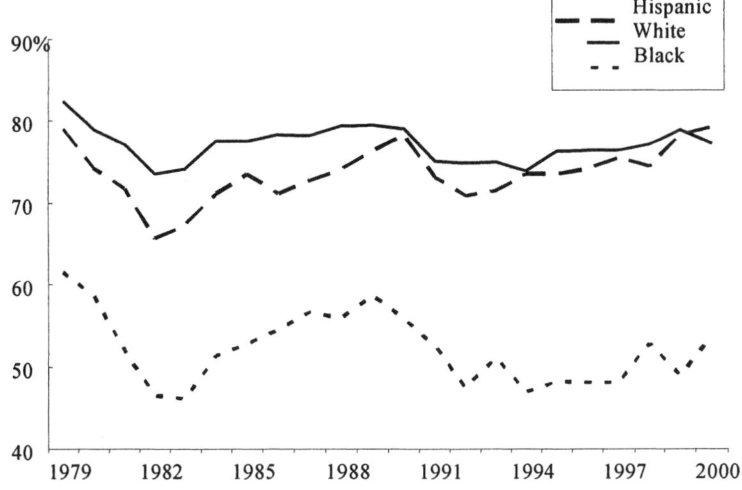

Figure 12.2 Employment–Population Rate, Males Aged 25–34, 1979–2000

trends rather than the business cycle, we do not include those years – the short run.

Furthermore, the data in Figures 12.1 to 12.4 no doubt understate the deterioration in employment activity for young Black men because they are based on the civilian non-institutional population, which leaves out a large group of young men: those who are incarcerated at the time of the survey. For young Black men, this group now constitutes about 12 per cent of the total population; and even among those released from prison, the traditional undercount of young Black men in these surveys suggests that a large group of the non-employed are not included in these data. Thus, the true trend in employment among young Black men is considerably worse than these data suggest.[4]

Finally, it is important to remember that employment and labor force participation are only two of the relevant dimensions of labor force activity. For those working, hourly wages are extremely important as well. It is, of course, widely known that wages of less-educated young men have deteriorated sharply in the past few decades, relative to those of women and more-educated young men.[5] So, even along this dimension, less-educated young minority men have done worse in recent years than have women or their more-educated male counterparts.

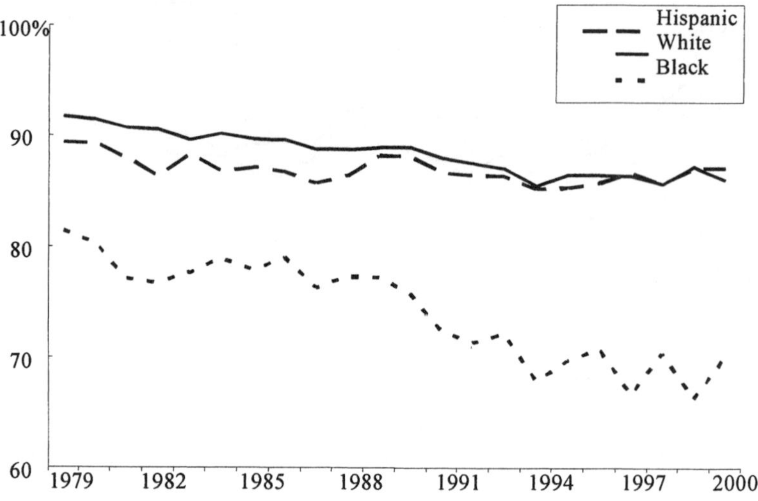

Figure 12.3 Labor Force Participation Rate, Males Aged 16–24, 1979–2000

THE CAUSES OF THESE TRENDS

Why have the employment trends of young less-educated young men, and especially African-Americans, declined over the past few decades? We focus on two sets of factors: 1) changes on the demand side of the labor market, reflecting structural shifts in the economy which have adversely affected job opportunities for young Black men; and 2) responses to these changes in labor supply, reflecting the choices of young men about work versus other activities.

Much has been written about changes in the labor market over the past few decades – and how these changes reflect trends in technology, globalization, and the like. These trends have generated a decline in demand for less-skilled workers, especially in manufacturing and blue-collar jobs more broadly. In addition, the weakening of institutions which had traditionally protected less-skilled workers from the vagaries of the labor market – such as unions and the minimum wage – have reinforced these trends and contributed to the declining relative wages of less-educated workers.

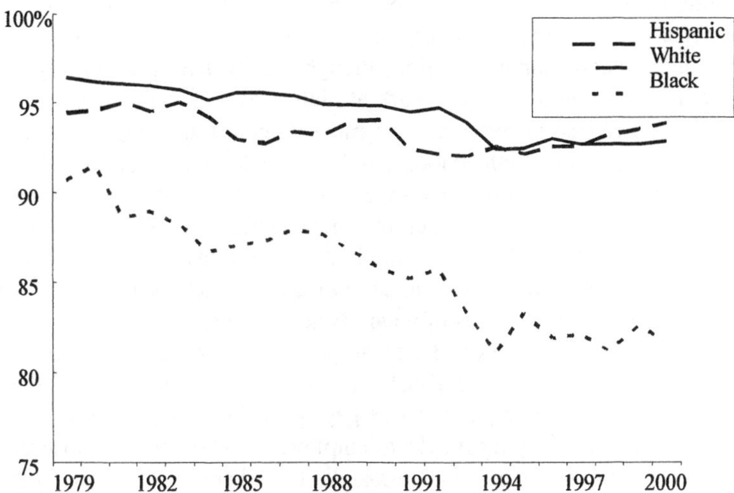

Figure 12.4 Labor Force Participation Rate, Males Aged 25–34

These trends have been somewhat more negative for less-educated young men than for women, as the latter have benefited more from growing labor market experience and a growing service sector in this time period. But young Black men have probably been more hurt than any other group. Rising skill requirements in manufacturing and blue-collar jobs, and the continuing outmigration of these jobs from large urban areas in the Northeast and Midwest, helped reduce the employment of Black men in these jobs more than that of any other group.[6]

In addition, employer demand for the labor of young Black men has been limited by some additional factors.[7] These include:

- Rising skill demands on jobs more broadly, and the growing association between skills and wages in the labor market;
- The persistence of employer discrimination against young Blacks and especially Black men;
- The continuing movement of jobs out of inner-city and inner-suburban areas towards more distant suburbs, generating 'spatial mismatch' between inner-city black residents and jobs;
- Deteriorating informal employment networks for young Blacks, especially relative to those of immigrants and other ethnic groups.

The continuing shift in labor demand towards jobs that require higher cognitive skills implies that high school graduation and some post-secondary education are the keys to higher standards of living. But even along this dimension, young minority men are lagging behind their White and especially their female counterparts. Young Hispanics have the highest rates of high school non-completion, though this is driven largely by the immigrant population; these men work at high rates, but in fairly low-wage jobs with little chance of future advancement. In contrast, young Black men continue to drop out of both school and the labor force at high rates. Post-secondary enrollments among young men lag behind those of young women in all race and ethnic groups, but this new gender gap in education is especially strong in the Black community.[8] And the test scores of Blacks continue to lag behind those of Whites, indicating an achievement gap that further erodes the relative status of young Blacks in the labor market.[9]

But, even at the same rates of educational attainment and achievement, the work experience of young Black men lags well behind that of their White and Hispanic counterparts. These gaps probably reflect other barriers that limit the access of young Blacks to employers, and especially those that pay somewhat better wages for less-skilled workers. For instance, the persistence of employer discrimination against Blacks has been clearly documented in a variety of tester studies and in ethnographic studies of employers as well. A continuing 'spatial mismatch' between Black residences and areas of job growth in major metropolitan areas has been clearly documented as well, which appears to reflect both transportation and informational gaps among these workers. And the continuing erosion of informal networks in the Black community further limits their access to employers, who often prefer young immigrants in jobs requiring little skill and who encourage the formation of informal networks in those communities.[10]

As a result of all these factors, young Black men have had fewer job offers in the labor market when they seek employment, and lower wages than other groups on the offers they do receive. Both their limited skills and their limited access to employers contribute to a lack of early work experience that hampers their advancement over time.

But in addition to the demand-side changes on the labor market, the labor supply responses of less-educated young men have become important as well. The labor force participation of all less-skilled young men has declined in response to declining wage rates and reduced incentives to work, and the particularly striking withdrawal of young Black men from the labor market. As wage offers in the legal labor market declined, young Black men increasingly opted for work in the illegal sector, where pecuniary rewards were growing – especially as a result of the crack trade in the 1980s. These choices were also probably reinforced by the declining presence of fathers in Black households during the 1970s and 1980s; and the growing isolation of the Black poor from middle-class Whites and Blacks.[11] Changing social norms and expectations among young Black men, and in particular a tendency to associate serious efforts in school and the labor market as 'acting white,' have also been noted and debated.[12]

The contrast between young immigrant Hispanics and native-born Blacks is very striking here. Young immigrant Hispanic men frequently arrive in the US (or leave school) without high school diplomas, but quickly become connected to the low-wage labor market and accumulate work experience that reinforces positive employer attitudes towards them. In fact, there is fairly little evidence of discrimination against immigrants in wages – most gaps can be fully accounted for by lower education and weaker language skills. But in their discouragement about future prospects, many young Black boys in their adolescent and teen years disengage (or 'disconnect') from both school and the labor market, never gaining a real foothold in the world of work. The gaps in early work experience between young Black men and other less-educated groups therefore become quite dramatic at fairly early ages, as we saw in Figures 12.1–12.4.[13]

But all these developments do not fully explain the trends in employment for young Black men in the 1990s; indeed, at least some improvements occurred in these factors, which should have generated at least some improvements in their employment. For example, the real wages of the least-skilled workers rose somewhat during the late 1990s, and also relative to workers in the middle of the earnings distribution. Crime rates declined dramatically as well, and high school graduation rates and test scores improved somewhat in the 1980s for those entering the labor market in the following decade. Even the 'spatial mismatch' between Black workers and jobs appeared to improve slightly over that decade. And, of course, the aggregate labor market was stronger in the late 1990s than at any time in the previous 30 years.[14]

So why did employment and labor force activity for young Black men continue to deteriorate? Recent analysis points largely to two relatively new factors: 1) the dramatic growth in incarceration rates among young Black men; and 2) growing enforcement of child support orders as well.

There are important reasons to believe that incarceration and child support impact on Black young men more than on other groups. As noted above, roughly 12 per cent of the young Black male population is incarcerated at any time; roughly twice that many are on parole or probation. It is estimated that about 30 per cent of all young Black men will be incarcerated at some point. The vast majority are released within three years, though large fractions of them recidivate. Furthermore, it is estimated that about one-fourth of all young Black men aged 16–24 are non-custodial fathers, as are as many as half of those aged 25–34. All these figures are vastly higher than the comparable numbers for Whites and Hispanics. Both incarceration rates and state efforts to enforce child support orders (by establishing paternity, identifying employers and withholding payments) have all risen consistently throughout the 1980s and 1990s.[15]

Furthermore, we have reason to believe that being an ex-offender or a non-custodial father reduces one's likelihood of employment – above and beyond any other disadvantages that one might already have – either through its effects on labor demand (employers) and/or supply (workers). For instance, survey evidence on employers indicates that they are much more reluctant to hire men with criminal records than any other category of unskilled employee. The reasons are varied. Some employers are legally prohibited from doing so by state laws; in other cases, their fear of legal liability (if an employee steals from or does bodily harm to coworkers or customers) and for their own safety and security might lead them to avoid offenders as well. Furthermore, a well-known study of job applicants in Milwaukee shows that employers are considerably more reluctant to hire Black men with criminal records than similar White men. And even those young Black men who do not have criminal records might face reduced demand from employers who want to avoid hiring offenders but do not do criminal background checks; in this case, there is evidence of 'statistical discrimination' against all less-educated young Black men by employers.[16]

In addition, having a criminal record probably impacts on one's decision to remain attached to the workforce. Offenders face low wages and benefits and very few advancement prospects when they do gain employment; their incentive to remain with any particular job, and in the overall labor market, is thus quite small. The 'pull' from their peers on the street is often considerable for many such young men, further reinforcing the trend toward high job turnover and recidivism.[17]

As for child support, there is evidence that the enforcement of child support orders tends to reduce the labor supply of some low-income men as well. This is because child support orders impose a 'tax' of sorts on the earnings of less-educated men. The tax averages 20–35 per cent of earnings for low-income fathers, but can be considerably higher in some cases. When combined with payroll and other state and local taxes, along with the implicit tax rate created by the loss of access to benefits as earnings rise, the total tax rates can be very substantial.[18]

For young men who are in 'arrears' – that is, in debt to the child support system for having fallen behind on their payments – the taxes associated with child support alone can be as high as 65 per cent; and in most states, these payments are automatically withheld from workers' paychecks. And the likelihood of being in arrears is especially high for young men who have been incarcerated, since the child support orders apply even when they are behind bars.

Of course, the idea that child support payments are a 'tax' might make little sense if the money went directly to the families and children of the non-custodial parents. But in a majority of states, little of the collected payments are 'passed through' to families that have been on public support, so the incentives of these men to make the payments are reduced. And if the work effort of these men is 'elastic' with respect to their earnings net of taxes, their tendency to work in the mainstream economy will decline (assuming they can escape detection by the authorities and avoid imprisonment for failure to pay support). Most econometric evidence does, in fact, suggest that the labor supply of low-income young men is elastic with respect to take-home pay.[19]

Overall then, a discouraging portrait appears of less-educated young men – and especially Black men – in the labor market. Given the relative disappearance of well-paid blue-collar jobs, low skills and educational attainment limit the abilities of young Black men to obtain good job offers. Discrimination, spatial mismatch, and lack of information further limit their access to employers and their ability to generate important early work experience. In response, these young men often withdraw from the labor market (either temporarily or permanently), and perhaps become involved in illegal activity. Their high incarceration rates then limit their long-term job prospects and their own inclination to remain attached to work, while child support orders drive many of them out of the formal labor market as well. In contrast, young Hispanic immigrants with poor education become more attached to the world of work, but face low wages and poor advancement prospects due to their very limited education and skills.

POLICY IMPLICATIONS

The discussion above implies that policies designed to improve the employment options of African-American youth should focus on the following:

- Improving a range of skills and educational outcomes among youth;
- Improving employer access and early labor market experience;
- Improving their incentives to work by supplementing their pay or benefits; and
- Preventing incarceration/early fatherhood or reducing the barriers to work faced by ex-offenders and non-custodial fathers.

Improving Skills and Educational Outcomes

As we noted above, young Black men suffer from a number of educational disadvantages that hinder their labor market performance. Specifically, they drop out of high school in large numbers, they graduate with poor basic skills, they lack occupational skills and labor market access while in school, and their access to (or retention in) post-secondary education is limited. In a labor market that increasingly rewards schooling and skills, these disadvantages limit their employment opportunities and often discourage many from attaching to or remaining in the labor market altogether.

To improve this set of outcomes, we need to improve educational outcomes well before high school. Since gaps in basic skills emerge very early, high-quality pre-Kindergarten programs, such as Head Start, could be expanded and universal pre-Kindergarten programs that a number of states are now implementing (such as Florida, Georgia, Oklahoma, New York) may disproportionately benefit young minority students as well. Reforms in the Kindergarten to Grade 8 years could also limit these gaps, though little consensus remains about which reforms are most beneficial. Early research on vouchers for private schools suggests gains for African-American students, though questions remain about these findings and the extent to which they can be generalized to larger citywide efforts. Doubts about reducing classroom sizes, charter schools, or other approaches remain as well.[20] And the impact of 'No Child Left Behind' (NCLB) on these gaps is unknown as well. A great deal more research and experimentation is needed before we can confidently assert 'what works' in closing the achievement gap at the elementary school level.

Given this fact, what to do at the high school level is even more problematic. High school reform has recently been touted by the Bush Administration, the National Governors' Association and Bill Gates, among others. But most of these proposals focus exclusively on academic skills and testing, as does NCLB. They run the risk of producing little in the way of improved test scores, and higher dropout rates among those who have difficulty improving their test scores.

Instead, a more promising approach might be to try to improve high schools for disadvantaged students across a range of areas – including academics, occupational skill building, and links to the labor market. Smaller schools with themes, such as the Talent Development High Schools, seem to generate improved academic outcomes. But for occupational skills and labor market experience, the Career Academies generate the most promising results. Recent evidence from MDRC shows that Career Academies raised employment and earnings among disadvantaged young men by nearly 20 per cent up to four years after school. This is one of the strongest positive impacts observed for any education or training program on this population.[21]

More broadly, School-to-Career programs appear to have been successful at improving employment rates among minority (or disadvantaged) young men, and perhaps their educational outcomes as well. While little hard evidence exists on internships and apprenticeships, the strong returns to private sector training among workers suggest that this is another potential route to higher employment and earnings among young minority men. To the extent that training and skill certification often require more advanced basic skills than many young men now have, they should be linked to high school curricula which reach these young men relatively early in their high school lives. And in a labor market where Baby Boomers will soon be retiring in large numbers, the willingness of employers to train non-college youth directly for their occupational openings should grow – assuming that they can get technical assistance and some public financial support for their efforts.[22]

Of course, some have objected that school-to-career efforts constitute 'tracking' that would discourage young minority students from attending college. But well-administered occupational training should raise basic skills, by integrating strong academic and occupational training and motivating students to take both more seriously. If anything, the Career Academies evaluation shows that these programs can raise post-school earnings without reducing post-secondary enrollments or educational outcomes, and other research on School-to-Career programs broadly suggests the same. Effective School-to-Career efforts should open doors and options to success, without closing any.

As for improving access to post-secondary education, a combination of approaches is needed that improves financial aid, provides more information and support services, and makes the curriculum more accessible for those with poor educational backgrounds. The 'Opening Doors' project that MDRC is evaluating in six community colleges across the country tries to provide this package of supports, and early results are encouraging. Alternatively, the 'Early College High School' programs that combine accelerated high school curricula and feed directly into community college are encouraging models as well, though none has been rigorously evaluated to date.[23]

Improving Access to Employers and Early Work Experience

Perhaps the best way to improve the early work experience of young Black men would be to implement some of the programs described above for high school students, before they disconnect from work and turn to crime or early fatherhood. However, additional efforts may be necessary for those who are out of school and have limited labor market experience. This is particularly true for high school dropouts and other at-risk youth, who have abysmally low rates of labor force activity among Black men.

The challenge of finding effective employment programs for out-of-school youth has been noted frequently. At this point, the Job Corps is the one program that has been rigorously evaluated and generates significant improvements in post-program earnings for at least 30 months. The Job Corps also reduces involvement in crime by young Black men, thereby further improving its cost-effectiveness.

Of course, the Job Corps is also an expensive program – costly at nearly $20,000 per participant/year. In contrast, the Youth Service Corps are much less expensive, since they do not provide residences for youth; and a short-term (15–month) evaluation shows positive impacts on employment and negative impacts on crime and pregnancy. The Service Corps also provide services for low-income communities that further improve its cost-effectiveness. Other programs, like Youth Build, might have similar impacts, though they have not been rigorously evaluated to date.[24]

More broadly, youth programs can generate success when they involve sustained and intensive efforts (as in Job Corps and the Youth Service Corps) or clear links to employers in the labor market. The Center for Employment and Training (CET) in San Jose, California, generated strong impacts on the earnings of youth, at least partly because of close links between program directors and local employers. More recent efforts to replicate CET have had more limited success, though the positive impacts might be underestimated in recent evaluations.[25]

Labor market intermediaries that can successfully bridge the gaps between the skills and worker characteristics sought by employers and those provided by job applicants might be helpful in placing young African-Americans in jobs that they have trouble reaching on their own. These intermediaries might include for-profit job placement firms (like temporary help agencies) or non-profits. The key is that they earn the confidence of employers by understanding employer skill needs and sending them strong applicants. If so, the employers might be induced to consider applicants whom they otherwise would not consider hiring. In fact, there is some evidence that temp agencies can improve the access of low-income workers to higher-wage jobs that they cannot reach on their own. Whether intermediaries work for young Blacks over the longer run is not known, but results are promising in a number of examples.[26]

What is also clearly needed is not just a set of disparate and disconnected programs for youth, but youth systems at the local level. This would counteract the tendency for so many young Black men to fall 'through the cracks' once they leave school, or to have limited access to services in so many local areas. To the extent that poor neighborhoods generate negative outcomes for youth above and beyond their own poor circumstances or characteristics, comprehensive approaches at the neighborhood level might be helpful in counteracting this.

Perhaps the most promising effort to date to build comprehensive community systems for youth was the Youth Opportunities program, initiated by the US Department of Labor in 2000. Grants were awarded to 36 low-income urban and rural neighborhoods in a competitive process which drew approximately 130 applicants. The grants were used to develop local infrastructures and management information systems to track local youth and to refer them to available resources in these neighborhoods. While the federal funding of the program has ended, local efforts to generate funding and to maintain the infrastructures developed are continuing, and deserve further federal support.[27]

Improving Work Incentives

As we noted earlier, one reason for the decline in work activity over time by young Black men, and for the corresponding rise in illegal activity, is the relative decline in wages that they have experienced. And one way to change the rewards associated with work for less-skilled young people is to supplement their wages publicly.[28] Indeed, the Earned Income Tax Credit already does so for low-income families with children, whose earnings can be increased by up to 40 per cent with this refundable credit. In turn, the EITC has been credited with helping to raise the labor force participation rate of low-income minority women, along with welfare reform and a strong economy in the 1990s.[29]

But the EITC is largely unavailable to youth or adults without custody of children.[30] This might be changed in a number of ways to make low-income young men eligible, and to encourage further their labor force participation. For instance, both the State of New York and the District of Columbia have recently considered paying a modest EITC to non-custodial fathers who are keeping up with their child support payments. Other proposals would improve and extend the childless credit from its very low current rate. Either way, the proposals would have to avoid creating disincentives for couples to marry or to improve their earnings above the maximum level rewarded by the credit – but adjustments can be made to avoid these problems.[31]

Another way to raise the rewards associated with low-wage work is simply to increase the minimum wage. Currently, the federal minimum (at $5.15 per hour) has fallen to less than one-third of the average wage in the economy – its lowest level in five decades. Accordingly, many states (up to 17 at last count) are raising their own statutory minimum wages above the federal level. While most labor economists have traditionally worried that the minimum wage will reduce employer demand for low-wage workers, recent evidence suggests that these negative impacts are small at worst and non-existent at best. And the positive effects on willingness to work among young African-Americans might outweigh any potential negative impacts on employer hiring.[32]

Preventing Incarceration/Early Fatherhood and Reducing Associated Barriers

The discussion above indicated that incarceration has strong negative effects on employment opportunities for young Black men, and that more stringent child support enforcement in the past two decades has driven some men out of the labor force as well. This implies that employment rates would be improved by preventing involvement in crime and early fatherhood in the first place; and by lessening its negative impact, when prevention efforts are not successful.

Anything that succeeds in improving school performance or early work experience for young Black men will probably help reduce risky behaviors and outcomes such as early fatherhood and illegal activity. We noted above that the Job Corps and the Youth Service Corps also appear to be successful at doing so.

But what might be done to improve the labor force activity of those who have already become offenders or non-custodial fathers? For ex-offenders, we could begin with efforts to raise employment activity among those who are still incarcerated. Recent evidence shows that such activity has positive effects on post-release employment. But expanding private-sector opportunities for offenders is highly controversial, and even work in Federal Prison Industries has faced potential cuts in recent legislation.[33]

Upon release, it is important to provide a range of 'reentry services' that help offenders become reintegrated into their families and communities. These men (and women) are in need of a wide range of supports at this time, including help with housing, health care, substance abuse issues. More successful reintegration of these men into their families and communities would probably reduce the high rates of recidivism among ex-offenders, and generate huge savings in public prison budgets.[34]

What services might be needed to improve employment outcomes among young ex-offenders? At a minimum, labor market intermediaries might be critically important, to overcome employer fears and suspicions regarding this population. Among the most prominent examples of these intermediaries are the Safer Foundation in Chicago and the Center for Employment Opportunities (CEO) in New York, each of which has placed hundreds of ex-offenders into jobs with local employers. These organizations not only work with local employers to find job opportunities; they also prepare the offenders themselves for the world of work. In the case of CEO, virtually all participants are given three to six months of paid 'transitional employment' to ease their return to the world of work. While rigorous evaluation of these program impacts is not yet available, some will hopefully be forthcoming shortly.[35]

Re-entry services have recently been funded through federal legislation, and more such support may soon be available – especially for 'faith-based' efforts. Other helpful efforts might include the following:

- Efforts by the federal government and states to review the legal barriers that now prevent employment of ex-offenders in many sectors, beyond what may be needed to enhance public safety;
- Better targeting of and outreach with the Work Opportunity Tax Credit (WOTC) and
- Updating the Federal Bonding program. Restrictions on employment opportunities for offenders in many states often seem punitive rather than based on public safety concerns, but in the end, they may raise recidivism by reducing opportunities for employment. For example, many states bar offenders from any employment in nursing homes or child care – even in janitorial work – and regardless of the nature of the offense. Given the large and growing proportions of jobs in the service sector that might be barred to offenders, their employment opportunities might be seriously limited. Other restrictions – such as driver's license revocations and bars from eligibility for Pell grants and other supports – probably further weaken their ability to connect to the labor market and gain rewarding jobs.[36]

The WOTC provides credits to employers who hire workers from particular disadvantaged groups, while the Federal Bonding program provides insurance against property damage that may be incurred by employers who hire ex-offenders. But take-up rates on both efforts are extremely low, especially the Bonding program. Both efforts could benefit from better outreach to employers and other reforms.[37]

As for non-custodial fathers, their labor force participation might be improved through the following kinds of reforms in the child support system:

- Reforming the process by which orders are established, and the orders themselves;
- Cancelling arrears in return for efforts to pay more of the current

orders;

- Pass-through of payments to low-income families; and
- More support for fatherhood programs.

Child support orders are often set by judges through default processes in hearings where the non-custodial father is absent and no information is provided about his earnings capabilities. One approach might be to set the order as a per cent of his annual earnings, rather than a fixed amount, as is done in Wisconsin. Cancelling arrears in return for efforts to pay on current orders might create better incentives for low-income men to gain legitimate employment and participate in the child support system; and passing more of the money collected through to the families would also improve these incentives and participation, as a demonstration in Wisconsin has shown.

But greater efforts to improve the earnings capabilities of the low-income fathers should also be part of this process. Fatherhood programs that provide employment assistance and perhaps even transitional jobs should go hand in hand with greater efforts to enforce child support orders. While the Parents Fair Share program based on this idea did not improve the earnings outcomes of fathers, other efforts with better combinations of services and requirements to participate might generate better outcomes. These efforts deserve greater study and evaluation.[38]

CONCLUSION

The continuing deterioration in employment and labor force participation of young minority men, especially African-Americans, is discouraging. Even the exceptionally strong labor market of the 1990s, combined with improved trends in crime and education, did not lead to progress. While employment rates and post-secondary school enrollment of women in these communities is growing, the trend for men continues to be downward.

But there is nothing inevitable about this development. Reversing it requires comprehensive efforts to improve the skills and access to employers of young men, especially in their high school years and right afterwards; to improve their early work experience; to raise the rewards they earn when they participate in the labor market; and to prevent early participation in crime and non-custodial fatherhood, as well as reducing the barriers and disincentives to work associated with these negative behaviors once they occur.

These efforts will certainly require some greater expenditure of public resources. Yet relative to what was spent in the 1990s to move a few million welfare mothers into the labor market, these new expenditures might be fairly modest.[39] At least some efforts, like Career Academies and private sector internships as well as higher minimum wages, would require no public resources at all. Wherever possible, marshaling private resources to this effort is possible and worthwhile. As Baby Boomers get ready to retire and employers in many sectors seek their replacements, efforts to connect workers to the labor market and give them the appropriate skills and experience they need to succeed might generate more private-sector interest than they did in the past.

What is also needed is the political will to move ahead. Young minority men are not viewed very favorably by the public – especially if they have been incarcerated and/or fathered children out of wedlock. Politicians frequently indulge in the temptation to vilify these individuals and impose punitive policies that may actually exacerbate recidivism problems.

But the public has a strong interest in generating productive workers who do not participate in crime and who take care of the children whom they father. And efforts to implement more constructive policies in this regard show some signs of bipartisan support. For instance, a bill to provide resources for fatherhood programs was supported by over 400 members of the US House of Representatives in 2000, before it died in the Senate. And recent efforts to provide public funds for 'prisoner re-entry' have also generated bipartisan support.

And, given the remaining uncertainty over exactly which approaches are cost-effective, any renewed efforts to address these issues should also include strong research and evaluation components.

NOTES

1. For employment trends among females see Meyer and Rosenbaum (2001) and Blank and Schmidt (2002). For employment trends among males see Holzer and Offner (2002).
2. See also Holzer, Offner, and Sorensen (2005). The figures are calculated from the Outgoing Rotation Groups of the Current Population Survey (CPS-ORG). The samples include only those who are not enrolled in school, not in the military or in any other institution.
3. See also Juhn (1992).
4. For evidence on business cycle effects since 2000 see Sum *et al.* (2003). See Holzer *et al.* (2005) for more evidence on incarceration and its estimated impact on employment of young Black men.
5. See, for instance, Autor and Katz (1999).
6. See Blau and Kahn (1997) or Blank and Shierholz (2005) for evidence on less-educated women over time. For evidence on how young Black men were more negatively impacted than other groups by industrial and regional shifts of output see Bound and Holzer (1993), Kasarda (1995), and Wilson (1996).
7. See Holzer (1996) and Holzer (2001).
8. Some authors suggest that the dropout rates from high school are worse than the Current Population Survey data imply, by comparing high school graduation rates with 9th grade populations within states. See Swanson (2004). Data on the relative enrollment rates in

post-secondary education of young men and women by race appear in Edelman, Holzer and Offner (2006).

9. See Neal and Johnson (1996) and Jencks and Phillips (1998).
10. See Kirschenman and Neckerman (1991), Fix and Struyk (1994), and Pager (2003) for evidence on hiring discrimination. See also Ihlanfeldt and Sjoquist (1998) for a review on 'spatial mismatch,' and Falcon and Melendez (2001) for evidence on informal networks across ethnic groups.
11. See Freeman (1992) and Grogger (1998) for evidence on the growth of participation in illegal activities, and Fryer, *et al.* (2005), for evidence on the crack trade specifically. See McLanahan and Sandefur (1994) for evidence on the effects of growing up in female-headed households. See Wilson (1996) and Jargowsky (1997) for a focus on the growing social isolation of the poor in the 1970's and 1980s. Whether female-headship of households has a truly causal effect has been disputed by some analysts. See, for example, Joyce and Korenman (2001). The causal effects of neighborhood isolation have also been debated, and have recently been analyzed using random assignment of families across neighborhoods in the Moving to Opportunity experiment. See Ludwig, Duncan and Hirschfield (2001) and Kling, Ludwig and Katz (2005). Results to date from this work have been mixed, with mobility to better neighborhoods generating much more positive outcomes for young females than young males. The geographic isolation of the poor also declined during the 1990s boom, after the increases of the 1970s and 1980s. See Jargowsky and Yang (2005).
12. See Cook and Ludwig (1998) and Austen-Smith and Fryer (2005).
13. See Borjas (1996) for evidence on the lack of wage gaps for immigrants after controlling for education and language skills, while Moss and Tilly (2001) document employer attitudes. See Besharov (1999), and Edelman *et al.* (2006) for discussions of disconnected youth.
14. See Hauser and Phang (1993); Grissmer, Flanagan and Wilkinson (1998); and Raphael and Stoll (2002); Autor, Katz and Kearney (2004);.
15. See Holzer *et al.* (2005) and Travis (2005).
16. See Pager (2003) for audit study evidence in Milwaukee, and Holzer, Raphael and Stoll (2004) for survey evidence on employer attitudes and hiring behavior. New evidence from an audit study of applicants and employers in New York City also shows the racial difference in employment effects of having a criminal record even more strongly.
17. See Travis (2005) and Bushway, Stoll and Weiman (2007).
18. See Pirog, Klotz and Byers (2000) and Primus (2002).
19. See Katz (1998) and Grogger (1998) on the responsiveness of work effort to wages among low-wage workers and young men respectively.
20. For varying opinions on school vouchers and their impacts see Howell *et al.* (2002); Heckman and Krueger (2003); Rothstein (2005). See Gormley and Gayer (2005) for evidence on pre-Kindergarten programs and Haskins and Rouse (2005) for a broader discussion on early childhood programs and their potential effects on achievement.
21. See Kemple (2004) for evidence on Career Academies.
22. See Neumark and Rothstein (2003) and Furstenberg and Neumark (2005) for evidence on School-to-Career programs and their impacts. For more discussions of these issues see Lerman (2002) and Bassi and Ludwig (2000).
23. See Bloom and Sommo (2005) for early evidence on 'Opening Doors'; and Steinberg *et al.* (2003) for discussion of Early College High School programs.
24. See Lalonde (1995) for a general discussion of difficulties in raising earnings among youth; and Schochet *et al.* (2001) for evidence on the Job Corps. See Jastrzab *et al.* (1997) for evidence on the Youth Service Corps.
25. The 30-month follow-up study in MDRC's replication of CET found only modest impacts on earnings of young people. See Bos et al. (2003). But the control groups in this study had unusually high levels of educational attainment and especially community college attendance for a sample of disadvantaged young people.

26. See Andersson, Holzer and Lane (2005) for evidence that temp agencies improve the subsequent earnings of low-wage workers, and Giloth (2004) for discussions of intermediaries more broadly.
27. See Edelman *et al.* (2006).
28. A smaller but more ambitious effort to improve the rewards for low-income young men and women associated with work was the New Hope project in Milwaukee. For evidence on the impacts of New Hope on the employment of young men over a five-year period see Huston *et al.* (2003).
29. See Meyer and Rosenbaum (2001) or Blank and Schmidt (2002).
30. A small annual credit, worth only about $400 per year, is available to low-income adults who do not have custody of children.
31. Edelman *et al.* (2006) discuss a range of approaches for reducing the marriage penalties and marginal taxes on earnings of second earners in the EITC.
32. See Card and Krueger (1995) and Chasanov (2004).
33. See Holzer, Raphael and Stoll (2003) for discussions of in-prison work experience, and Rostad (2002) for a discussion of private-sector employment for the incarcerated.
34. See Travis (2005).
35. The US Department of Health and Human Services is sponsoring a rigorous evaluation of programs for the 'Hard-to-Serve,' and CEO is one of the sites being evaluated.
36. See Love (2005) for a state-by-state review of legal barriers facing ex-offenders. The Federal Pell Grant Program is the government's main need-based grant program for post-secondary students.
37. Hamersma (2005) shows modest impacts of the WOTC on employment for disadvantaged groups, though this could improve with better targeting and outreach. The bonding program now provides only $5000 worth of coverage per bond, which is far too little to cover potential damages and legal liabilities.
38. Cancian and Meyer (2005). See also Primus (2002).
39. Expenditures on the EITC, which mostly benefit single mothers, now exceed $30 billion each year. Major portions of the TANF block grant, which costs the federal government $16.5 billion per year, are now used to finance work supports for single mothers as well.

13. Does Job Corps Training Boost the Labor Market Outcomes of Young Latinos?

Alfonso Flores-Lagunes, Arturo Gonzalez and Todd Neumann

Hispanics are the largest minority group in the United States, accounting for 14 per cent of the population in 2005. However, they are on average one of most economically disadvantaged ethnic groups in the country despite having a high labor-force attachment rate.[1] Most of the explanations for their low socioeconomic status center on low levels of human capital: the 'status' dropout rate for US-born Hispanics ages 16–24 is around 15 per cent and the 'event' dropout rate for all 15 to 16 year old Hispanics is 8.8 per cent, both of which are the highest of any group in the country.[2,3] Since the human capital model argues that educational achievement is a prerequisite for sustained economic mobility, the prospects for Hispanic success in the labor market are limited by their below-average levels of education. One way out-of-school Hispanic youths can compensate for this shortcoming is to take advantage of job training and education programs that provide, for example, a General Education Diploma (GED), vocational training, English proficiency, or job placement assistance.

One such effort is the federally funded Job Corps (JC) training program that targets young individuals with the aim of improving their skills. However, the 48-month follow up of the National Job Corps Study (NJCS), an evaluation of the JC program, found that Hispanics in the 'treatment' group were the only racial/ethnic group that did not earn higher weekly earnings compared to Hispanics in the 'control' group.[4,5] Our previous work showed that the NJCS results were robust to alternative estimation methods, and that the lack of a program effect on earnings was due to non-treated Hispanics accumulating significantly higher levels of labor market experience during the NJCS relative to treated Hispanics, which led to a weekly earnings advantage that treated individuals were not able to surpass by the 48-month follow-up survey.[6] This variable alone accounted for the lack of earnings gain for Hispanics, while it had virtually no effect on

lack of earnings gain for Hispanics, while it had virtually no effect on the original estimates for Whites and Blacks. Whereas that work shed light on the process generating the NJCS finding, it did not address the issue of *why* Hispanic youth were alone in accumulating enough work experience to offset the earnings gain from JC training at 48 months: the difference in accumulated labor market experience between treated and non-treated individuals is statistically significant only for Hispanics.

This chapter considers whether local labor market conditions and job networks in Hispanic enclaves can explain why Hispanic youth are able to find and keep jobs to a greater extent than other young workers. These two factors uniquely affect Hispanics if the regions of the country where they are concentrated have particularly high demand for unskilled young workers, and also if their residence within heavy concentrations of Hispanics provides them access to job networks.[7] In this chapter we focus on the mean outcomes of three labor market variables: earnings, employment rates, and post-treatment labor market experience of trained and non-trained Hispanics.

Our findings suggest that the performance of Hispanics with respect to these labor market outcomes is correlated both with the local unemployment rate and the degree of concentration of Hispanics in the areas where they live. More importantly, we find a disparate effect of these two community-level variables on treated and non-treated Hispanics, which is consistent with the notion that treated Hispanics (perhaps mistakenly) neglect their job network when using Job Corps placement services after training. In particular, we find evidence that Hispanic enclaves provide young non-treated Hispanics access to employment opportunities during expansionary periods, but JC-trained Hispanics tend to do relatively better in labor markets with high unemployment, especially in areas with a lower concentration of Hispanics. These results provide initial evidence that Hispanic enclaves provided young Hispanics not selected for Job Corps with employment opportunities; this resulted in the relatively large accumulation of labor market experience that dominated the positive effect that Job Corps training had on trained Hispanics. Since the evaluation of Job Corps spanned a period of time characterized by generally declining unemployment rates, this chapter provides a foundation to contextualize the apparent lack of a treatment effect previously noted by the NJCS and reinforced in our previous study.

DESCRIPTION AND EVALUATION OF THE JOB CORPS

The Job Corps (JC) program was created in 1964 as part of the War on

Poverty under the Economic Opportunity Act, and since then has served over 2 million young persons ages 16–24.[8] The purpose of JC is to provide low-skilled and less-educated young people with marketable skills to enhance their labor market outcomes. It does this by offering academic, vocational, and social skills training at 122 centers throughout the country. In fiscal year 2005, JC received $1.5 billion to enroll 68,000 new students, at a per-student cost of $22,300.[9] The program's educational, job training, and post-completion services are provided at JC centers, which are either operated by Civilian Conservation Centers or by private and non-profit organizations under contract to the Department of Labor.[10] What distinguishes JC from other job training and educational programs are the residential centers, run by federal agencies or by private contractors, where nearly all students reside during their enrollment period. In addition to the educational and vocational training, JC also provides health services and a stipend during program enrollment.

Students are selected based on several criteria, including age (16–24), poverty status, residence in a disruptive environment, not on parole and ability to benefit from additional training or education; all students must be US citizens or permanent residents. The typical JC student is from a minority ethnic or racial group (70 per cent of all students), 18 years of age, who has dropped out of high school (80 per cent) and reads at a seventh grade level.[11] Job Corps applicants become familiar with the program in various ways, the most common being by word of mouth, with approximately 2 out of 3 applicants hearing about it from either friends or relatives, and another 20 per cent through direct mailings or from radio and television.[12] Rarely are applicants referred to JC by schools, a JC counselor or probation officers. Younger applicants are more interested in completing high school or a GED course, while older applicants have greater interest in job training in a specific field. Above all, applicants see JC training as a means of finding employment since the majority has never held a full-time job.

During the late 1990s, the Department of Labor sponsored the National Job Corps Study (NJCS), a randomized experimental study of JC-eligible young persons, to assess its effectiveness and social value. Overall, the NJCS report found that program participants earned 12 per cent more than control-group members during the 48-month follow-up survey.[13] At the same time, however, the NJCS revealed that Hispanics who undertook JC training did not have higher earnings or a higher employment rate than Hispanics randomized out of JC services. The average weekly earnings of the control group was $15.1 more (not statistically significant) than treatment-group Hispanics. The lack of effects for Hispanics could not be explained by differences in education and training, length of program enrollment, or quality of JC centers, or differences within specific age, language, education and region groups.[14]

WHY HAVE PAST STUDIES FOUND NO JOB CORPS EFFECTS ON HISPANICS?

Since Hispanics represent a significant and growing proportion of the population, and disproportionately exhibit disadvantaged characteristics, it is *important* to understand the reasons behind the lack of impacts first noted by the NJCS. Flores-Lagunes, Gonzalez and Neumann (FGN hereafter) examined whether the NJCS created statistically comparable treatment and control groups for Hispanics using alternative methods to estimate the average treatment effect on the treated (ATT) that relax the assumptions of a valid randomization, and estimated the 'net treatment difference' parameter to identify a plausible channel by which JC training fails to operate for Hispanics.[15]

The conclusions regarding the lack of effect of JC training for Hispanics in the NJCS rest on the assumption that randomization created two statistically comparable groups. FGN tested this assumption because the original randomization did not explicitly consider race or ethnicity, and hence the analysis of a relatively small and geographically concentrated subsample (18 per cent of the sample) may yield treatment and control groups that are not comparable. Indeed, comparing Hispanics of both groups right after randomization revealed statistically significant differences with regards to the percentage of females, number of children, percentage living in a Primary Metropolitan Statistical Area (PMSA), percentage living in a Metropolitan Statistical Area (MSA), percentage unemployed at randomization, and per cent employed at randomization. Consequently, FGN estimated the ATT using the propensity score estimator, the bias-corrected simple matching estimator, and the linear difference-in-difference and difference-in-difference matching estimators.[16] Despite using alternative estimators, the FGN results corroborated the NJCS findings of statistically insignificant JC effects for Hispanics.

FGN then focused on possible causes for the lack of effects of JC on Hispanics. The analysis of randomization undertaken for Hispanics revealed a pervasive difference between the Hispanic groups in the accumulation of post-treatment labor market experience during the 48 months of the NJCS, which was in turn strongly (positively) related to differences in the type of metropolitan area of residence.[17] In particular, treated Hispanics were under-represented in PMSAs and over-represented in MSAs while the reverse is true for non-treated Hispanics. Furthermore, the largest difference in average hours of work per week during the NJCS between treated and non-treated Hispanics occurred in PMSAs (a highly statistically significant 3.2). These differences in location and labor market experience affected the distribution of earnings for Hispanics. Treated Hispanics earned on average about $19 per week less than non-treated Hispanics, and this effect is statistically significant at the 10 per cent level. Therefore, it is plausible that the accumulation of labor market experience by non-treated Hispanics results in higher earnings for them that treated Hispanics are not able to overcome by the end of the NJCS.

Controlling for post-treatment experience, however, no longer identifies the ATT since this variable is affected by the treatment itself (that is, it is an outcome variable), and instead estimates the 'net treatment difference' or NTD.[18] The interpretation of the NTD is that, if there is a positive effect of Job Corps on Hispanics net of post-treatment experience, this variable is a likely mechanism by which Job Corps 'fails' to work for Hispanics. Indeed, the NTD yielded a positive and statistically significant (non-causal) effect of Job Corps, similar in magnitude to the ATT estimate for Blacks and Whites. Interestingly, the NTD estimates for Whites and Blacks are virtually identical to the ATT estimates, implying that accumulated labor market experience during the study is not a factor for these two groups.

SOME FEATURES OF HISPANIC YOUTH IN THE LABOR MARKET

The two main conclusions in the literature regarding Hispanics in the labor market are that they earn less and have higher unemployment rates than Whites, and that differences in observable characteristics explain most of these gaps.[19] However, *young* Hispanics are an exception to this generalization. The few empirical studies focusing on inter-ethnic earnings differences among young workers find that young second- and third-generation Hispanics earn more than young Whites and Blacks, although their unemployment rate is still 50 per cent higher than the rate for White youths.[20] Also, the unemployment rate for young Hispanics improves relative to Whites during expansionary periods, but falls more than proportionally at the start of recessionary periods.[21]

The finding of high earnings and experience for young Hispanics has important implications for participants in job training programs. Since higher earnings are directly related to the probability of employment, and the growth of earnings depends on experience, the ability to find stable employment may be an important attribute distinguishing Hispanics from other groups. For this reason, it is important to consider the determinants of employment and accumulation of weeks of work. We conjecture that non-treated Hispanics may be at an advantage in the labor market relative to other young persons for at least two reasons. First, given evidence that the economic expansion of the 1990s benefited Hispanics after 1995[22] – at the start of the evaluation of the JC program – it is possible that non-treated Hispanics benefited from this expansion sooner since they entered the labor market before those that delayed their entry because of participation in JC. In addition, economic expansions do not occur simultaneously in all local labor markets across the nation. Instead, some locations experience booms while others still experience stagnation.

The second reason young Hispanics may have an early-career advantage in the labor market is due to access to employment enclaves. The relevant literature in economics and sociology considers Hispanic employment networks to be important for Hispanics in the labor market.[23] Conditional on a critical mass of Hispanics, employment networks enhance the likelihood of a positive outcome because the potential worker and the potential employer do not have sufficient or perfect information to make an efficient match, or the costs necessary for this match outweigh the gains.[24] Of course, any early and favorable labor-market conditions enjoyed by young non-treated Hispanics may be outweighed by their lack of skills in the long run.[25]

The ability of the network to provide a valuable outcome, however, depends on the 'quality' of the network (measured by the labor force participation or employment status among established members of the enclave), as well as the ability to access this network (usually based on a shared connection like place of origin or family ties). The review of the literature finds that:

1. Hispanics are more likely to search for jobs through friends than Whites or Blacks;
2. Social contacts with extensive employment experience increase the likelihood of labor force participation for individuals;
3. Unemployed persons in large areas are more likely to use contacts than those in smaller cities;
4. The majority of studies find that young persons are more likely to use employment networks than older persons; and
5. Persons without a high school diploma living in high- poverty areas use informal job-search strategies more so than those from low-poverty areas.[26]

These factors suggest that Hispanic youth potentially differ from White and Black youth in their use of social networks to find employment.

Additionally, although treated Hispanics can also access these networks, it is possible that they did so to a lesser extent during the period of the NJCS because they utilized the Job Corps placement services, since this is one of the most sought-after component of JC.[27]

Combined with the relatively expansionary labor market of the mid-1990s, non-treated Hispanics may have been acquiring on-the-job training and experience at the same time that the treated group was out of the labor market acquiring training. Therefore, it is important to assess the separate effects of Hispanic employment networks and local labor market conditions on the outcomes of Hispanics, since each variable measures different labor market dynamics within the same geographic area. In other words, it is possible that the quality of the Hispanic job network is correlated with local labor demand as suggested by the literature review, and so it is necessary to consider the interaction effect between these two variables. In the following sections, we provide some initial evidence on how these two important factors – local unemployment rates and employment networks – influence the labor market outcomes of non-treated and treated Hispanics.

DATA

We use publicly available data from the NJCS together with the restricted-use NJCS data that contain the ZIP code of residence for individuals in the NJCS sample. We use the ZIP code information to match the individual's location to the corresponding labor market's unemployment rate for Hispanics between the ages of 16 and 35 and the local concentration of Hispanics. The location's concentration of Hispanics is used as a proxy variable for employment networks. However, besides capturing the positive effect of employment networks, the concentration of Hispanics in the location potentially has the opposite effect of reducing individual labor market outcomes since a higher concentration is related to higher competition in the local labor market, and hence reduces the quality of the network.[28] Therefore, by using this variable, we only identify this combined effect and not exclusively the effect of employment networks, although looking simultaneously at Hispanic concentration and local unemployment rates can in principle ameliorate this issue. A brief description of the data follows.

NJCS Data[29]

The publicly available NJCS data is a nationally representative sample of 15,386 people drawn from the universe of first-time Job Corps eligible applicants from November 1994 through December 1995 (N = 80,883) that were randomly assigned into a control group (N = 5,977 or 39 per cent) or treatment group (N = 9,409 or 61 per cent). The latter group was allowed to enroll in JC and 73 per cent eventually enrolled, while the former was barred from enrolling in JC for a period of three years but not from other programs, some of which also offer job training and vocational opportunities that might be similar in nature or content to some of the JC training. The control and treatment groups were tracked with a series of interviews immediately after randomization and continuing 12, 30, and 48 months after randomization. The outcomes at these times are the basis for the evaluation of JC. The actual sample used in this chapter, however, contains only 9,105 individuals that are White, Black or Hispanic, and that report information on all the relevant variables used in our analysis. The restricted-use NJCS data was obtained directly from Mathematica Policy Research, Inc., and contains ZIP codes of residence at the baseline and 48-month interviews. The more recent ZIP codes of residence were used since it is plausible that individuals look for work after JC in the location where they have undertaken the training.[30]

Labor Markets and Enclave Variables

Data on local unemployment rates for Hispanics between 16 and 35 years of age (which we refer to as the 'local unemployment rate') and Hispanic concentration are obtained from two different sources: the 2000 5 per cent PUMS and the 2000 Census SF-3 data files. County-level variables including unemployment estimates for different group of workers (16–35 year-olds, Hispanics, Whites, Blacks), as well as the county's overall population and concentration of Hispanics (a proxy for a Hispanic enclave) are derived from these data. These variables were then merged with the NJCS data using the ZIP code of each respondent. For a more detailed discussion regarding these variables, see Appendix 13.1.

EMPIRICAL ANALYSIS

Table 13.1 presents several variables by city type (PMSA, MSA and Other areas) for each of the three racial and ethnic groups. The classification into city type is performed by aggregating from ZIP code of residence at the 48-month interview, such that the variables measured at the ZIP code level are averages weighted by the corresponding population. This table reveals some interesting points, but before proceeding we note that all the evidence presented here is based on simple differences in means and thus has no causal interpretation. First, looking at mean earnings in quarter 16, it is evident that living in a PMSA is strongly associated with negative differences in earnings between treated and non-treated Hispanics. Perhaps surprisingly, Whites also have a somewhat heterogeneous pattern across city type, since it is only for those who live in Other areas that the difference in earnings between treated and non-treated individuals is statistically significant. Blacks are a relatively more homogeneous group across type of city of residence, as they show a positive and statistically significant difference in mean earnings in both MSA and Other areas. Interestingly, both Black and White treated individuals in non-PMSAs mostly perform relatively worse than their non-treated counterparts in PMSAs, where we also find a dismal performance between treated and non-treated Hispanics. Lastly, the employment rate in quarter 16 shows a very similar pattern to that of earnings.

In terms of post-treatment labor market experience (third row in each panel), the average hours worked per week during the 208 weeks of the NJCS reveal that, regardless of city type and racial/ethnic group, non-treated individuals attain higher labor market experience. This is to be expected because treated individuals cannot gain labor market experience during training.[31] What is probably unexpected is that non-treated Hispanics attain markedly more labor market experience than their treated counterparts over the same period. Looking at the aggregate over city types (last panel), non-treated Hispanics accumulate 2.72 more hours per week than treated Hispanics, compared to a difference of 0.76 and 0.73 for treated/non-treated Blacks and Whites respectively.[32] In fact, in PMSAs, where non-treated Hispanics are more concentrated, the difference is almost twice as large: 4.35, which correspond to an advantage of almost one-half year's worth of labor market experience over the 208 weeks of the NJCS.

Looking at the breakdown by city type, it is evident that the accumulation of labor market experience by non-treated Hispanics is relatively constant: 21.54, 21.23 and 21.21 hours per week in PMSA, MSA and Other, respectively. Therefore, the source of difference is probably due to treated Hispanics 'underachieving' in PMSA and to a lesser extent in Other areas: Hispanics accumulate 20.05 hours of experience per week in MSA, but only 17.19 and 18.77 in PMSA and Other areas, respectively. Of course, these differences could also be due to non-treated Hispanics 'overachieving' due to the effects of enclaves and labor demand.

Why do non-treated and treated Hispanics have divergent labor market outcomes? In Table 13.1 we undertake a first attempt to relate accumulation of labor market experience to Hispanic concentration and local unemployment rate (both of which have been aggregated from ZIP code level to city type). The table shows that there is a very close correspondence in the values of these two variables within each city type between treated and non-treated Hispanics. The largest differences in Hispanic concentration occur in Other areas (2.25 percentage points) and PMSA (1.47 percentage points) with non-treated Hispanics living in areas with more Hispanic concentration, which would be consistent with an employment network advantage provided by the enclave. However, neither of the differences is statistically significant. As for the local unemployment rate, the same statistically insignificant pattern arises, with the higher local unemployment rate faced by treated Hispanics in Other areas (0.83 percentage points higher) and PMSA (0.09 percentage points higher). The lack of statistically significant differences by city type in these variables may be a consequence of comparing simple averages rather than different points of the distribution of Hispanic concentration and unemployment. In what follows, we take a closer look at each of these two variables in turn at three percentiles in their distributions.

Table 13.2 presents some outcome variables over the distribution of Hispanic concentration, population concentration (for comparison purposes) and local unemployment rates. Each of the panels divides the distribution into three equally sized percentiles (Low, Medium, and High). While splitting the distribution into more percentiles is desirable, the trade-off we face is having too few individuals in each percentile.[33] The top panel of Table 13.2 looks at mean earnings, employment rate and labor market experience over the distribution of the Hispanic concentration variable. For the most part, the best-observed outcomes for both treated and non-treated Hispanics occur in areas with 'medium' Hispanic concentration. This is consistent with the notion that there are two effects of a high Hispanic concentration working in opposite directions: it may lead to better outcomes through the availability of better job networks, while it may also lead to worse outcomes due to more competition for the available jobs. Nevertheless, the observed outcomes for treated Hispanics worsen more than proportionately in high Hispanic concentrated areas relative to non-treated Hispanics. Given that treated Hispanics have accessibility to JC placement services after training and that job networks for Hispanics are typically effective, this observation is consistent with treated Hispanics replacing informal employment networks with this service. In this case, the only effect of a larger enclave is the higher competition for available jobs.[34]

Hispanic concentration is obviously positively correlated with population concentration, so it is a valid question to ask if the pattern of the top panel holds when we substitute Hispanic concentration with population concentration, in which case the enclave story would be undermined. The middle panel of Table 13.2 shows the observed outcomes over the distribution of population concentration. Interestingly, contrary to Hispanic concentration, the best outcomes for non-treated individuals are found in the highly populated areas, while for treated individuals the best outcomes are found in the medium populated areas. This result is consistent with the notion that Hispanic concentration is informative about 'enclave effects' for non-treated Hispanics, whereas the evidence of enclave effects for treated Hispanics is minimal, consistent again with them not utilizing informal employment networks. In addition, it is evident again that treated Hispanics in highly populated areas have disproportionately unfavorable outcomes, while their outcomes are best (even relative to non-treated individuals) in the bottom third of the population concentration distribution, where the enclave effect is expected to be weak.

Finally, the bottom panel of Table 13.2 presents observed outcomes over the distribution of the local unemployment rate. As expected, the best outcomes for both treated and non-treated Hispanics are found in low unemployment rate areas. It is noteworthy that treated Hispanics in these areas have higher mean earnings and employment rates than non-treated Hispanics. However, treated Hispanics do extremely poorly in areas with both medium and high unemployment rates.

Table 13.2 shows how different outcomes vary over the distribution of Hispanic concentration and the local unemployment rate separately, but it is quite possible that there is interplay between those two variables. It is thus of interest to consider how the outcome variables (mean earnings, employment rate, and the accumulation of labor market experience) change over the joint distribution of Hispanic concentration and the local unemployment rate. However, a simple cross-tabulation of the outcome variables over the joint distribution of Hispanic concentration and local unemployment rate is too coarse to reveal any clear patterns.

Therefore, in order to analyze the interplay of Hispanic concentration and local unemployment rate on the outcome variables, we look at differences in outcome variables over the two conditional distributions of these two variables. In other words, Table 13.3 (and Table 13.4) present differences in the outcome variables over the distribution of Hispanic concentration (local unemployment rate), fixing the level of the local unemployment rate (Hispanic concentration). In this way, we compare the association of the outcome variables and changes in the level of one variable while holding constant the other variable at a particular level.

Table 13.3 provides the differences in outcomes when changing the level of Hispanic concentration, holding fixed the level of the local unemployment rate. Diverging patterns between non-treated and treated Hispanics are present in this table. The table reveals that the relative employment rate for non-treated Hispanics is greater in areas with higher concentration of Hispanics, but this advantage is conditional on the labor market conditions of the area being considered. In areas with a Low unemployment rate, there is a small advantage (3.1 per cent) for persons in Low Hispanic concentration compared to Medium concentration, but the change from Medium to High Hispanic concentration results in a relative increase of 17.3 per cent, and thus a net gain of 14.2 per cent from Low to High Hispanic concentration. Interestingly, as the level of unemployment increases, the relative gains for non-treated Hispanics residing in High Hispanic concentration areas declines.

Conversely, the relative average employment rate for treated Hispanics tends to decline as the level of Hispanic concentration increases, especially between the Medium to High concentration areas. However, the relative employment rate within Hispanic areas worsens as the local unemployment rate increases, regardless of Hispanic concentration (for example, -1.1 per cent in Low unemployment/High-Low Hispanic concentration compared to -9.2 per cent in High unemployment/High-Low Hispanic concentration).

With regard to earnings and experience, Table 13.3 shows again that within the Low level of the unemployment rate, a relative increase in Hispanic concentration is associated with a greater gain in both variables for non-treated Hispanics, but this pattern does not hold when moving to the Medium or High levels of the unemployment rate. Conversely, for treated Hispanics, the best differences over Hispanic concentration occur in the Medium-Low column across *all* three unemployment rate levels. They are still adversely affected by the level of Hispanic concentration, but to a lesser extent in the High level of unemployment rate (especially for experience).

The panel labeled 'Differences in Differences' (DID) refers to changes in the difference in the outcomes between treated and non-treated individuals due to changes in the level of Hispanic concentration, holding the local unemployment rate constant. In general, these estimates provide further support for the possibility that the level of Hispanic concentration is correlated with higher mean employment rates for non-treated Hispanics, but this advantage is predicated on low unemployment rates. It is also interesting to note that treated Hispanics tend to do relatively better as the unemployment levels rise in all outcome variables. Taking earnings as an example, although non-treated Hispanics have a large relative advantage in mean earnings in areas with low unemployment rates if they live in high Hispanic concentration areas ($127.2 and $98.8), this advantage declines as labor markets worsen, and eventually treated Hispanics have an earnings advantage of $34.8.

Table 13.4 presents the differences in outcomes when changing the level of the local unemployment rate, holding fixed the level of Hispanic concentration. The main conclusion still holds from Table 13.3 that non-treated and treated Hispanics' outcomes are affected differently by each of these two variables. For example, the employment rate and earnings of non-treated Hispanics are mostly greater in areas with lower unemployment and higher level of Hispanic concentration. Treated Hispanics, on the other hand, benefit more from lower unemployment areas where the concentration of Hispanics is at the Medium level.

In this table, the DID columns consider the changes in the outcome variables between treated and non-treated individuals due to changes in the level of the unemployment rate, within the same level of Hispanic concentration. Again, these estimates generally support the previous interpretations, namely, non-treated Hispanics have better relative outcomes than their treated counterparts in areas with higher levels of Hispanic concentration. For example, in the Low-High unemployment rate column, the slight relative employment advantage of treated Hispanics in low Hispanic concentration areas decreases from 0.2 per cent to -5.9 per cent in high Hispanic concentration areas, relative experience changes from -0.2 to -4.1 hours per week, and relative earnings decline from $67.5 to -$66.1.

The DID panel in Table 13.4 also supports the previous finding that treated Hispanics tend to have better outcomes than non-treated Hispanics in areas with higher levels of unemployment, although this conclusion is tempered by the size of Hispanic concentration in the area. The incremental effect of an increase in the unemployment level from Medium to High, shows that treated Hispanics increase their level of employment by 5.3 percentage points in areas with Low Hispanic concentration, -2.9 percentage points in areas with Medium Hispanic concentration, and 3.9 percentage points in areas with High Hispanic concentration. The incremental change in earnings is $43.9 in Low Hispanic areas, but in larger Hispanic areas, this figure declines to -$8.0. Similarly, the incremental change in average hours per week of work experience declines from -4.8 to -5.3 due to an increase in enclave size.

Taken together, Tables 13.3 and 13.4 are consistent with two reinforcing patterns of the effect of Hispanic concentration and unemployment levels for young Hispanics. First, access to Hispanic social networks provides employment opportunities for Hispanics, provided that there are sufficient jobs in the local labor market. If jobs are scarce, however, then treated Hispanics tend to have better relative outcomes than non-treated Hispanics in smaller Hispanic enclaves. This suggests that the 'quality' of the Hispanic network matters.[35] At the same time, in areas where such quality is low or lacking altogether (that is, high unemployment, high Hispanic concentration), JC-trained Hispanics tend to have higher employment rates, higher earnings, and similar levels of work experience to their non-treated counterparts. This suggests that JC renders Hispanic youth less vulnerable to downturns in the economy or when their employment network is not beneficial.

CONCLUSIONS AND DIRECTIONS FOR FUTURE RESEARCH

In this chapter we present an initial analysis of the role of two important factors that potentially influence the labor market outcomes of young Hispanics: local unemployment rates and employment networks. This study is motivated by previous findings that Job Corps was not beneficial for Hispanics 48 months after randomization. While our previous work points out that the lack of effects of JC is most probably due to higher accumulation of labor market experience during the study, an open question is why only for Hispanics is this variable significantly different.

We collected data about local unemployment rates and Hispanic concentrations from various sources that are then matched to our sample of individuals that participated in the evaluation of Job Corps. We regard the local unemployment rate as a measure of the economic conditions faced by individuals residing in the area (for example local labor demand), and Hispanic concentration as a measure of employment networks available to Hispanic individuals (and we also point out that it may also be measuring the extent of Hispanic labor supply in the area).

In general, our findings support the notion that Hispanic concentration and local labor market conditions are important factors that can explain at least part of the lack of JC effects on Hispanic earnings 48 months after randomization. However, these factors seem not to operate in isolation from one another, and the local unemployment rate seems to dominate any positive benefits of Hispanic employment networks, particularly for non-treated individuals. More specifically, our analysis reveals that access to Hispanic social networks provides employment opportunities for Hispanics, *provided* that there are sufficient jobs in the local labor market. This finding suggests that the 'quality' of the Hispanic network is important. At the same time, we find that JC-trained Hispanics tend to have relatively better labor market outcomes in areas where the quality of the network is low or non-existent, suggesting that training obtained in JC mitigates the negative effects of high local unemployment rates.

A number of steps are left in our research agenda, the first of which is to undertake a multivariate analysis that can better determine the role of these two factors on Hispanic outcomes by controlling for relevant characteristics of the individual. In addition, other measures of local labor demand, such as the mean manufacturing wage, and Hispanic enclaves, measured as the number of employed Hispanics, need to be considered in future studies for a better assessment of their effects on the labor market outcomes of Hispanic youths.

APPENDIX 13.1

This appendix describes the community-level variables used for this study, and some of the issues arising in matching these variables to the restricted-use NJCS. Matching the various data by county posed some challenges, and the steps taken to arrive at our sample are described here. The geographic unit of analysis is the county or county group, and all county-level variables are obtained from data widely available from the Census Bureau. The restricted-use NJCS data contains the respondent's ZIP code of residence at the time of the 48-month follow-up interview, between December 1998 and May 2000.[36] The Census data is organized at the PUMA level for the PUMS (public use micro sample), and the county-level information from the SF-3 data is based on quasi-ZIP code information gathered in 1999.

Each data set has unique characteristics. The 5 per cent PUMS data is organized around the PUMA, a geographic construct that may span several counties or may also lie within a county so that each PUMA is approximately the same population size (approximately 100,000 persons). Thus, it is possible that three counties with a population the size of 35,000 will be combined into one PUMA, while a large city will be broken up into multiple PUMAs. For this reason, the common geographic measure is the county or county-group. That is, observations in PUMAs that spanned multiple counties are grouped into a 'county group,' while observations taken from PUMAs within one county are defined as belonging to that particular county. A crosswalk between the PUMA, county, MSA, PMSA, and a quasi-ZIP code variable was obtained from the MABLE 1998/Geocorr Geographic Correspondence Engine, available at http://mcdc2.missouri.edu/websas/geocorr2k.html. This engine provides a crosswalk between the ZIP Census Tabulation Areas variable (ZCTA) and the other Census geographic units. The ZCTA 'in most instances' are the same as the ZIP codes for an area, but differ in the sense that ZCTA are defined to have a geographic meaning, which is not the case for ZIP code, and are based on ZIP codes that existed in 2000. See www.census.gov/geo/ZCTA/zcta.html for further details regarding ZCTAs.

Therefore all the 2000 Census data was organized into a county or county group and the corresponding ZCTA was merged. The ZTCA was then merged with the NCJS data using the ZIP code reported at the 48-month interview. Since the NJCS ZIP code is self-reported, we assume that the most recent ZIP code is used, and are therefore confident that the ZIP code is merged with the correct county. Because the NJCS data were merged 'up' to the county level, this minimized geographic mismatch between the Census and NJCS data sets. In certain cases (about 30 per cent), a single ZTCA is found in more than one county or county group. In this case the labor market statistics assigned to this Zip code are an average of the county or county groups that contain that Zip code weighted by the number of people in that Zip code that live in a certain county or county group. Finally, in a small number of cases (2.6 per cent), there was no match between the ZIP code reported by the JC participant and the ZTCA. In this case the closest ZTCA was used. The results are not materially different if these observations are excluded.

Data pertaining to enclaves and the labor force in 2000 are derived from the 5 per cent PUMS file and the Summary File-3. The Summary File-3 from the 2000 Census is a 100 per cent count of the population. The wide coverage of the SF-3 data makes it possible to measure the size of Hispanic enclaves. The 5 per cent PUMS makes it possible to obtain unemployment estimates for Whites, Blacks, and Hispanics ages 16–35, although these estimates are based on a 5 per cent count of the population, rather than a count of all individuals. To the extent that young persons and minorities are less likely to be counted in the Census, these estimates will be less than ideal. The sample selection excludes persons living in group quarters, in the military, or with missing employment status. Additionally, for precision, all county groups with fewer than 25 observations are excluded from these calculations.

Table 13.1 Means of Selected Variables for Treated and Non-Treated Groups, by Metro Type, Race and Ethnicity

	Hispanic		White		Black	
	Not Treated	Treated	Not Treated	Treated	Not Treated	Treated
PMSA						
Earnings $	244.59	206.5*	289.76	308.42	190.17	192.47
Employ/pop.%	74.21	65.7*	79.67	82.42	65.51	66.62
Hours work/week	21.54	17.2*	26.60	25.49	18.81	17.5*
County pop(000s)	2585	2601	1097	952	1734	1614
Hispan. Conc.%	32.92	30.62	15.54	13.56	17.35	18.21
Unempl. Rate%	9.68	9.77	4.64	4.68	14.96	15.09
N	476	362	292	239	1034	845
MSA						
Earnings $	196.74	217.25	255.88	265.20	177.36	198.7*
Employ/pop.%	69.66	74.79	78.74	80.66	65.84	70.4*
Hours work/week	21.23	20.05	26.14	25.08	19.32	18.92
County pop(000s)	649	654	388	379	465	472
Hispan. Conc.%	34.69	34.16	8.17	7.76	5.08	5.7*
Unempl. Rate%	10.30	10.35	5.02	4.98	14.14	13.87
N	428	369	776	605	1403	1147
Other Areas						
Earnings $	195.10	196.27	207.37	247.5*	131.38	169.5*
Employ/pop.%	63.16	69.31	72.71	77.84	53.88	60.8*
Hours work/week	21.21	18.77	24.97	24.85	17.00	16.65
County pop(000s)	47	44	45	45	38	41.8*
Hispan. Conc.%	28.69	26.06	4.60	5.39	3.10	3.03
Unempl. Rate%	11.68	10.85	6.31	6.20	15.96	15.64
N	114	88	504	370	435	365

Notes: *Difference between Treated and Not Treated is statistically significant at 5 per cent level. Unemployment Rate is of all 16–35 year olds of the same race/ethnicity

Table 13.2 Mean Outcome Variables for Hispanics, by Local Jobless Rate, Population and Hispanic Concentration

	LOW			MEDIUM			HIGH		
	Not Treated	Treated	Diff.	Not Treated	Treated	Diff.	Not Treated	Treated	Diff.
Panel 1: Hispanic Concentration[a]									
Earnings $	212.40	202.18	-10.22	251.96	254.30	2.34	199.80	175.70	-24.10
Employ/pop %	68.78	70.49	1.71	73.65	75.81	2.16	71.92	64.34	-7.58
Hours work/week	21.41	18.81	-2.6*	22.40	19.58	-2.8*	20.65	17.73	-2.9*
N	341.00	261.00		324.00	277.00		334.00	258.00	
Panel 2: Population Concentration[b]									
Earnings $	198.01	204.37	6.36	224.38	218.31	-6.07	240.10	213.31	-26.79
Employ/pop %	0.67	0.71	0.04	0.72	0.72	0.00	0.75	0.68	-7.3*
Hours work/week	21.34	19.72	-1.62	21.63	19.01	-2.6*	21.44	17.36	-4.1*
N	326.00	283.00		339.00	253.00		334.00	260.00	
Panel 3: Local Unemployment Rate For Hispanic Youth[c]									
Earnings $	238.24	262.24	24.00	230.21	200.47	-29.74	201.95	174.68	-27.27
Employ/pop %	0.74	0.78	0.04	0.73	0.68	-0.05	0.70	0.65	-0.05
Hours work/week	22.19	20.75	-1.44	22.93	18.12	-4.8*	19.69	17.64	-2.05
N	320.00	271.00		325.00	250.00		322.00	255.00	

Notes:
* Significant at the 5 per cent level.
a. Low<16.2 per cent, Medium<39.8 per cent, high<98.3 per cent.
b. Low<442,008, Medium<1,336,839, High<8,080,826.
c. Low<8.33 per cent, Medium<10.67 per cent, High<34.25 per cent.

Table 13.3 Differences in Outcomes over Hispanic Concentration,[a] Holding Local Unemployment Rate Fixed

	NOT TREATED			TREATED			DIFFERENCES in DIFFS.		
	Med.-Low	**High-Med.**	**High-Low**	**Med.-Low**	**High-Med.**	**High-Low**	**Med.-Low**	**High-Med.**	**High-Low**
Employ/pop %									
Low Unemp.[b]	-3.10	17.30	14.20	7.70	-8.80	-1.10	10.80	-26.1*	-15.30
Medium Unemp.	8.00	-5.70	2.30	-5.70	-2.61	-8.30	-13.70	3.10	-10.60
High Unemp.	6.10	-6.10	0.00	0.60	-9.80	-9.20	-5.50	-3.71	-9.20
Earnings $									
Low Unemp.[b]	12.10	29.80	41.90	40.50	-97.4*	-56.90	28.40	-127.20	-98.80
Medium Unemp.	$86.3*	$-88.4*	-2.10	33.30	-52.50	-19.20	-53.00	35.90	-17.10
High Unemp.	5.10	-38.30	-33.20	35.30	-33.70	1.60	30.20	4.60	34.80
Hours work/week									
Low Unemp.[b]	0.00	4.70	4.70	0.90	-1.34	-0.44	0.90	-6.04	-5.14
Medium Unemp.	-2.20	-5.5*	-7.7*	-3.40	-6.00	-9.4*	-1.20	-0.5*	-1.70
High Unemp.	1.80	0.80	2.60	1.10	0.30	1.40	-0.70	-0.50	-1.20

Notes: * Significant at the 5 per cent level.

[a] Low<16.2 per cent, Medium<39.8 per cent, High (<98.3 per cent)

[b] Low<8.33 per cent, Medium<10.67 per cent, High<34.25 per cent

Table 13.4 Differences in Outcomes Over Local Unemployment,[a] Holding Hispanic Concentration Level Fixed

	NOT TREATED			TREATED			DIFFERENCES in DIFFS.		
	Med.-Low	**High-Med.**	**High-Low**	**Med.-Low**	**High-Med.**	**High-Low**	**Med.-Low**	**High-Med.**	**High-Low**
Employ/pop %									
Low Conc.[b]	4.20	0.70	4.90	-0.90	6.00	5.10	-5.10	5.30	0.20
Med. Conc.[b]	-6.90	2.60	-4.30	12.5*	-0.30	12.20	19.4*	-2.90	16.50
High Conc.[b]	16.10	3.00	19.1*	6.30	0.07	13.20	-9.80	3.90	-5.90
Earnings $									
Low Conc.[b]	23.40	-10.80	12.60	47.00	33.10	80.1*	23.60	43.90	67.50
Med. Conc.[b]	-50.80	70.40	19.60	54.20	31.10	85.3*	105.0*	-39.30	65.70
High Conc.[b]	67.40	20.30	87.70	9.30	12.30	21.60	-58.10	-8.00	-66.10
Hours work/week									
Low Conc.[b]	-5.6*	9.3*	3.7*	-1.00	4.5*	3.50	4.60	-4.80	-0.20
Med. Conc.[b]	-3.4*	5.3*	1.90	3.3*	0.00	3.3*	6.7*	-5.30	1.40
High Conc.[b]	6.8*	-1.00	5.80	7.96	-6.30	1.66	1.16	-5.30	-4.14

Notes: * Significant at the 5 per cent level.
[a] Low (<8.33 per cent) Medium (<10.67 per cent) High (<34.25 per cent)
[b] Low (<16.2 per cent) Medium (<39.8 per cent) High (<98.3 per cent)

NOTES

1. Chapa (1989), DeFreitas (1991), Gómez-Quiñones (1994), Gonzalez (2002), Smith (1991), Tienda (1983), Trejo (1997), and Vélez-Ibáñez (1996).
2. US Department of Education (2004) Tables 1 and 3.
3. The 'event' dropout rate measures persons who have recently dropped out of high school (and hence were enrolled at one point), while the 'status' dropout rate measures whether a certain age cohort, such as 16–24 year olds, have completed high school. The status dropout rate thus may include immigrants who had never enrolled in high school in the US.
4. Schochet, Burghardt and Glazerman (2001).
5. 'Treatment' and 'control' groups refer to the original groups created by randomization and used by the NJCS to estimate the effects of JC. In contrast, given the large amount of non-compliance in the sample, our analysis divides individuals into those who actually undertook JC (treated) and those who didn't (non-treated), regardless of their random assignment.
6. Flores-Lagunes, Gonzalez and Neumann (2005).
7. Munshi (2003).
8. Currently the Congressional mandate for JC is derived from the Workforce Investment Act of 1998 and administered by the Department of Labor's Employment and Training Administration. From 1982 to mid-2000, JC operated under the Job Training Partnership Act.
9. US Department of Labor (2005).
10. Burghardt *et al.* (2001).
11. Schochet (1998).
12. Schochet (1998) and US Department of Labor (1999).
13. Schochet *et al.* (2001, Table D-15).
14. *Ibid.*, 171–175.
15. Flores-Lagunes *et al.* (2005) and Rosenbaum (1984).
16. Abadie and Imbens (2006) and Rosenbaum (1984).
17. Flores-Lagunes *et al.* (2005), Table 3.
18. Rosenbaum (1984).
19. DeFreitas (1991), Gonzalez (2002), and Trejo (1997).
20. DeFreitas (1991) and Fry and Lowell (2002).
21. DeFreitas (1991).
22. There is speculation that low-skilled Hispanics may benefit during economic booms if employers believe they have a better work ethic than non-Hispanics. See Suro and Lowell (2002).
23. Gonzalez (1998), Ioannides and Datcher Loury (2004), Munshi (2003), Spener and Bean (1999), Waldinger (1999), and Weinberg, Reagan and Yankow (2004).
24. Edin, Fredriksson and Aslund (2003), Ioannides and Datcher Loury (2004), Montgomery (1991), Munshi (2003), Spener and Bean (1999), and Wilson and Portes (1980).
25. This is a common occurrence predicted by human capital models. For example, it takes a certain period of time for people fresh out of college to catch up with their peers who have worked continuously since high school.
26. Ioannides and Datcher Loury (2004).
27. Schochet (1998).
28. Munshi (2003).
29. A more detailed discussion of the NJCS can be found in Schochet *et al.* (2001), and Flores-Lagunes, Gonzalez and Neumann (2005).
30. In addition, a small cross-check was undertaken to gauge how much mobility of individuals occurs between the baseline and 48-month interviews, concluding that the

mobility is relatively low and most of the time within the same three-digit ZIP code, which is consistent with mobility within the same local labor market.

31. Recall that JC is an intensive training program in which participants spend on average 8 months.
32. While 2.72 hours per week might seem a small amount, it corresponds to over one-quarter of a year's worth of labor market experience (assuming 2,000 hours of work a year) during the 208 weeks of the NJCS.
33. On the other hand, an analysis splitting the sample into below- and above-the-median yields essentially the same insights.
34. Ioannides and Datcher Loury (2004), Munshi (2003), Spener and Bean (1999), and Weinberg *et al.* (2004).
35. Edin *et al.* (2003), Ioannides and Datcher Loury (2004), and Munshi (2003).
36. Schochet (2001).

14. Have Young Workers Lost Their (Collective) Voice? Youth–Adult Preferences for Workplace Voice in Canada

Michele Campolieti, Rafael Gomez and Morley Gunderson[1]

Nowhere is the phrase 'the future is our youth' more true than with respect to the labor movement. This is so because union density has generally plummeted in industrialized countries so that recruiting young workers is regarded as necessary to stem the decline. The issue will be even more important in the near future given that the aging baby-boom population in industrialized countries will be retiring, often from unionized jobs that are often replaced by non-union jobs involving non-standard or contingent forms of employment. The fact that plant closures and job losses are frequently in unionized jobs is highly detrimental to unions since virtually every new firm is 'born non-union'. Furthermore, 'young blood' is often regarded as an important ingredient to restore the vibrancy of a union movement that has been on the defensive for nearly three decades. Organizing youths is particularly important since, as detailed subsequently, unionization has elements of an 'experience good' such that the benefits of membership tend to be revealed only after union attributes have been experienced. There is an inter-generational and social capital transmission mechanism associated with unionization whereby the likelihood of being unionized is enhanced if family and peers are also unionized – in essence, unionization begets further unionization and conversely, as is the legitimate fear of the trade union movement, union decline begets further decline.

Analyzing youth–adult differences in preferences for collective forms of voice in Canada is particularly informative for a number of reasons. Canada is one of the few industrialized countries with decentralized bargaining where unionization was sustained or at least did not plummet dramatically in the 1990s. Nevertheless, there has been a recent decline which has raised the issue of whether Canada's unionization rate will converge towards the lower level of many other countries, and in particular its major trading partner – the United States. What happens to youth will obviously affect that pattern. While the collective bargaining regimes in Canada and the US are fairly similar (that is, based on the Wagner Act model), Canada does have a number of institutional and legal features that differentiate it from the United States.[2] This is especially the case since labor matters are largely under provincial jurisdiction in Canada and there has been considerable variation in labor policies both over time and across such jurisdictions, often providing a natural laboratory for analyzing the impact of such policy initiatives. These include many 'union friendly' policies such as the prominence of the agency shop whereby all members of the bargaining unit are required to pay union dues, and the existence of certification through card signing rather than a vote. Canada also differentiates itself with respect to the US in that it allows potential non-union forms of voice at the workplace that could, in theory, be substitutes or even complements for more formal voice through unions.

These background facts on unionization and the legal environment in Canada are developed in the next section, with comparisons made mainly with the US. Youth–adult differences in unionization as well as preferences for union and non-union forms of voice in Canada are then documented. Particular attention is paid to youth–adult differences in the frustrated or unmet demand for unionization and non-union forms of voice, as well as the possible oversupply of unionization that may occur from union members who would prefer to be non-union but who are prevented from being so by the agency shop. Reasons for youth–adult differences in unionization and voice are then outlined. The chapter concludes with a discussion of implications for the future.

The chapter draws extensively from our earlier studies on unionization and non-union voice in Canada (as well as the US and Britain); it focuses on youth–adult differences in Canada from those earlier papers cited in the references.[3] Many of those papers in turn utilized the Lipset-Meltz 1996 Canada-US Labor Attitudes Survey that is used in this chapter.[4]

BACKGROUND TO UNIONIZATION IN CANADA

Sustained Union Density

Union density in Canada[5] is slightly above 30 per cent – one of the highest levels amongst industrialized countries with decentralized bargaining. Canada is also one of the few Anglo-American countries where unionization has not plummeted in recent years. Of particular note, both Canada and the

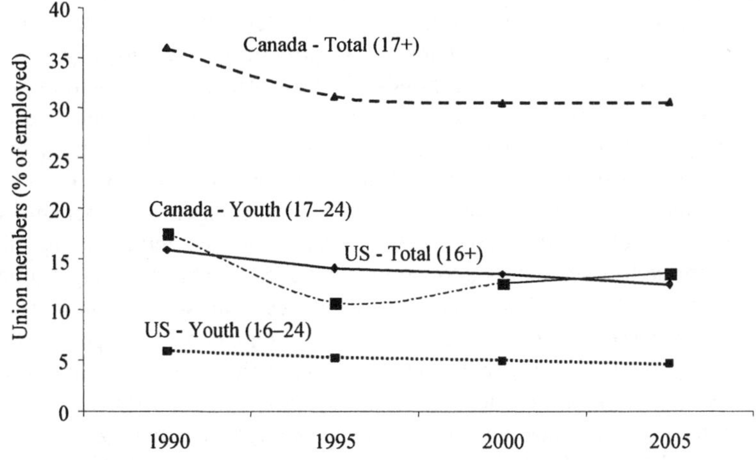

Source: US data from Bureau of Labor Statistics, various years. www.bls.gov
Canada data from Labour Market Activity Survey, 1990, and various Labor Force Surveys

Figure 14.1 Unionization Rate in Canada and US by Age, 1990–2005

US had similar levels of union density of around 30 per cent in the mid-1960s. Since then, unionization has declined steadily in the US to 12.5 per cent in 2005. In contrast, unionization has fluctuated somewhat over the period in Canada, but it remains at over twice the US rate today. There has, however, been a slow decline since the early 1990s (as seen in Figure 14.1) – a possible 'trend' that is being watched carefully to see if it will converge to the lower US levels. Young workers, it should be noted, have roughly one-third the unionization rate of their respective older worker counterparts in both countries.

Reasons for Sustained Density in Canada

There is general agreement that the sustained union density in Canada reflects supply-side considerations whereby the legislative, political and employer environment is more conducive to the formation and retention of unions, as opposed to any greater demand for unions in Canada on the part of workers. This may be surprising to some since there is a general impression that Canadians are more amenable to collective solutions to social problems as evidenced by such facts as our universal public health care, gun control legislation, higher taxes to finance greater expenditure on social programs, and the existence of viable left-wing social democratic parties (sometimes winning majorities in provincial elections). This is in contrast to the image of a more individualistic American orientation. The differences between Canada and the US have often been attributed to the fact that the US was founded on a revolution built on the distrust of a foreign state, while Canada remained 'loyal' to that same foreign state.

In spite of the perception of Canadians as being more amenable to collective solutions than Americans, survey evidence indicates that the desire for collective solutions to workplace issues is actually stronger in the US than in Canada. For example, 58 per cent of workers in the US expressed a preference for being unionized, compared to 53 per cent in Canada[6]. All of this greater demand for unionization in the US came from stronger preferences for unionization and not as a result of differences in the characteristics of Canadian and American workers that may give rise to different demands for unionization. Since the actual unionization rate is much lower in the US (around 16 per cent at that time) compared to Canada (around 34 per cent – 36 per cent at that time) the frustrated or unmet component of demand for unionization is greater in the US compared to Canada. The fact however that there is a frustrated or unmet demand in both countries for unionization suggests that constraints in the supply of unionization exist and play an important role in the representation gap in both countries. The fact that frustrated demand is greater in the US than in Canada suggests that these supply-side constraints play a stronger role in the US than in Canada. What, then, are these supply-side factors that constrain unionization in both countries but more so in the US than in Canada and more so for youth than for adults in both countries?

Supply-Side Factors Accounting for Higher Union Density in Canada[7]

In Canada compared to the US, there has been less restructuring away from extensively unionized industries and especially the public sector. As well, management opposition to unions is not as prominent. The political system in Canada also has viable left-wing parties and a parliamentary system where the head of state is not elected directly but is head of the party in power. In contrast, in the US the President is elected directly and the House and Senate serve as checks and balances. In such circumstances change is more feasible in Canada, and while this could work for or against unions, it appears to have worked in their favor. As well, Canadian unions have been fairly innovative and aggressive especially in the area of organizing.

Most importantly, the legal regime in Canada is more 'union friendly' and conducive to the formation and retention of unions. Canada has strong union security provisions via the agency shop (termed the Rand formula in Canada) whereby all persons in the bargaining unit are required to pay union dues or contribute the equivalent to charity. There are also, unlike many US states, no right-to-work laws in any of the ten provinces and three territories. Numerous restrictions exist on how employers can campaign during a certification drive, and unlike the US, provincial labor boards can (and often do) impose the first collective bargaining contract in newly unionized establishments. Restrictions also exist on the extent to which employers can shed collective agreements through bankruptcy and succession rights. Until recently, certification was generally allowed through signing of cards rather than requiring a vote.

Unlike the US, where section 8a2 provisions of the National Labor Relations Act inhibit the formation of non-union forms of representation at the workplace, no such prohibitions exist in Canada. Employers and employees are relatively free to establish non-union forms of representation. These are often regarded as substitutes for unions (essentially 'company' or sham unions), yet research has not established with any degree of certainty whether this is the case. The presence of non-union voice could very well be complementary to more formal unions in the sense of establishing the foundations or the stepping-stones leading to more formal unionization. The non-union employee associations that were prominent in the public sector prior to the 1960s in Canada were generally regarded as providing the infrastructure for the rapid evolution into formal public sector unions that began, often through legislative fiat, in the late 1960s and led to the public sector largely being unionized in Canada today.[8]

While these various factors have been influential in sustaining unionization in Canada, there has been some recent decline, reflecting such factors as a shift from card signing regimes to the requirement of a vote[9]. This decline has increased the attention paid to union renewal, including organizing young workers. In such an environment it is important to understand the preferences of youth for unionization as well as other forms of employee voice. Prior to looking at the empirical evidence, we briefly discuss factors that may shape the preferences of youths for unionization and other collective forms of voice at the workplace and contrast these factors with adults.

POTENTIAL REASONS FOR YOUTH–ADULT UNIONIZATION DIFFERENCES

There are a considerable number of reasons for expecting unionization to be lower for young as compared to older persons.[10] Youths often obtain their initial employment in small firms, non-standard jobs (for example, limited-term contracts) and in sectors like services that are not organized. New plants, often in greenfield sites that tend to be non-union (since companies are born non-union), disproportionately employ younger workers. Such workers may see little point in joining unions, which tend to emphasize policies like seniority, job security and pensions that benefit older workers. Moreover, given that their turnover rates are high, especially as they are often hunting for the right job, youth may see fewer benefits than adults in unionization if they intend to leave. Consequently, they have a shorter period over which to amortize those benefits. This is compounded by the fact that the benefits come in the distant future (seniority, pensions, health plans) while the costs of queuing for a union job are immediate in the present. Youths may regard exit as an alternative to union voice to deal with their workplace issues. Union emphasis on fringe benefits, many of which are geared to families, may alienate youth who prefer cash wages to such fringe benefits. Union actions will reflect the preferences of the median voter and youths are unlikely to be median voters within the union. Youths, as compared to adults, may also have more of an individualistic rather than collective orientation and hence regard many institutions, such as unions, as being outmoded and out of touch with their values.[11]

Unionization also has elements of an 'experience good' – that is, something that has to be experienced to be understood and appreciated in terms of its real value.[12] Only by sampling an experience good will its hard-to-observe attributes be revealed. Since young workers often start off in non-union jobs, they do not get the opportunity to experience unionization and hence to sample the many attributes of membership such as protection from unfair dismissal, clear and objective promotional criteria, and the provision of family friendly policies. This is especially important because youths are at a stage in their life cycle where their attitudes may be malleable and capable of being shaped, especially by life experiences and the attitudes of family and friends.[13]

DEFINITIONS AND CONCEPTS

How do these theoretical expectations about youth–adult differences in unionization play out in the numbers? Prior to providing the evidence, it is informative to outline some definitions. The framework is based on concepts related to the demand and supply of unionization as outlined in Farber (1983) and Riddell (1993).

Proportion Union and Non-Union

The proportion unionized (that is, union density) representing the probability of being unionized is represented as $P(U=1)$ while $P(U=0)$ is the proportion non-unionized, representing the probability of being a non-union worker. The data for these concepts are based on the Labor Force Survey in 1996. All other figures below are based on the Lipset-Meltz survey of 1996.

Satisfied Demand amongst Unionized and Non-Unionized

The probability that a union member desires to remain a union member (that is, the proportion of union members who desire to remain unionized) is $P(D=1| U=1)$, and is derived by responding 'yes' to the question: "If an election were held tomorrow, would you vote to remain part of the union at your workplace?" It is taken here to represent the preference of union members to retain union representation, and hence is a measure of satisfied demand amongst union members.

$P(D=0| U=0)$ is the probability that a non-union worker desires to remain non-unionized (that is, the proportion of non-union workers who desire to remain without union representation) as indicated by responding 'no' to the question: "If an election were held tomorrow, would you vote for unionization at your workplace?" It is taken here to represent the preference to remain non-union amongst those who are non-union, and hence is a measure of satisfied demand amongst non-union workers.

Unsatisfied demand for Non-Unionized and Oversupply for Unionized

$P(D=1| U=0)$ is the probability that a non-union worker desires to be unionized (that is, the proportion of non-union workers who desire to be unionized) as indicated by responding 'yes' to the question: "If an election were held tomorrow, would you vote for unionization at your workplace?" It is taken here to represent the preference for being unionized amongst the non-unionized, and hence is a measure of unsatisfied demand for unionization amongst non-union workers. The demand is perhaps not met, for example, because such persons are not able to persuade their fellow employees to form a union or because they are unwilling to switch to unionized jobs, since jobs and unionization often come as a package that cannot be unbundled.

$P(D=0| U=1)$ is the probability that a union member desires to be non-union (that is, the proportion of union members who desire to be non-union) as indicated by responding 'no' to the question: "If an election were held tomorrow, would you vote to remain unionized at your workplace?" It is taken here to represent the preference for being non-union amongst the unionized, and hence is a measure of oversupply of unionization amongst union members. The oversupply can occur, for example, because such persons are not able to persuade their fellow employees to decertify the union or because they are unwilling to switch to a non-union job. Oversupply may be expected to be prominent in Canada, in part, because of the agency shop provisions embodied in the Rand formula whereby all members of the union must pay union dues or the equivalent to a charity, as well as the absence of right-to-work legislation. In addition, oversupply may be fostered by card signing regimes to the extent that individuals are pressured into signing, but would not have voted for a union if there were a secret ballot (as implied in the question).

The previous measures were conditional measures, based on being in the sub-samples of union or non-union workers. Equivalent unconditional measures for the workforce as a whole can be calculated by multiplying the conditional estimates by their respective proportions in the workforce as a whole. The conditional and unconditional measures will differ depending upon the size of the group in the workforce. For example, oversupply of unionization may be prominent amongst unionized workers, but this may not translate into a high degree of oversupply in the total workforce if such unionized workers are a small proportion of the workforce. Since these components of satisfied demand, oversupply and unmet demand are weighted by the proportions of the respective youth and adult workforces in each component, they will sum to one within each of the youth and adult workforces.

Satisfied Demand in the Workforce

The preference to remain unionized amongst workforce (satisfied demand for unionization amongst the workforce) is calculated by $P(D{=}1, U{=}1) = P(D{=}1|\ U{=}1)*P(U{=}1)$, which is the probability of union members desiring to remain unionized times the proportion of union members in the workforce.

The preference to remain non-unionized amongst the workforce (satisfied demand for non-unionization amongst the workforce) is calculated by $P(D{=}0, U{=}0) = P(D{=}0|\ U{=}0)*P(U{=}0)$, which is the probability of a non-union worker desiring to remain non-union times the proportion of non-union workers in the workforce.

Unsatisfied Demand and Oversupply in the Workforce

The preference for unionization that is not being met amongst workforce (unsatisfied demand for unionization amongst the workforce) is calculated by $P(D{=}1, U{=}0) = P(D{=}1|\ U{=}0)*P(U{=}0)$, which is the probability of a non-union worker preferring to be unionized, times the proportion of non-union workers in the workforce.

The preference for non-unionization that is not being met amongst the workforce (oversupply of unionization amongst the workforce) is calculated by $P(D{=}0, U{=}1) = P(D{=}0|\ U{=}1)*P(U{=}1)$, which is the probability of a union worker preferring to be non-unionized, times the proportion of union workers in the workforce.

Gross and Net Demand for Unionization

A measure of the gross or total demand for unionization in the workforce can be calculated by summing the realized or satisfied demand and the unsatisfied demand in the workforce. This would indicate the potential unionization rate in the economy if all demand were satisfied. It is a gross demand, however, since it still includes the oversupply that exists from unionized workers who would prefer to be non-union. A measure of net demand can be calculated by subtracting the oversupply from net demand. This indicates the hypothetical unionization rate that would prevail, if all preferences were satisfied. These measures are as follows:

Gross demand (realized demand + unsatisfied demand in workforce) as measured by $P(D{=}1) = P(U{=}1) + P\ (D{=}1, U{=}0)$.

Net demand (realized demand + unsatisfied demand - oversupply in workforce) as measured by $P(D^*{=}1) = P(U{=}1) + P(D{=}1, U{=}0) - P(D{=}0, U{=}1)$.

Probability of Achieving Desired Union Status

An alternative way of presenting the data is to calculate the probability of achieving one's desired union status conditional upon desiring a particular status. For those who answered 'yes' to the question: "If an election was held tomorrow, would you vote for unionization at your workplace?" the proportion who have achieved that desired status is $P(U{=}1|\ D{=}1)$. This is a measure of the probability of being unionized conditional on desiring unionization. The proportion which has achieved that status is simply 1 minus the proportion which has not achieved it since these are exhaustive and mutually exclusive states. That is, $P(U{=}0|\ D{=}1)$ gives the probability of being non-union conditional on desiring unionization.

Similarly for non-union workers, $P(U=1|\ D=0)$ gives the probability of being unionized conditional on not desiring unionization and $P(U=0|\ D=0)$ gives the probability of being non-union conditional on desiring to be non-union.

YOUTH–ADULT DIFFERENCES IN UNIONISATION AND PREFERENCES

Given the aforementioned reasons for differences in the unionization of youths and adults, what is the evidence in this area based on the definitions and concepts outlined? Table 14.1 provides evidence of preferences for unionization based on the Lipset-Meltz 1996 Canada-US Labor Attitudes Survey, with the actual unionization rates coming from the Labor Force Survey at the same time.

Satisfied Demand, Oversupply and Unsatisfied Demand

As indicated in the first row, only 13 per cent of youths (15–24) were unionized, slightly over one-third of the rate of 36 per cent for adults (25–64). This lower unionization rate of youths is common across a wide range of countries.[14] To what extent do these differences in unionization reflect differences in preferences on the part of youths compared to adults? More specifically, does the lower unionization rate of youths reflect less demand for collective action in the form of unions, perhaps reflecting a more individualistic orientation and a perception that unions would do little for them, or is it a reflection of greater supply-side constraints? The answer to this question, as illustrated below, is unequivocal: 'it's the supply-side stupid!'

As shown in the first row of the second panel of calculations, for both youths and adults who are unionized, almost three-quarters prefer to remain unionized, [P(D=1|U=1)]; that is, a clear majority are satisfied. This also implies, as indicated, in the second row, P(D=0|U=1), that slightly over one-quarter of both youths and adults who are unionized would prefer to be non-union; for these workers there is an excess supply of unionization. However, as indicated in the third row, [P(D=1|U=0), only 20 per cent of adults who are non-union would prefer to be unionized while almost half (46 per cent) of youths who are non-union would prefer to be unionized. In essence, the extent of unmet demand for unionization (the union representation gap) is much higher for youths than it is for adults. The potential gains for unionization are much higher amongst youths than amongst adults. Alternatively stated, as indicated in the last row of that panel, [$P(D{=}0|U{=}0)$], amongst non-union workers, the demand for remaining non-union is satisfied for 80 per cent of adults but only half (54 per cent) of youths.

Table 14.1 Supply and Demand Components of Unionization, Canada

Component	Definition	Adult 25–64	Youth 15–24
1. Proportions (that is, union density)			
$P(U{=}1)$	Proportion union	0.36	0.13
$P(U{=}0)$	Proportion non-union	0.64	0.87
2. Conditional preferences			
$P(D{=}1\| U{=}1)$	Desire for union by unionized	0.73	0.73
$P(D{=}0\| U{=}1)$	Desire for non-union by unionized	0.27	0.27
$P(D{=}1\| U{=}0)$	Desire for union by non-unionized	0.20	0.46
$P(D{=}0\| U{=}0)$	Desire for non-union by non-unionized	0.80	0.54
3. Unconditional preferences			
$P(D{=}1, U{=}1){=} P(D{=}1\| U{=}1)*P(U{=}1)$	Desire for union by unionized	0.26	0.09
$P(D{=}0, U{=}1){=} P(D{=}0\| U{=}1)*P(U{=}1)$	Desire for non-union by unionized	0.10	0.03
$P(D{=}1, U{=}0){=} P(D{=}1\| U{=}0)*P(U{=}0)$	Desire for union by non-unionized	0.13	0.40
$P(D{=}0, U{=}0){=} P(D{=}0\| U{=}0)*P(U{=}0)$	Desire for non-union by non-unionized	0.51	0.47
4. Total gross and net demand			
$P(U{=}1) + P(D{=}1, U{=}0)$	$P(D{=}1)$ = Gross demand	0.49	0.53
$P(U{=}1) + P(D{=}1, U{=}0) - P(D{=}0, U{=}1)$	$P(D^*{=}1)$ = Net demand	0.39	0.49

Table 14.1(cont.)

Component	Definition	Adult 25–64	Youth 15–24
5. Conditional probabilities			
$P(U=1\mid D=1)$	Probability of being union conditional on desiring	0.79	0.31
$P(U=0\mid D=1)$	Probability of being non-union conditional on desiring	0.21	0.69
$P(U=1\mid D=0)$	Probability of being union conditional on not desiring	0.26	0.12
$P(U=0\mid D=0)$	Probability of being non-union conditional on not desiring	0.74	0.88

Sources: Union density from Labor Force Survey; other figures from 1996 Lipset-Meltz Survey.

The previous discussion was based on the preferences of union and non-union workers. As indicated in the discussion of the definitions and concepts above, those conditional demands (that is, conditional upon being a union or a non-union worker) must be multiplied by the proportion of union and non-union workers to convert them into demands for the workforce as a whole. This is done in the third panel of Table 14.1. The conditional demands can differ from the unconditional demands depending upon the size or weight of the different groups in the workforce.

Satisfied Demand, Oversupply and Unsatisfied Demand: Youth and Adult Workforces

As indicated in the first row of the third panel of calculations, the satisfied demand for unionization for adults in the workforce as a whole is:

$$P(D=1, U=1)= P(D=1\mid U=1)*P(U=1) = 0.728* 0.36 = 0.262.$$

That is, multiplying the 72.8 per cent of adults who are union members and who want to remain unionized, by their 36 per cent unionization rate yields

26.2 per cent of the adult workforce as a whole being satisfied remaining unionized. For youth, multiplying the 72.7 per cent who are union members and want to remain unionized by their 13 per cent unionization rate yields 9.5 per cent of the youth workforce as a whole being satisfied remaining unionized. Clearly a much smaller proportion of the youth compared to the adult workforce is satisfied with remaining unionized because a much smaller proportion of the youth workforce is unionized (9.5 per cent for youths compared to 36 per cent for adults), not because youths who are unionized have a lower preference for remaining unionized compared to adults (those preferences being identical with 73 per cent of both youths and adults who are unionized wanting to remain unionized). In essence, the satisfied demand for unionization amongst the youth is less than that of the adult workforce because the youth unionization rate itself is lower, not because of a lower preference for unionized youths to remain unionized.

As shown in the second row of the third panel, the extent of excess supply of unionization in the youth workforce as a whole is much smaller than in the adult workforce because of the much smaller proportion of youths who are unionized, not because of a difference in the extent of oversupply amongst youths and adults who are unionized. The extent of oversupply, conditional upon being a union member, is identical, with 27 per cent of each of youths and adults who are unionized preferring to be non-union. It is because that identical preference is multiplied by a much smaller proportion of youths who are unionized that this gets translated into a smaller degree of excess supply of unionization amongst the youth workforce as a whole.

The third row of the third panel indicates that the extent of unsatisfied demand for unionization is much greater among non-union youth compared to the adult workforce as a whole. Specifically, almost 40 per cent (39.7 per cent) of the total youth workforce would prefer to be unionized but is not, compared to nearly 13 per cent (that is, 12.9 per cent) of the adult workforce that has a desire for unionization that is not being met. Clearly there is a large growth potential for unionization amongst youths. This much larger unsatisfied demand for unionization amongst young workers compared to the adult workforce occurs both because the desire for unionization amongst youths who are not unionized is much higher than amongst adults who are not unionized and because of the much lower unionization rate of youths compared to adults. The contribution of both of these components can be illustrated more clearly by plugging the numbers into the formula for calculating the unsatisfied demand for unionization:

$P(D=1, U=0) = P(D=1 | U=0) * P(U=0)$

$= 0.456 * 0.87 = 0.397 = 0.40$ for the youth workforce as a whole

=0.201*0.64 = 0.129= 0.13 for the adult workforce as a whole.

In other words, the unmet demand for unionization at 40 per cent of the youth workforce is over three times that of 13 per cent in the adult workforce, both because a much higher proportion (45.6 per cent) of youths compared to adults (20.1 per cent) who are not unionized would prefer to be unionized, and a much higher proportion of the youth workforce (87 per cent) that is not unionized, compared to the adult workforce (64 per cent). Put simply, the greater latent demand for unionization amongst youths is multiplied by a much larger base of non-unionized workers. This greater demand for unionization amongst non-union youths as well as the lesser extent to which their demands are being met, translates into a large potential market for unionization.

As indicated in the last row of the third panel, the extent of satisfied demand for remaining non-union is fairly similar amongst youths (47 per cent of the youth workforce) compared to adults (51 per cent of the adult workforce). This occurs because of the offsetting effect of two components, as illustrated by plugging the numbers into the formula for satisfied demand for remaining non-union:

$P(D=0, U=0)= P(D=0|\ U=0)*P(U=0)$
= 0.544 * 0.87 =0 .47 for the youth workforce as a whole
= 0.799 * 0.64 = 0.51 for the adult workforce as a whole.

These figures reveal that satisfied demand for remaining non-union is fairly similar for youths and adults, at about half of their respective workforces. This is because the preference for non-union workers to remain non-union is smaller amongst youths (54 per cent) compared to adults (80 per cent) but this is offset by the fact that a larger proportion of youths (87 per cent) are non-union, compared to adults (64 per cent). As such, this gets translated into fairly similar shares of the youth and adult workforces as a whole preferring to remain non-union.

Decomposing Components across Youth and Adult Workforces

An alternative portrayal of the relative importance of the different components of satisfied demand, unsatisfied demand and excess supply of unionization can be given when the components are weighted by the proportions of the youth and adult workforces in each of the components. These components sum to one within each of the youth and adult workforces.

As indicated by the panel 3 results, 9.5 per cent of the total youth workforce has their preference for remaining union satisfied and 47 per cent are content to remain non-union so that in total, slightly over half (57 per cent) of the total youth workforce has their preferences for union status satisfied. Conversely, a sizable number do not have their preferences satisfied, with the vast majority – unsatisfied demand for unionization amongst non-union workers – substantially outweighing the oversupply amongst union workers (3.5 per cent). In essence, 6 of 10 young workers do have their preference for union status being met, with most of them content to remain non-union. However, 4 out of 10 young workers do not have their preferences met, with almost all of them being non-union workers who would prefer to be unionized.

In contrast, about three quarters of the adult workforce have their preferences for union status satisfied, with 26 per cent having their preference for remaining union status satisfied and 51 per cent content to remain non-union. Conversely, almost one-quarter do not have their preferences satisfied, with slightly more having an unsatisfied demand for unionization (13 per cent) compared to an oversupply of unionization (10 per cent). In essence, 77 per cent of the adult workforce have their preference for union status met, with most of those content to remain non-union. However, 23 per cent do not have their preferences met, with slightly more being non-union workers having an unmet demand in that they would prefer to be unionized (13 per cent) compared to union workers who have an excess supply in that they would prefer to be non-union (10 per cent).

Clearly, there is unsatisfied demand for unionization amongst both youths and adults, but it is much more prominent amongst youths. This unsatisfied demand amongst non-union workers who would prefer to be unionized, is greater than any oversupply amongst union workers who would prefer to be non-union, and this is especially the case for youths, where unsatisfied demand is extensive and oversupply small.

Potential Unionization Rates

The previous information can be used to calculate the potential or hypothetical unionization rate that would prevail if all desires for unionization were fulfilled by adding the unsatisfied demand to the actual or realized demand as measured by the actual unionization rate. We term this the gross demand since it is the existing demand plus the unsatisfied demand (first row of the fourth panel). A measure of net demand can also be calculated by also subtracting any oversupply. This measure indicates the hypothetical unionization rate that would prevail if the unsatisfied demand and oversupply were both eliminated (second row of fourth panel).

As indicated in the first row of the fourth panel, the potential unionization rate if unsatisfied demands were met would be about 53 per cent for youths and 49 per cent for adults, clearly much higher than their actual unionization rates of 13 per cent and 36 per cent respectively. The larger change for youths compared to adults comes about both because a much higher proportion (45.6 per cent) of youths compared to adults (20.1 per cent) are not unionized but would prefer to be unionized, and a much higher proportion of the youth workforce (87 per cent) is not unionized, compared to the adult workforce (64 per cent). This potential unionization rate would correspond to the scenario where unsatisfied demands were met, but oversupply was not eliminated.

The second row of the fourth panel indicates the potential unionization rate if the net demands for unionization were met in that the excess supply of unionization was also subtracted from the unsatisfied demand, with that net demand being then added to the actual unionization rate for youths and adults. The potential unionization rate under net demand (unsatisfied demand minus excess supply) would be lower than the scenario where only gross demand was used (satisfied plus unsatisfied demand) because the excess supply is being subtracted from the unsatisfied demand. It is still higher than the actual unionization rate, however, since unsatisfied demand is always greater than excess supply. The potential unionization rate if both unsatisfied demand and excess supply were eliminated would be nearly 50 per cent (49.2 per cent) for youths and 39 per cent for adults. Again the difference between this potential rate for youths at 50 per cent and their actual rate at 13 per cent is much greater than the difference between the potential rate for adults at 39 per cent and their actual rate at 36 per cent for three reasons: 1) youths have greater unmet demands for unionization; 2) they have lesser excess supplies of unionization; and 3) they have a much lower actual unionization rate. In fact the potential unionization rate for adults is not that much higher than their actual rate since their unmet demand for unionization (12.9 per cent) is not much greater than their excess supply (9.8 per cent).

Probability of Achieving Desired Union Status

As indicated previously, an alternative way of presenting the data is to calculate the probability of achieving one's desired union status conditional upon desiring a particular status. These are given in the bottom panel of Table 14.1. For those who desire union status (D=1), the proportion who have achieved that status, $P(U=1|\ D=1)$, is 79 per cent for adults but only 31 per cent for youths. Again, this reflects the combination of youths having both a higher desire for union status and lower actual unionization rates compared to adults. Alternatively stated, the proportion who are non-union but who desire to be unionized, $P(U=0 | D=1)$, is 21 per cent for adults but 69 per cent for youths (the proportions summing to one within each group).

For those who desire to be non-union ($D=0$), the proportion who have achieved that status, $P(U=0 | D=0)$, is 74 per cent for adults and 88 per cent for youths. Alternatively stated, the proportion who are unionized but who desire to be non-union $P(U=1 | D=0)$, is 26 per cent for adults and 12 per cent for youths (the proportions again summing to one within each group). In essence, for both youths and adults, those who desire to be non-union tend to be able to achieve that status more easily, in part because non-union status is more common than union status.

YOUTH–ADULT DIFFERENCES IN UNIONIZATION AND WORKPLACE VOICE

The previous discussion focused on youth adult differences in unionization and preferences for unionization. While unionization is the most prominent form of voice at the workplace, there certainly are other non-union forms of employee representation such as professional associations, staff associations and non-union grievance procedures.[15]

Non-Union Representation and Preferences for Collective versus Individual Representation

As indicated in the analysis presented in 2005 by Campolieti, Gomez and Gunderson, the Lipset-Meltz survey asked questions that can be used to identify non-union forms of voice at the workplace as those who responded 'yes' to either or both questions: 'Are you a member of an organization other than a union that bargains on your behalf?' or 'Are you covered by any non-union employee representation at your workplace?' In the Canadian workforce 9.1 per cent are covered by one of these non-union forms of representation and an additional 4.5 per cent by both union and non-union forms. While youths are much less likely to be covered by union voice they are more likely to be covered by non-union representation. Specifically, based on logistic regression to control for the effect of other variables that can affect union and non-union representation, youths aged 18–24 were 19.6 per cent less likely to be covered by a union but 3.9 per cent more likely to be covered by non-union representation, when compared to adults aged 45–54. When compared to adults aged 35–44, youths aged 18–24 were 15.4 per cent less likely to be covered by a union but 5.4 per cent more likely to be covered by non-union representation.

In terms of their desire for different forms of voice, the Lipset-Meltz survey asked the following questions: 'How would you prefer to solve a workplace problem of your own? Would you feel more comfortable dealing directly with management yourself, or would you feel more comfortable having a group of your fellow employees help you deal with management?' Most Canadian workers (57.8 per cent) preferred to deal directly with management, rather than to use collective forms of voice to deal with their own workplace problems. However, young workers (age 18–24) were around 8 percentage points less likely than older workers to prefer to deal directly with management over their workplace problems, as opposed to using a collective response (after controlling for the effect of other variables). Perceptions of their individualistic orientation notwithstanding, younger workers were less likely than older workers to want direct individual solutions to their workplace problems.

In terms of their desire for representative voice, workers were also asked if they would be interested 'in joining an organization that would engage in collective bargaining (or negotiate) over wages and benefits' and separately whether they would be interested 'in joining an organization that would represent employees who have filed grievances against their superiors or managers.' Overall, the proportion of the Canadian workforce that expressed a preference for collective representation for bargaining over these issues was: 36 per cent for bargaining for both wage/benefits and grievances; 50.3 per cent for wages/benefits only; and, 44.6 per cent for grievances only. Young workers (age 18–24) were much more likely than the various older worker age groups to prefer collective representation for these issues. Specifically, their likelihood of preferring collective bargaining over these issues was 10 to 15 percentage points higher for both wages/benefits and grievances; 17–21 percentage points higher for wages/benefits only; and, 8–13 percentage points higher for grievances only. In essence, compared to older workers, younger workers had a stronger preference for collective representation, even more so for wages than for grievances. Again, contrary to perceptions of their individualistic orientation, younger workers were more likely than were older workers to want collective solutions to the key workplace issues of wages/benefits and grievances.

Reasons for Youth–Adult Differences in Desire to Belong to a Union

As indicated in the 2002 analysis of Gomez, Gunderson and Meltz, the stronger expressed preferences of youths for collective solutions to workplace problems can also be illustrated by using logistic regression to decompose the adult-youth differences in desiring to belong to a union into two components: one that can be attributed to differences in the characteristics or exposure of youths and adults that give rise to their desire to belong to a union; the other is attributed to differences in their pure preferences after netting out the effect of the differences in characteristics or exposure to factors that influence the desire for unionization. The characteristics that can influence the desire to belong to a union were:

1. Social capital indicators (union member in the family, and family and friends support unions);
2. Attitudes towards traditional union policies (positive attitude towards pay standardization; positive view of worker political power; preference for layoffs based on seniority; perception that collective solutions to work problems are best);
3. Perceptions about the employer and the job (feels no loyalty to employer; feels employees are treated unfairly at work; perceives poor opportunity for advancement at work; worried about layoffs);
4. Union-voice substitutes (no progressive human resources management, (HRM) practices at the job; feels unprotected by workplace law); and,
5. Individual characteristics (gender; union status; political position). The desire to belong to a union was measured as responding 'yes' to the Lipset-Meltz survey question: 'All things considered, if you had a choice, would you personally prefer to belong to or remain in a labor union or not?'

The empirical results yielded the following specific findings (all effects for the different variables are net effects that control for the effect of the other variables via logistic regression):

- 56.7 per cent of youths compared to 49.8 per cent of adults stated a desire to belong to a union, for an overall difference of 6.9 percentage points in favor of youths preferring unions.
- Almost two-thirds (62 per cent) of the higher desire of youths for unionization can be attributed to the greater preferences of youths for unionization, and somewhat more than one-third (38 per cent) can be attributed to the fact that youths have characteristics or are more exposed to the social capital, workplace issues or attitudes that give rise to a greater desire for unionization to deal with such issues in general.
- Persons who had a union member in the family or who had family and friends that supported unions were themselves much more likely to desire unionization, with the effect being much stronger for youths compared to adults. Families and peers were a more important influence in shaping the preferences of youths than was the case for adults.
- The desire for unionization was higher amongst persons who preferred pay standardization as opposed to merit-based pay, with the effect being

almost twice as large for youths compared to adults.

- Not surprisingly, the desire for unionization was much greater for those persons who felt that workers should have more political power, with the effect being greater for youths compared to adults. Youths were also more likely than adults to think that workers should have more political power.
- The proportion of youths who supported the traditional union policy of preferring layoffs based solely on seniority was smaller for youths (36 per cent) compared to adults (42 per cent), but not hugely so. This is somewhat surprising since layoffs based on seniority as opposed to merit would disproportionately benefit adults. Adults were more likely than were youths, however, to translate those preferences into reality by indicating a desire for unionization.
- About one-third of both youth and adults felt that individual solutions to workplace problems were best, around 20 per cent felt that collective solutions were best and about half of each group did not know. The latter fact suggests that substantial numbers could be persuaded to support either collective or individual policies (for example, unions or progressive HRM practices). Adults were more willing to act on their views, however, through supporting unions.
- About two-thirds of both adults and youth felt a loyalty to their employer. Only adults, however, translate that loyalty into action by indicating that they were less likely to prefer a union. The effect of loyalty on youths' preferences for unionization is statistically insignificant.
- 58 per cent of youths compared to only 13 per cent of adults perceived employees as being treated unfairly at their workplace. Youths were also much more likely than adults to support unionization as a result. Substantial numbers of both youths (19 per cent) and especially adults (30 per cent) indicated that they 'did not know' whether employees were treated unfairly at work, suggesting that substantial numbers could be influenced by unions or by progressive HRM practices that would facilitate fair treatment at work.
- 31 per cent of both youths and adults thought they had poor opportunity for advancement at work. Adults who felt that way were more likely to prefer unions (presumably because the seniority principle was more likely to help them advance) while such youths preferred to be non-union (presumably because they felt that the seniority principle harms their prospects for advancement).
- While almost one-third of adults (31.5 per cent) worried about layoffs, only about 19 per cent of youths had such a worry. Presumably this reflects the lower cost of layoffs to youths and the fact that they expected to be laid off given their lower seniority. The expectation of being laid

off, however, had a large effect on preferring unionization for youths but no effect for adults. This is puzzling since unions would tend to foster the seniority principle that tends to put youths at more risk of layoffs, compared to adults.

- Youths were somewhat more likely (41 per cent) than adults (33.5 per cent) to have no progressive HRM practices at work (for example, self-directed work teams, total quality management, quality circles, employee involvement programs). Youths who had such progressive HRM policies, however, were much less likely to prefer unionization, although the lack of such practices had no such effect for adults.
- This highlights the potential for such progressive HRM practices to be a substitute for unionization for youths who are at a stage in their life cycle when such preferences are being shaped. It also highlights why unions understandably may regard such practices as threats, especially for youths who have not had the opportunity to experience unionization.
- 50 per cent each of adults and youths felt protected by workplace law. However, only youths who did not feel protected translated this into a strong preference for unionization; the lack of protection had no effect on the preference of adults for unionization. This highlights that legal protection could be a potential substitute for unionization, at least for youths, again at a stage in their life cycle where preferences are being shaped.
- For both youths and adults who were currently union members compared to those who were not union members, the preferences to remain unionized were very strong. This highlights that only small numbers of union members preferred decertification.
- Perhaps somewhat surprisingly, the proportion of youths and adults on the left, right and center of the political spectrum were remarkably similar. This is contrary to the notion that people become more conservative as they age, but it is consistent with the possibility that the youths of today are more conservative than the youths of yesterday. Adults at the centre and especially on the left in the political spectrum were more likely to prefer unions than persons on the right. The same pattern prevails for youths, but the effects are statistically insignificant.

CONCLUDING OBSERVATIONS AND IMPLICATIONS

A number of broader generalizations and implications emerge from this study as well as others we have conducted on youth–adult differences in unionization rates and preferences for union and non-union forms of voice at the workplace. The main generalizations are:

- There is substantial unsatisfied demand in Canada for unionization amongst both youths and adults, but it is much more prominent amongst youths. This unsatisfied demand amongst the non-union workers who would prefer to be unionized is greater than any oversupply amongst union workers who would prefer to be non-union, and this is especially the case for youths where the unsatisfied demand is extensive and the oversupply small.
- The potential unionization rate if both unsatisfied demand and excess supply were eliminated would be almost 50 per cent for youths and 39 per cent for adults. The difference between this potential rate for youths at 50 per cent and their actual rate at 13 per cent is much greater than the difference between the potential rate for adults at 39 per cent and their actual rate at 36 per cent for three reasons: youths have greater unmet demands for unionization; they have lesser excess supplies of unionization; and, they have a much lower actual unionization rate.
- About two-thirds of the stronger desire of youths for unions emanates from a stronger preference of youths for unions to deal with workplace issues, and one-third reflects their characteristics or exposure to issues that create a demand for unionization.
- Youth preferences for unionization are malleable and strongly shaped by such factors as the attitudes of family and friends towards unions and whether family members are unionized. This highlights the cumulative and inter-generational effects that can be involved in the transmission of union status – unionization begets further unionization.
- Progressive HRM practices and legislative protection can strongly reduce the preferences of youth for unionization, suggesting that they may be substitutes for unions. This highlights a trade-off for unions. They may support protective legislation for reasons of social justice and because it can protect their own members by raising the cost of non-union labor. But the protective legislation may reduce the demand for union protection if it can be provided by the state.
- Large number of youths seemed to be at a tipping point with respect to being persuaded into individual solutions (for example, progressive HRM practices) or collective solutions (for example, unions) to deal with many workplace issues. This is evidenced by the fact that youth were more likely to indicate that they 'did not know' whether collective or individual solutions were better, whether employees were treated unfairly at work, and whether they felt unprotected by workplace law as compared to adults.
- As such, there is a large potential among youths either to support or oppose unionization, depending on conditions inside the workplace as well as the views of family and friends about unions. In essence, there is

a 'potential youth market' for unions, especially in workplaces where youths believe that employees are not being fairly treated and if they are given the opportunity to experience unionization.
- Our results provide a possible explanation of the cumulative, snowballing effect that seems to be associated with union decline, as in the US. Declining union membership means that it is less likely that there will be a union member in the family, and less likely that family and friends will support unions because they will be less familiar with them. As such, union decline begets further union decline, given the much stronger effect that these variables have on youths as compared to adults.
- Our analysis suggests that there are strong reasons for unions to target youths for the purpose of organizing them or informing them about unions. Moreover, our analysis shows that this targeting strategy should not focus on the short-run costs and benefits. Rather, there is a longer-run investment component with a potential long-term payoff through multiplier and inter-generational effects on successive generations.

Reasons for the targeting of youth that flow from our analysis are:

- Youths do have a preference for unionization and for collective solutions to deal with workplace issues.
- Those preferences are not being met given their low unionization rate.
- As such, they have considerable unmet demand that makes them a labor market segment offering growth potential for unions.
- Their preferences in this area are quite malleable and not yet fixed. In addition, youth preferences for or against unions seem to influence their desire for unionization somewhat more than their characteristics or their exposure to issues that affect the desire for unionization.
- Many are at a tipping point in that they could easily be influenced by unions or by possible union substitutes in the form of progressive HRM practices or legislative initiatives.
- Whichever way they go will probably have multiplier effects (through influencing family and friends and through experience effects) as well as long-term consequences through intergenerational transmission mechanisms.

Of course, the various reasons for unions to target youth provide a similar rationale for employers, especially if they are trying to maintain a non-union status. The future of trade unionism in Canada may well hinge on who wins that battle. Unions may have a slight advantage to the extent that the preferences of youths seem to be in their favor; nevertheless, these preferences are malleable and likely to be influenced by their experiences and social relations.

NOTES

1. Financial assistance for this research from the Social Science and Humanities Research Council (SSHRC) is gratefully acknowledged as is support from the Leverhulme Trusts 'Future of British Trade Unions' Project Fund..
2. On the Wagner model set by the 1935 National Labor Relations Act in the US, see for example Taras (1997b).
3. Gomez, Lipset and Meltz (2001), Bryson, Gunderson and Meltz (2005); Gomez, Gunderson and Meltz (2002), Gomez and Gunderson (2004).
4. The survey is described in detail in Lipset, et al. (2004, Appendix B). Many of the survey questions were intentionally borrowed from the Freeman and Rogers (1999) Workplace Representation and Participation Survey (WRPS) so as to foster comparability with the US.
5. Canada–US comparisons of union density are given in Murray (2005, p. 86) and international comparisons in Lipsig-Mumme (2005, p.489).
6. Campolieti, Gomez and Gunderson (2005). This greater preference for collective solutions at the workplace in the US compared to Canada was found across a wide range of measures such as worker political power, collective solutions to work, grievance representation, and collective bargaining over wages as well as belonging to a union. It is also found in other studies including Bryson, et al. (2005), Gomez, Lipset and Meltz (2001) and Lipset *et al.* (2004).
7. Reasons for the higher union density in Canada compared to the US are outlined in Lipset *et al.* (2004), Murray (2005), Riddell (1993) and Taras (2001) and references cited therein.
8. The evolution from non-union associations to unions in the Canadian public sector is discussed in (Gunderson 2002) and references cited therein.
9. The recent decline in unionization is documented and discussed in (Riddell 2004 and Riddell and Riddell 2004).
10. Theoretical reasons for youth–adult differences in unionization are outlined in Gomez, Gunderson and Meltz (2002), Haynes, Vowles and Boxall (2005) and references cited therein.
11. This alleged individualistic attitude on the part of youth is discussed in Alvin and Sverke (2000) and in O'Bannon (2001).
12. The experience-good model of unionization is developed and discussed in Bryson and Gomez (2003), Gomez and Gunderson (2004) and Gomez, Gunderson and Meltz (2002).
13. The malleable preferences of youths in this area and the importance of family, peers and the socialization process is emphasized in Barling, Kelloway and Bremermann (1991), Dekker, Greenberg and Barling (1998), Freeman and Diamond (2003), Fullagar and Barling (1989), Fullagar *et al.* (1995), Gallagher (1999), Kelloway, Barling and Agar (1996), Loughlin and Barling (2001), Lowe and Rastin (2000) and Payne (1989).
14. See Bryson, et al. (2005, p. 156) for Canada, the US, and Britain, and Haynes, Vowles and Boxall (2005) for evidence for New Zealand and Australia, and for references to other international evidence on youth–adult differences in unionization.
15. Non-union representation is discussed in Campolieti, Gomez and Gunderson (2005) and Taras (2000, 2002).

References

Abadie, Alberto and Guido W. Imbens (2006), 'Simple and Bias–Corrected Matching Estimators for Average Treatment Effects,' *Econometrica*, **74**, 235–67.

Abe, Y. (2001), 'Chiikibetsu Saitei Chingin ga Part Chingin ni Ataeru Eikyo' (The Influence of the Prefectural Minimum Wages on the Wages of Part–time Workers), in Takenori Inoki and Fumio Ohtake (eds), *Koyo Seisaku no Keizai Bunseki (Economic Analysis of Employment Policy)*, Tokyo: Tokyo University Press, 259–302.

Abowd, J. M., F. Kramarz, T. Lemiux and D. Margolis (2000), 'Minimum Wages and Youth Employment in France and the United States,' in D. G. Blanchflower and R. B. Freeman (eds), *Youth Unemployment and Joblessness in Advanced Countries,* Chicago: University of Chicago Press, 427–72.

Ackum, S. (1991), 'Youth Unemployment, Labour Market Programmes and Subsequent Earnings,' *Canadian Journal of Economics*, **93** (4), 531–43.

Advisory Committee on Student Financial Assistance, US Dept. of Education (2002), *Empty Promises: The Myth of College Access in America*, Washington DC: US Dept. of Education.

AFL-CIO (1999), *High Hopes, Little Trust*, Washington DC: AFL-CIO Mediacenter.

Aldrich, Howard and Roger Waldinger (1990), 'Ethnicity and Entrepreneurship,' *Annual Review of Sociology*, **16**, 111–35.

Allen, S. (2001), 'Technology and the Wage Structure,' *Journal of Labour Economics*, 19, 440–83.

Altonji, Joseph and David Card (1991), 'The Effects of Immigration on the Labor Market Outcomes of Less-Skilled Natives,' in R. B. Freeman and G. Borjas (eds), *Immigration, Trade, and the Labor Market*, Chicago: University of Chicago Press, 201–34.

Alvin, M. and M. Sverke (2000), 'Do New Generations Imply the End of Solidarity? Swedish Unionism in the Era of Individualization,' *Economic and Industrial Democracy,* **21**, 71–95.

Andersson, Fredrik, Harry J. Holzer and Julia Lane (2005), *Moving Up or Moving On: Who Advances in the Low-Wage Labor Market?* New York: Russell Sage Foundation.

Andrews, M., S. Bradley and R. Upward (1999), 'Estimating Youth Training Wage Differentials during and after Training,' *Oxford Economic Papers*, **51** (3), 517–44.

Arulampalam, W. and A. Booth (2000), 'Union Status of Young Men in Britain: A Decade of Change,' *Journal of Applied Econometrics*, **15**, 289–310.

Austen-Smith, David and Roland Fryer (2005), 'An Economic Analysis of Acting White,' *Quarterly Journal of Economics*, **120** (2), 551–84.

Autor, David and Lawrence Katz (1999). 'Changes in the Wage Structure and

Earnings Inequality,' in O. Ashenfelter and D. Card (eds), *Handbook of Labor Economics, Vol. 3A,* Amsterdam: North Holland.

Autor, David, Lawrence Katz and Melissa Kearney (2004), 'Trends in US Wage Inequality: Reassessing the Revisionists,' Working Paper, Harvard University.

Autor, D. H., L. F. Katz and A. B. Krueger (1998), 'Computing Inequality: Have Computers Changed the Labor Market?' *Quarterly Journal of Economics*, **113** (4), 1169–1213.

Bailey, Mark and Tony Mallier (1999), 'The Summer Vacation: Influences on the Hours Students Work,' *Applied Economics*, **31** (1), 9–15.

Bailey, Thomas (1987), *Immigrant and Native Workers: Contrasts and Competition*, Boulder, CO: Westview Press.

Barling, J., E. Kelloway and E. Bremermann (1991), 'Pre-employment Predictors of Union Attitudes: The Role of Family Socialization and Work Beliefs,' *Journal of Applied Psychology*, **76**, 725–31.

Bartik, Timothy J. (2001*), Jobs for the Poor: Can Labor Demand Policies Help?* New York: Russell Sage Foundation.

Bassanini A. and R. Duval (2006), 'Employment Patterns in OECD Countries: Reassessing the Role of Policies and Institutions,' OECD Economics Department Working Paper No. 486.

Bassi, Laurie and Jens Ludwig (2000), 'School to Work Programs in the United States: A Multi-Firm Case Study of Training, Benefits and Costs,' *Industrial and Labor Relations Review*, **53** (2), 219–39.

Batty, David (2006), 'Immigration Surge Tips UK Population Over 60m,' *The Guardian*, London: August 24, 1.

Bean, Frank, and Daniel Hammermesh (eds), (2000), *Help or Hindrance? The Economic Implications of Immigration for African Americans,* New York, NY: Russell Sage Foundation.

Bean, Frank, B. L. Lowell and L. J. Taylor (1988), 'Undocumented Mexican Immigrants and the Earnings of Other Workers in the United States,' *Demography,* **25** (1), 35–49.

Beaulieu, E. (2000), 'The Canada-US Free Trade Agreement and Labor Market Adjustment in Canada,' *Canadian Journal of Economics*, **33** (2), 540–63.

Becker, Gary (1985), 'Human Capital, Effort, and the Sexual Division of Labor,' *Journal of Labor Economics*, special supplement, S33–S58.

Becker, Sascha O., Samuel Bentolila, Ana Fernandes and Andrea Ichino (2004), 'Job Insecurity and Children's Emancipation,' *Discussion Paper no. 1046*, Bonn: IZA.

Berman, E., J. Bound and Z. Griliches (1994), 'Changes in the Demand for Skilled Labour within US Manufacturing: Evidence from the Annual Survey of Manufacturers,' *Quarterly Journal of Economics,* **109**, 367–98.

Bertola, G., F. D. Blau and L. M. Kahn (2002), 'Labor Market Institutions and Demographic Employment Patterns,' *NBER Working Paper No. 9043.*

Besharov, Douglas (ed.), (1999), *America's Disconnected Youth,* Washington DC: CWLA Press.

Biancotti, Claudia, Giovanni D'Alessio and Andrea Neri (2004), 'Errori di Misura nell'Indagine sui Bilanci delle Famiglie Italiane,' *Temi di Discussione no. 520*, Roma: Servizio Studi, Banca d'Italia.

Bishop, J. (1991), 'Achievement, Test Scores and Relative Wages,' in M.H. Kosters (ed), *Workers and Their Wages,* Washington DC: AEI Press, 146–86.

Blanchard, O. and A. Landier (2002), 'The Perverse Effects of Partial Labour

Market Reform: Fixed-Term Contracts in France,' *The Economic Journal*, **112** (480), F214–F244.

Blanchflower, D. G. and R. B. Freeman (eds), (2000a), *Youth Unemployment and Joblessness in Advanced Countries,* Chicago: University of Chicago Press.

Blanchflower, D. G. and R. B. Freeman (2000b), 'Introduction,' in D. G. Blanchflower and R. B. Freeman (eds), *Youth Unemployment and Joblessness in Advanced Countries,* Chicago: University of Chicago Press, 1–16.

Blanchflower, D. G. and R. B. Freeman (2000c), 'The Declining Economic Status of Young Workers in OECD Countries' in D. G. Blanchflower and R. B. Freeman (eds), *Youth Unemployment and Joblessness in Advanced Countries*, Chicago: University of Chicago Press, 19–55.

Blank, Rebecca (1999), 'Race and Gender in the Labor Market,' in Orley C. Ashenfelter and David Card (eds), *Handbook of Labor Economics, Vol. 3A*, Amsterdam: North Holland.

Blank, Rebecca and Heidi Shierholz (2005), 'Explaining Employment and Wage Trends among Less-Skilled Women,' presented at the *National Poverty Center Conference*, Georgetown University, June 9–10.

Blank, Rebecca and Lucie Schmidt (2002), 'Work, Wages and Welfare,' In R. Blank and R. Haskins (eds), *The New World of Welfare,* Washington DC: Brookings Institution.

Blau, Francine and Lawrence Kahn (1997), 'Swimming Upstream: Trends in the Gender Wage Differential in the 1980's,' *Journal of Labor Economics*, **15** (1), 1–42.

Bloom, Dan and Colleen Sommo (2005), *Opening Doors: Building Learning Communities*, New York: MDRC.

Boal, W. M. and J. Pencavel (1994), 'The Effects of Labor Unions on Employment, Wages and Days of Operation: Coal Mining in West Virginia,' *Quarterly Journal of Economics*, **109**, 267–98.

Bohning, W. R. and M-L. Schloeter-Paredes (eds), (1994), *Aid in Place of Migration,* Geneva: International Labour Organization.

Borjas, George (1996), *Labor Economics*, New York: McGraw Hill.

Borjas. George J. (1998), 'Do Blacks Gain or Lose from Immigration?' in Daniel S. Hamermesh and Frank D. Bean (eds), *Help or Hindrance? The Economic Implications of Immigration for African Americans*, New York: Russell Sage Foundation.

Borjas, George (1999), *Heaven's Door*, Princeton: Princeton University Press.

Borjas, George (2003), 'The Labor Demand Curve is Downward Sloping: Reexamining the Impact of Immigration on the Labor Market,' *Quarterly Journal of Economics,* **118** (4), 1335–74.

Borjas, George J. (2004), 'Native Internal Migration and the Labor Market Impact of Immigration,' *NBER Working Paper No. 11610.*

Bos, Johannes, Susan Scrivener, Jason Snipes, and Gayle Hamilton (2003), *Center for Employment* Training*: Five Year Summary Report*, New York: MDRC.

Bound, John and Harry Holzer (1993), 'Industrial Shifts, Skill Levels and the Labor Market for White and Black Males,' *Review of Economics and Statistics*, **75** (3), 387–96.

Bowers, N., A. Sonnet and L. Bardone (1999), 'Giving Young People a Good Start: The Experience of OECD Countries,' in OECD, *Preparing Youth for the 21st Century: The Transition from Education to the Labour Market*, OECD, Paris, 7–86

Brandolini, Andrea 1999, 'The Distribution of Personal Income in Post-War Italy: Source Description, Data Quality and the Time Patterns of Income Inequality' *Giornale degli Economisti e Annali dell'Economia*, **58** (2), 183–239.

Brandolini, Andrea, Piero Cipollone and Eliana Viviana (2006), 'Does the ILO Definition Capture All Unemployment?' *Journal of the European Economic Association*, **4** (1), 153–79.

Briggs, Vernon M. (2001), *Immigration and American Unionism*, Ithaca, NY: Cornell University Press.

Brown, B. (2001), *Teens, Jobs and Welfare: Implications for Social Policy*, Washington DC: Child Trends, www.childtrends.org.

Bryson, A., R., M. Gunderson, and N. Meltz (2005), 'Youth-Adult Differences in the Demand for Unionization: Are American, British and Canadian Workers All That Different?' *Journal of Labor Research*, **26** (1), 155–67.

Büchtemann, C., J. Schupp and D. Soloff (1993), 'Roads to Work: School to Work Transition Patterns in Germany and the US,' *Industrial Relations Journal*, **24**, 97–111.

Burghardt, John, Peter Z. Schochet, Sheena McConnell, Terry Johnson, R. Mark Gritz, et al. (2001), *Does Job Corps Work? Summary of the National Job Corps Study*, Princeton, NJ.: Mathematica Policy Research, Inc.

Bushway, Shawn, Michael Stoll and David Weiman (eds), (2007), *Barriers to Reentry? The Labor Market for Released Prisoners in Post-Industrial America*, New York: Russell Sage Foundation.

Butcher, Kristin and David Card (1991), 'Immigration and Wages: Evidence from the 1980s,' *American Economic Review*, **81**, 292–96.

Campolieti, M., R. Gomez and M. Gunderson (forthcoming), 'Say What? Employee Voice in Canada,' in R. Freeman, P. Boxall and P. Haynes (eds), *Voice and Voicelessness in the Anglo-American World: Continuity and Transformation in the Anglo-American World.*

Cancian, Maria and Daniel Meyer (2005), 'Child Support and the Economy,' presented at the National Poverty Center Conference, Georgetown University, June 9–10.

Card, David (1990), 'The Impact of the Mariel Boatlift on the Miami Labor Market,' *Industrial and Labor Relations Review*, **43** (1), 245–57.

Card, D., L. F. Katz and A. B. Krueger (1994), 'Comment on David Neumark and William Wascher, Employment Effects of Minimum and Subminimum Wages: Panel Data on State Minimum Wage Laws,' *Industrial and Labor Relations Review*, **47** (3), 487–96.

Card D., F. Kramarz and T. Lemieux (1996), 'Changes in the Relative Structure of Wages and Employment: A Comparison of the United States, Canada, and France,' NBER Working Paper 5487.

Card D., F. Kramarz and T. Lemieux (1999), 'Changes in the Relative Structure of Wages and Employment: A Comparison of the United States, Canada, and France,' *Canadian Journal of Economics*, **32**, 843–77.

Card, D. and A. B. Krueger (1994), 'Minimum Wages and Employment: A case study of the Fast Food Industry in New Jersey and Pennsylvania,' *American Economic Review*, **84** (4), 772–93.

Card, D. and A. B. Krueger (1995), *Myth and Measurement: The New Economics of the Minimum Wage*, Princeton: Princeton University Press.

Card, D. and A. B. Krueger (2000), 'Minimum Wages and Employment: A Case

Study of the Fast-Food Industry in New Jersey and Pennsylvania: Reply,' *American Economic Review*, **90** (5), 1397–1420.

Card, D. and DiNardo, J. (2002), 'Skill-biased technological change and rising wage inequality: some problems and puzzles,' *Journal of Labor Economics*, **20** (4), 733–83.

Card, David and Thomas Lemieux (2000), 'Adapting to Circumstances: The Evolution of Work, School, and Living Arrangements Among North American Youth,' in D. G. Blanchflower and R. B. Freeman (eds), *Youth Employment and Joblessness in Advanced Countries,* Chicago: University of Chicago Press, 171–214.

CEREQ (2002), *Quand L'Ecole est Finie: Premiers pas dans la Vie Active de la Generation* **98**, Marseilles: CEREQ.

CEREQ (2004), 'Generation 2001: S'Inserer Lorsquq la Conjuncture se Degrade,' *CEREQ Bref, 214.*

Chapa, Jorge (1989), 'The Myth of Hispanic Progress: Trends in the Educational Ad Economic Attainment of Mexican Americans,' *Journal of Hispanic Policy*, 4**,** 3–18.

Chaplin, Duncan (1999), 'Limit Children's Work Hours, Report Says,' *Public Health Reports*, **114** (2), 105–12.

Chasanov, Amy (2004), 'No Longer Getting By: An Increase in the Minimum Wage is Long Overdue,' *EPI Working Paper,* Economic Policy Institute, Washington DC.

Choy, Susan (1998), 'College Access and Affordability,' *Education Statistics Quarterly*, **1** (2), 1–8.

Christopoulou, R., *Youth Unemployment in Advanced Economies*, doctoral dissertation in progress, Faculty of Economics, Cambridge University.

Clark, K. and L. Summers (1982), 'The Dynamics of Youth Unemployment,' in R. B. Freeman and D.A. Wise (eds), *The Youth Labor Market Problem: Its Nature, Causes and Consequence,* Chicago: University of Chicago Press, 199–234.

Cook, Philip and Jens Ludwig (1998), 'The Burdens of Acting White: Do Black Adolescents Disparage Academic Achievement?' in C. Jencks and M. Phillips (eds), *The Black-White Test Score Gap,* Washington DC: The Brookings Institution.

Cooper, P. and B.S. Schone, (1997), 'More Offers, Fewer Takers for Employment-Based Health Insurance: 1987 and 1996,' *Health Affairs*, **16** (6), 142–49

Corak, Miles (2004a), 'Do Poor Children Become Poor Adults? Lessons for Public Policy from a Cross-Country Comparison of Generational Earnings Mobility, paper presented at the *Colloque sur le Devenir des Enfants de Familles Defavourisees en France*. Paris, April.

Corak, Miles (ed.), (2004b), *Generational Income Mobility in North America and Europe*, Cambridge: Cambridge University Press.

Costrell, R.M., G. E. Duguay, and G.I. Treyz (1986), 'Labour Substitution and Complementarity among Age-Sex Groups,' *Applied Economics* **18** (7), 777–91.

Crawford D.L., A.W. Johnson and A.A. Summers (1997), 'Schools and Labor Market Outcomes,' *Economics of Education Review*, June, **16** (3), 255–69.

Crouter, Ann C. and Susan M. McHale (2005), 'Work Time, Family Time, and Children's Time: Implications for Child and Adolescent Relationships, Development, and Well-being,' in S. Bianchi, L. Casper, K. E. Christensen, and R. B. King (eds), (2005), W*orkforce/Workplace Mismatch? Work, Family, Health, and Well-Being*, Mahwah, NJ: Lawrence Erlbaum Associates.

Curtis, Susan and Najah Shani (2002), 'The Effect of Taking Paid Employment During Term-time on Students' Academic Studies,' *Journal of Further and Higher Education*, **26** (2), 129 – 38.

Darity, William A. and Patrick L. Mason (1998), 'Evidence on Discrimination Employment: Codes of Color, Codes of Gender,' *Journal of Economic Perspectives*, **12** (2), 63–90.

DeFreitas, Gregory (1988), 'Hispanic Immigration and Labor Market Segmentation,' *Industrial Relations*, **27** (2), 195–214.

DeFreitas, Gregory (1991), *Inequality at Work: Hispanics in the US Labor Force*, New York: Oxford University Press.

DeFreitas, Gregory (1993), 'Unionization Among Racial and Ethnic Minorities,' *Industrial and Labor Relations Review*, **46** (1), 284–301.

DeFreitas, Gregory (1996a), 'Nonimmigrant Visa Programs: Problems and Policy Reforms,' In Lindsay Lowell, ed. *Temporary Migrants in the US*, Washington DC: US Commission on Immigration Reform, 189–98.

DeFreitas, Gregory (1996b), *The Impact of Immigration on Youth Employment in New York City: Findings from an Employer Survey*, Washington DC: US Dept. of Labor, ILAB.

DeFreitas, Gregory (1998), 'Immigration, Inequality and Policy Alternatives,' in Gerald Epstein and Robert Pollin (eds), *Globalization and Progressive Economic Policy*, New York: Cambridge University Press.

DeFreitas, Gregory (2002), 'Fear of Foreigners: Immigrants as Economic Scapegoats,' in Ronald Takaki (ed), *Debating Diversity: Clashing Perspectives on Race and Diversity in America,* New York: Oxford University Press.

DeFreitas, Gregory (2006), 'Can Construction Unions Organize New Immigrant Workers?' *Regional Labor Review*, **9** (1), 28–32.

DeFreitas, Gregory and Niev Duffy (2004), 'Young Workers, Economic Inequality and Collective Action,' in Michael Zweig (ed), *What's Class Got To Do With It? American Society in the 21st Century*, New York: Cornell University Press, 143–60.

DeFreitas, Gregory, David Marsden, and Paul Ryan (1991), 'Youth Employment Patterns in Segmented Labor Markets in the US and Europe,' *Eastern Economic Journal*, **17** (2), 223–36.

DeFreitas, Gregory and Bhaswati Sengupta (2007), 'The State of New York Unions 2007,' *Regional Labor Review*, **10** (1), 3–12.

Dekker, I., L. Greenberg and J. Barling (1998), 'Predicting Union Attitudes in Student Part-time Workers,' *Canadian Journal of Behavioural Science,* 30, 49–55.

Del Boca, Daniela, Marilena Locatelli and Silvia Pasqua (2000), 'Employment Decisions of Married Women: Evidence and Explanations,' *Labour*, **14** (1), 35–52.

Delgado, Hector (2000), 'Immigrant Nation: Organizing America's Newest Workers,' *New Labor Forum* (Fall/Winter), 29–39.

Dembe, Allard (2005), 'Long Working Hours: The Scientific Basis for Concern,' *Perspectives on Work*, **8** (2), 200–20.

Djankov, S., R. La Porta, F. Lopez de Silanes, A. Shleifer and J. C. Botero (2003), 'The Regulation of Labor,' Social Science Research Network Working Paper.

Dolado, J. J., F. Kramarz, S. Machin, A. Manning, D. Margolis and C. Teulings (1996), 'The Economic Impact of Minimum Wages in Europe,' *Economic Policy*, **23**, 319–72.

Doms, M., T. Dunne and K. R. Troske (1997), 'Workers, Wages and Technology,' *Quarterly Journal of Economics*, **112**, 253–90.

Draut, Tamara (2005), *Strapped: Why America's 20- and 30-Somethings Can't Get Ahead,* New York: Doubleday.

Duffy, Niev J. (2002a) 'The Coming Health Care Crisis for New York Parents,' *Regional Labor Review,* **4** (1), 29–33.

Duffy, Niev J. (2002b), *A Crisis in Coverage: Falling Adolescent Health Insurance: Its Impact on Youth and their Health Care Providers*, Mt Sinai Adolescent Health Center Policy Report, New York: Mt. Sinai Adolescent Health Center.

Dundes, Lauren and Jeff Marx (2006–07), 'Balancing Work and Academics in College: Why Do Students Working 10 To 19 Hours Per Week Excel?' *Journal of College Student Retention,* **8** (1), 107–20.

Edelman, Peter, Harry Holzer and Paul Offner (2006), *Reconnecting Disadvantaged Young Men*, Washington DC: Urban Institute Press.

Edin, Per-Anders, Peter Fredriksson, and Olof Aslund (2003), 'Ethnic Enclaves and the Economic Success of Immigrants – Evidence from a Natural Experiment,' *The Quarterly Journal of Economics*, **118**, 329–57.

Ehrenberg, Ronald and Daniel Sherman, 'Employment While in College, Academic Achievement, and Post-college Outcomes,' *Journal of Human Resources*, **22** (1), 1–23.

European Training Village (1999a), *Apprenticeship in Finland 1999*, www2.trainingvillage.gr/etv/library/apprenticeship/country/fi.asp.

European Training Village (1999b), *Apprenticeship in France 1999*, www2.trainingvillage.gr/etv/library/apprenticeship/country/f.asp.

Eurostat (2004), *Work and Health in the EU: A Statistical Portrait 1994–2002* http://epp.eurostat.cec.eu.int/cache/ITY_OFFPUB?KS-57-04-807-EN.pdf.

Falcon, Luis and Edwin Melendez (2001), 'Racial and Ethnic Differences in Job Searching in Urban Centers,' in A. O'Connor, C. Tilly and L. Bobo (eds), *Urban Inequality: Evidence from Four Cities,* New York: Russell Sage Foundation.

Farber, H. (1983), 'The Determination of Union Status of Workers,' *Econometrica.* **51**, 1417–38.

Farber, H. and D. Saks (1980), 'Why Workers Want Unions: The Role of Relative Wages and Job Characteristics,' *Journal of Political Economy*, **88**, 349–69.

Fenwick, R. and M. Tausig (2001), 'Scheduling Stress: Family and Health Outcomes of Shift Work and Schedule Control,' *The American Behavioral Scientist*, **44** (7), 1179–98.

Fix, Michael and Jeffrey S. Passel (1994), *Immigration and Immigrants: Setting the Record Straight*, Washington DC: Urban Institute Press.

Fix, Michael and Raymond Struyk (eds), (1994), *Clear and Convincing Evidence*, Washington DC: Urban Institute Press.

Flores-Lagunes, Alfonso, Arturo Gonzalez, and Todd Neumann (2005), 'Learning but Not Earning? The Value of Job Corps Training for Hispanic Youths,' Discussion Paper No. 1638, Institute for the Study of Labor (IZA), Bonn.

Freeman, R. B. (1992), 'Crime and the Employment of Disadvantaged Youth,' in G. Peterson and W. Vroman (eds), *Urban Labor Markets and Job Opportunities*, Washington DC: Urban Institute Press.

Freeman, R. B. (1994), 'Minimum Wages Again!' *International Journal of Manpower*, **15** (2), 8–25.

Freeman, R. B. (1996), 'Why Do So Many Young American Men Commit Crimes and What Might We Do About It?' *Journal of Economic Perspectives*, **10** (1), 25–42.

Freeman, R. and W. Diamond (2003), 'Young Workers and Trade Unions,' in H. Gospel and S. Woods (eds), *Representing Workers: Union Recognition and Membership in Britain*, London: Routledge.

Freeman, R. B. and Harry Holzer (eds), (1986), *The Black Youth Employment Crisis*, Chicago: University of Chicago Press.

Freeman R. B. and S. Nickell (1988), 'Labour Market Institutions and Economic Performance,' *Economic Policy*, **3** (6), 63–80.

Freeman, R. B. and Joel Rogers (1999), *What Workers Want*, Ithaca, NY: Cornell University Press.

Freeman, R. B. and David Wise (eds), (1982), *The Youth Labor Market Problem*, Chicago: University of Chicago Press.

Fry, Richard and B. Lindsay Lowell (2002), 'Work or Study: Different Fortunes of US Latino Generations,' Washington DC: Pew Hispanic Center.

Fryer, Roland, Paul Heaton, Steven Levitt and Kevin Murphy (2005), 'Measuring the Impact of Crack Cocaine,' *National Bureau of Economic Research Working Paper*.

Fullagar, C. and J. Barling (1989), 'A Longitudinal Test of a Model of the Antecedents and Consequences of Union Loyalty,' *Journal of Applied Psychology*, **74**, 213–27.

Fullagar, C., D. Gallagher, M. Gordon and P. Clark (1995), 'Impact of Early Socialization on Union Commitment and Participation: A Longitudinal Study,' *Journal of Applied Psychology*, **80**, 147–57.

Funkhouser, Edward and Stephen Trejo (1995), 'The Labor Market Skills of Recent Male Immigrants: Evidence from the Current Population Survey,' *Industrial and Labor Relations Review*, **48** (3), 792–811.

Furstenberg, Frank and David Neumark (2005), 'School-to-Career and Post-Secondary Education: Evidence from the Philadelphia Educational Longitudinal Study,' NBER Working Paper.

Galinsky, E., S. Kim and J. Bond (2001), *Feeling Overworked: When Work Becomes Too Much*, New York: Families and Work Institute.

Gallagher, D. (1999), 'Youth and Labor Representation,' in J. Barling and E. Kelloway (eds), *Young Workers: Varieties of Experience*, Washington DC: American Psychological Association.

Garonna, P. and P. Ryan (1991), 'The Regulation and Deregulation of Youth Economic Activity,' in P. Ryan, P. Garonna and R. C. Edwards (eds), *The Problem of Youth: The Regulation of Youth Employment and Training in Advanced Economies*, London: Macmillan, 25–81.

Genda, Y. (1997), 'Chance wa ichido (One Chance),' *Monthly Journal of Japan Institute of Labor*, **449**, 2–14.

Genda, Y. (2001), 'Who Really Lost Jobs in Japan?' in T. Tachibanaki and D. Wise (ed.), *Labor Markets and Firm Benefit Policies in Japan and the United States*, Chicago: University of Chicago Press.

Genda, Yuji (2005), *A Nagging Sense of Job Insecurity*, Tokyo: International House of Japan.

Genda, Y. and M. Kurosawa (2001), 'Transition from School to Work in Japan,' *Journal of the Japanese and International Economies*, **15**, 465–88.

Giannelli, Gianna and Chiara Monfardini (2003), 'Joint Decisions on Household

Membership and Human Capital Accumulation of Youths: The Role of Expected Earnings and Local Markets,' *Journal of Population Economics*, 16, 265–285.

Gibson, Campbell J. and Emily Lennon (1999), 'Historical Census Statistics on the Foreign-born Population of the United States: 1850–1990,' Population Division Working Paper, no. 29, Washington DC: US Bureau of the Census

Giloth, Robert (2004), *Workforce Intermediaries for the Twenty-First Century*, Philadelphia: Temple University Press.

Gittleman, Maury and David R. Howell (1995), 'Changes in the Structure and Quality of Jobs in the United States: Effects by Race and Gender, 1973–1990,' *Industrial and Labor Relations Review*, **48** (3), 420–40.

Gober, Patricia (2000), 'Immigration and North American Cities,' *Urban Geography*, **21** (1), 83–90.

Golden, Lonnie (2005), 'Overemployment in the US: Which Workers Face Downward Constrained Hours?' in M. Boulin, et al. (eds), *Decent Working Time: New Trends, New Issues*, Geneva: International Labour Organization: Chapter 8.

Gomez, R and M. Gunderson (2004), 'The Experience-Good Model of Union Membership,' In Phanindra V. Wunnava (ed), *The Changing Role of Unions: New Forms of Representation*, Armonk, NY: M.E. Sharpe.

Gomez, R., M. Gunderson and N. Meltz (2002), 'The Demand for Unionization Among Youth and Adult Workers,' *British Journal of Industrial Relations,* **40** (3), 521–42.

Gomez, R., M. Lipset and N. Meltz (2001), 'Frustrated Demand for Unionization: the Case of the United States and Canada Revisited,' in *Proceedings of the 53rd Annual Meeting of the Industrial Relations Research Association,* Urbana-Champagne: Industrial and Labor Relations Association, 163–172.

Gómez-Quiñones, Juan (1994), *Mexican American Labor, 1790–1990*, Albuquerque, NM: University of New Mexico Press.

Gonzalez, Arturo (1998), 'Mexican Enclaves and the Price of Culture,' *Journal of Urban Economics*, **43** (March), 273–91.

Gonzalez, Arturo (2002), *Mexican Americans and the US Economy: Quest for Buenos Días*, Tucson, AZ: University of Arizona Press.

Gordon, Jennifer (2005), *Suburban Sweatshops: The Fight for Immigrant Rights*, Cambridge, MA: Harvard University Press.

Gormley, William and Ted Gayer (2005), 'Promoting School Readiness in Oklahoma: An Evaluation of Tulsa's Pre-K Program,' *Journal of Human Resources*, **43** (3), 533–58.

Greenhouse, S. (2006), 'Labor Federation Forms a Pact with Day Workers,' *New York Times*, August 10.

Grenier, Guillermo J., A. Stepick, D. Draznin, A. LaBorwit and S. Morris (1992), 'On Machines and Bureaucracy: Controlling Ethnic Interaction in Miami's Construction and Apparel Industries,' in Louise Lamphere (ed), *Structuring Diversity: Ethnographic Perspectives on the New Immigration,* Chicago: University of Chicago Press.

Grissmer, David, Ann Flanagan and Stephanie Wilkinson (1998), 'Why Did the Black-White Test Score Gap Narrow in the 1970s and 1980s?' in C. Jencks and M. Phillips (eds), *The Black-White Test Score Gap,* Washington DC: The Brookings Institution.

Grogger, Jeffrey (1998), 'Market Wages and Youth Crime,' *Journal of Labor Economics* **16** (4), 756–91.

Grubb, W. N (1996), *Learning to Work: The case for Reintegrating Job Training and Education*, New York: Russell Sage Foundation.

Guendelman, S., Pearl, M. (2001), 'Access to care for children of the working poor,' *Archives of Adolescent Medicine,* **155** (6), 651–58

Gunderson, M. (2002), 'Collective Bargaining and Dispute Resolution in the Public Sector,' in C. Dunn (ed), *Oxford Handbook of Canadian Public Administration*, London: Oxford University Press.

Hægeland, T. (2001), *Experience and Schooling: Substitutes or Complements?* Statistics Norway Research Department Working Paper No. 301.

Hall, P. and D. Soskice (2001), *Varieties of Capitalism,* Oxford: Oxford University Press.

Hamermesh, Daniel S. (1985), 'Substitution between Different Categories of Labour, Relative Wages, and Youth Unemployment,' *OECD Economic Studies*, **5**, 57–85.

Hamermesh, Daniel and M. Lee (2002), 'Stressed Out on Four Continents: Time Crunch or Yuppie Kvetch?' Unpublished, Economics Dept., University of Texas, Austin.

Hamersma, Sarah. (2005), 'The Effects of an Employer Subsidy on Employment Outcomes: A Study of the Work Opportunity and Welfare-to-Work Tax Credits,' *Working Paper,* University of Florida.

Hannah, Richard and Charles Baum (2001), 'An examination of college-bound high school students' labor market behavior: Why some students work and why some do not,' *Education*, **121** (4), 787–94.

Haskins, Ron and Cecelia Rouse (2005), 'Closing Achievement Gaps,' *Policy Brief: The Future of Children*, Washington DC: Princeton-Brookings.

Hauser, Robert and Hanam Samuel Phang (1993), 'Trends in High School Dropout Among White, Black and Hispanic Youth,' *Institute for Research on Poverty Discussion Paper*, University of Wisconsin at Madison.

Haynes, P., J. Vowles and P. Boxall (2005), *Explaining the Younger-Older Workers Union Density Gap: Evidence from New Zealand*, Auckland: University of Auckland, Business School.

Heckman, James and Alan Krueger (2003), *Inequality in America: What Role for Human Capital Policies?* Cambridge, MA: MIT Press.

Heer D.M (1996), *Immigration in America's Future: Social Science Findings and the Policy Debate*, Boulder, CO: Westview Press.

Heer, D. M., V. Agadjanian, F. Hammad, Y. Qiu and S. Ramasundaram (1992), 'A Comparative Analysis of the Position of Undocumented Mexicans in the Los Angeles County Work Force in 1980,' *International Migration*, **3** (2), 101–26.

Heer D.M., and Jeffrey S. Passel (1987), 'Comparison of Two Methods for Computing the Number of Undocumented Mexican Adults in Los Angeles County,' *International Migration Review* **21** (4), 1446–73.

Hertz, Tom (2006), *Understanding Mobility in America*, Center for American Progress Report, Washington DC: Center for American Progress.

Holahan, J. and J. Kim (2000), 'Why does the number of uninsured Americans continue to grow?' *Health Affairs*, **19** (4), 188–96.

Holl, J. L., P. G. Szilagyi, L. E. Rodewald, R. S. Byrd and M. L. Weitzman (1995), 'Profile of Uninsured Children in the United States,' *Archives of Pediatric and Adolescent Medicine*, **149**, 398–406

Holzer, Harry J. (1996), *What Employers Want: Job Prospects for Less-Educated Workers*, New York: Russell Sage Foundation.

Holzer, Harry J. (2001), 'Racial Differences in Labor Market Outcomes of Men,' in N. Smelser, W. J. Wilson and F. Mitchell (eds), *America Becoming: Racial Trends and their Consequences,* Washington DC: National Academy Press.

Holzer, Harry and Paul Offner (2002), 'Trends in Employment among Less-Skilled Young Men,' Discussion Paper, Institute for Research on Poverty, University of Wisconsin at Madison.

Holzer, Harry, Paul Offner, and Elaine Sorensen (2005), 'Declining Employment among Less-Educated Young Men: The Role of Incarceration and Child Support,' *Journal of Policy Analysis and Management,* **24** (2), 329–50.

Holzer, Harry, Steven Raphael and Michael Stoll (2003). 'Employment Barriers Facing Ex-Offenders,' paper presented at the Reentry Roundtable, The Urban Institute, New York University, May 19–20.

Holzer, Harry, Steven Raphael and Michael Stoll (2004), *The Effect of an Applicant's Criminal History on Employer Hiring Decisions and Screening Practices: New Evidence from Los Angeles*, Discussion Paper, Institute for Research on Poverty, University of Wisconsin at Madison.

Howell, D. R. and J. Schmitt (2006), *Employment Regulation and French Unemployment: Were the French Students Right After All?* New York: New School Center for Economic Policy Analysis.

Howell, William, Paul Peterson, Patrick Wolf and David Campbell (2002), *Education Gaps: Vouchers and Urban Schools,* Washington DC: Brookings Institution.

Hum, Tarry (2005), 'Immigration Grows to Half of New York's Labor Force,' *Regional Labor Review,* **8** (2), 28–32.

Huston, Aletha, C. Miller and L. Richburg-Hayes (2003), *New Hope for Children and Families: Summary Report,* New York: MDRC.

Ihlanfeldt, Keith and David Sjoquist (1998), 'The Spatial Mismatch Hypothesis: A Review of Recent Studies and their Implications for Welfare Reform, *Housing Policy Debate,* **9** (4), 849–92.

Inoki, T. and F., Ohtake (1997), 'Roudoujijyou ni okeru Sedai Kouka ni tuite' (Cohort Effects in the Japanese Labour Market), in K. Asako, S. Fukuda and N. Yoshino eds, *Gendai Makuro Keizai Bunseki: Tenkanki no Nihon Keizai (The Japanese Economy in Transition: A Macroeconomic Analysis)*, Tokyo University Press, Tokyo.

International Labour Organization (2004), *Global Trends for Youth*, Geneva: ILO.

Ioannides, Yannis M. and Linda Datcher Loury (2004), 'Job Information Networks, Neighborhood Effects, and Inequality,' *Journal of Economic Literature*, **42** (December), 1056–96.

Japan Cabinet Office (1998), *The Sixth Survey on the Attitudes of Youth in the World*, Tokyo: Cabinet Office.

Japan Cabinet Office (2005), *Jyakunen Mugyosya ni Kansuru Chosa (Chukanhoukoku) (Study on Inactive Young People)*, www8.cao.go.jp/youth/kenkyu/shurou/chukan.pdf.

Japan Institute of Labour (2002), *The Labour Situation in Japan: 2002*, Tokyo: Japan Institute of Labour.

Japan Institute of Labour (2003), *From School to Workplace: Current Status and Problems of Employment of High School Graduates*, Research Report 154; Tokyo.

Japan Institute of Labor Policy and Training (2006), *Labor Situation in Japan and*

Analysis: General Overview 2006/2007, Tokyo: Japan Institute of Labor Policy and Training.

Japan Ministry of Education, Culture, Sports and Technology (2005), *Survey on Senior High School Dropouts,* Tokyo: Japan Ministry of Education, Culture, Sports and Technology.

Japan Ministry of Labour (2005), *Rate of Promised Employment for New High School Graduates,* Tokyo, Japan Institute of Labour.

Japan Ministry of Labour (1985, 1997), *Survey on Young Employees,* Tokyo, Japan Institute of Labour.

Japan Ministry of Labour and Welfare (2004), *Basic Survey on Wage Structure,* Tokyo, Japan Ministry of Labour and Welfare.

Japan Statistics Bureau (2005), *Labour Force Survey*, Tokyo, Japan Statistics Bureau.

Jargowsky, Paul (1997), *Poverty and Place*, New York: Russell Sage Foundation

Jargowsky, Paul and Rebecca Yang (2005), *The Underclass Revisited: A Social Problem in Decline?* Washington DC: Brookings Institute.

Jastrzab, Joann *et al.* (1997), *Youth Corps: Promising Strategies for Young People and their Communities,* Cambridge MA: Abt Associates.

Jencks, Christopher and Meredith Phillips (eds), (1998), *The Black-White Test Score Gap*, Washington DC: Brookings Institute.

Jimeno, Juan F. and Rodriguez-Palanzuela, Diego (2002), *Youth Unemployment in the OECD: Demographic Shifts, Labour Market Institutions and Macroeconomic Shocks*, Working Paper Series no. 155, Frankfurt: European Central Bank.

Johnson, George E. (1977), 'Changes in Earnings Inequality: The Role of Demand Shifts,' *Journal of Economic Perspectives*, **11**, 41–54.

Joyce, Theodore and Sanders Korenman (2001), 'Unintended Pregnancy and the Consequences of Nonmarital Childbearing,' in L. Wu and B. Wolfe (eds), *Out of Wedlock: Causes and Consequences of Nonmarital Childbearing*, New York: Russell Sage Foundation.

Juhn, Chinhui (1992), 'Decline of Male Labor Force Participation: The Role of Declining Market Opportunities,' *Quarterly Journal of Economics*, **107** (1), 79–121.

Juhn, Chinhui, K. M. Murphy and B. Pierce (1993), 'Wage Inequality and the Rise in Returns to Skill,' *Journal of Political Economy,* **101** (3), 410–42.

Kamenetz, Anya (2006), *Generation Debt: Why Now Is A Terrible Time To Be Young*, New York: Riverhead Books.

Kariya, T. (1999), 'Transition from School to Work and Career Formation of Japanese High School Students,' in David Stern and Daniel A. Wagner (eds), *International Perspectives on the School-To-Work Transition,* Series on Literacy, Cresskill, NJ: Hampton Press, 273–309.

Kasarda, John (1995), 'Industrial Restructuring and the Changing Location of Jobs,' in R. Farley (ed), *State of the Union, Vol. 1*, New York: Russell Sage Foundation.

Katz, L. F and K. M. Murphy (1992), 'Changes in Relative Wages, 1963–1987: Supply and Demand Factors,' *Quarterly Journal of Economics*, **107** (1), 35–78.

Katz, L. F. and D. H. Autor (1999), 'Changes in the Wage Structure and Earnings Inequality,' in O. Ashenfelter and D. Card (eds), *Handbook of Labor Economics*, 3A, New York: Elsevier, 1464–555.

Katz, Lawrence (1998), 'Wage Subsidies for the Disadvantaged,' in R. Freeman and P. Gottschalk (eds), *Generating Jobs,* New York: Russell Sage Foundation.

Kelloway, E., J. Barling and S. Agar (1996), 'Pre-employment Predictors of

Children's Union Attitudes: The Moderating Role of Identifying with Parents,' *Journal of Social Psychology*, **136**, 413–15.

Kelly, Karen (1998), 'Working Teenagers: Do After-School Jobs Hurt? High Schoolers Who Work More than 20 Hours a Week May Be At Higher Risk for Failure,' *Harvard Education Letter*, **18** (3), www.edletter.org/past/issues/1998-ja/working.shtml.

Kemple, James (2004), *Career Academies: Impacts on Labor Market Outcomes and Educational Attainment*, New York: Manpower Development Research Corporation.

King, Tracey and Ellyne Bannon (2002), 'At What Cost? The Price That Working Students Pay for a College Education,' *US Public Interest Research Group Reports*: www.uspirg.org/report.

Kirschenman, Joleen and Kathryn Neckerman (1991), 'We'd Love to Hire Them But...,' in C. Jencks and P. Peterson (eds), *The Urban Underclass*, Washington DC: The Brookings Institution.

Klein, J. D., K. M. Wilson, M. McNulty, C. Kapphahn and K. S. Collins (1999), 'Access to Medical Care for Adolescents: Results from the 1997 Commonwealth Fund Survey of the Health of Adolescent Girls,' *Journal of Adolescent Health* **25**, 120–30

Kling, Jeffrey, Jens Ludwig and Lawrence Katz (2005), 'Neighborhood Effects on Crime for Female and Male Youth: Evidence from a Randomized Housing Voucher Experiment,' *Quarterly Journal of Economics*, **120** (1), 87–130.

Kochhar, Rakesh (2006), *Growth in the Foreign-Born Workforce and Employment of the Native Born*, Pew Hispanic Center Report, Washington DC: Pew Hispanic Center (August).

Korenman, S. and D. Neumark (2002), 'Cohort Crowding and Youth Labor Markets,' in D. G. Blanchflower and R. B. Freeman (eds), *Youth Unemployment and Joblessness in Advanced Countries*, Chicago: University of Chicago Press, 57–105.

Korpi, T. (1997), 'Is Utility Related to Employment Status? Employment, Unemployment, Labour Market Policies and Subjective Well-Being Among Swedish Youth,' *Labour Economics*, **4** (2), 125–48.

Krueger, A. B. and J. S. Pischke (1997), 'Observations and Conjectures on the US Employment Miracle,' Princeton University Industrial Relations Section Working Paper No. 39.

Krugman, P. (1994), 'Past and Prospective Causes of High Unemployment,' *Federal Reserve of Kansas City Economic Review*, **79** (4), 23–43.

Laferrière, Anne, and François-Charles Wolff (2006), 'Microeconomic Models of Family Transfers,' in Serge-Cristophe Kolm and Jean M. Ythier (eds), *Handbook on the Economics of Giving, Reciprocity and Altruism*, Vol. 2, Cheltenham, UK and Northampton, MA, USA: Edward Elgar, 889–969.

Lalonde, Robert (1995), 'The Promise of Public Sector-Sponsored Training Programs,' *Journal of Economic Perspectives*, **9** (2), 149–68.

Lalonde, Robert and Robert Topel (1991), 'Immigrants in the American Labor Market: Quality, Assimilation, and Distributional Effects,' *American Economic Review*, **81** (May), 297–302.

Layard, R., S. Nickell and R. Jackman (eds), (1991), *Unemployment: Macroeconomic Performance and the Labour Market*, Oxford: Oxford University Press.

Lerman, Robert I. (2000), *Are Teens in Low-Income and Welfare Families Working*

Too Much? Policy Briefs, B–25, Washington DC: Urban Institute.

Levitan, Mark and Robin Gluck (2002), *Mothers' Work: Single Mother Employment, Earnings, and Poverty in the Age of Welfare Reform*, New York: Community Service Society.

Levy, Frank and Richard Murnane (1992), 'US Earnings Levels and Earnings Inequality: A Review of Recent Trends and Proposed Explanations,' *Journal of Economic Literature*, **30**, 1333–381.

Light, Ivan and Steven Gold (2000), *Ethnic Economies*, New York: Academic Press.

Lillydahl, Jane (1990), 'Academic Achievement and Part-Time Employment of High School Students,' *Journal of Economic Education*, **21** (3), 307–16.

Lindbeck, A. and D. J. Snower (1986), 'Wage Setting, Unemployment and Insider-Outsider Relations,' *American Economic Review*, **76**, 235–39.

Lindell, M. and K. Abrahamsson (2002), *The Impact of Lifelong Learning on Vocational Education and Training in Sweden*, Adelaide: National Center for Vocational Education Research.

Lipset, S. M. (1989), *Continental Divide: The Values and Institutions of the United States and Canada*, New York: Routledge.

Lipset, S.M., N. Meltz, R. Gomez and I. Katachanovski (2004), *The Paradox of American Unionism*, Ithaca, NY: Cornell University Press.

Lipsig-Mumme, C. (2005), 'Trade Unions and Labour-Relations Systems in Comparative Perspective,' in M. Gunderson, A. Ponak and D. Taras (eds), *Union Management Relations in Canada* (5th ed), Toronto: Pearson-Addison Wesley, 476–93.

Lofstrom, Magnus (2002), 'Labor Market Assimilation and the Self-Employment Decision of Immigrant Entrepreneurs,' *Journal of Population Economics*, **15**, 83–114.

Loughlin, C. and J. Barling (2001), 'Young Workers' Work Values, Attitudes, and Behaviours,' *Journal of Occupational and Organizational Psychology*, **74**, 543–58.

Love, Margaret Colgate (2005), *Relief from the Collateral Consequences of a Criminal Conviction: A State-by-State Resource Guide,* Washington DC: The Sentencing Project.

Lowe, G. and S. Rastin (2000), 'Organizing the Next Generation: Influences on Young Workers' Willingness to Join Unions in Canada,' *British Journal of Industrial Relations*, **38**, 203–22.

Ludwig, Jens, Greg Duncan and Paul Hirschfield (2001), 'Urban Poverty and Juvenile Crime: Evidence from a Randomized Housing-Mobility Experiment,' *Quarterly Journal of Economics*, **116** (2), 665–79.

Manacorda, Marco and Enrico Moretti (2006), 'Why Do Most Italian Young Men Live with Their Parents? Intergenerational Transfers and Household Structure,' *Journal of the European Economic Association*, **4** (4), 800–29.

Manning, A. (1996), 'The Equal Pay Act as an Experiment to Test Theories of the Labour Market,' *Economica*, **63**, 191–212.

Marcelli, Enrico A. (1999), 'Undocumented Latino Immigrant Workers: The L.A. Experience,' In Haines, D.W. and K.E. Rosenblum (eds), *Illegal Immigration in America: A Reference Handbook*, Westport, CT: Greenwood Press, 193–231.

Marcelli, Enrico A. (2004a), 'The Unauthorized Residency Status Myth: Health Insurance Coverage and Medical Care Use among Mexican Immigrants in California,' *Migraciones Internacionales*, **2** (4), 5–35.

Marcelli, Enrico A. (2004b), 'Unauthorized Mexican Immigration, Day Labor and other Lower-wage Informal Employment in California,' *Regional Studies,* **38** (1), 1–13.

Marcelli, Enrico A. and D. M. Heer (1997), 'Unauthorized Mexican Workers in the 1990 Los Angeles County Labor Force,' *International Migration,* **35** (1), 59–83.

Marcelli, Enrico A. and D. M. Heer (1998), 'The Unauthorized Mexican Immigrant Population and Welfare in Los Angeles County: A Comparative Statistical Analysis,' *Sociological Perspectives,* **41** (2), 279–302.

Marcelli, Enrico A. and B. L. Lowell (2005), 'Transnational Twist: Pecuniary Remittances and Socioeconomic Integration Among Authorized and Unauthorized Mexican Immigrants in Los Angeles County,' *International Migration Review* **39** (1), 69–102.

Marcelli, Enrico A., M. Pastor Jr., and P. M. Joassart (1999), 'Estimating the Effects of Informal Economic Activity: Evidence from Los Angeles County,' *Journal of Economic Issues,* **33** (3), 579–607.

Marcelli, Enrico A. (2004c), 'The Institution of Unauthorized Residency Status, Neighborhood Context, and Mexican Immigrant Earnings in Los Angeles County,' in D. C. Knoedler (ed), *The Institutionalist Tradition in Labor Economics,* Armonk, New York: M.E. Sharpe: 206–28.

Marsden, D. W. and P. Ryan (1991), 'Initial Training, Labor Market Structure and Public Policy: Intermediate Skills in British and German Industry' in P. Ryan, (ed.), *International Comparisons of Vocational Education and Training for Intermediate Skills,* The Falmer Press, 251– 85.

McCormick, M. C., B. Kass, A. Elixhauser, J. Thompson and L. Simpson (2000), 'Annual Review of Child Health Care Access and Utilization,' *Pediatrics* **105**, 219–30

McLanahan, Sara and Gary Sandefur (1994), *Growing Up with a Single Parent: What Hurts, What Helps,* Cambridge, MA: Harvard University Press.

McPherson, Michael S. and Morton O. Shapiro (1998), *The Student Aid Game: Meeting Need and Rewarding Talent in American Higher Education,* Princeton: Princeton University Press.

Merz, J. (2002), 'Time and Economic Well–Being—A Panel Analysis of Desired versus Actual Working Hours,' *The Review of Income and Wealth,* **48** (3), 317–46.

Meyer, Bruce and Daniel Rosenbaum (2001), 'Welfare, The Earned Income Tax Credit and the Labor Supply of Single Mothers,' *Quarterly Journal of Economics,* **116** (3), 1063–114.

Migration Policy Institute (2004), 'Immigrant Union Members: Numbers and Trends,' *Immigration Facts.* Washington DC: Migration Policy Institute.

Min, Pyong Gap (1996), *Caught in the Middle: Korean Communities in New York and Los Angeles,* Berkeley and Los Angeles, CA: University of California Press.

Mitani, N. (1999), 'The Japanese Employment System and Youth Labour Market,' in OECD, *Preparing Youth for the 21st Century: The Transition from Education to the Labour Market,* OECD, Paris, 305–28.

Mitani, N. (2001a), 'Koureisya Koyo Seisaku to Roudou Jyuyo' (Employment Policies for Older Workers and Labor Demand), in Takenori Inoki and Fumio Ohtake (eds), *Koyo Seisaku no Keizai Bunseki (Economic Analysis of Employment Policy),* Tokyo University Press, Tokyo, 339–88

Mitani, N. (2001b), 'Chouki Fukyo to Jyakunen Situgyo' (Long-term Recession and Youth Unemployment), *Kokumin Keizai Zassi (Journal of Economics and Business Administration),* **183** (5), 45–62.

Montgomery, James D. (1991), 'Social Networks and Labor-Market Outcomes: Toward an Economic Analysis,' *American Economic Review*, **81** (December), 1408–18.

Mora, Virginie (2001), 'When the transition to work process grinds to a halt,' *Training and Employment*, **62** (May), CEREQ, Marseilles.

Moss, Philip and Chris Tilly (1996), 'Soft Skills and Race: An Investigation of Black Men's Employment Problems,' *Work and Opportunity*, **23** (3), 252–76.

Moss, Philip and Chris Tilly (2001), *Stories Employers Tell*, New York: Russell Sage Foundation.

Munshi, Kaivan (2003), 'Networks in the Modern Economy: Mexican Migrants in the US Labor Market,' *Quarterly Journal of Economics*, **118**, 549–597.

Murray, G. (2005), 'Union Membership, Structure, Actions and Challenges,' in M. Gunderson, A. Ponak and D. Taras (eds), *Union Management Relations in Canada.* (5th ed), Toronto: Pearson-Addison Wesley, 79–111.

Myers, Dowell (1999), 'Demographic Dynamism and Metropolitan Change: Comparing Los Angeles, New York, Chicago and Washington DC,' *Housing Policy Debate,* **10** (4), 919–54.

National Academy of Sciences (1998), *Protecting Youth at Work: Health, Safety and Development of Working Children and Adolescents in the United States*, Washington DC: Committee on the Health and Safety Implications of Child Labor, National Research Council and Institute of Medicine.

National Center for Public Policy and Higher Education (2002), *Losing Ground: A National Status Report on the Affordability of American Higher Education*, San Jose, CA: NCPPHE.

National Center for Public Policy and Higher Education (2006), *Measuring Up: The National Report Card on Higher Education*, San Jose, CA: NCPPHE.

National Research Council (1997), *The New Americans: Economic, Demographic, and Fiscal Effects of Immigration*, Washington DC: National Academy Press.

Neal, Derek and William Johnson (1996), 'Black-White Wage Differences: The Role of Pre-market Factors,' *Journal of Political Economy,* **104** (6), 869–95.

Ness, Immanuel (2005), *Immigrants, Unions, and the New US Labor Market*, Philadelphia: Temple University Press.

Neumark, David and Donna Rothstein (2003), 'School-to-Career Programs and Transitions to Employment and Higher Education,' NBER Working Paper.

Neumark, D. and W. Wascher (1992), 'Employment Effects of Minimum and Subminimum Wages: Panel Data on State Minimum Wage Laws,' *Industrial and Labor Relations Review*, **46** (1), 55–81.

Neumark, D. and W. Wascher (2000), 'The Effect of New Jersey's Minimum Wage Increase on Fast-Food Employment: A Reevaluation Using Payroll Records,' *American Economic Review*, **90** (5), 1362–396.

Neumark, David, and W. Wascher (1994), 'Employment Effects of Minimum and Subminimum Wages: Reply to Card, Katz, and Krueger,' *Industrial and Labor Relations Review*, 47 (3), 497–512.

New York City Planning Department (2004), *The Newest New Yorkers 2000*, New York: New York City Planning Dept.

Newacheck, P.W., J. J. Stoddard, D. C. Hughes, and M. Pearl (1998), 'Health Insurance and Access to Primary Care for Children,' *New England Journal of Medicine*, **338**, 513–19.

Newman, Katherine and Chauncy Lennon (1995), 'Finding Work in the Inner

City: How Hard is it Now? How hard will it be for AFDC Recipients?' Working Paper #76, New York: Russell Sage Foundation.
Nickell, S. (1997), 'Unemployment and Labour Market Rigidities: Europe versus North America,' *Journal of Economic Perspectives*, **11** (3), 55–74.
Nickell, S. J. and B. Bell (1996), 'Changes in the Distribution of Wages and Unemployment in OECD Countries,' *American Economic Review, AEA Papers and Proceedings*, **86** (2), 302–8.
Nitta, M (1995), 'The Employment Practices and Employment of Young Workers in Japan: Past Experience and Present Situation,' *Japan Labour Bulletin*, October.
Nohara, H. (1999), 'Male and Female Patterns of Labor Force Participation: A Comparison between France and Japan,' in M. Maurice and A. Sorge (eds), *Societal Analysis in Comparative Research*, New York: De Gruyter.
O'Bannon, P. (2001), 'Managing Our Future: The Generation X Factor,' *Public Personnel Management*, **30** (1) 112–32.
O'Higgins, N. *(1992)*, 'School-Leaving at Sixteen: An Empirical Analysis using Individual Data,' *Economia e Lavoro*, **26** (1), 3–22.
O' Higgins, N. (1994), 'YTS, Employment and Sample Selection Bias,' *Oxford Economic Papers*, 46 (4), 605–28.
O' Higgins, N. (1997), *The Challenge of Youth Unemployment*, Employment and Training Paper No. 7, Geneva: ILO.
O'Higgins, N. (2001), *Youth Unemployment and Employment Policy: A Global Perspective*, Geneva: ILO.
O'Higgins, N. (2003), *Trends in the Youth Labour Market in Developing and Transition Countries*, Social Protection Discussion Paper Series no. 0321, Washington DC: World Bank.
O'Higgins, N. (2005), 'I Giovani nel Mercato di Lavoro Meridionale,' in Emiliano Rustichelli and Adalgiso Amendola (eds), *Rapporto sul Mercato del Lavoro nel Mezzogiorno*, monografie sul mercato del lavoro e le politiche per l'impiego no. 12/05, Vol. II, Rome: Instituto per la Formazione dei Lavoratori, 34–49.
OATELS/ BAT (2000), *The National Apprenticeship System Programs and Apprentices, Fiscal Year 2000*, US: OATELS/BAT.
OECD (1982), *Youth Unemployment: the Causes and Consequences*, Paris: OECD.
OECD (1994), *The OECD Jobs Study: Facts, Analysis, Strategies*, Paris: OECD.
OECD (1996), 'Growing into Work: Youth and the Labour Market over the 1980s and 1990s,' in *OECD Employment Outlook*, Paris: OECD, 109–59.
OECD (1998), 'Getting Started, Settling In: The Transition from Education to the Labour Market,' in *OECD Employment Outlook*, Paris: OECD, 81–122.
OECD (1999a), 'Employment Protection and Labour Market Performance' in *OECD Employment Outlook*, Paris: OECD, 47–132.
OECD (1999b), *Implementing the Jobs Strategy: Assessing Performance and Policy*, Paris: OECD.
OECD (1999c), 'Preparing Youth for the 21st Century: The Transition from Education to the Labour Market,' Proceedings of the Washington D. C. Conference, Paris: OECD.
OECD (2002), *OECD Employment Outlook 2002*, Paris: OECD.
OECD (2004a), 'Wage-setting Institutions and Outcomes,' in *OECD Employment Outlook*, Paris: OECD, 127–81.
OECD (2004b), 'Employment Protection Regulation and Labour Market Performance' in *OECD Employment Outlook*, Paris: OECD, 61–125.
OECD (2004c), *Labour Force Statistics*, www.oecd.org/topicstatsportal.

OECD (2004d), *Main Economic Indicators*, www.oecd.org/topicstatsportal.

OECD (2006), *OECD Economic Outlook 2006*, www.oecd.org/dataoecd.

Office for National Statistics (2002), *Social Trends*, London: ONS.

Ohta, S. (1999), 'Keikijyunkan to Tensyoku Kodo (Business Cycles and Turnover Behavior),' in J. Nakamura and M. Nakamura (eds), *Nihonkeizai no Kozochousei to Rodoshijyo (Structural Adjustment and Labor Market in the Japanese Economy),* Tokyo: Nihon Hyoron Sya.

Ohtake, F. (2005), *Nihon no Fubyodo (Inequality of Japan)*, Tokyo: Nihon Keizai Sinbun Sya.

Oi, W. Y. (1962), 'Labor as a Quasi-Fixed Factor,' *Journal of Political Economy*, **70** (6), 538–55.

Okamura, K. (2000), 'Nihon ni okeru Kouhouto Saizu Kouka–Kyaria Dankai Moderu ni yoru Kensyou' (Effects of Cohort Size in Japan: Examination by Career Phase Model), *Monthly Journal of Japan Institute of Labour*, **481**, 36–50.

Orrenius, Pia M. and Madeline Zavodny (2003), *Does Immigration Affect Wages? A Look at Occupational Level Evidence*, Fed Working Paper 0302, Dallas: Federal Reserve Bank of Dallas Research Dept.

Orszag, Jonathan, et al. (2001), *Learning and Earning: Working in College*, Newton, MA: Upromise, Inc.

Ortega, Bob (1998), *In Sam We Trust: The Untold Story of Sam Walton and How Wal-Mart is Devouring America*, New York: Times Books.

Ottaviano, Gianmarco and Giovanni Peri (2005), 'Rethinking the Gains from Immigration: Theory and Evidence from the US,' NBER Working Paper (August).

Oulton, N. and H. Steedman (1994), 'The British System of Youth Training: A Comparison with Germany,' in L. M. Lynch (ed), *Training and the Private Sector: International Comparisons*, Chicago: University of Chicago Press, 61–76.

Pager, Devah (2003), 'The Mark of a Criminal Record,' *American Journal of Sociology,* **108** (5), 937–75.

Paley, Irina (2005), 'Right Place, Right Time: Parents' Employment Schedules and the Allocation of Time to Children,' unpublished manuscript, Providence, RI: Brown University.

Papademetriou, Demetrios G. (ed.), (2006), *Europe and Its Immigrants in the 21st Century: A New Deal or a Continuing Dialogue of the Deaf?* Washington DC: Migration Policy Institute.

Park, F., Y.-B. Park, G. Bechterman, and A. Dar, (eds) (2001), *Labor Market Reforms in Korea: Policy Options for the Future*, Seoul: Korean Labour Institute/World Bank.

Passel, Jeffrey S. (2005a), *Estimates of the Size and Characteristics of the Undocumented Population*, Washington DC: Pew Hispanic Center, http://pewhispanic.org/files/reports.

Passell, Jeffrey S. (2005b), *Unauthorized Migrants: Numbers and Characteristics*, Pew Briefing Paper, Washington DC: Pew Hispanic Center.

Passell, Jeffrey S. and Roberto Suro (2005), *Rise, Peak and Decline: Trends in US Immigration 1992–2004*, Pew Hispanic Center Report, Washington DC: Pew Hispanic Center (September).

Pastor, Jr., Manuel and E. A. Marcelli (2000), 'Men N the Hood: Skill, Spatial, and Social Network Mismatch among Male Workers in Los Angeles County,' *Urban Geography*, **21** (6), 474–96.

Pastor Jr., M and E.A. Marcelli (2003), 'Somewhere over the Rainbow? African Americans, Unauthorized Mexican Immigration, and Coalition Building,' *Review of Black Political Economy*, **31** (1–2), 125–55.

Payne, J. (1989), 'Trade Union Membership and Activism Among Young People in Great Britain,' *British Journal of Industrial Relations*, **27**, 111–32.

Payne, J. (1995), 'Options at 16 and Outcomes at 24: A Comparison of Academic and Vocational Educations and Training Routes,' Youth Cohort Report No. 35, Sheffield: Department for Education and Employment.

Pegula, Stephen M. (2005), 'Occupational Injuries among Groundskeepers, 1992–2002,' *Compensation and Working Conditions*, ww.bls.gov/opub/cwc/home.htm.

Pew Hispanic Center (2006), *America's Immigration Quandary*, Pew Hispanic Center Report (August), Washington DC: Pew Hispanic Center.

Pew Research Center (2006), *Once Again the Future Ain't What It Used To Be*, Social Trends Report, (May), Washington DC: Pew Center.

Pirog, Maureen, Marilyn Klotz and Katherine Byers (2000), 'Interstate Comparisons of Child Support Orders Using State Guidelines,' *Family Relations*, **47** (2), 289–95.

Pocock, Barbara (2001), *The Effect of Long Hours on Family and Community Life: A Survey of Existing Literature*, Queensland, AZ: Queensland Department of Industrial Relations.

Portes, Alejandro and Min Zhou (1996), 'Self–employment and the Earnings of Immigrants,' *American Sociological Review*, **61**, 219–30.

Primus, Wendell (2002), 'Child Support Policy Changes and Demonstration Projects,' Washington DC: Center on Budget and Policy Priorities.

Raphael, Steven and Michael Stoll (2002), 'Modest Progress: The Narrowing Spatial Mismatch Between Blacks and Jobs in the 1990's,' Washington DC: The Brookings Institution.

Rau, William and Durand, Ann (2000), 'The Academic Ethic and College Grades: Does Work Help Students to Make the Grade?' *Sociology of Education*, **73**, 19–38.

Rich, Lauren (1996), 'The Long-Run Impact of Teenage Work Experience: A Rexamination,' *Review of Black Political Economy*, **25** (2), 11–36.

Riddell, Chris (2004), 'Union Certification Success Under Voting Versus Card-Check Procedures: Evidence from British Columbia, 1978–1998,' *Industrial and Labor Relations Review*, **57** (4), 493–517.

Riddell, Chris and Craig Riddell (2004), 'Changing Patterns of Unionization: The North American Experience,' in Thomas Kochan and Anil Verma (eds), *Unions in the 21st Century: An International Perspective*, London: Palgrave MacMillan.

Riddell, Craig (1993), 'Unionization in Canada and the United States: A Tale of Two Countries,' In David Card and Richard Freeman (eds), *Small Differences That Matter: Labor Markets and Income Maintenance in Canada and The United States*, Chicago: University of Chicago Press.

Ridley, M. (2000), *Genome: The Autobiography of a Species in 23 Chapters*, New York: Harper Collins.

Roisman, Glenn (2002), 'Beyond Main Effects of Adolescent Work Intensity, Family Closeness and School Disengagement,' *Journal of Adolescent Research*, **17** (4), 331–46.

Rosenbaum, Paul R. (1984), 'The Consequences of Adjustment for a Concomitant Variable That Has Been Affected by the Treatment,' *Journal of the Royal Statistical Society, Series A*, **147**, 656–66.

Rothstein, Richard (2005), *Class and Schools*, Washington DC: Economic Policy Institute.
Ruggles, Steven, Matthew Sobek, Trent Alexander, Catherine A. Fitch, Ronald Goeken, Patricia Kelly Hall, Miriam King, and Chad Ronnander (2004), *Integrated Public Use Microdata Series: Version 3.0* [Machine-readable database]. Minneapolis, MN: Minnesota Population Center [producer and distributor].
Ruhm, Christopher (1997), 'Is High School Employment Consumption or Investment?' *Journal of Labor Economics*, **15** (4), 735–76.
Ryan, Paul (1987), 'Trade unionism and the Pay of Young Workers,' in P. N. Junankar (ed), *From School to Unemployment?* London: Macmillan, 119–42.
Ryan, Paul (1998), 'Is Apprenticeship Better? A Review of the Economic Evidence,' *Journal of Vocational Education Targeting*, **50** (2), 289–325.
Ryan, Paul (2000), 'The Institutional Requirements of Apprenticeship: Evidence from Smaller EU Countries,' *International Journal of Training and Development*, **4** (1), 42–65.
Ryan, Paul (2001), 'The School-to-Work Transition: a Cross-National Perspective,' *Journal of Economic Literature*, **39**, 34–92;
Ryan, Paul (2007), 'Has the Youth Labour Market Deteriorated in Recent Decades? Evidence from Developed Countries,' Working Paper, forthcoming, Stockholm: Institute for Future Studies.
Ryan, Paul, Paolo Garonna and Richard Edwards (eds), (1991), *The Problem of Youth: The Regulation of Youth Employment and Training in Advanced Economies, London*: Macmillan.
Ryan, Paul and D. Miyamoto (2005), 'The Pay and Employment of Young Workers in Japan, 1988–2003,' Paper presented to Youth Employment in the Global Economy Conference, Hofstra University, September 15–16.
Sakai, T. and Y. Higuchi (2005), 'Fri-ta- no Sonogo – Syugyo, Syotoku, Kekkon, Syussan' (After Being Young Part-time Workers: Employment, Income, Marriage, Childbirth), *Monthly Journal of Japan Institute of Labour*, **535**, 29–41.
Scarpetta, S. (1996), 'Assessing the Role of Labor Market Policies and Institutional Settings on Unemployment: A Cross-Country Study,' *OECD Economic Studies*, 2 (26), 43–82.
Schochet, Peter Z. (1998), *National Job Corps Study: Eligible Applicants' Perspectives on Job Corps Outreach and Admissions*, Princeton, NJ: Mathematica Policy Research, Inc.
Schochet, Peter Z. (2001), *National Job Corps Study: Methodological Appendixes on the Impact Analysis*, Princeton, NJ.: Mathematica Policy Research, Inc.
Schochet, Peter Z., John Burghardt, and Steven Glazerman (2001), *National Job Corps Study: The Impacts of Job Corps on Participants' Employment and Related Outcomes*, Princeton, NJ: Mathematica Policy Research, Inc.
Schwabish, Jonathan A. and Jane E. Lynch (2005), 'Job and Business Growth Among New Migrants: Rising Self-Employment in New York City,' *Regional Labor Review*, **8** (1), 33–44.
Sciolino, Elaine (2006), 'French Protests Over Youth Labor Law Spread to 150 Cities,' *New York Times* (March 19), 16.
Shackleton, J. R. (1995), *Training for Employment in Western Europe and the United States,* Cheltenham: Edward Elgar.
Sharpe, A. (1999), *Apprenticeship in Canada: A Training System Under Siege?*

Report prepared for the Canadian Labour Force Development Board National Apprenticeship Committee.

Singh, Kusum and Mehmet Ozturk (2000), 'Effect of Part-Time Work on High School Math and Science Course Taking,' *Journal of Educational Research,* **94** (2), 67–74.

Smith, J. P. (1991), *Hispanics and the American Dream: An Analysis of Hispanic Male Labor Market Wages 1940–1980*, Los Angeles: Rand.

Smith, J. P. and B. Edmonston (eds), (1997), *The New Americans: Economic, Demographic, and Fiscal Effects of Immigration*, Washington DC: National Academy Press.

Smith, J. P. and B. Edmonston (eds), (1998), *The Immigration Debate: Studies on the Economics, Demographic, and Fiscal Effects of Immigration*, Washington DC: National Academy Press.

Soskice, D. (1994), 'Reconciling Markets and Institutions: The German Apprenticeship System' in L. M. Lynch (ed), *Training and the Private Sector, International Comparisons*, Chicago: University of Chicago Press, 25–60.

Sparks, K., B. Faragher and C. Cooper, (2001), 'Well-being and Occupational Health in the 21st Century Workplace,' *Journal of Occupational and Organizational Psychology*, **74** (4), 489–509.

Spener, David and Frank D. Bean (1999), 'Self-Employment Concentration and the Earnings of Mexican Immigrants in the U.S,' *Social Forces*, **77**, 1021–45.

Steedman, H. (1993), 'The Economics of Youth Training in Germany,' *Economic Journal*, **103**, 1279–91.

Steinberg, Adria, Cheryl Almeida, Lili Allen and Sue Goldberger (2003), *Four Building Blocks for a System of Educational Opportunity*, Boston: Jobs for the Future.

Steinberg, Lawrence (1996), *Beyond the Classroom*, New York: Simon and Schuster.

Stinebrickner, Ralph and Todd Stinebrickner (2003), 'Working During School and Academic Performance,' *Journal of Labor Economics,* 21(2), 473–91.

Stinebrickner, Ralph and Todd Stinebrickner, (2004), 'Time-Use and College Outcomes,' *Journal of Econometrics*, **121** (1–2), 243–69.

Sugeno, K. (1992), *Japanese Labor Law*, Seattle: University of Washington Press.

Sullivan, Oriel and Jonathan Gershuny (2001), 'Cross-National Changes In Time-Use: Some Sociological (Hi)Stories Re-Examined,' *British Journal of Sociology,* **52** (2), 331 – 47.

Sum, Andrew, Ishwan Khatiwada, Nathan Pond and Mykheylo Trubskyy (2003), 'Left Behind in the Labor Market: Labor Market Problems of the Nation's Out-of-School Youth,' Working Paper, Northeastern University, Boston MA.

Suro, Roberto and B. Lindsay Lowell (2002), *New Losses from New Highs: Latino Economics Losses in the Current Recession*, Washington DC: Pew Hispanic Center.

Swanson, Chris (2004), *Who Graduates? Who Doesn't? A Statistical Portrait of Public High School Graduation*, Washington DC: The Urban Institute.

Tannock, Stuart (2001), *Youth At Work: The Unionized Fast-Food and Grocery Workplace*, Philadelphia: Temple University Press.

Taras, D.G. (1997a), 'Why Nonunion Representation is Legal in Canada,' *Relations Industrielles/Industrial Relations*, **52** (4), 761–80.

Taras, D.G. (1997b), 'Collective Bargaining Regulation in Canada and the United

States: Divergent Cultures, Divergent Outcomes,' in B. Kaufman (ed), *Government Regulation of the Employment Relationship*, Madison, WI: Industrial Relations Research Association Annual Volume.

Taras, D. G. (2000), 'Portrait of Nonunion Employee Representation in Canada: History, Law, and Contemporary Plans,' in B. Kaufman and D. Taras (eds), *Non-Union Employee Representation*, Armonk, NY: M. E. Sharpe.

Taras, D.G. (2001), *Employee Representation and Voice in the North American Workplace*, Working Paper 2001–24, University of Calgary.

Taras, D. G. (2002), 'Alternative Forms of Employee Representation and Labour Policy,' *Canadian Public Policy*, **28** (1), 105–16.

Tienda, Marta (1983), 'Market Characteristics and Hispanic Earnings: A Comparison of Natives and Immigrants,' *Social Problems*, 31 (October), 59–72.

Travis, Jeremy (2005), *But They All Come Back: Facing the Challenges of Prisoner Reentry*, Washington DC: Urban Institute Press.

Trejo, Stephen J. (1997), 'Why Do Mexican Americans Earn Low Wages?' *Journal of Political Economy*, **105** (December), 1235–68.

Tyler, John (2003), 'Using State Child Labor Laws to Identify the Effect of School-Year Work on High School Achievement,' *Journal of Labor Economics*, **21** (2), 381–408.

UK Department of Education and Skills (2003, 2006), *Participation in Education, Training and Employment by 16–18 Year-Olds in England*, Statistical First Releases, SFR 31/2003 and 21/2006, London: Office for National Statistics.

US Bureau of Labor Statistics (1983–2007), *Employment and Earnings* (January), Washington DC: BLS.

US Bureau of the Census (2003), *Census 2000 Brief: Foreign-Born Population* 2000, www.census.gov/population/www/socdemo/foreign.

US Bureau of the Census (2006), *2005 American Community Survey*, Washington DC: Census Bureau.

US Department of Education (2004), *Dropout Rates in the United States: 2001*, Washington DC: National Center for Educational Statistics.

US Department of Labor (2005), 'FY 2006 Budget Overview,' Retrieved August 13, 2005, www.dol.gov/_sec/budget2006/overview.pdf.

US Government Accounting Office (1998), *Immigration Statistics: Information Gaps, Quality Issues Limit Utility of Federal Data to Policymakers* (GAO/GGD–98–164), Washington DC: http://www.gao.gov/archive/1998/gg98164.pdf.

US Government Accounting Office (2004), *Workforce Investment Act: Labor Actions Can Help States Improve Quality of Performance Outcome Data and Delivery of Youth Services*, Washington DC: US GAO.

Van Hook, J. and Frank Bean (1998), 'Estimating Underenumeration among Unauthorized Mexican Migrants to the United States: Applications of Mortality Analyses,' in Mexican Ministry of Foreign Affairs, US Commission on Immigration Reform (eds), *Migration between Mexico and the United States:Binational Study*, Austin, TX: Morgan Printing: 551–70.

Van Long, N. and H. Siebert (1983), 'Layoff Restraints and the Demand for Labor,' *Zeitschrift Für Die Gesamte Staatswissenschaft*, **139**, 612–24.

Vélez-Ibáñez, Carlos G. (1996), *Border Visions: Mexican Cultures of the Southwest United States*. Tucson, AZ: University of Arizona Press.

Waddington, J. and A. Kerr (2002), 'Unions Fit for Young Workers?' *British Journal of Industrial Relations*, **41**, 298–315.

Waldinger, Roger (1986), *Through the Eye of the Needle: Immigrants and*

Enterprise in New York's Garment Trades, New York: NYU Press.

Waldinger, Roger (1996), *Still the Promised City? African-Americans and New Immigrants in Post-industrial New York*, Cambridge, MA: Harvard University Press.

Warren, R. (2003), Estimates of the Unauthorized Immigrant Population Residing in the US: 1990 to 2000, Washington DC: US Immigration and Naturalization Service.

Weinberg, Bruce A., Patricia B. Reagan, and Jeffrey J. Yankow (2004), 'Do Neighborhoods Affect Hours Worked? Evidence from Longitudinal Data,' *Journal of Labor Economics*, **22**, 891–923.

Weinick, R.M., Weigers M.E., Cohen, J.W. (1998), 'Children's health insurance, access to care, and health status: New findings,' *Health Affairs*, **17**, 127–36.

Wiatrowski, William J. (2005), 'Fatalities in the Ornamental Shrub and Tree Services Industry,' *Compensation and Working Conditions Online*, www.bls.gov/pub/cwc.

Wilson, Kenneth and Alejandro Portes (1980), 'Immigrant Enclaves: An Analysis of the Labor Market Experiences of Cubans in Miami,' *American Journal of Sociology*, **86** (September), 295–319.

Wilson, William J. (1996), *When Work Disappears*, New York: Alfred Knopf.

Windau, Janice and Samuel Meyer (2005), 'Occupational Injuries among Young Workers,' *Monthly Labor Review*, **128** (10), 11–23.

Winegarden, C.R. and L. B. Khor (1991),'Undocumented Immigration and Unemployment of US Youth and Minority Workers: Econometric Evidence,' *Review of Economics and Statistics*, **73** (1), 105–12.

Wood, A (1994), 'How Trade Hurts Unskilled Workers,' *Journal of Economic Perspectives*, 9, 57–80.

Working Group on New York City's Low-Wage Labor Market (2000), *Building a Ladder to Jobs and Higher Wages*, New York: Community Service Society.

Yamada, M. (1999), *Parasaito singuru no jidai* (The Era of Parasite Singles), Tokyo: Chikuma-syobo.

Zellner, Wendy (2002), 'How Wal-Mart Keeps Unions at Bay,' *Business Week*, October 28.

Zolberg, Aristide (2006), *A Nation by Design: Immigration Policy in the Fashioning of America*, New York and Cambridge, MA: Russell Sage Foundation and Harvard University Press.

Zweig, Michael (2000), *The Working Class Majority*, Ithaca, NY: Cornell University Press.

Index

Abe, Y. 122
Abowd, J. 57
Ackum, S. 57
advanced labor markets
  affluence in 5
  bias against youth 22
  deindustrialization 38
  educational participation 28–9, 31, 143–4
  institutions *see* institutions
  labor market outcomes, trends in 140–5, 149
  low-skilled and internationalization 38
  part-time employment 30, 31, 114, 116–17, 128, 138–9, 154–5
  pay determination institutions 147–8
  pay-setting 141
  recent outcomes 23–31
  relative pay and employment changes 142, 143
  school-to-work institutions 148–56
  school-to-work transitions 141
  unemployment, long-term 138
  young adults versus prime-age adults 23–30, 52–3, 137
  youth employment problems 137–59
  youth identity, problems with 139
  youth labor market outcomes, causes of 145–9
  youth labor market outcomes, trends in 140–5, 149
  youth-unfriendly economic trends 145–7
  see also individual countries
agricultural industry
  and immigration, US 233, 234–5, 237, 238, 240
  occupational fatalities 177–9, 184, 185
Aldrich, H. and R. Waldinger 224
Allen, S. 158
Altonji, J. and D. Card 224
Alvin, M. and M. Sverke 310
Andersson, F., H. Holzer and J. Lane 263
Andrews, M., S. Bradley and R. Upward 57
apprenticeship opportunities 48, 50, 150–1, 152, 255
  construction industry 82–3
  see also education; vocational training
Asia
  emigration 207, 219, 232, 235–6, 239
  see also individual countries
Austen-Smith, D. and R. Fryer 262
Australia
  apprenticeship registrations 50
  earnings ratio 25–7, 28, 36–7
  educational participation and employment rates 34–5
  employment-to-population ratios by age 24–5
  labor market institutions 49
  pay-setting regulation 148
  relative pay and employment changes 142, 143
  tertiary education 143–4
  unemployment insurance 47, 49
  unemployment rates 32–3, 39
  union membership 310
Autor, D.H., and L.F. Katz 56, 261, 262

baby boom generation
  delayed retirement 1, 5
  earnings decline 6
  retirement age, Japan 115, 116, 121
  and youth labor market problem 41, 115–16, 121
Bailey, M. and T. Mallier 172
Bailey, T. 224
Barling, J., E. Kelloway and E.

Bremermann 310
Bartik, T.J. 88
Bassanini, A. and R. Duval 57
Bassi, L. and J. Ludwig 262
Batty, D. 223
Bean, F. 241, 285, 286
Beaulieu, E. 56
Becker, G. 162
Becker, S.O. 107
Belgium
earnings ratio 25–7, 31, 36–7
employment-to-population ratios by age 24–5
labor market institutions 49
pay-setting regulation 148
relative pay and employment changes 142, 143
tertiary education 143
unemployment insurance 49
unemployment rates 29, 32–3, 39
Berman, E., J. Bound and Z. Griliches 56
Bertola, G., F.D. Blau and L.M. Kahn 55, 57
Biancotti, C., G. D'Alessio and A. Neri 106
Bishop, J. 57
Blanchard, O. and A. Landier 57
Blanchflower, D.G. and R.B. Freeman 18, 55, 57, 145, 157
Blank, R. 87, 261, 263
Blau, F. 55, 57, 261
Bloom, D. and C. Sommo 262
Boal, W.M. and J. Pencavel 57
Bohning, W.R. and M.-L. Schloeter-Pareded 225
Borjas, G. 212, 213, 214, 241, 262
Bos, J. 262
Bound, J. 56, 261
Bowers, N., A. Sonnet and L. Bardone 55
Brandolini, A. 106, 107
Briggs, V. 213
Bryson, A.R., M. Lipset and N. Meltz 310
Büchtemann, C., J. Schupp and D. Soloff 158
Burghardt, J. 285
Bushway, S., M. Stoll and D. Weiman 262
Butcher, K. and D. Card 215

Campolieti, Michele 287–310
Canada
apprenticeship registrations 50
collective bargaining contracts 291
earnings ratio 25–7, 28, 36–7
educational participation and employment rates 34–5
employment-to-population ratios by age 2, 3, 4, 23, 24–5
intergenerational earnings mobility 10–11
labor market institutions 49
non-union representation 291, 293–4, 296–8, 299, 301, 302–4, 306
pay-setting by labor unions 45
pay-setting regulation 53, 148
provincial labor boards 291
relative pay and employment changes 142, 143
tertiary education 143–4
unemployment insurance 49
unemployment rates 32–3, 39
union agency shop (Rand formula) 290–1, 294
union membership *see* union membership, Canada
youth-adult preferences for workplace voice 287–310
Cancian, M. and D. Meyer 263
Card, D. 215, 224
Card, D. and A.B. Krueger 44, 45, 57, 263
Card, D., F. Kramarz and T. Lemieux 56, 57
Card, D. and J. NiNardo 56, 146
Card, D. and T. Lemieux 106, 107
Career Academies 254–5
Chapa, J. 285
Chasanov, A. 263
Choy, S. 18
Christopoulou, Rebekka 21–58, 158
Clark, K. and L. Summers 57, 107, 121
construction industry
apprenticeship opportunities, US 82–3
and immigration, US 208, 215–16, 220–1, 233, 237, 240
occupational fatalities 179–80, 184, 185

contract employment 114, 139
Cook, P. and J. Ludwig 262
Cooper, P. and B.S. Schone 200
Corak, M. 10, 18
Costrell, R.M. 224
Crawford, D.L., A.W. Johnson and A.A. Summers 172
crime *see* prison
Crouter, A.C. and S.M. McHale 172
Cuba, emigration 207, 219
Curtis, S. and N. Shani 172
Czech Republic, emigration 203

Darity, W.A. and P.L. Mason 87
DeFreitas, Gregory 1–18, 203–25, 241, 285
Dekker, I., L. Greenberg and J. Barling 310
Del Boca, D. 107
Delgado, H. 225
Dembe, A. 172
Denmark, intergenerational earnings mobility 10–11
developing countries
  and debt relief 12, 223
  marginal employment 138
  powerlessness of young people 139
  youth unemployment 137–8
dispatch employment 114, 139
Djankov, S. 57
Dolado, J.J. 57
Doms, M., T. Dunne and K.R. Troske 56
Draut, T. 18
Duffy, Niev J. 18, 189–200
Dundes, L. and J. Marx 172

earnings *see* wage levels
economic activity, geographic distribution of 63
economic decline
  explaining youth's 13–14
  youth response to 11–13
economic impact, of youth employment 4–7, 41, 218, 246–7
Edelman, P. 262, 263
Edin, P.-A., P. Fredriksson and O. Aslund 285, 286
education
  in advanced labor markets 28–9, 31, 143–4
  barriers to 9–11
  Career Academies 254–5
  and class background 9–10
  college degrees of migrants 213, 240
  college-going costs 6, 9
  college-going, increased 42
  dropouts 117, 165–6, 254, 256, 265
  Early College High School programs 255
  gap and immigration 212–13, 214, 235–6, 239, 240, 250, 251
  high school reforms 254
  Krugman hypothesis 38, 147–8
  No Child left Behind (NCLB) 254
  Opening Doors project 255
  parental support 5, 6
  participation and employment ratios 29–30, 34–5
  pre-Kindergarten and Kindergarten programs 254
  private schools' vouchers 254
  rising standards 5
  school-employer hiring networks 46, 151–6
  school-to-work institutions 1, 41, 46–7, 48, 111–12, 120, 127, 144, 148–56
  school-to-work transitions 109, 111–12, 114, 117, 120–1, 127, 141, 155–6, 159, 255
  'second chance' system 81
  and skill age gap 22
  and skills mismatch 64, 78–81
  and student employment, effect of 6
  student loans 9
  Talent Development High Schools 254
  and technological change 40, 146
  tertiary 29–30, 92, 99–100, 118, 132, 143–4
  and unemployment rates 29, 99, 117–19, 132, 251
  and voluntary inactivity 29, 251
  and wage levels 6, 7–11, 29, 97–8, 247, 248
  young black males 64, 245–61
  young Hispanics 265, 267–8
  see also apprenticeship opportunities; individual countries; vocational training
Ehrenberg, R. and D. Sherman 172

employment discrimination, racial preferences, United States 63–4, 77, 249, 250, 252
employment networks, and immigration 249, 270–1
employment protection 42–3, 47, 49, 115–16
employment-to-population ratios by age *see* individual countries
EU
  Schengen Accord 203
  see also individual countries

Falcon, L. and E. Melendez 262
Farber, H. 18, 292
Farber, H. and D. Saks 18
fatherhood programs, resources for, United States 261
Fenwick, R. and M. Tausig 172
Finland
  apprenticeship registrations 50
  earnings ratio 25–7, 31, 36–7
  educational participation and employment rates 34–5
  employment-to-population ratios by age 24–5, 28
  intergenerational earnings mobility 10–11
  labor market institutions 49
  recession 149
  relative pay and employment changes 142, 143
  school-to-work institutions 149
  unemployment insurance 49
  unemployment rates 29, 32–3, 39
  youth labor market outcome trends 144, 149
Fix, M. 224, 241, 262
Flores-Lagunes, Alfonso 265–86
France
  apprenticeship registrations 50
  earnings ratio 25–7, 28, 36–7
  educational participation and employment rates 34–5
  employment-to-population ratios by age 3, 4, 24–5, 140–1
  First Employment Contract (CPE) 1, 11, 43
  intergenerational earnings mobility 10–11
  labor market institutions 49
  part-time employment 138
  pay-setting by labor unions 45, 48
  pay-setting regulation 53, 148
  relative pay and employment changes 142, 143
  school-to-work transition 121, 155, 156, 159
  temporary employment 138
  tertiary education 143
  unemployment insurance 49
  unemployment, long-term 138
  unemployment rate and GDP growth rate 126
  unemployment rates 11, 29, 32–3, 39, 110, 111, 125
  vocational training 46
  youth employment, economic impact of 41
  youth labor market outcome trends 140, 141
  youth protests 6, 11
Freeman, R. 57, 87, 145, 157, 224, 262
Freeman, R. and D. Wise 18
Freeman, R. and H. Holzer 18, 87
Freeman, R. and J. Medoff 13
Freeman, R. and J. Rogers 310
Freeman, R. and S. Nickell 56
Freeman, R. and W. Diamond 310
freeters 139, 154–5
Frey, W. 215
Fry, R. and B.L. Lowell 285
Fryer, R. 262
Fullagar, C. and J. Barling 310
Funkhauser, E. and S. Trejo 224
Furstenberg, F. and D. Neumark 262

Galinsky, E. 172
Gallagher, D. 310
Garonna, P. and P. Ryan 18, 57
Genda, Y. 157, 159
Genda, Y. amd M. Kurosawa 121, 122
gender pay gap 7–9
Generation X, education levels, advantages of 14
Germany
  apprenticeship registrations 48, 50, 150–1, 152
  earnings ratio 25–7, 31, 36–7, 40
  economic growth 150

educational participation and employment rates 34–5
employment-to-population ratios by age 3, 4, 24–5, 28, 40
intergenerational earnings mobility 10–11
labor market institutions 49
pay-setting by labor unions 45
relative pay and employment changes 142, 143
school-to-work institutions 1, 41, 46, 144, 149–50
school-to-work transition 121
unemployment insurance 49
unemployment rate and GDP growth rate 126, 145, 150
unemployment rates 32–3, 39, 110, 125, 150, 151
youth labor market outcome trends 140, 144
Giannelli, G. and C. Monfardini 106, 107
Gibson, C.J. and E. Lennon 223
Giloth, R. 263
Gittleman, M. and D.R. Howell 87
Gober, P. 224
Golden, Lonnie M. 161–72
Gomez, Rafael 287–310
Gómez-Quiñones, J. 285
Gonzalez, Arturo 265–86
Gordon, J. 225
Gormley, W. and T. Gayer 262
Greece, school-to-employment transition 159
Greenhouse, S. 225
Grenier, G.J. 224
Grissmer, D., A. Flanagan and S. Wilkinson 262
Grogger, J. 262
Grubb, W.N. 57
Guendelman, S. and M. Pearl 200
Gunderson, Morley 287–310

Hægeland, T. 57
Hall, P. and D. Soskice 158
Hamermesh, D. 224, 241
Hamersma, S. 263
Hannah, R. and C. Baum 166
Haskins, R. and C. Rouse 262
Hauser, R. ad H.S. Phang 262
Haynes, P., J. Vowles and V. Boxall 310
health insurance
Child Health Plus (CHIP) 199
employer-sponsored 189, 190, 191–4, 197, 198–9
falling private coverage 189–200
family coverage 190, 193, 194–6, 198–9
and health care costs 198
individual coverage 190, 193, 194, 197
Medicaid 198, 199, 218
uninsurance, effects of 199
Heckman, J. and A. Krueger 262
Heer, D.M. 231
Hertz, T. 18
Holahan, J. and J. Kim 198
Holl, J.L. 200
Holzer, Harry J. 18, 87, 245–63
Howell, D.R. 57, 87
Howell, W. 262
Hum, T. 224
Huston, A. 263

ICT *see* technological change
Ihlanfeldt, K. and D. Sjoquist 262
immigration
and agricultural industry, US 233, 234–5, 237, 238, 240
basic economic model 210–11
college degrees of migrants 213, 240
and consumer demand 218–19
and debt relief 223
and education gap 212–13, 214, 235–6, 239, 240, 250, 251
employment impact, empirical findings 214–18
and employment networks 249, 270–1
and employment-population ratios 214
and ethnic networks 215–16
EU Schengen Accord 203
and family reunification 207, 215–16
foreign-born population, US 205–6, 212, 216, 218–19
Illegal Immigration Reform and Immigrant Responsibility Act, US 229
and job displacement 210–12, 214–18, 219, 220, 222, 229, 233–4
labor market impacts 209–18,

227–41
Legal Permanent Resident Immigrants (LPRs), US 204, 207, 208–9, 213
and low-grade jobs 5, 6, 220
management positions, immigrants in 233, 237, 238, 240
and manufacturing industry 215–16, 233, 235, 237, 238
Mexican *see* Mexico
National Day Laborer Organizing Network, US 221
New York City Youth Employment Survey 216–18
and occupational distribution 232–5, 237, 238, 239, 240
Personal Responsibility and Work Opportunity Reconciliation Act, US 229
and productivity 210–11
public perception of 209–10
quality of migrants, US, alleged 212–13
and self-employment 219–20
and technological change 208, 233, 235, 237, 240
Temporary Legal Nonimmigrants (TLNs), US 204–5
Unauthorized Migrants, US 205, 208–9, 210, 213, 214, 220, 227–41
and unemployment rates 214
and union membership 213, 220–1, 223
in United States *see* United States, immigration
and wage levels 5, 6, 77, 210–14, 218, 229, 230–1, 234–6, 238, 251
and welfare system 212, 229
and youth employment, recent debates and research findings 203–25
youth in US 207
see also individual countries
Inoki, T. and F. Ohtake 122
institutions
demand-side 42–3, 47
and employment protection 42–3, 47
measuring 47–8
pay-setting 44–6, 141, 148
school-to-work 46–7, 48, 111–12, 120, 127, 144, 148–56
supply demand institutions (SDI) approach 48–54
supply-side 43–4, 47
intergenerational earnings mobility 10–11
internal labor markets, protectionism 38
internationalization, and low-skilled 38
Ioannides, Y.M. and L.D. Datcher 285, 286
Ireland
apprenticeship system 57
educational participation and employment 30
Italy
discouraged workers group 107
earnings ratio 25–7, 31, 36–7
educational participation and employment 30, 90, 91, 92, 93, 97, 104–5
employment-to-population ratios by age 24–5, 28, 92, 93, 98–9, 100, 101
geographical differences in employment 103–5
immigration 203
labor market institutions 49
marriage rates by age 90, 91, 93, 95, 101, 102
pay-setting regulation 148
relative pay and employment changes 142, 143
school-to-employment transition 159
tertiary education 92, 99–100
time differences in employment 103–4
unemployment insurance 49
unemployment rates 29, 32–3, 39, 99
wage levels 95–6, 97–9, 100, 101
youth labor market 89–107
youth labor market, empirical findings 97–105
youth labor market, research strategy 94–7
youth living with parents 90–2, 100–1, 139

Japan
aging labor force 115–16
baby boomers 115–16, 121
consumption tax 113
contract employment 114, 139

discouraged worker effects 112, 113
dispatch employment 114, 139
earnings ratio 25–7, 36–7
economic growth 150
educational participation and
employment rates 34–5
employment path dependency and
inequality 118–19
employment protection legislation
115–16
employment rate, decomposition of
112–14, 133
employment-to-population ratios by
age 3, 24–5, 28, 113, 116, 129,
133
freeters 154–5
inactive jobless (NEETs) 139
inactivity rate 117–18, 134
IT recession (2001) 115
job matching 119, 155
labor force participation rate 113, 116,
117–18, 121, 133
labor market institutions 49
labor unions and pay-setting 48
Labour Standard Law 115
lifetime earnings distribution 118–19
manufacturing industries 113
minimum wage 48, 122
older workers, employment of 115–16
part-time employment 114, 116–17,
128, 138–9, 154–5
pay and employment data, validity of
144
pay-setting regulation 53
regular employment contracts 144,
154
relative pay and employment changes
142, 143
retirement age 115, 116, 121
school dropouts and unemployment
117
school-employer hiring networks
151–6
school-to-work institutions 46, 48,
111–12, 120, 127, 144, 148,
149–50
school-to-work transition 109, 111–12,
114, 117, 120, 127
service industries 113–14
SMEs and credit crunch 113
temporary employment 138–9, 154–5
tertiary education 118, 132
unemployment and educational
attainment 117–19, 132
unemployment insurance 47, 49
unemployment, long-term 110, 124
unemployment rates 32–3, 39, 110–11,
114, 116–18, 120–1, 123, 125–6,
130–1, 150
unemployment, and re-employment
114
vocational training 115
wage level path dependency 118–19,
130, 131
wage rigidity 116–17
youth employment after 1990s
recession 109–34
youth employment, economic impact
of 41
youth labor market outcome trends
140, 141, 144
youth living with parents (parasite
singles) 114, 139, 155
youth unemployment, recent trends
110–11, 113
Jargowsky, P. 262
Jastrzab, J. 262
Jencks, C. and M. Phillips 262
Jimeno, J.F. and D. Rodriquez-
Palenzuela 55, 57, 107
Job Corps 256
description and evaluation 266–8
empirical analysis on young Hispanics
272–8
National Job Corps Study (NJCS)
267–9, 271–2, 273, 279–80
New York City, establishment of 82,
84–5
placement services 271
results of past studies on young
Hispanics 268–9
training for young Hispanics, benefits
of 265–86
job displacement, and immigration
210–12, 214–18, 219, 220, 222,
229, 233–4
job matching, Japan 119, 155
job placement firms 256
Johnson, G.E. 87
Joyce, T. and S. Korenman 262

Juhn, C. 56, 87, 261

Kamenetz, A. 18
Kariya, T. 121, 158
Kasarda, J. 87, 261
Katz, L. 56, 57, 158, 261, 262
Kelly, K. 172
Kemple, J. 262
King, T. and E. Bannon 172
Kirschenman, J. and K. Neckerman 262
Klein, J.D. 200
Kling, J., J. Ludwig and L. Katz 262
Kochhar, R. 215
Korea
  earnings ratio 25–7
  economic growth 149
  emigration 219
  employment-to-population ratios by age 23, 24–5, 28
  labor market institutions 49
  relative pay and employment changes 142, 143
  school-to-work transition 121, 149
  unemployment insurance 49
  unemployment rates 29, 32–3, 39
  youth labor market outcomes 142, 143, 144, 149
Korenman, S. 30, 56, 57, 122, 262
Korpi, T. 57
Kreuger, A.B. 44, 45, 56, 57, 262, 263
Krugman, P. 38, 147–8

labor unions *see* union membership
Laferrière, A. and F.-C. Wolff 107
Lalonde, R. 262
Lalonde, R. and R. Topel 212–13
Latin America
  emigration 204, 207–8, 208, 210
  see also Mexico
Layard, R., S. Nickell and R. Jackman 56
Lerman, R.I. 172, 262
Levitan, Mark 59–88
Levy, F. and R. Murnane 140, 158
Light, I. and S. Gold 224
Lillydahl, J. 172
Lindbeck, A. and D.J. Snower 57
Lipset, S.M and N. Meltz 293, 298, 303–4, 310
Lipsig-Mumme, C. 310

Lofstrom, M. 224
Loughlin, C. and J. Barling 310
Love, M.C. 263
low-skilled
  and immigration 5, 6, 220
  and internationalization 38
Lowe, G. and S. Rastin 310
Ludwig, J., G. Duncan and P. Hirschfield 262

McCormick, M.C. 200
McLanahan, S. and G. Sandefur 262
Manacorda, M. and E. Moretti 107
management positions, immigrants in 233, 237, 238, 240
Manning, A. 57
manufacturing industry 113
  and immigration 215–16, 233, 235, 237, 238
  occupational fatalities 181–2, 184, 185
  skill requirements 248, 249
Marcelli, Enrico A. 227–41
Marsden, D. 18, 57
Martinez, A. 220–1
Mexico
  emigration 204, 207–8, 219
  unauthorized emigration to California 227–41
  unauthorized emigration to California, data and methods used 230–2
  unauthorized emigration to California, empirical findings 232–6
Meyer, B. and D. Rosenbaum 261, 263
Millennial Generation 2
Min, P.G. 219
Mitani, Naoki 109–34, 159
Montgomery, J.D. 285
Mora, V. 157
Moss, P. and C. Tilly 87, 262
Munshi, K. 285, 286
Murray, G. 310
Myers, D. 224

Neal, D. and W. Johnson 262
Ness, I. 225
Netherlands
  apprenticeship registrations 48, 50
  earnings ratio 25–7, 40
  educational participation and employment rates 34–5

employment population ratio 2, 3, 4
employment-to-population ratios by age 23, 24–5, 28, 40
labor market institutions 49
part-time (student) employment 30, 31
pay-setting regulation 148
relative pay and employment changes 142, 143
school-to-work institutions 41, 149
unemployment insurance 49
unemployment rate and GDP growth rate 126
unemployment rates 29, 32–3, 39, 110–11, 125
youth labor market outcome trends 140
youth sub-minimum wage levels 44–5, 149
Neumann, Todd 265–86
Neumark, D. 30, 44, 45, 56, 57, 122, 262
New Zealand, union membership 310
Newacheck, P.W. 200
Newman, K. and C. Lennon 217–18
Nickell, S.J. 56, 57
Nitta, M. 57
Norway, intergenerational earnings mobility 10–11

O'Bannon, P. 310
occupational distribution, and immigration 232–5, 237, 238, 239, 240
occupational fatalities
agriculture, forestry and fishing 177–9, 184, 185
by event 176–7
by industry 177–87
child labor regulations, federal 182, 183
construction industry 179–80, 184, 185
and Hazardous Orders for Agriculture, US Department of Labor 178–80
manufacturing industries 181–2, 184, 185
public sectors 184–5
retail trade 181, 184, 185
service industries 180–1, 184, 185
transportation and public utilities 182–3, 184, 185
wholesale trade 183, 184, 185
O'Higgins, Niall 18, 57, 89–107
Ohta, S. 122
Oi, W.Y. 121
Opening Doors project 255
Orrenius, P. and Zavodny, M. 213
Orszag, J. 172
Ortega, B. 18
Ottaviano, G. and G. Peri 214
Oulton, N. and H. Steedman 57

Pager, D. 262
Paley, I. 172
Papademetriou, D.G. 223
parents, youth living with 90–2, 100–1, 114, 139, 155
part-time employment
advanced labor markets 30, 31, 114, 116–17, 128, 138–9, 154–5
and employer-provided health insurance decline 191
Passel, J.S. 223, 224, 241
Pastor, M. and E.A. Marcelli 241
pay-setting *see* wage levels
Payne, J. 57, 310
Pirog, M., M. Klotz and K. Byers 262
Pocock, B. 172
Poland
college enrollment and completion 9
emigration 203
unemployment rates 106
Portes, A. 225, 285
Portugal
college enrollment and completion 9
educational participation and employment 30
Primus, W. 262, 263
prison
ex-offenders, re-entry of, United States 258–60, 261
incarceration rates, male black youth, United States 247, 251–3, 256, 258–60
and paid transitional employment 84–5
public sector
jobs programs 84
occupational fatalities 184–5

Raphael, S. and M. Stoll 262, 263

Rau, W. and A. Durand 172
retirement
  age, Japan 115, 116, 121
  delayed 1, 5
Rich, L. 172
Riddell, C. 292, 310
Roisman, G. 172
Rosenbaum, P.R. 285
Rothstein, R. 262
Ruhm, C. 172
Ryan, Paul 18, 28, 38, 41, 48, 55, 56, 57, 88, 137–59

Sakai, T. and Y. Higuchi 122
Scarpetta, S. 57
Schochet, P.Z. 262, 285, 286
Schochet, P.Z., J. Burghardt and S. Glazerman 285
school-to-work institutions and transitions *see* education
Schwabish, J. and Lynch, J. 219–20
Sciolino, E. 18
self-employment, and immigration 219–20
service sector 113–14
  employment growth 249
  and immigration 215–16, 217–18, 233, 235, 237, 238, 240
  occupational fatalities 180–1, 184, 185
Shackleton, J.R. 57
Singh, K. and M. Ozturk 172
Slovakia, unemployment rates 106
Smith, J.P. 241, 285
Soskice, D. 57, 158
Soviet Union, emigration 207
Spain
  educational participation and employment 30
  immigration 203
  school-to-employment transition 159
  youth sub-minimum wage levels 44–5
Sparks, K. 172
Spener, D. and F.D. Bean 285, 286
Steinberg, L. 172, 262
Stinebrickner, R. and T. 172
Sugeno, K. 121
Sullivan, O. and J. Gershuny 172
Sum, A. 261
Suro, R. 223, 285
Swanson, C. 261
Sweden
  apprenticeship registrations 50
  earnings ratio 25–7
  educational participation and employment rates 34–5
  employment population ratio 3
  employment-to-population ratios by age 24–5, 28, 140–1
  inactive jobless (NEETs) 139
  intergenerational earnings mobility 10–11
  labor market institutions 49
  pay-setting regulation 53, 148
  recession 149
  relative pay and employment changes 142, 143
  school-to-work institutions 149
  school-to-work transition 121
  unemployment insurance 47, 49
  unemployment rate and GDP growth rate 126
  unemployment rates 29, 32–3, 39, 110, 125
  youth employment, economic impact of 41
  youth labor market outcome trends 144
  youth labor market outcomes 144, 149

Tannock, S. 18
Taras, D.G. 310
technological change
  computer use at work 146–7
  and education 40, 146
  experience-biased 146
  and immigrant workers 208, 233, 235, 237, 240
  and skill levels 38–40, 63, 80, 145–6, 248, 250
  and wage levels 146
temporary employment
  and employer-provided health insurance decline 191
  protection 49
  temp-agencies 256
  work contracts 43, 47, 138–9, 154–5
Tienda, M. 285
transition countries
  youth unemployment 138
  see also individual countries

transitional jobs programs 84
Travis, J. 262, 263
Trejo, S.J. 224, 285
Tyler, J. 172

UK
- apprenticeship registrations 50
- earnings ratio 25–7, 28, 36–7
- educational participation and employment rates 34–5
- employment-to-population ratios by age 2, 3, 4, 23, 24–5
- immigration 203
- inactive jobless (NEETs) 139
- intergenerational earnings mobility 10–11
- labor market institutions 49
- part-time (student) employment 30, 31
- pay-setting by labor unions 45
- pay-setting regulation 148
- relative pay and employment changes 142, 143
- school-to-work transition 121
- unemployment insurance 47, 49
- unemployment, long-term 138
- unemployment rate and GDP growth rate 126
- unemployment rates 32–3, 39, 110, 111, 125
- union membership 310
- wages levels 140
- youth labor market outcome trends 140

unemployment insurance 43–4, 47, 49
unemployment rates
- advanced labor economies 32–3, 39, 110–11, 114, 116–18, 120–1, 123, 125–6, 130–1, 150
- black male youth in New York City *see* United States, black male youth
- cyclical nature of 145
- and discouraged workers group 107, 112, 113
- economic factors 145, 269
- and education 29, 99, 251
- and employment networks for Hispanics, US 270–1, 274
- and GDP growth rate 126, 145, 150
- global 137–8
- and immigration 214
- inactive jobless (NEETs) 117–18, 134, 139
- and labor unions 45, 306–7
- long-term 110, 124
- voluntary inactivity and education 29, 251
- and wage levels, Japan 116, 117
- young Hispanics, US 270–1, 273–4, 275–8, 281, 283–4

union membership 12–13, 49, 310
- definitions and concepts 292–6
- and employer loyalty 306
- and immigration 213, 220–1, 223
- and internationalization 38
- Justice for Janitors 220
- oversupply 293–4, 295
- and pay-setting 44, 45–8, 53, 147, 148, 213, 248, 305–6
- and political leanings 307
- and political power 306
- public sector unionization 290
- satisfied demand in the workforce 294
- and unemployment 45, 306–7
- United States 12–13, 288, 289, 290, 291, 310
- unsatisfied demand 295
- and workplace protection 307
- and workplace treatment 306

union membership, Canada 287–8
- collective bargaining contracts 291
- collective versus individual 303–4, 306
- non-union representation 291, 293–4, 296–8, 299, 301, 302–4, 306
- pay-setting by labor unions 45
- potential 301–3
- reasons for targeting youth 309–10
- satisfied and unsatisfied demand 296–301, 302
- sustained 288–90
- sustained, supply-side factors accounting for 290–1
- unionized oversupply 294, 296–300, 301, 302
- youth-adult union differences 291–2, 296–303
- youth-adult union differences, reasons for 304–7
- youth-adult union differences and

workplace voice 303–7
see also individual countries
United States
American Time Use Survey 161, 163, 167–8
apprenticeship opportunities 50, 82–3, 83–4
Bureau of Citizenship and Immigration Services (BCIS) 205
Career Academies 254–5
Center for Employment Opportunities, New York City 259
Center for Employment and Training (CET), San Jose, California 256
Child Health Plus (CHIP) 199
Civil Rights Act 207
and colonialism 227–8
Commission on Construction Opportunity 82–3
computer use at work 146–7
debt-for-diploma system 6
Early College High School programs 255
Earned Income Tax Credit 257
earnings ratio 25–7, 28, 36–7
education *see* United States, education
employment discrimination, racial preferences 63–4, 77, 249, 250, 252
employment structure, change in, New York City 69–72
employment-to-population ratios by age 3, 4, 23, 24–5, 61–3
ex-offenders, re-entry of 258–60, 261
fatherhood programs, resources for 261
Federal Bonding program 259
Federal Pell education grants 9, 259
Federal Prison Industries 258
first-year seminar (FYS) campus survey 168–9
foreign military and financial policies and immigration 223
foreign-born population US 205–6, 212, 216, 218–19
Hazardous Orders for Agriculture, Department of Labor 178–80
health insurance *see* health insurance
intergenerational earnings mobility 10–11
Job Corps *see* Job Corps
Justice for Janitors 220
labor market institutions 49
Legal Permanent Resident Immigrants (LPRs) 204, 207, 208–9, 213
'living wage' campaigns 12
Medicaid 198, 199, 218
Mexican immigration *see* Mexico
minimum wage effects 44, 223, 257–8
Moving to Opportunity experiment 262
National Day Laborer Organizing Network 221
National Labor Relations Act 291
New Hope project, Milwaukee 263
No Child left Behind (NCLB) 254
non-union representation 291
occupational fatalities among young workers *see* occupational fatalities
Opening Doors project 255
out-of-school male youth *see* United States, out-of-school male youth
part-time (student) employment 31
pay-setting by labor unions 45
pay-setting regulation 53, 148
Personal Responsibility and Work Opportunity Reconciliation Act 229
publicly subsidized employment 84
relative pay and employment changes 142, 143
Safer Foundation, Chicago 259
school-to-work transition 121, 159, 162
self-employment 219
single mothers 64–5, 72–4, 75
skill-biased technical change 145–6
sweatshop wages 12
Talent Development High Schools 254
technical change, effects of 146–7
Temporary Legal Nonimmigrants (TLNs) 204–5
Unauthorized Migrants 205, 208–9, 210, 213, 214, 220, 227–41
unemployment insurance 49
unemployment rate and GDP growth rate 126
unemployment rates 29, 32–3, 39, 110, 111, 125, 145–6

unemployment rates of black male youth *see* United States, black male youth
union membership 12–13, 288, 289, 290, 291, 310
upward mobility of youth, falling 6
wage inequality 38, 63, 64, 77, 145
wage levels 12, 140, 146, 162
Work Opportunity Tax Credit 259
Workforce Investment Act 83
working hours 163–6
Youth Build 256
Youth Employment Survey, New York City 216–18
youth labor market outcome trends 140
Youth Opportunities program 257
youth protests 11–12
Youth Service Corps 256
youth sub-minimum wage levels 44–5
United States, black male youth
child support orders 251–3, 257, 258–60
'disconnected' rate in New York City 59, 61
education 64, 245–61
illegal sector employment 250–1, 257, 258
improving employment outcomes for 245–63
improving employment outcomes for, employment trends 245–8
improving employment outcomes for, employment trends, causes of 248–53
incarceration rates 247, 251–3, 256, 258–60
labor force participation rate 248, 249, 250
policy implications 253–60
school and work status in New York City 61–3
skills and educational outcomes, improving 254–5
unemployment rates 59–88, 281
unemployment rates, analysis of 65–81
unemployment rates, explanations of 63–5
unemployment rates, immigration effect 72–4, 75–8
unemployment rates, share effect 64–5, 71, 72–4
unemployment rates, and skills mismatch 78–81
wage levels 250, 257–8, 281
work experience and employer access, improving 255–7
work incentives, improving 257–8
United States, education
attainment for out-of-school males 78–80, 81
black male youth 64, 245–61
and class background 10
college dropouts and working hours 165–6
college employment, economic reaction to 161–3
college enrollment and completion 9
college students, work and non-work time use 161–72
college students, work and working hours, effects of 163–6, 170
financial aid 6, 166
participation and employment rates 34–5
'second chance' system 81
Young Hispanics 265, 267–8
United States, immigration 6, 203
effects of 64–5, 72–4, 75–8, 80, 203–4, 223
flows and features 204–9
foreign military and financial policies 223
Illegal Immigration Reform and Immigrant Responsibility Act 229
Immigration Act (1990) 207
Immigration Reform and Control Act (IRCA) 207, 220, 229, 230
legislative changes 207
policy, early 228
states 209, 215, 216, 219, 227–41
United States, out-of-school male youth
employment-population ratios 61–3
by job tier 65–9, 70, 74–5, 76, 77–8, 79–81, 83–4
by race/ethnicity 71–2
distribution of 65–9, 79–80, 85–6
labor market initiatives 81–4

and local policy implications 81–5
'second chance' system 81
United States, young Hispanics
education 265, 267–8
employment features 269–71
employment networks and unemployment rates 270–1, 274
enclave effects 273, 274, 275, 277, 278–9
Job Corps, results of past studies on 268–9
Job Corps empirical analysis on 272–8
Job Corps training for, benefits of 265–86
network advantages 270–1, 274, 277
wage levels 267–8, 269, 273, 275, 276, 277–9, 282

Van Hook, J. and F. Bean 241
Van Long, N. and H. Siebert 57
Vélez-Ibáñez, C.G. 285
vocational training 44, 46, 255
Job Corps *see* Job Corps
technological change and skill levels 38–40, 63, 80, 145–6, 248, 250
work experience 44, 255–7
see also apprenticeship training; education

wage levels 22, 95–6, 97–9, 100, 101, 282
and college employment, United States 162
and continuing education decisions 97–9
earnings ratios 25–7, 31, 36–7
and education 6, 7–11, 29, 97–8, 247, 248
and immigration 5, 6, 77, 210–14, 218, 229, 230–1, 234–6, 238, 251
intergenerational earnings mobility 10–11
Krugman hypothesis 38
and labor demand and supply 48–54
'living wage' campaigns, United States 12
minimum wage legislation 44–5, 48, 49, 122, 223, 248, 257–8
path dependency, Japan 118–19, 130, 131
pay determination institutions 44–6, 141, 147–8
pay-setting in advanced economies 53, 141, 148
pay-setting and union membership 44, 45–8, 53, 147, 148, 213, 248, 305–6
reservation wage 5
and skills 249
sweatshop wages, United States 12
and technological change 146
and transitional jobs programs 84
and unemployment, Japan 116, 117
wage inequality, United States 38, 63, 64, 77, 145
youth sub-minimum 44–5
see also individual countries
Waldinger, R. 87, 224, 285
Warren, R. 241
Weinberg, B.A., P.B. Reagan and J.J. Yankow 285, 286
Weinick, R.M., M.E. Weigers and J.W. Cohen 200
welfare system
and immigration 212, 229
unemployment insurance 43–4, 47, 49
see also unemployment rates
Wilson, K. and A. Portes 285
Wilson, W.J. 261, 263
Windau, Janice 175–87
Winegarden, C.R. and L.B. Khor 214, 241
Wood, A. 56
working hours 163–6, 273, 281, 282

Yamada, M. 121
youth employment
cross-country perspective of problem 21–58
economic impact of 4–7, 41, 218, 246–7
employment-to-population ratio, young Black men, US 245–6, 247
and labour demand and supply 14, 38, 41–2, 48–54, 63, 64
under-employment 138
see also individual countries

Zolberg, A. 241